The English Legal System

We work with leading authors to develop the strongest educational materials in law, bringing cutting-edge thinking and best learning practice to a global market.

Under a range of well-known imprints, including Longman, we craft high quality print and electronic publications which help readers to understand and apply their content, whether studying or at work.

To find out about the complete range of our publishing please visit us on the World Wide Web at: www.pearsoneduc.com

The English Legal System

John Wheeler

Senior Lecturer in Law,
University of Surrey Roehampton

Longman

An imprint of **Pearson Education**

Harlow, England · London · New York · Reading, Massachusetts · San Francisco
Toronto · Don Mills, Ontario · Sydney · Tokyo · Singapore · Hong Kong · Seoul
Taipei · Cape Town · Madrid · Mexico City · Amsterdam · Munich · Paris · Milan

Pearson Education Limited
Edinburgh Gate
Harlow
Essex CM20 2JE
England

and Associated Companies around the world

Visit us on the World Wide Web at:
www.pearsoneduc.com

───────────────

First published 2002

ISBN 0 582 42405 4

British Library Cataloguing-in-Publication Data
A catalogue record for this book can be obtained from the British Library.

10 9 8 7 6 5 4 3 2
06 05 04 03 02

Typeset by 35 in 10/13pt Palatino
Printed in Great Britain by Henry Ling Limited, at the Dorset Press, Dorchester, DT1 1HD

In memory of Sheila

Contents

Preface   xvii
Table of cases   xix
Table of statutes   xxiv
Table of statutory instruments   xxx
EU treaties   xxxi
EU secondary legislation   xxxii
Abbreviations   xxxiii
Glossary of legal terms   xxxv

1 Introduction   1

Part One THE LEGAL PROFESSION   7

2 The legal profession   9

   1 Introduction   9
   2 Solicitors   9
   3 Qualifying as a solicitor   10
   4 The work of solicitors   11
   5 Courts and Legal Services Act 1990   11
   6 Legal executives   13
   7 Complaints against solicitors   14
   8 Office for the Supervision of Solicitors 15
   9 Discipline   15
  10 Barristers   16
  11 Qualifying as a barrister   17
  12 The work of barristers   18
  13 Career progression   19
  14 Barristers and professional negligence   19
  15 Complaints against barristers   20
  16 Legal Services Ombudsman   23
  17 Legal Services Complaints Commissioner   24
  18 Is there a case for a unified legal profession? 24
     Progress test   25
     Further reading   26

3 Magistrates, judges and the courts   27

   1 Introduction   27
   2 Magistrates   28

  3 Circuit judges and district judges   30
  4 Judges of the High Court   31
  5 Eligibility for appointment to the High Court   33
  6 Judges of the Court of Appeal   33
  7 Judges of the House of Lords   34
  8 Judicial appointments and tenure   35
  9 The Judicial Studies Board   36
     Progress test   37
     Further reading   38

Part Two THE LAW-MAKING PROCESS   39

4 The law-making process 1: Case law and law reporting   41

   1 Introduction   41
   2 Case studies   42
   3 *Ratio decidendi* and *obiter dicta*   43
   4 Precedent and the hierarchy of the courts   45
   5 Flexibility or rigidity?   48
   6 Importance of law reports   50
   7 Historical development of common law   51
   8 Deficiencies in common law   53
   9 The development of equity   54
 10 Common law and equity in conflict   55
 11 Nineteenth-century reforms   57
 12 The modern relationship   58
 13 Equitable remedies in modern litigation   59
     Progress test   60
     Further reading   61

5 The law-making process 2: Primary legislation   62

   1 Introduction   62
   2 Constitutional arrangements past and present   62
   3 Composition of the Westminster Parliament   63
   4 Proposals for new legislation   64
   5 Time pressures   65
   6 Establishing priorities   65
   7 Role of Parliamentary Counsel to the Treasury   66
   8 The process of enactment   66
   9 Royal Assent   70
 10 Other forms of Public General Act   71
 11 Private Acts of Parliament   72
 12 Citation   72
 13 Supremacy of statute law over case law   72
 14 Supremacy of EU law over national law   73
 15 The effect of the Human Rights Act 1998 on UK law   75

16 The clarity of legislation   75
   Progress test   77
   Further reading   78

6 The law-making process 3: Subordinate legislation   79

 1 Introduction   79
 2 The extent of delegation   79
 3 Statutory Instruments Act 1946   80
 4 Drafting of statutory instruments   81
 5 Citation   81
 6 Parliamentary awareness   81
 7 Deregulation orders   83
 8 Remedial orders   85
 9 Orders in Council   86
10 The case for scrutiny of statutory instruments   86
11 Joint Committee on Statutory Instruments   87
12 The validity of subordinate legislation   88
   Progress test   90
   Further reading   91

7 The impact of the European dimension   92

 1 Introduction   92

THE INSTITUTIONS   93
 2 The Council of the European Union   93
 3 The European Commission   94
 4 The European Parliament   96
 5 The European Court of Justice   97
 6 The Court of Auditors   98

THE EUROPEAN COMMUNITY   98
 7 The Community and the Union   98

SOURCES OF EU LAW   100
 8 The EC Treaty   100
 9 Supremacy of EC law   101
10 Secondary legislation   102
11 Secondary legislation and subsidiarity   103
12 Consultation procedure   104
13 Co-decision procedure   105
14 Cooperation procedure   106
15 Assent procedure   106
16 Voting in the Council   106
17 Application of secondary legislation   107
18 Jurisdiction and jurisprudence of the ECJ   108
19 Jurisdiction under Article 234   110
20 Expansion of the doctrine of direct effect   111
21 State liability   115

FUNDAMENTAL RIGHTS IN EU LAW 119
22 Fundamental human rights 119
23 General principles of EU law 121
24 Proportionality 121
25 Equality 122
26 Legal certainty 122
27 Procedural justice 123
28 A note on citizenship of the EU 125
Progress test 125
Further reading 126

8 Interpretation of UK and EU legislation 127

1 Introduction 127
2 The normal rule 127
3 Case study 129
4 Intrinsic aids 131
5 Extrinsic aids 132
6 Search for the underlying purpose 133
7 Adding words to the text 135
8 Human Rights Act 1998 137
9 European law 140
10 Case study 143
11 Transposed legislation 144
Appendix 145
Progress test 149
Further reading 150

Part Three LAW IN ACTION 153

9 Resourcing legal services 155

1 Introduction 155
2 The Community Legal Service 156
3 Eligibility for assistance 161
4 The Criminal Defence Service 162
5 Eligibility for financial assistance 163
6 Contingency and conditional fee agreements 164
7 Contingency fee agreements 167
8 Pro bono publico 168
Progress test 169
Further reading 169

10 Criminal justice system 1 170

1 Introduction 170
2 The regulatory framework 170
3 Stop and search 172
4 Search under warrant 174

 5 Helping police with inquiries   175
 6 The alternative to arrest and charge   175
 7 Arrest   176
 8 Arrest without a warrant   177
 9 Making an arrest   179
10 Role of the custody officer   180
11 The power of search after arrest   181
12 Search of premises following arrest   183
13 Detention without charge   183
14 Decision-making by the custody officer   184
15 Review of detention   185
16 Questioning of suspects   187
17 The right to remain silent   190
18 The decision to charge   190
19 Police discretion   192
20 The role of the Crown Prosecution Service   194
21 The decision to prosecute   194
22 Other prosecuting agencies   196
23 Jurisdiction of the criminal courts   196
24 Charge bargaining   197
25 Consent for a prosecution   197
26 Immunity from prosecution   198
   Progress test   198
   Further reading   199

11 Criminal justice system 2   **200**

 1 Introduction   200
 2 Classification of offences   201

SUMMARY TRIAL FOR ADULTS   201
 3 Conduct of the trial   201
 4 A submission of 'no case'   203
 5 The defence   203
 6 The verdict   203
 7 Remanding the accused   204

EITHER WAY OFFENCES   206
 8 Mode of trial   206
 9 Committal proceedings   207

TRIAL ON INDICTMENT   208
10 Pre-trial disclosure of information   208
11 Plea bargaining prior to trial   210
12 Meetings between advocates and judge   211
13 The indictment   211
14 Pre-trial and preparatory hearings   212
15 Empanelling the jury   214
16 Conduct of the trial   215

17 The prosecution case   216
18 Evidence and admissibility   216
19 Submission of 'no case to answer'   218
20 The case for the defence   219
21 The judge's summing up   220
22 Retirement of jury and verdict   220
23 Sentencing – some introductory remarks   221
24 Sentencing procedure   221
25 Evidence of character and antecedents   222
26 Reports on the offender   223
27 Mitigation of sentence   223
28 Types of sentence   223
29 Concurrent and consecutive sentences   225
30 Statutory criteria and custodial sentences   225
31 Pronouncing sentence   226

APPEALS   227
32 Appeals from magistrates' courts   227
33 Appeals to the Crown Court   228
34 Appeal by way of case stated   229
35 Appeal by claim for judicial review   230
36 Appeals to the Court of Appeal (Criminal Division)   230
37 Determination of an appeal against conviction   231
38 Appeal against sentence   233
39 Appeal to the House of Lords   234
40 Application to the European Court of Human Rights   234
41 The Criminal Cases Review Commission   235
    Progress test   236
    Further reading   236

12 Dispute resolution 1: Civil litigation   **238**

 1 Introduction   238
 2 The quiet revolution   238
 3 The scenario   239
 4 Pre-action protocols   240
 5 Issue and service of proceedings   241
 6 Responding to the particulars of claim   244
 7 Agreed settlements: Part 36 Offers and Payments   246
 8 Allocation of the case   249
 9 The small claims procedure   253
10 The listing questionnaire   254
11 Trials on the fast track   255
12 Multi track trials   256
13 Conduct of the trial   257
14 Delivering judgement   258
15 Remedies   258
16 Enforcement of judgements   259

17 Appeals 260
   Progress test 262
   Further reading 263

13 Dispute resolution 2: The role of tribunals 264

1 Introduction 264
2 Administrative tribunals 265
3 Employment tribunals 267
4 Discrimination in employment 268
5 Expansion of jurisdiction under the Conservatives 268
6 Expansion in jurisdiction since 1997 270
7 Employment tribunal procedure 271
8 Appeals from employment tribunals 272
9 Domestic tribunals 273
10 Procedural fairness 274
   Progress test 277
   Further reading 277

14 Dispute resolution 3: Alternative forms of resolution 279

1 Introduction 279
2 Mediation 280
3 Conciliation 282
4 Other forms of ADR 285
5 Arbitration 286
6 Arbitration schemes 289
7 Appeals from an arbitrator's award 291
8 ADR and arbitration compared 293
   Progress test 293
   Further reading 293

15 Dispute resolution 4: Judicial review 295

1 Introduction 295
2 Form of the action 296
3 Exclusion of judicial review 299
4 The established categories 299
5 Illegality 300
6 Procedural fairness in general 309
7 Procedural fairness: the rule against bias 309
8 Procedural fairness: the duty to act fairly 312
9 Irrationality or unreasonableness 320
10 Proportionality 325
11 Procedure: making an application 327
12 Appeals 330
13 Remedies 330

14 Liability in tort   332
    Progress test   333
    Further reading   334

16 Law reform and the Law Commission   335

1 Introduction   335
2 Royal Commissions   336
3 The Law Reform Committee   337
4 The Criminal Law Revision Committee   338
5 The Law Commission   338
6 Personnel of the Law Commission   338
7 The statutory remit of the Law Commission   339
8 Methods of working   340
9 The Seventh Programme and beyond   341
10 An evaluation of the Law Commission   341
    Progress test   342
    Further reading   343

Part Four LEGAL SKILLS   345

17 Legal skills 1   347

1 Introduction   347
2 Older law reports   348
3 Reports of the ICLREW   349
4 Modern reports of the ICLREW   351
5 Other law reports   352
6 Using the *Current Law Case Citator*   352
7 Locating recent case reports   353
8 Legislation   354
9 Strategy for using *Halsbury's Statutes of England*   355
10 Subordinate legislation   356
11 Locating European materials   356
12 Legal textbooks   357
13 Legal periodicals   358
14 Legal dictionaries   359
    Further reading   359

18 Legal skills 2   360

1 Introduction   360
2 Locating material   361
3 Researching legal problems   362
4 Using *Halsbury's Law of England*   362
5 The Lexis and Westlaw databases   364
6 Format of a modern law report   364
7 Reading case law   365

8 Preparing and delivering a seminar paper   366
9 Essay writing   367
10 Examinations   369
Further reading   371

Index   **373**

Preface

One of the problems that I have experienced in the year that it has taken to write this book has been ensuring that the content of the earlier chapters remains up to date. It has been necessary to revisit some completed chapters to include material that takes account of the most recent developments and excise the material that has become outdated. For example, Chapter 7 had to be revisited in order to include new material necessitated by the signing of the Treaty of Nice in February 2001 and revisited again to reflect the 'no' vote in the Irish referendum in June 2001. The creation of a companion website is intended to ensure that the text does not become dated too soon. Unfortunately, it has not been possible to incorporate the findings and recommendations of the report by Sir Andrew Leggatt on tribunals and the system of administrative justice as publication has been delayed. The same applies to the long awaited final report of Lord Justice Auld on the criminal courts which is likely to suggest far-reaching changes. I hope to be able to deal with these developments on the website in due course.

In writing the book, I have aimed to produce an accessible text that covers the topics forming an English legal system course of an LLB or similar under-graduate degree programme in reasonable depth. I hope that this book will provide the reader with a bridge to the more scholarly texts and articles that have been listed at the end of each chapter. These will enable the reader to develop his/her understanding of the various topics still further. They should also raise the reader's awareness of the fact that not everything in law is as cut and dried as might at first appear and that there is scope for debate and controversy. It is this which makes law such a stimulating academic discipline.

A number of people have helped me in the course of writing the book by providing constructive criticism and suggestions. I should like to express my thanks to Pat Bond at Pearson Education, my colleague at Roehampton, Jane Offler, Dr Ann Brady, Jeff Kenner, Barry Sweeney and to one other who cannot be specifically acknowledged for his comments on Chapter 11. None of these is in any way responsible for any errors that might have crept into the text although it has been checked and double-checked. Special thanks are due to Eileen Thorogood and Mary Clare McNamara who did so much to improve the general readability of the text. I have endeavoured to state the law as at 30 June 2001.

John Wheeler
Roehampton

Table of cases

Alderson *v* Booth [1969] 2 QB 216 *176*

Amministrazione delle Finanze dello Stato *v* Simmenthal (Case 106/77) [1978] ECR 629 *102*

Anisminic Ltd *v* Foreign Compensation Commission [1969] AC 147 *299*

Appleby Bros *v* Myers (1867) LRCP 651 *44*

Arthur J.S. Hall and Co. *v* Simons [2000] 3 All ER 673 *19*

Associated Provincial Picture Houses Ltd *v* Wednesbury Corporation [1948] 1 KB 223 *296*

Attorney General *v* BBC [1981] AC 303 *264*

Bank of Credit and Commerce (in liquidation) *v* Ali and others [2000] 3 All ER 51 *59*

Barber *v* Guardian Royal Exchange Assurance Group (Case C-262/88) [1990] ECR I-1889 *144*

Bayerische HNL Vermehrungsbetriebe GmbH & Co. KG *v* Council and Commission (Cases 83, 94/76; 4, 15, 40/77) [1978] ECR 1209 *110*

Bela-Muhle Josef Bergmann KG *v* Grows-Farm GmbH & Co. KG (Case 114/76) [1977] ECR 1211 *121, 326*

Bilka-Kaufhaus GmbH *v* Weber von Hartz (Case 170/84) [1986] ECR 1607 *144*

Boddington *v* British Transport Police [1999] AC 143 *80, 298*

Bonsor *v* Musicians' Union [1955] 3 All ER 518 *276*

Boys *v* Chaplin [1968] 2 QB 1 *48*

Brasserie du Pecheur SA *v* Germany and R *v* Secretary of State for Transport *ex p*. Factortame Ltd and others (Joined Cases C-46/93 and 48/93) [1996] 1 CMLR 889 [1999] 4 All ER 906 *75, 116*

Brind and others *v* Secretary of State for the Home Department [1991] 1 All ER 720 *307*

British Railways Board *v* Herrington [1972] AC 877 *46*

British Railways Board *v* Picken [1974] 1 AC 765 *75*

British Telecommunications Plc *v* Sheridan [1990] IRLR 27 *272*

Bushell *v* Secretary of State for the Environment [1981] AC 75 *315*

Carrington and others *v* Therm-A-Stor Ltd [1983] ICR 208 *129, 131*

Carltona Ltd *v* Commissioners of Works [1943] 2 All ER 560 *307*

Central London Property Trust *v* High Trees House Ltd [1947] KB 130 *45*

Chief Constable of North Wales *v* Evans [1982] 1 WLR 1155 *317*

Chiron Corporation *v* Murex Diagnostics Ltd [1995] All ER (EC) 88 *142*

CILFIT *v* Ministro della Sanità (Case 283/81) [1982] ECR 3415 *142*

Cocks *v* Thanet County Council [1983] 2 AC 286 *297*

Commission *v* Germany (Case 249/86) [1989] ECR 1263 *120*

Commission *v* Hellenic Republic (Case C-387/97) (As yet unreported) *109*

Commission *v* Italy (Case 22/87) [1989] ECR 143 *116*

Commissioners of Customs and Excise *v* Samex Ap S [1983] 1 All ER 1042 *141, 143*

Condron *v* UK [2000] Crim. LR 679 *190, 232*

Conway v Rimmer [1968] AC 910 46
Council for the Civil Service Unions v
   Minister for the Civil Service [1985]
   AC 374 299, 300, 314
Costa v ENEL (Case 6/64) [1964] ECR
   585 101, 111, 141

DPP ex p. Manning [2000] 3 WLR 463
   195
Defrenne v SABENA (Case 43/75)
   [1976] ECR 455 101
Denkavit International BV v
   Bundesamt für Finanzen (Cases
   C-283/94, C-291/94 & C-292/94)
   [1996] ECR I-5063 118
Dillenkofer and others v Germany
   (Cases C-178/94, C-179/94,
   C-188/94, C-189/94 and C-190/94)
   [1996] ECR I-4845 118
DPP v Jordan [1977] AC 699 131
Duncan v Cammell Laird & Co. [1942]
   AC 124 46

Elder, Dempster & Co. Ltd v Paterson,
   Zochonis & Co. Ltd [1924] AC 522 44
Ellis v Dubowski [1921] 3 KB 621 306
European Parliament v Council (Case
   C-295/90) [1992] ECR I-4193 110
Exportation des Sucres v Commission
   (Case 88/76) [1997] ECR 709 123

Faccini Dori v Recreb Srl (Case
   C-91/92) [1994] ECR I-3325 115
Factortame Ltd and others v Secretary
   of State for Transport [1989] 2 All
   ER 692 74
Factortame Ltd and others v Secretary
   of State for Transport No. 2 [1991]
   1 All ER 70 73
Foster v British Gas (Case C-188/89)
   [1990] ECR 3313 114
France v UK (Case C-141/78) [1979]
   ECR 2923 109
Francovich and Bonifaci v Italian State
   (Cases 6 and 9/90) [1991] ECR
   I-5357 115

Garland v British Rail Engineering
   (Case 12/81) [1982] ECR 359 144

Glamorgan C.C. v Rafferty [1987] 1 All
   ER 1005 324
Grad v Finanzamt Traunstein (Case
   9/70) [1970] ECR 825 111
Griffin v South West Water Services
   Ltd [1995] IRLR 15 114
Gross v O'Toole (1982) 4 Cr. App. R.
   (S) 283 223

Hall & Co. Ltd v Shoreham by Sea
   UDC [1964] 1 WLR 240 326
Harz v Deutsche Tradax (Case 79/83)
   [1984] ECR 1921 115
Hayter v L and another [1998] 1 WLR
   854 193
Hazell v Hammersmith & Fulham LBC
   [1992] 2 AC 1 303
Hedley Byrne Ltd v Heller & Partners
   Ltd [1964] AC 465 45
Heil v Rankin [2000] 2 WLR 1173 340
Herne Bay Steam Boat Co. v Hutton
   [1903] 2 KB 683 49
HM Treasury v British
   Telecommunications Plc (Case
   C-392/93) [1996] 2 CMLR 217 118
Hoffman La Roche v Secretary of State
   for Trade [1975] AC 295 88
Hotel and Catering Industry Training
   Board v Automotive Proprietary Ltd
   [1969] 1 WLR 1 89, 267
H.P. Bulmer Ltd v J. Bollinger SA
   [1974] 2 WLR 202 141

Inco Europe Ltd and others v First
   Choice Distribution and others
   [2000] 2 All ER 109 77, 136
Ingram v Little [1961] 1 QB 31 46
Inland Revenue Commissioners v
   National Federation of Self
   Employed and Small Businesses
   [1982] AC 617 328
Internationale Handelsgesellschaft
   GmbH v Einfuhr-und Vorratstelle
   für Getreide und Futtermittel (Case
   11/70) [1970] ECR 1125 102, 119

James v Eastleigh Borough Council
   [1990] 1 AC 751 322
Johnson v Moreton [1980] AC 37 132

Johnston v Chief Constable of the Royal Ulster Constabulary (Case 222/84) [1986] ECR 1651 *114, 120*

Kampelmann v Landschaftsverband Westfalen-Lippe (Joined Cases C-253/96 and C-258/96) [1997] ECR I-6907 *114*

Krell v Henry [1903] 2 KB 740 *49*

Ladd v Marshall [1954] 1 WLR 1489 *261*

Lee v Showmen's Guild [1952] 2 QB 329 *275*

Les Vert-Parti Ecologiste v Parliament (Case 294/83) [1986] ECR 1339 *99*

Lewis v Avery [1972] 1 QB 198 *46*

Litster v Forth Dry Dock and Engineering Co. Ltd [1989] IRLR 161, [1989] ICR 341 *144*

Mandla v Dowell Lee [1983] ICR 385, [1983] IRLR 209 *132*

Marleasing SA v La Commercial Internacional de Alimentacion SA (Case C-106/89) [1990] ECR 4135, [1992] 1 CMLR 305 *115, 145*

Marshall v Southampton and South West Hampshire Area Health Authority (Teaching) (Case 152/84) [1986] ECR 723 *112, 113*

McKay v Northern Ireland Public Service Alliance [1995] IRLR 146 *135*

McLeod v UK [1998] 27 EHRR 493 *175*

Mirehouse v Rennell (1833) 1 CL & F 527, 546 *41*

Nickoll and Knight v Ashton [1901] 2 KB 126 *43*

Nold v Commission (Case 4/73) [1974] ECR 491 *120*

NUT and others v Governing body of St Mary's Church of England (Aided) Junior School [1997] 1 ICR 334 *114*

NV Algemene Transporten-Expeditie OndernemingVan Gend en Loos v Nederlandse Administratie der Belastingen (Case 26/62) [1963] ECR 1 *see* Van Gend en Loos

O'Reilly v Mackman [1983] 2 AC 237 *296*

Padfield v Minister of Agriculture, Fisheries and Food [1968] AC 997 *300*

Pengelly v Bell Punch Co. Ltd [1964] 1 WLR 1055 *132*

Pepper (HM Inspector of Taxes) v Hart [1993] 1 All ER 42 *133, 135*

Phillips v Brooks [1919] 2 KB 243 *46*

Pickstone v Freemans Plc [1982] All ER 803 *135*

Plaumann & Co. v Commission (Case 25/62) [1963] ECR 95 *109*

Pubblico Ministero v Ratti (Case 148/78) [1979] ECR 1629 *112*

R v A [2001] 3 All ER 1 *139*

R v Brosch [1988] Crim. LR 743 *176*

R v Civil Service Board ex p. Cunningham [1991] 4 All ER 310 *319*

R v Davidson [1988] Crim. LR 442 *184*

R v Disciplinary Committee of the Jockey Club ex p. Aga Khan [1993] 2 All ER 853 *298*

R v DPP ex p. Association of First Division Civil Servants *The Times* 24 May 1988 *307*

R v DPP ex p. Manning [2000] 3 WLR 463 *195*

R v Forde [1923] 2 KB 400 *231*

R v Gough [1993] AC 646 *310*

R v Gray [1900] 2 QB 36 *300*

R v Guppy [1994] Crim. LR 614 *223*

R v Herrod ex p. Leeds County Council [1976] QB 540 *317*

R v Hillingdon LBC ex p. Royco Homes Ltd [1974] 1 QB 720 *325*

R v Hughes *The Times* 12 November 1993 *182*

R *v* Huntingdon Crown Court *ex p.* Jordan [1981] QB 857 *227*

R *v* Inland Revenue Commissioners *ex p.* Matrix Securities Ltd [1994] 1 WLR 334 *322*

R *v* Kent Kirk (Case 63/83) [1985] 1 All ER 453 *120, 123*

R *v* Law Society *ex p.* Reigate Projects [1993] 1 WLR 1531 *318*

R *v* Liverpool Corporation *ex p.* Liverpool Taxi Fleet Operators' Association [1972] 2 QB 299 *313*

R *v* Liverpool University *ex p.* Caesar-Gordon [1991] 1 QB 124 *305*

R *v* Lord Chancellor *ex p.* Witham [1997] 2 All ER 779 *89*

R *v* McMullen [2000] QB 520 *232*

R *v* Metropolitan Police Commissioner *ex p.* Blackburn [1968] 2 QB 118 *192*

R *v* Ministry of Agriculture, Fisheries and Food *ex p.* Hedley Lomas (Case C-5/94) [1996] 2 CMLR 391 *118*

R *v* Newton (1982) 77 Cr. App. R. 13 *222*

R *v* North and East Devon Health Authority *ex p.* Coughlan (Secretary of State for Health and another intervening) [2000] 3 All ER 850 *307, 321*

R *v* Nottingham Justices *ex p.* Davies [1981] QB 38 *204*

R *v* Panel on Takeovers and Mergers *ex p.* Datafin [1987] QB 815 *299*

R *v* Port Talbot B.C. and others *ex p.* Jones [1988] 2 All ER 207 *322*

R *v* Secretary of State for the Environment *ex p.* Rose Theatre Trust [1990] 1 QB 504 *328*

R *v* Secretary of State for Foreign Affairs *ex p.* World Development Movement Ltd [1995] 1 WLR 356 *304, 329*

R *v* Secretary of State for Health *ex p.* United States Tobacco International Inc. [1992] QB 353 *314*

R *v* Secretary of State for the Home Department *ex p.* Bentley [1994] QB 349 *302*

R *v* Secretary of State for the Home Department *ex p.* Dannenberg [1984] QB 766 *308*

R *v* Secretary of State for the Home Department *ex p.* Doody [1994] 1 AC 531 *315*

R *v* Secretary of State for the Home Department *ex p.* Fayed [1997] 1 All ER 228 *319*

R *v* Secretary of State for the Home Department *ex p.* Fire Brigades Union [1995] AC 583 *302*

R *v* Secretary of State for the Home Department *ex p.* Venables [1997] 1 WLR 23 *324*

R *v* Secretary of State for Trade and Industry *ex p.* Eastway [2001] 1 All ER 27 *329*

R *v* Secretary of State for Transport *ex p.* Factortame Ltd and others (Case C-213/89) [1990] ECR I-2433 *74*

R *v* Secretary of State for Transport *ex p.* Pegasus Holidays (London) Ltd and Airbro (UK) Ltd [1988] 1 WLR 990 *326*

R *v* Turner [1970] 2 QB 321 *211*

R *v* West London Coroner *ex p.* Dallagho and another [1994] 4 All ER 139 *310*

R (on the application of Alconbury Developments Ltd) *v* Secretary of State for the Environment, Transport and the Regions [2001] 2 All ER 929 *139*

Racke *v* Hauptzollamt Mainz (Case 98/78) [1979] ECR 69 *123*

Rakhit *v* Carty [1990] 2 All ER 202 *47*

Raymond *v* Honey [1983] 1 AC 1 *300, 308*

Ricards *v* Ricards [1989] 3 All ER 193 *47*

Ridge *v* Baldwin [1964] AC 40 *312, 317*

Rinner-Kuhn *v* FWW (Case 171/88) [1989] ECR 2743 *144*

Robert Addie & Sons (Collieries) Ltd *v* Dumbreck [1929] AC 358 *46*

Rondel v Worsley [1967] 3 All ER 993
19
Roquette Frères v Council (Case
138/79) [1980] ECR 3333 104
Roy v Kensington and Chelsea and
Westminster FPC [1992] 1 All ER
705 298

Schmidt v Secretary of State for Home
Affairs [1969] 2 Ch 149 314
Scruttons Ltd v Midland Silicones Ltd
[1962] AC 466 44
Showboat Entertainment Centre Ltd v
Owens [1984] IRLR 7 135

Taff Vale Railway Co. Ltd v ASRS
[1901] AC 426 72
Taylor v Caldwell (1863) 3 B & S 826
42, 43, 44, 45, 49
The Post Office v Lewis [1997] LS Gaz.
94/18, 32 273
Transocean Marine Paint Association
v Commission (Case 17/74) [1974]
ECR 1063 123

UK v Council (Case C-84/94) [1996]
ECR I-5755 269

Van Gend en Loos v Nederlandse
Administratie (Case 26/62) [1963]
ECR 1 98, 111, 140

Van Duyn v Home Office (Case 41/74)
[1974] ECR 1337 112
Victoria Square Property Co. Ltd v
Southwark LBC [1978] 2 All ER 281
323
Von Colson and Kamann v Land
Nordrhein-Westfalen (Case 14/83)
[1984] ECR 1891 115

Wandsworth Corporation v Winder
[1985] AC 461 297
Warwickshire C.C. v Johnson [1993]
1 All ER 299 134
Weathersfield Ltd v Sargent [1998]
IRLR 14 136
Wilson v First County Trust Ltd [2001]
3 All ER 229 139
Wordingham v Royal Exchange Trust
Co. Ltd [1992] 3 All ER 204 60
Worringham v Lloyds Bank (Case
69/80) [1981] ECR 767 144

Yaxley v Golls [1999] 3 WLR 1217 132
Young v Bristol Aeroplane Co. Ltd
[1944] KB 718 46

Zarczynska v Levy [1978] 1 All ER 814,
[1979] ICR 184, [1978] IRLR 532 135,
136
Zuckerfabrik Schoppenstedt v Council
(Case 5/71) [1971] ECR 975 110

Table of statutes

Access to Justice Act 1999
  s. 1(1) *156*
  s. 1(2) *156*
  s. 3 *156*
  s. 4(1) *156*
  s. 4(2) *157*
  s. 4(6) *157*
  s. 5(1) *157*
  s. 5(3) *157*
  s. 5(6) *157*
  s. 12(1) *162*
  s. 12(2) *163*
  s. 16 *163*
  s. 27 *165*
  s. 36 *11*
  s. 40(2) *13*
  s. 49 *24*
  s. 51 *24, 164*
  Schedule 2 *160*
Acquisition of Land Act 1981 *80*
Acts of Parliament Numbering and
    Citation Act 1962 *72*
Administration of Justice Act 1960
  s. 1 *330*
Administration of Justice
    (Miscellaneous Provisions)
    Act 1933
  s. 2(1) *212*
  s. 2(2) *212*
Agricultural Marketing Act 1958
  s. 19(3) *301*
Ancient Monuments and
    Archaeological Areas Act
    1979
  s. 1(1) *328*
Appellate Jurisdiction Act 1876 *34,
    58*
Appropriation Act 1994 *303*
Arbitration Act 1950
  s. 26 *286*
  s. 32 *287*

Arbitration Act 1996 *77*
  s. 1(a) *288*
  s. 1(b) *288*
  s. 9(1) *287*
  s. 9(4) *288*
  s. 23 *288*
  s. 24 *288*
  s. 26 *286*
  s. 26(1) *128*
  s. 33 *291*
  s. 33(b) *288*
  s. 45 *287*
  s. 46(1) *288*
  s. 48(5) *288*
  s. 57 *292*
  s. 68(1) *291*
  s. 68(2) *291, 292*
  s. 68(3) *291*
  s. 68(4)–(6) *292*
  s. 69 *292*
  s. 69(2) *292*
  s. 69(3) *292*
  s. 69(4)–(6) *292*
  s. 69(7) *292*
  s. 70(2) *292*
  s. 82(1) *292*
  Schedule 3 para. 37(2) *136*
Asylum and Immigration Appeals
    Act 1993 *330*
Attachment of Earnings Act 1971
  s. 6(1) *260*

Bail Act 1976
  s. 3A(5) *184*
  s. 7 *213*
  Schedule 1 *205*
    paras 2–6 *205*
    para. 11A *204*
Betting and Gaming and Lotteries Act
    1963
  s. 49 *317*

Schedule 6 *317*
  para. 3 *317*
  para. 4 *317*
British Nationality Act 1981 *330*
  s. 44(2) *320*

Caravan Sites Act 1968
  s. 6(1) *324*
Children Act 1989 *33, 342*
Children and Young Persons Act 1933
  s. 42 *217*
  s. 53(1) *324*
Cinematograph Act 1909 *306*
Civil Aviation Act 1982 *197*
Civil Procedure Act 1997 *239*
Companies Act 1985 *251*
Computer Misuse Act 1990 *342*
Consolidation of Enactments
  (Procedure) Act 1949 *71*
Consumer Credit Act 1974
  s. 127(3) *139*
Consumer Protection Act 1987
  s. 20(1) *134*
  s. 20(2) *134*
Contracts (Rights of Third Parties)
  Act 1999 *342*
Coroners Act 1988
  s. 16(3) *311*
County Courts Act 1984
  s. 66 *257*
Courts Act 1971 *336*
Courts and Legal Services Act 1990 *11*
  s. 21 *23*
  s. 22 *23*
  s. 56 *29*
  s. 58 *164*
  s. 58(1) *165*
  s. 58A(1) *165*
  s. 58A(2) *165*
  s. 58(3) *165*
  s. 62 *20*
Crime and Disorder Act 1998
  s. 50 *163*
  s. 51 *208, 213*
  s. 65 *193*
  s. 66 *193*
Criminal Appeal Act 1968
  s. 1 *231*
  s. 2(1) *231*

s. 7(1) *233*
s. 9(1) *233*
s. 102 *233*
s. 33 *234*
s. 34 *234*
Criminal Appeal Act 1995 *235*
Criminal Courts (Sentencing) Act 2000
  s. 79(2) *225*
  s. 79(4) *227*
  s. 81 *223*
  s. 155(1) *227*
Criminal Justice Act 1967
  s. 1 *208*
  s. 9 *217*
  s. 10 *215*
Criminal Justice Act 1987
  s. 2 *192*
Criminal Justice Act 1988
  s. 23 *217*
  s. 25 *217*
  s. 40(1) *212*
  ss 108–117 *302*
  s. 171(1) *303*
  Schedule 6 *303*
  Schedule 7 *303*
Criminal Justice Act 1991
  s. 35 *324*
Criminal Justice Act 1993 *337*
  ss 1–6 *196*
Criminal Justice and Public Order Act
  1994 *342*
  s. 34 *190*
  s. 35 *190, 219*
  s. 36 *190*
  s. 37 *190*
  s. 60 *173*
Criminal Justice (Terrorism and
  Conspiracy) Act 1998
  ss 5–8 *196*
Criminal Law Act 1967
  s. 6 *210*
Criminal Law Act 1977
  s. 14 *201*
Criminal Procedure and Investigations
  Act 1996
  s. 3 *209*
  s. 5(8) *219*
  ss 28–38 *214*
  s. 39 *212*

s. 40 *212*
Schedule 2
  para. 1(4) *217*

Data Protection Act 1998 *108*
Deregulation and Contracting Out Act
  1994 *83, 87*
Diplomatic Privileges Act 1964 *198*
Disability Discrimination Act 1995 *270*

Education (No. 2) Act 1986
  s. 43 *306*
Employment Act 1980 *268*
Employment Relations Act 1999
  ss 7–9 *270*
  ss 10–11 *270*
  s. 16 *270*
Employment Rights Act 1996 *71*
  s. 67 *269*
  s. 68 *269*
  s. 70(1) *269*
  s. 70(4) *269*
Employment Protection Act 1975 *222*
Environmental Protection Act 1990
  s. 82 *165*
Equal Pay Act 1970 *268*
European Communities Act 1972 *73*
  s. 2(1) *99*
  s. 2(2) *79, 108*

Family Law Act 1996 *342*
Finance Act 1976
  s. 61 *133*
  s. 61(1) *133*
  s. 63 *133*
Firearms Act 1968
  s. 47 *173*
Foreign Compensation Act 1950
  s. 4(4) *299*

Government of Scotland Act 1998 *35,
  63*
Government of Wales Act 1998
  s. 44 *80*
  s. 58 *88*

Highways Act 1959
  s. 11 *315*
  Schedule 2 *315, 316*

Highways Act 1980 *332*
House of Lords Act 1999 *63*
Housing Act 1957 *297, 323*
  s. 17(2) *297, 323*
Housing (Homeless Persons) Act 1977
  297
Human Rights Act 1998
  s. 1(2) *138*
  s. 2(1) *48, 232*
  s. 3 *138*
  s. 3(1) *138, 232*
  s. 3(2)(b) *75*
  s. 4 *139*
  s. 4(2) *75*
  s. 4(6) *139*
  s. 5(2) *139, 146*
  s. 6 *307*
  s. 6(1) *48, 138, 256*
  s. 6(2) *138*
  s. 7 *138*
  s. 7(1) *137*
  s. 7(7) *137*
  s. 10 *85*
  s. 14 *138*
  s. 15 *138*
  s. 19 *67*
  Schedule 1 *75, 137*
    Article 2 *145*
    Article 3 *146, 189*
    Article 4 *146*
    Article 4(1) *146*
    Article 4(2) *146*
    Article 4(3) *146*
    Article 5 *146, 174*
    Article 6 *147, 190*
    Article 6(1) *147*
    Article 7 *147*
    Article 8 *148, 174, 175*
    Article 9 *148*
    Article 10 *148*
    Article 11 *148*
    Article 12 *149*
    Article 14 *149*
  Schedule 3 *138*

Immigration Act 1971 *330*
  s. 5(1) *308*
  s. 6(1) *308*
  s. 6(2) *308*

s. 13(5) *307*
s. 14(3) *307*
s. 15(4) *307*
Industrial Training Act 1964
  s. 1 *89*
  s. 4 *89*
  s. 12 *267*
Industrial Tribunals Act 1996 *272*
International Transport Conventions
    Act 1983 *87*
  s. 8 *87*
  s. 9 *87*

Judicial Committee Act 1833 *35*
Juries Act 1974
  s. 12(1)(b) *215*

Landlord and Tenant Act 1927 *241*
Landlord and Tenant Act 1954 *241*
Land Registration Act 1997 *342*
Law Commissions Act 1965 *338*
  s. 3(1) *339*
Law Reform (Frustrated Contracts)
    Act 1943 *337*
Law Reform (Year and a Day) Act 1996
  197
Legal Aid Act 1988 *164*
Life Peerages Act 1958 *63*
Local Government Act 1972 *80, 303,*
  304
Local Government Act 1988 *269*
Local Government Finance Act 1982
  304

Magistrates' Courts Act 1980
  s. 1(1) *176, 200*
  s. 1(4) *176*
  s. 2 *201, 207*
  s. 5 *200*
  s. 6(1) *208, 232*
  s. 6(2) *208, 232*
  s. 10 *200*
  s. 12 *202*
  s. 17A *206*
  s. 18 *206*
  s. 19 *206, 207*
  s. 20 *206*
  s. 20(2) *206, 207*
  s. 21 *206*

s. 22 *206*
s. 97A *217*
s. 108 *228*
s. 109 *228*
s. 110 *228*
s. 111(1) *229*
s. 113(1) *228*
s. 125 *177*
s. 128 *204*
s. 128A *205*
Mental Health Act 1983 *241*
Merchant Shipping Act 1988 *74, 309*
Merchant Shipping Act 1995
  s. 282 *196*
Misrepresentation Act 1967
  s. 2(1) *75, 128*
Misuse of Drugs Act 1971
  s. 23 *173*

National Assistance Act 1948
  s. 21 *322*
National Health Act 1977
  s. 1 *322*
  s. 3 *322*
National Minimum Wage Act 1998
  270
Northern Ireland Act 1998 *35, 63, 80,*
  88

Occupiers' Liability Act 1957 *337*
Offences against the Person Act 1861
  193
Official Secrets Act 1911 *197*
Overseas Development and
    Cooperation Act 1980
  s. 1(1) *304*

Parliament Act 1911 *70*
Parliament Act 1949 *70*
Parliamentary Constituencies Act 1986
  63
Partnership Act 1890 *71*
Police Act 1996
  s. 30 *177*
Police and Criminal Evidence Act
    1984
  s. 1(1) *172*
  s. 1(2) *172*
  s. 1(3) *172*

s. 1(7)(b) *172*
s. 2(9)(a) *172*
s. 3 *172*
s. 4(1) *173*
s. 8(1) *174*
s. 8(2) *174, 175*
s. 8(3) *174*
s. 10(1) *174*
s. 11(1) *174*
s. 17(1) *178*
s. 18(4) *183*
s. 24 *177*
s. 24(4) *177*
s. 24(7) *177*
s. 25 *177, 178*
s. 29 *175*
s. 30(1) *183*
s. 32(1) *181*
s. 32(2)(b) *183*
s. 32(4) *181*
s. 32(5) *184*
s. 34(1) *184*
s. 34(2)(b) *184*
s. 34(5)(b) *184*
s. 35 *184*
s. 36(1) *180*
s. 36(5) *180*
s. 37(1) *181*
s. 37(2) *184, 185*
s. 37(7)(a) *185*
s. 40(13) *186*
s. 42(1) *186*
s. 42(10) *186*
s. 44(1) *187*
s. 46(2) *200*
s. 54(1) *181*
s. 54(6) *182*
s. 55(1)(a) *182*
s. 55(1)(b) *182*
s. 58 *188*
s. 67(1) *171*
s. 67(4) *171*
ss. 83–106 *171*
Schedule 2 *178*
Powers of the Criminal Courts
        (Sentencing) Act 2000 *342*
s. 52(4) *225*
s. 79(2) *225*
s. 79(4) *227*

s. 80 *226*
s. 80(2)(a) *226*
s. 80(2)(b) *226*
s. 81 *223*
s. 109 *226*
s. 109(2) *226*
s. 109(5) *225*
s. 110(2) *225*
s. 111(2) *225*
s. 155(1) *227*
Prison Act 1952
s. 47 *300*
Prosecution of Offences Act 1985
s. 1 *197*
s. 1(7) *197*
s. 3(2) *194*
s. 22 *205*
Public Interest Disclosure Act 1998 *64,
        270*
Public Order Act 1986 *193*
s. 4(1) *178*
s. 5(4) *179*
s. 12 *179*
s. 13(10) *179*
s. 14(4) *179*
s. 18(3) *179*

Race Relations Act 1968 *268*
Race Relations Act 1976 *268*
s. 1(1)(a) *135, 136*
s. 4(2)(c) *135*
s. 30 *136*
Rehabilitation of Offenders Act 1974
        222
Road Traffic Act 1988
s. 7 *187*
Road Traffic Offenders Act 1988
s. 24 *204*
Royal Assent Act 1967 *70*
Rules of Publication Act 1893 *80*

Sale of Goods Act 1979 *71*
s. 11(3) *128*
Sex Discrimination Act 1975 *268*
Sex Discrimination (Amendment) Act
        1986 *113*
Sexual Offences Act 1956 *197*
Sexual Offences (Conspiracy and
        Incitement) Act 1996 *196*

Solicitors Act 1974 *274*
  s. 36 *318*
  s. 36(2)(a) *318, 319*
  s. 87(1) *167*
State Immunity Act 1978
  s. 20 *198*
Statutory Instruments Act 1946
  s. 1(1) *80*
  s. 1(2) *80*
  s. 2(1) *80*
  s. 4(1) *87*
Suicide Act 1961 *197*
Supreme Court Act 1981
  s. 16 *329*
  s. 18 *329*
  s. 29(3) *230*
  s. 31 *296, 297, 330*
  s. 31(2) *331*
  s. 31(3) *328*
  s. 31(4) *332*
  s. 48 *229*
  s. 49(1) *58*
  s. 59 *232*
  s. 69 *257*
  s. 80(2) *176*
  s. 81(1)(b) *228*
  s. 130 *90*
Supreme Court of Judicature Act 1873
  31, 58

Supreme Court of Judicature Act 1875
  58

Terrorism Act 2000
  s. 43(1) *173*
  s. 43(4) *173*
  s. 116(2) *173*
Theft Act 1968 *172, 338*
Theft Act 1978 *338*
Timeshare Act 1992 *77*
Trade Union and Labour Relations
  (Consolidation) Act 1992
  s. 152 *129*
  s. 152(1) *129*
  s. 152(1)(a) *129*
  s. 153 *129, 130*
Transport Act 1985
  s. 46 *87*
Tribunals and Inquiries Act 1958 *266*
Tribunals and Inquiries Act 1971
  s. 12 *319*
Tribunals and Inquiries Act 1992 *266*
  Schedule 1 *266*
Trustee Delegation Act 1999 *342*
Trustees Act 2000 *341*

Unfair Contract Terms Act 1977 *342*

War Crimes Act 1991 *197*

Table of statutory instruments

Conditional Fee Agreements Order
    1998 (SI 1998 No. 1860) *165*
Conditional Fee Agreements Order
    2000 (SI 2000 No. 823) *165*
Conditional Fee Agreements
    Regulations 2000 (SI 2000
    No. 692) *165*
Criminal Procedure and Investigations
    Act 1996 (Preparatory Hearings)
    Rules 1997 (SI 1997 No. 1052) *214*
Crown Court (Advance Notice of
    Expert Evidence) Rules 1987
    (SI 1987 No. 716)
  r. 3(1)(a) *210*
  r. 3(1)(b) *210*
Crown Court Rules (SI 1982 No. 1109)
    228

High Court and County Court
    Jurisdiction Order 1991 (SI 1991
    No. 724) *250*

Institute of Legal Executives Order
    1998 (SI 1998 No. 1077) *81*

Magistrates' Courts Rules 1981
    (SI 1981 No. 522)
  r. 7 *207*
  r. 13 *203*

Magistrates' Court (Advance
    Information) Rules 1985 (SI 1985
    No. 601)
  r. 5 *209*
Maternity and Parental Leave Etc.
    Regulations 1999 (SI 1999
    No. 3312) *81*

Part-time Workers (Prevention of
    Less Favourable Treatment)
    Regulations 2000 (SI 2000/1551)
    270

Transfer of Undertakings (Protection
    of Employment) Regulations 1981
    (SI 1981 No. 1794)
  Regulation 5(3) *144*
Transnational Information and
    Consultation of Employees
    Regulations 1999 (SI 1999
    No. 3323) *82*

Working Time Regulations 1998
    (SI 1998 No. 1833) *270*

EU treaties

EC Treaty
Article 2 *98*
Article 3 *98*
Article 4 *98*
Article 5 *103*
Article 6 *117*
Article 7 *92*
Article 10 *108, 115*
Article 12 *105, 122*
Article 12(2) *122*
Article 17 *125*
Article 19 *125*
Article 20 *125*
Article 21 *125*
Article 25 *100*
Article 28 *100*
Article 30 *117*
Article 34(2) *122*
Article 39 *101, 112, 122*
Article 43 *122*
Article 49 *122*
Article 50 *122*
Article 52 *117*
Article 62 *105*
Article 63 *105*
Article 65 *105*
Article 81 *101, 123*
Article 82 *101*
Article 87(1) *308*
Article 141 *122*

Article 157 *105*
Article 159 *105*
Article 191 *105*
Article 192 *103*
Article 194 *125*
Article 195 *125*
Article 202 *93*
Article 205 *106*
Article 205(1) *106*
Article 217 *95*
Article 220 *97*
Article 226 *108, 109*
Article 227 *109*
Article 228(2) *109*
Article 230 *98, 109*
Article 232 *98, 110*
Article 234 *110, 111*
Article 235 *98, 110*
Article 249 *103, 107, 113, 116*
Article 251 *105*
Article 252 *106*
Article 253 *104*
Article 288(2) *109, 110*
Article 308 *110*
Merger Treaty 1965
Article 4 *94*
Single European Act 1986 *106*
Treaty of Amsterdam 1997 *104, 105, 106*
Treaty of European Union 1992
Article 6 *124, 125*

EU secondary legislation

Directive 64/221/EEC on free
movement of workers *309*
Article 6 *309*
Article 9 *309*
Directive 75/442/EEC on development
of clean technologies and
recycling *109*
Directive 76/207/EEC on equal
treatment of men and
women *113, 114, 268*
Directive 77/187/EEC on safeguarding
employees' rights in the event of
transfers of undertakings *144, 269*
Directive 78/319/EEC on toxic and
dangerous waste *109*
Directive 80/987/EEC on the
protection of employees in the
event of insolvency of employers
115
Directive 85/577/EEC on contracts
negotiated away from business
premises *115*
Directive 90/314/EEC on package
holidays *118*
Directive 90/366/EEC on rights of
residence for students *110*
Directive 90/435/EEC on the taxation
of parent and subsidiary
companies in different states
Article 3(2) *119*

Directive 90/531/EEC
Telecommunications: Procurement
Procedures *118*
Directive 91/533/EEC proof of
employment contracts
Article 2(2)(c) *114, 269*
Directive 92/85/EEC on pregnant
workers *269*
Directive 93/104/EC on the
organisation of working time *110,
269*
Directive 96/34/EC on parental leave
270
Directive 97/74/EC on the extension
to the UK of Directive 94/45/EC
on the establishment of European
Works Councils *82*
Directive 97/81/EC on part-time work
270
Recommendation 92/131/EEC on
protection of the dignity of
women and men at work *108*
Regulation 17/62 on competition *123*
Regulation 1612/68 on free movement
of persons
Article 10 *120*
Regulation 563/76 on compulsory
purchase of skimmed-milk
powder *121*
Regulation 170/83 derogation
concerning common fisheries
policy *123*

Abbreviations

AC	Appeal Cases
ACAS	Advisory, Conciliation and Arbitration Service
ACI	Arbitration a Commercial Initiative
ADR	Alternative (Appropriate) dispute resolution
All ER	All England Reports
BVC	Bar Vocational Course
CBI	Confederation of British Industry
CEDR	Centre for Effective Dispute Resolution
CFI	Court of First Instance (Luxembourg)
Ch.	Chancery Division of High Court
CIA	Chartered Institute of Arbitrators
CLS	Community Legal Service
CPE	Common Professional Examination
CPR	Civil Procedure Rules
CPS	Crown Prosecution Service
DPP	Director of Public Prosecutions
EAT	Employment Appeal Tribunal
ECHR	European Convention on Human Rights and Fundamental Freedoms
ECJ	European Court of Justice (Luxembourg)
ECSC	European Coal and Steel Community
EDM	Early day motion
EEC	European Economic Community (now the European Community)
ETS	Employment Tribunals Service
EU	European Union
ICC	International Chamber of Commerce
ICLREW	Incorporated Council for Law Reporting in England and Wales
ILO	International Labour Organisation
JSB	Judicial Studies Board
LPC	Legal Practice Course
LRC	Learning resources centre
LSC	Legal Services Commission
LSCC	Legal Services Complaints Commission
LSO	Legal Services Ombudsman

MEP	Member of the European Parliament
ODA	Overseas Development Administration
OSS	Office for the Supervision of Solicitors
PACE	Police and Criminal Evidence Act 1984
PCC	Professional Conduct and Complaints Committee of Bar
PDH	Plea and Directions Hearings
QB	Queen's Bench Division of High Court
TUC	Trades Union Congress

Glossary of legal terms

A fortiori	With stronger reason
Ab initio	From the beginning
Acte clair	The law is so clear that no reference is necessary to the European Court of Justice
Action	A civil claim commenced under the Civil Procedure Rules
Actus reus	Conduct, which if combined with the necessary *mens rea*, is a crime
Adduce	Used in relation to producing evidence
Administrator	A person appointed by the court to distribute the property of a deceased person who did not make a will
Admissibility	Whether something is permitted to be given or allowed in evidence
Admonishment	A warning
Adversarial	Refers to the nature of civil and criminal litigation where both sides are in opposition to each other
Advocacy	The pleading of a case in court
Advocate	A solicitor or barrister who pleads a case in court
Affidavit	Written statement in the name of a person (the deponent) who swears and signs it
Affirm	(1) Where taking an oath is contrary to a person's religious belief he/she may affirm under the Oaths Act 1878; (2) an appellate court that upholds a judgement on appeal is said to affirm it
Appellant	The person who brings an appeal to a court or tribunal superior to the one that originally decided the issue(s)
Appellate	A court or tribunal whose jurisdiction entails the hearing of appeals
Arraignment	The procedure of calling a person to the bar of the court to plead to the charge(s) laid against him/her in the indictment
Attorney General	The principal legal advisor to the Crown who is appointed by letters patent – he/she is *ex officio*

	leader of the Bar and is a member of the government
Bail	Effectively the release from custody of a person who has been arrested but where the release is conditional on complying with whatever conditions are imposed
Beneficiary	A person for whose benefit a trust is created
Brief	A document instructing a barrister to appear in court
Case law	Law as contained in precedent – *see ratio decidendi*
Case stated	A statement of a case prepared by a lower court for consideration by a higher court
Cause of action	A recognised form of liability, for example a tort or breach of contract based on a set of facts
Caveats	These may be notes of caution to be heeded
Chancery	The term used to describe the office or court of the Chancellor
Commissioner for Oaths	A person appointed by the Lord Chancellor to administer oaths or affirmations and take affidavits
Common law	This term has a number of meanings but its primary meaning is in relation to rules developed in the old courts of common law. It is sometimes used to distinguish judge-made law from statute law
Conditional fee agreement	An agreement between a solicitor and client whereby the solicitor takes the risk that if he/she does not win the case, no fee will be charged but an additional amount based on the normal fee will be recovered if the case is won
Contempt of court	Failing to comply with an order of a superior court or an insult to the court or the judge(s)
Contentious proceedings	In general, these are proceedings begun before a court or arbitrator in the England and Wales
Contingency fee agreement	A agreement whereby a lawyer agrees to take a case on the basis that if the case is won the lawyer will receive a percentage of the damages
Convention	A form of treaty
Conveyancing	This is a process whereby the legal title to land is transferred from the seller to the purchaser

Coroner	These are usually persons with medical qualifications who convene inquests to inquire into the circumstances surrounding death of a person who has died in unusual or suspicious circumstances
Cross appeal	This is where both parties to a case appeal
Custom	Certain local customs have the force of law but it must have existed since 1189, be reasonable, certain and not contrary to any statute
Damages	Financial compensation
Deed	A document executed under seal and witnessed but which must also be delivered to the party in whose favour it is made
Director of Public Prosecutions	Head of the Crown Prosecution Service but the office was originally created in 1879 for a person to carry on criminal proceedings under the supervision of the Attorney General
Disbar	Expel a barrister from his/her Inn
Disbursements	Payment of expenses usually incurred with litigation or some legal service
Divisional Court	A court normally comprising two or three High Court judges
Empanelled	Refers to the swearing in of jury
Enactment	A general word denoting an Act of Parliament
Equity	The rules and remedies developed in the Court of Chancery but it can be used in a general sense to mean fairness or natural justice
Euratom	European Atomic Energy Community
Ex gratia	Literally, 'as a favour', but it is normally used in the context of payments made without legal liability to do so
Ex officio	By virtue of office
Ex parte (**often abbreviated** *ex p.***)**	An application in legal proceedings made (1) by an interested person who is not a party or (2) by one party in the absence of the other
Exchequer	Medieval court dealing with royal revenue but from 1550 it developed a common law jurisdiction
Executor	A person appointed to carry out the directions of a deceased person contained in a will

Factual distinguishing	Differentiating an earlier precedent on its facts from the case under consideration
Fiduciary duties	Duties owed by a person placed in a position of trust and confidence
Fiscal	To do with taxation
Frustration of contract	Premature termination of a contract because performance has been rendered impossible or so different that it would be unreasonable to hold the parties bound
Garnishee proceedings	A procedure whereby a person's bank is ordered to pay over money to a court having deducted the amount from the person's account
Habeas corpus	A court order for obtaining the release of a subject who has been imprisoned
Incorporated	A legal process whereby a group of people are collectively recognised as being a separate legal person
Indemnity	An undertaking to be responsible for the debts of another irrespective of whether the debtor is able to pay
Indictable offence	An offence, which if committed by an adult, can only be tried in a Crown Court
Indictment	The document containing the counts to which the accused must plead
Injunction	A court order requiring the person to whom it is addressed to refrain from doing some act or to do an act
Inns of Court	Voluntary unincorporated societies where persons used to study to become barristers
Inquest	An inquiry held by a coroner
Insolvency	The state of being unable to pay one's debts as and when they fall due
Interlocutory order	An interim order pending the determination of the rights of the parties
Ipse dixit	An assertion unsupported by legal authority
Judicial	Of judges
Judicial activism	An allegation often made against the judges of the European Court of Justice that they seek to interpret EU law creatively rather than literally

Jurisdiction	Literally, the legal authority to decide
Jurisprudence	Can refer to legal theory but can also refer to the body of case law created by a particular court such as the European Court of Justice
Justiciable	Capable of being decided by a court
Legacy	A gift of personal property under a will
Legal person	All natural persons are legal persons but so are entities known as corporations, the most numerous being companies
Legal title	In effect, legal ownership
Letters patent	Open letters containing public directions from the monarch bearing the Great Seal
Levy	A form of tax
Litigant	Someone who goes to law
Litigation	Resolving disputes through the courts
Lobby	To petition for some cause
Locus standi	The right to be heard in court
Mandatory order	An order addressed to a lower court or tribunal usually requiring it to rehear a case
Mens rea	The necessary mental state required for the commission of certain crimes
Misfeasance	Literally, wrongdoing
Mitigate	Literally, to make less of
Monist	Where international law and national law are part of the same legal order
Municipal	A large unit of local government
Negligence	A tort that enables a person who suffers loss or damage from the defendant's breach of duty of care to recover compensation provided the other conditions of liability are satisfied
Obiter dicta	That part of the judgement that does not refer to the facts as established at trial
Ombudsman	A Swedish word that refers to a person who deals with complaints
Per curiam	By the court
Per incuriam	A decision of the court that is mistaken

Personal representative	An administrator or executor
Plaintiff	The old term for a person who brings a legal action
Plenary session	Literally, a session comprising all members of a legislature or a court hearing with all the judges of the court in attendance
Pluralism	A form of society where the members of groups maintain their independence and traditions without encroachment by government
Precedent	A decided case the *ratio* of which can be applied in future cases
Prerogative orders	These are the quashing, mandatory and prohibiting orders that can be made by the Administrative Court
Prima facie	On first impression
Privy Council	(1) An appeal court that hears appeals from certain Commonwealth countries; (2) an advisory body to the monarch
Probate	A certificate granted by a court indicating that the last will and testament of a deceased person has been proved
Proportionality	Doing no more than is necessary to achieve an end or outcome
Protocol	Part of a treaty usually found at the end
Pupillage	A period of apprenticeship undertaken by barristers
Quorum	The requisite number of persons who must be present before any business of an organisation may be transacted
Ratio decidendi	The principle of law which is the basis of the decision that can be applied in subsequent cases – it is always linked to the facts of the earlier case
Recognisances	These are the obligations entered into to secure the performance of an act, usually the appearance of another in court to stand trial
Rectification	An equitable remedy that puts right an error in a document
Remission	Part of a person's prison sentence that is not served

Remit	(1) To send a case back to the court that originally heard it; (2) 'statutory remit' meaning what an organisation or body was established to do
Repeal	The nullifying of a statute or part of a statute
Res judicata	The principle that a matter, having been adjudicated on by a competent court, may not be reopened subsequently or challenged
Rescission	An equitable remedy that ends a contract
Respondent	The party that responds to an appeal that is brought
Retrospective effect	Having effect from a date earlier than that date of the measure itself
Sine die	Indefinitely
Specific performance	An equitable remedy requiring the person to whom it is addressed to perform that which was promised in a contract
Standing order	An order passed by the House of Commons intended to speed the progress of business
Statute	This term is used to refer to an Act of Parliament
Statutory instrument	A form of subordinate legislation
Subpoena	A court order requiring a person to come before the court at a certain place and time subject to a penalty if he/she does not
Summons	An order issued by magistrates requiring attendance at court
Sureties	Persons who enter into recognisances to secure the appearance of another in court
Tenure	A feudal land holding or can be used more generally to signify a period that an office is held
Tort	A civil wrong that is neither a breach of contract nor a breach of trust
Tortious	Conduct that involves committing a tort
Treaty	A legally binding agreement between two states
Trustee	A person who holds the legal title to some right or property not for his/her benefit but for the benefit of others
Ultra vires	Literally, 'beyond the powers of . . .' and an act which so designated has no legal effect

Vested rights   Rights owned by a person in whom they are
                                  vested

Vicarious liability   A substitution of liability whereby a person
                                  becomes liable (in certain circumstances) for
                                  the acts of another where there is a special
                                  relationship such as employer/employee

Warrant of execution   A court order entitling a bailiff to seize property

Wingers   Persons who sit on a tribunal to assist the
                                  chairperson

Writ   A written order or warrant – prior to the Civil
                                  Procedure Rules a writ was an order issued in the
                                  name of the sovereign to commence an action
                                  before a court

1

Introduction

You have chosen to study the English legal system at a particularly exciting time because it is in the throes of a process of dynamic change. This book has been written specifically to explain how the various elements that combine to make up the legal system of England and Wales relate to each other and function at a time of change. The book is divided into four parts.

Part One

The first objective of Part One is to provide you with an insight into the legal profession and its regulation. The Courts and Legal Services Act 1990 brought to an end the monopoly that barristers enjoyed to appear as advocates in the superior courts. The government wished to introduce greater competition into the provision of legal services with a view to reducing costs by abolishing what it perceived as restrictive practices. For the first time, solicitors were to be able to acquire 'rights of audience' in the superior civil and criminal courts so that they could represent their clients. The Access to Justice Act 1999 has since streamlined the procedure whereby the Law Society and other professional bodies are able to grant rights of audience to their members. These developments and others continue to impact on the organisation and structure of the legal profession. The profession's system of self-regulation remains under scrutiny. Even though members of the public have been able to complain to the Legal Services Ombudsman since 1991, it is possible that self-regulation may not survive. The second objective of Part One is to examine the courts, the magistracy and judiciary. The 'winds of change' are blowing through the ranks of the judiciary. Having changed the rules relating to rights of audience in the superior courts, the Courts and Legal Services Act 1990 also changed the rules governing the eligibility for judicial appointments. Solicitors are now entering the lower ranks of the judiciary in increasing numbers and those who show flair are being promoted. Women are still under-represented among the ranks of the judiciary as are members of ethnic minorities, and this represents a challenge for the future.

Part Two

Part Two focuses on the law-making processes that are either embedded in or impact directly on the system. This entails an examination of the judicial contribution to the law-making process through the creation of case law and development of precedent. However, legislation is the dominant form of law-making in the system and so the legislative process comes under scrutiny. There is also a consideration of the concept and extent of parliamentary sovereignty. European Union law has been firmly implanted in the English legal system. The doctrine of 'direct effect' devised by the Court of Justice in Luxembourg means that the English and Welsh courts routinely apply EU law in appropriate cases. When they encounter difficulties of interpretation, they continue to make applications to Luxembourg. As the process of European integration proceeds apace, government is required to respond to the directives that are adopted at the European level by implementing them, mainly through the medium of subordinate legislation. The creation of the concept of state liability by the Court of Justice means that government can be sued by its own citizens in their national courts over its failure to implement directives on time – where these directives confer rights on them. Moreover, it is clear that the state itself can be held liable in damages for any 'serious breach' of EU law by those affected, whether they are nationals or not. Part Two concludes with an examination of the problems that can arise in interpreting and applying legislation, whether national or European.

Part Three

Part Three opens with a consideration of the funding of legal advice and representation. A major change has occurred recently in the resourcing of legal services. The Access to Justice Act 1999 created the Legal Services Commission (LSC) to replace the Legal Aid Board. The LSC, which was inaugurated in April 2000, has overall responsibility for its sub-entities: the Community Legal Service and the Criminal Defence Service. The former was responsible for creating the Community Legal Service which has developed local 'partnerships' to coordinate legal services at a local level. The latter launched its Public Defender Service in May 2001 which employs lawyers to provide advice to those arrested by the police and representation for accused persons appearing in court. An investigation of the new arrangements for the provision of legal services paves the way for a survey of key aspects of the criminal justice system. The criminal justice system is a major sub-system of the English legal system. Widespread deviant behaviour obviously poses a serious threat to any civilised society. It is the role of the criminal justice system to deal effectively with this by ensuring that those who have engaged in criminal activity are apprehended, punished and, if possible, reformed and rehabilitated. Despite the reforms that have been made in recent times, there are still parts of the criminal justice system that are not functioning as effectively as they might. In its Command Paper *Criminal Justice: The Way Ahead*, published in February 2001, the government stated that public confidence in the criminal justice system had been seriously undermined by the fall in clear-up rates (for certain crimes) and by the fall in conviction rates. It did, however, acknowledge that there were complex reasons for this state of affairs. In January 2001, the Director of Public Prosecutions, as head of the Crown Prosecution Service, announced that, in future, the most serious criminal cases would be 'fast-tracked' to the Crown Court to reduce unnecessary delays in the system. In the previous month, the Lord Chancellor had announced that Lord Justice Auld would conduct a thoroughgoing review of the practices and procedures, including the rules of evidence, of the criminal courts at every level. Lord Justice Auld's final report has been delayed and is eagerly awaited. Part Three also includes a fairly detailed survey of the civil justice system which is the other major sub-system within the English legal system. Disputes between individuals and organisations need to be settled justly but it is advantageous to both sides if they can also be settled quickly and cheaply. Solicitors and barristers who engage in civil litigation on behalf of clients have been required to adjust to the new climate in which civil litigation is now conducted under the Civil Procedure Rules that were introduced in April 1999. The rules, made under the Civil Procedure Act 1997, were the government's response to Lord Woolf's report *Access to Justice* in which he heavily criticised the old culture of civil litigation which was renowned for its delay and expense. The new regime has resulted in a huge reduction in delays. This is directly attributable to the new system of judicial case management and cost penalties. It is not clear, however, whether costs of litigation have been reduced significantly. Parties are now actively encouraged to settle their differences at an early stage through the medium of the Pre-action Protocol, and this innovation seems to have produced a higher rate of early settlements. The rules also encourage parties in dispute to consider alternatives to litigation such as mediation and conciliation. Lawyers are now seeking to qualify as mediators in ever greater numbers under schemes operated by bodies such as the Centre for Effective Dispute Resolution as they increasingly perceive mediation and conciliation to be income-generating activities. Arbitration, a long-established system of dispute resolution, was completely revamped under the Arbitration Act 1996 to encourage parties in dispute to make greater use of it. In consequence, a number of new arbitration schemes have been launched by lawyers. It may be that in the near future there will actually be a decline in court-based dispute resolution as alternative dispute resolution (ADR) becomes more widely known and accepted as a realistic alternative. Although most disputes concern private law rights and obligations, a significant number come within the province of public law because they take the form of grievances with government and other public bodies. Historically, the judges have considered it to be part of their role to protect individuals and groups in society against the abuse of power by local and national government through the process of judicial review. In recent years, this jurisdiction has expanded beyond all expectations. A new Administrative Court has been established within the High Court structure to deal exclusively with public and administrative law cases as recommended by the Bowman Committee. Part Three concludes with a consideration of the need for ongoing law reform and focuses on the role of the Law Commission.

Part Four

Part Four represents something of an innovation for a textbook on the English legal system because it contains two chapters on the acquisition of some basic legal skills. Chapter 17 aims to help the new undergraduate navigate the law section of the Learning Resources Centre of his/her university, whilst Chapter 18 offers guidance on researching source material for seminars and essays. There is also some guidance on the preparation of seminar papers, writing essays as well as some practical tips on coping with law examinations.

The Human Rights Act 1998

The Human Rights Act 1998 is a recurring theme throughout the book. The Act has been sending tremors through the entire legal system since October 2000 when the rights available under the European Convention of Human Rights and Fundamental Freedoms became available in national law. The Act marks a fundamental shift from a legal system in which the civil and political rights of individuals were largely residual to one where individuals now enjoy positive rights. Irrespective of whether it was enacted before or since October 2000, all legislation is now to be interpreted, in so far as it is possible to do so, in a way that is compatible with the Convention rights contained in Schedule 1 of the Act. Since it is unlawful for a public authority to act in a way that is incompatible with a Convention right (unless it is required to do so by primary legislation), there is now far greater scope for challenging the actions of government by way of claims for judicial review. The Act also continues to make a great impact in the sphere of criminal justice and there are references to Convention rights in Chapters 10 and 11. There is an obvious link between the fundamental rights recognised by the European Court of Justice as considered in Chapter 7 and the Convention rights considered in Chapter 8. Strictly speaking, the Convention is not part of EU law but the English and Welsh courts continue to have regard to the fundamental rights recognised by the European Court of Justice as they implement EU law.

PART ONE

The legal profession

2

The legal profession

1. Introduction

A functioning legal system depends upon there being a corps of highly trained professional people who are able to undertake a range of varied tasks. The most distinctive feature of the legal profession in England and Wales is its division into two branches: solicitors and barristers. Anyone considering a legal career must still decide at the outset whether to qualify as a solicitor or as a barrister even though the rigid distinctions between the roles of these two branches of the profession are becoming a little blurred. In the past, those persons who wished to have the option of undertaking a wide variety of legal work and were not particularly attracted by advocacy in the higher courts would decide to train and qualify as solicitors by taking the examinations prescribed by the Law Society of England and Wales. The Law Society originated in 1845 and is the organisation which sets the educational and professional standards for solicitors. Those persons who are attracted by a career in advocacy especially in the higher courts, still opt to train and qualify as barristers by taking the qualifying examinations prescribed by the Council for Legal Education. This chapter focuses initially on solicitors before examining the emerging profession of legal executive. It will then be appropriate to consider the profession of barrister which is the longest established and, some would argue, the most prestigious. This chapter is also the most apt place to deal with the disciplinary framework for the profession including the office of the Legal Services Ombudsman.

2. Solicitors

Statistics taken from the 1999 annual report of the Law Society indicate that there were over 100,000 solicitors in England and Wales on the official Roll. Of this number, almost 80,000 held practising certificates issued by the Law Society, but as the remainder held salaried posts in commerce, industry and education, they were not obliged to have practising certificates. Two-thirds of solicitors with practising certificates were men but the numbers of women joining the profession continues to increase each year. In the region of

80 per cent of solicitors holding practising certificates in 1999 worked in private practice offering legal services to businesses and individuals. A significant number of solicitors with practising certificates held posts in commerce, local government and in government agencies. Approximately 40 per cent of solicitors' firms were 'sole practices' (employing about 10 per cent of solicitors in private practice), but most solicitors either form partnerships with other solicitors or work as salaried employees for larger partnerships in the capacity of assistant solicitors. In some of the large international law firms with headquarters in London some solicitors have the hybrid status of being 'salaried partners'.

3. Qualifying as a solicitor

The quickest way to qualify as a solicitor is to study law at a university. Provided the course covers the core subjects prescribed for the Common Professional Examination (CPE)/Postgraduate Diploma in Law and is approved by the Law Society the graduate can, on obtaining student membership of the Law Society, undertake the Legal Practice Course (LPC) at an approved centre. Litigation and advocacy skills are now a compulsory part of the LPC. Having passed all the examinations and assessments prescribed for this course it is then necessary to obtain a training contract with an established firm of solicitors or with certain approved agencies of central or local government. This is vital in the process of qualifying but every year there are still more young people searching for training contracts than there are contracts available, although the number of contracts on offer continues to increase. All trainees must now undertake the Professional Skills Course during their training contract in which the advocacy skills module is a compulsory part. After two years have been spent as a trainee with an established firm of solicitors or some other agency approved by the Law Society, the former trainee must apply to have his/her name entered on the Roll of solicitors maintained by the Law Society. This confers the status of being an admitted solicitor. Only at this point does the former trainee become fully qualified. Even though he/she has attained the status of qualified solicitor, he/she must continue to attend seminars or courses for three years after qualifying as part of the Law Society's Continuing Education Scheme. For someone who does not study law at university it is necessary to take a one-year preparatory course at a university or at some other approved centre before being eligible to enrol on the Legal Practice Course. This preparatory course is known as the CPE/Postgraduate Diploma in Law referred to above. The core subjects are: law of obligations I (contract); law of obligations II (torts); foundations of the criminal law; foundations of equity and law of trusts; foundations of the law of the EU; foundations of property law; and foundations of public law. Satisfactory completion of this course does not, however, guarantee a place on the Legal Practice Course.

4. The work of solicitors

Traditionally solicitors have engaged in a wide variety of legal work ranging from the drafting of legal documents such as contracts and wills to company formations and conveyancing (the transfer of the legal title of business premises or residential property from seller to buyer). Many firms of solicitors derive a substantial part of their income from administering the wills of deceased persons once they have been validated by a process known as probate. Solicitors have long been able to represent their clients in proceedings in magistrates' courts and in county courts. They also deal with the preparatory stages of civil litigation in the higher courts entailing the actual commencement of legal proceedings and the interviewing of witnesses. Prior to 1990, those solicitors who wished to develop advocacy skills in the higher courts had to apply to have their names deleted from the Roll of Solicitors so that they could become barristers, but this is no longer necessary.

5. Courts and Legal Services Act 1990

The Courts and Legal Services Act 1990 made fundamental changes in the legal profession reflecting the desire of the government of the day to introduce greater competition into the provision of legal services. One of its key provisions put an end to the monopoly that barristers had long enjoyed in relation to advocacy in the superior courts because the Law Society was empowered to grant its members rights of audience under conditions specified in Regulations made in 1992 and subsequently in 1998. By the end of July 1998 the Law Society had granted rights of audience to 651 solicitors in England and Wales to appear in the superior courts, and by January 2000 this total had reached 999. However, a significant number of those who had been granted rights of audience in the higher courts were former barristers who had transferred to the solicitors' branch of the profession. The Access to Justice Act 1999 s. 36 has substituted a new s. 31 into the Court and Legal Services Act 1990 which now provides that:

> Every solicitor shall be deemed to have been granted by the Law Society (a) a right of audience before every court in relation to all proceedings (exercisable in accordance with the qualification regulations and rules of conduct of the Law Society approved for the purposes of s. 27 in relation to the right); and (b) a right to conduct litigation in relation to every court and all proceedings (exercisable in accordance with the qualification regulations and rules of conduct of the Law Society approved for the purposes of s. 28 in relation to the right).

In view of the coming into operation of this new provision, the council of the Law Society has made the Higher Courts Qualification Regulations 2000 to replace its previous regulations. The new regulations came into effect from 1 October 2000. Regulation 2(3) makes it clear that no solicitor is entitled to exercise any right of audience (other than those that could be exercised before 7 December 1989) unless he/she holds a Higher Courts Advocacy Qualification granted under these or the earlier regulations entitling him/her to exercise that right of audience. The Law Society can grant one of three qualifications to solicitors who meet the necessary requirements as follows:

(a) Higher Courts (All Proceedings) Qualification which entitles the solicitor to exercise rights of audience in all proceedings in the higher civil and criminal courts.

(b) Higher Courts (Civil Proceedings) Qualification which entitles the solicitors to exercise rights of audience in all civil proceedings in the higher courts including judicial review in any court arising from any criminal cause.

(c) Higher Courts (Criminal Proceedings) Qualification which entitles the solicitor to exercise rights of audience in all criminal proceedings in the higher courts including judicial review proceedings in any court arising out of any criminal cause.

New entrants to the profession must satisfy the Law Society that they have successfully undertaken a training course that includes assessment in evidence, procedure and ethics applicable to the higher civil and/or criminal courts. They must also successfully undertake training and assessment in advocacy skills applicable to these higher courts. In addition, the Law Society requires evidence of one year's experience of litigation and advocacy and at least six months of this must have been gained after admission to the Roll. This will be evidenced by a portfolio that must be attested by another experienced solicitor who has been appointed as mentor. Any solicitor may opt to gain a Higher Courts Qualification at any stage in his/her career by this route which is referred to as the Development Route. For solicitors who have already gained extensive experience of litigation there is an opportunity to gain a Higher Courts Qualification by the Accreditation Route or by the Exemption Route to which special requirements apply. All solicitor advocates are required by Regulation 13 to undertake at least five hours' continuing professional development a year relating to the provision of advocacy services in the higher courts. The Law Society anticipates that the number of solicitor advocates will grow steadily in the years ahead.

6. Legal executives

Not all of the staff working in a solicitor's practice are fully qualified solicitors. This is obviously true of the reception and secretarial staff but there will be other staff apart from trainee solicitors who are engaged in legal work under the supervision of a qualified solicitor. These people are quite likely to be members of the Institute of Legal Executives, a professional body formed in 1963, but not one enjoying the same status and prestige as the Law Society. The Institute prescribes a course of study that is divided into two parts that enables those who join it to become qualified members and subsequently, fellows. The total membership is in the region of 22,000 including trainees but it is only fellows of the Institute who are permitted to use the designation 'legal executive'. A number of legal executives specialise in conveyancing or in the drafting of wills or in the administration of the affairs of those deceased persons who have made wills. For many years some legal executives have been undertaking advocacy of a low level and limited nature, mainly appearing before tribunals and before judges in chambers. The Courts and Legal Services Act 1990 has expanded the opportunities for persons other than barristers to undertake advocacy. It is expressly provided in s. 27 that an 'authorised body' may grant rights of audience to their members and the Access to Justice Act 1999 s. 40(2) specifies that the Institute is an 'authorised body'. Only fellows of the Institute working under the supervision of solicitors are eligible to apply for the necessary training to be accorded rights of audience by the Institute's Rights of Audience Committee. Three separate certificates are available from the Committee for the three areas in which legal executives may function as advocates. These are:

(a) Civil Proceedings Certificate

(b) Matrimonial Proceedings Certificate

(c) Coroners Proceedings Certificate.

A candidate making an application for (a) or (b) above must have completed 36 hours of directed private study on the rules of evidence and pre-trial procedure after which it is necessary to pass a three-hour written examination. In addition, it is necessary to satisfactorily complete the advocacy skills programme. This is in two parts comprising 18 hours of study and the satisfactory completion of a two-hour test after which it is necessary to undergo 18 hours of face-to-face training that incorporates an assessment of advocacy skills. Candidates wishing to obtain a Coroners Proceedings Certificate must undertake a programme of 8 hours' tuition prior to taking 12 hours of examinations. All applications for rights of audience must be accompanied by evidence of some previous advocacy experience. The minimum necessary is 20 appearances a year during the preceding two years either before a judge in chambers or before tribunals including appearances on contested matters.

The Civil Proceedings Certificate entitles the legal executive advocate to appear in the county court on all matters within the normal jurisdiction of a district judge or to appear in a magistrates' court in relation to all matters originating by complaint or application. The Certificate will also entitle the legal executive advocate to appear before any tribunal that is under the supervision of the Council on Tribunals.

The Family Proceedings Certificate enables him/her to appear as an advocate before magistrates in cases that come before the Family Proceedings Court and in certain family proceedings before a district judge in the county court. All advocacy certificates have to be renewed annually by the Institute's Rights of Audience Committee who will require evidence of at least eight hours of continuing professional development, sight of a log book showing details of the advocacy experience gained and a statement from the employer of the rights of audience to be exercised during the next year. In March 2000 the Institute announced that the first six legal executive advocates had qualified under the Courts and Legal Services Act 1990. Members of the Institute may also become Commissioners for Oaths and are therefore able to attest to swearing of legal documents that require this degree of formality.

Each year between 100 and 150 qualified members of the Institute opt to qualify as solicitors. As from October 2000, duly qualified members and fellows can be exempted from the CPE/Postgraduate Diploma in Law provided that they apply for a place and commence the Legal Practice course within four years of gaining their membership qualification. Fellows of the Institute will be exempted from the normal two-year training contract that trainee solicitors must undertake before being admitted as solicitors. Fiona Bawdon in an article entitled 'Second class status' published in the *New Law Journal* on 17 October 1997, suggests that former legal executives who have taken the initiative to qualify as solicitors meet with discrimination from some solicitor colleagues. Sadly this seems to be attributable to 'academic snobbery' on the part of graduate solicitors who tend to look down on non-graduates.

7. Complaints against solicitors

The system for dealing with complaints against lawyers in England and Wales operates in two stages. In the first instance there is self-regulation by the profession and then a referral to the Legal Services Ombudsman (*see* **16**) if the complainant is dissatisfied with the way in which the complaint has been handled by the profession. The Solicitors' Costs Information and

Client Care Code – drawn up by the Council of the Law Society – requires solicitors in private practice to operate a complaints handling procedure. The Code stipulates that every firm must:

(a) ensure that the client is informed of the name of the person in the practice to contact regarding any problem(s) with the service provided,

(b) have a written complaints procedure and ensure that complaints are handled in accordance with it, and

(c) ensure that the client is given a copy of the complaints procedure on request.

In August 2000, the Office for the Supervision of Solicitors distributed 40,000 copies of a guide to solicitors in private practice in England and Wales entitled *Handling Complaints Effectively*. The guide gives advice on establishing good in-house complaints procedure including an appeals stage. Clients who have not been able to obtain satisfaction under the Code can then complain to the Office for the Supervision of Solicitors.

8. Office for the Supervision of Solicitors

In September 1996, the Law Society replaced its much criticised Solicitors Complaints Bureau (SCB) with another agency known as the Office for the Supervision of Solicitors (OSS) which took over the work in progress of the SCB. The OSS also assumed responsibility for the operation of the Solicitors' Compensation Fund which had been established to provide compensation to clients in appropriate cases. It was hoped that the recruitment of a number of competent laypersons by the OSS to work alongside the solicitor caseworkers would engender greater confidence in the new body. Yet, as recently as May 1999, it was being heavily criticised by Martin Mears, a former president of the Law Society, for its delays and complacency. In view of the fact that the OSS was under-resourced from the outset, and given the rising annual number of complaints against solicitors, the Law Society has promised substantial additional resources following a critical report prepared by the management consultants Ernst & Young. As a result of this report, the OSS is recruiting additional staff and is streamlining some of its procedures. It will be interesting to see whether these changes will result in a higher level of public confidence in the performance of the OSS.

9. Discipline

Practising solicitors are regarded as officers of the Supreme Court subject to the direct discipline of the judges, but in practice it is the Law Society that is responsible for supervising its members in private practice and it has extensive powers to intervene in the functioning of any solicitor's practice. Solicitors who are considered to have been involved in some form of professional misconduct may be required to appear before the Solicitors' Disciplinary Tribunal which was established under the Solicitors Act 1974. The tribunal is completely independent of the Law Society as its members are appointed by the Master of the Rolls (the senior judge of the civil division of the Court of Appeal) from among solicitors who have at least 10 years' post-qualifying experience. Laypersons are also appointed so that each tribunal panel comprises two solicitors and a layperson. At the close of its proceedings, a tribunal panel can make whatever order it sees fit. For example, it may remove the solicitor's name from the official Roll, suspend him/her from practising for a time, order a penalty not exceeding £5,000 and make an order for costs and expenses against him/her. The tribunal itself is obliged to make an annual report to the Lord Chancellor and this must be published for distribution to interested members of the public.

10. Barristers

The word 'barrister' seems to have entered the language around the middle of the fifteenth century to refer to members of the Inns of Court. From the fourteenth century it was to these institutions that those who wished to undertake the programme of vocational training that would enable them to practise as advocates in the courts of common law, would come. Today the Bar, as practising barristers are collectively known, is a thoroughly modern profession, albeit one with a distinguished tradition. Practising barristers are not permitted to form partnerships but must operate as self-employed, independent professionals. A cluster of barristers will usually join together to occupy a suite of offices that are always referred to as chambers. A set of chambers will usually be presided over by one or more senior barristers who have reached the rank of Queen's Counsel. Grouping together in a set of chambers enables the barristers to pool the costs of employing support staff and to share the other operating expenses. According to the Bar Council, there were 10,132 practising barristers in England and Wales (7,494 men and 2,638 women) at 1 October 2000, and there were 604 sets of chambers. Most of these chambers (311) were situated in and around the four Inns of Court in London, and of the total number of practising barristers, 6,591 were London-based. In recent years there has been an expansion of the Bar outside London in the important regional centres. As at 1 October 2000 there were 3,541 practising barristers based in these centres and a total of 293 sets of chambers. The day-to-day management of a set of chambers will be entrusted to one or more barristers' clerks. It is they who negotiate barristers' fees with firms of solicitors and allocate the incoming briefs to members of the chambers. In recent years some well-established barristers have decided to set up their 'chambers' in their own homes because they prefer to work from home, taking advantage of the latest electronic information services and communications technology. A barrister may only do this if he/she has spent at least three years with an established set of chambers and has access to an adequate law library. This is an interesting development and it remains to be seen whether it will become a popular method of working for barristers in the future.

11. Qualifying as a barrister

Anyone aspiring to become a barrister must be a graduate and must apply to join one of the four Inns of Court (Inner Temple, Middle Temple, Gray's Inn and Lincoln's Inn). If the person concerned does not have a law degree, he/she must take the course leading to the CPE/Postgraduate Diploma in Law before enrolling on the Bar Vocational Course (BVC) on either a full-time or a part-time basis. Having become a student member of one of the Inns, it is necessary to attend the Inn on a certain number of occasions to dine there. This can be done whilst the student is taking the BVC at the Inns of Court Law School. For those who take the BVC outside London, officials of the Inns visit these provincial centres and dine with the entire student cohort.

On successful completion of the BVC the candidates are 'called to the bar' at a ceremony at the Inn that they elected to join. It is then necessary to secure 'pupillage' in a set of chambers if the newly qualified barrister wishes to practise as an advocate in the English and Welsh courts. Fortunately there is an online system for pupillage applications although not all chambers participate in the scheme. Some well established sets of chambers provide a limited number of generously funded pupillages; others provide limited funding, whilst a few provide no funding even though the Bar Council has recommended that all pupil barristers be paid a guaranteed income of £10,000 during pupillage.

The period of pupillage lasts 12 months and is divided into two six-month periods, but not all chambers will offer a pupillage for the entire 12 months and so it may be necessary to change to another set at the half-way point. The first six-month period in chambers is likely to be spent becoming conversant with the legal paperwork under the general supervision of a 'pupil master'. In a set of chambers specialising in particular branches of the civil law the pupil barrister may be set to work drafting documents and writing opinions, albeit under supervision. On satisfactory completion of this initial period, the pupil is issued with a practising certificate. If the pupil barrister intends to work at the 'employed Bar' rather than in private practice, the first six-month period of pupillage may be undertaken in the government legal service, Crown Prosecution Service or in local government under the supervision of an 'employed' barrister pupil master. In the second six-month period the pupil barrister may be given some briefs and may appear in court and thereby generate some income. A final certificate is issued at the end of the second six-month period. Once pupillage is over, unless the young barrister is offered a tenancy in the chambers where he/she has undertaken pupillage, it will be necessary for him/her to find a tenancy in another set of chambers in order to be able to practice.

Well over one thousand men and women complete the BVC each year but only half will obtain a pupillage, and of these only 60 per cent or so will obtain tenancies. Recently qualified barristers who do not succeed in establishing themselves in practice at the Bar can often look forward to very well paid career opportunities at the 'employed Bar' working in the government legal service or Crown Prosecution Service where their legal skills are very much in demand. Some barristers even choose to work as salaried employees for the large London-based international law firms and provide advocacy services to clients of these firms.

12. The work of barristers

Most people have seen films or television series in which actors have taken the parts of barristers either prosecuting or defending persons charged with criminal offences. Although a large number of practising barristers do specialise in criminal law, many others opt to perfect their advocacy skills in one or more of the branches of civil law or public law. These barristers are likely to spend as much time on legal paperwork as they do in court. The paperwork will involve them in drafting pleadings for the clients that they are to represent and in drafting opinions, at the request of solicitors, on difficult points of law prior to the commencement of any litigation. Whilst it is correct in principle that any barrister is supposed to be technically competent to perform advocacy for either side in criminal or civil cases, the reality is somewhat different. A degree of specialisation is necessary in order to keep abreast of the vast amount of reading that needs to be done to keep up to date. Indeed, entire sets of chambers are known within the profession to specialise in particular branches of the law and they will obviously seek to attract as tenants those possessing the relevant specialisms. The pace of change at the Bar is such that new entrants may now be expected to retrain and respecialise two or even three times during their careers in order to generate sufficient income. The Bar operates as a 'referral' profession in that the public does not have direct access. Access is normally through a solicitor, but in recent times the BarDIRECT scheme has been established to give organisations that have the appropriate knowledge and experience direct access to the advisory and advocacy skills of members of the Bar without the need to instruct a solicitor. In April 2001, qualified members of the Institute of Financial Services were granted direct access.

13. Career progression

Many practising barristers are ambitious and hope to achieve great distinction in their profession and perhaps eventually enter the ranks of the judiciary. Some even use the Bar as a 'launching pad' to a career in politics. After about ten years or so in successful practice a barrister can apply to the Lord Chancellor to become a Queen's Counsel (QC). This will only be done by those barristers who genuinely consider that they have achieved some distinction within the profession. Although the applications are made annually to the Lord Chancellor, the actual appointment is made by HM the Queen albeit on his advice. In a typical year there are in the region of 500 applications but only approximately 15 per cent of applicants are likely to succeed. Unsuccessful applicants are at liberty to make further applications in subsequent years. According to the Bar Council, as at 1 October 2000 there were 1,072 QCs, but of this number only 82 were women. Although it is possible to become a judge without first becoming a QC, it is often a helpful first step and serves to confer an enhanced status on the person concerned. In future he/she will often appear in court with a 'junior' (an ordinary barrister) who will assist with the more routine aspects of the case such as the drafting of pleadings. The QC normally presents the legal argument in court and will always receive a much higher fee than the junior barrister. Since September 1995, solicitors who practise as solicitor advocates have been eligible to apply to become QCs but few bother to avail themselves of the opportunity. In April 2000 just six practising solicitors made applications but none was appointed; in the previous year there were nine applications and one appointment.

14. Barristers and professional negligence

In *Arthur J.S. Hall & Co.* v *Simons* [2000] the House of Lords reversed its long-standing decision in the case of *Rondel* v *Worsley* [1967] that barristers cannot be sued by their clients for professional negligence in the provision of advocacy services. All seven Law Lords ruled in favour of abolishing this long-standing immunity in civil litigation and a majority decided that it should no longer be applicable in criminal proceedings. In the course of his judgement, Lord Steyn stated:

There is no reason to fear a flood of negligence suits against barristers. The mere doing of [his/her] duty to the court by the advocate to the detriment of his client could never be called negligent.

The Courts and Legal Services Act 1990 s. 62 had extended the immunity that had been enjoyed by barristers to solicitor advocates and it is interesting to note that in *Arthur J.S. Hall & Co.* v *Simons* that the appellants were in fact solicitors who had acted as advocates. The decision of the House of Lords to end the immunity for professional negligence therefore applies to both barristers and solicitor advocates.

15. Complaints against barristers

In 1997, a new system was established for dealing with complaints against barristers. The General Council of the Bar produces a leaflet on what is now an elaborate complaints system entitled *How to Complain About a Barrister*. This makes it clear that, although a barrister has an overriding duty to the court to ensure that justice is properly administered, he/she also has a duty to clients to act in their best interests. If a client considers that a formal complaint ought to be made against a barrister, a complaint form can be obtained from the Bar Council together with a set of guidance notes on how to complete the form. The complaints procedure is set in motion once the complaints department receives the completed form. It may take between two and six months to resolve the matter unless the complaint is deemed unjustified, but more serious complaints are likely to take longer to resolve. The complaint form is examined by the Complaints Commissioner – a non-lawyer who will decide on one of three possible courses of action:

(a) to dismiss the complaint because it is not justified

(b) that the complaint may be resolved by conciliation between the client and the barrister

(c) that the complaint should be investigated.

If the complaint is dismissed the client will be informed of this decision and of the reasons for it and it is then for the client to decide whether to refer the matter to the Legal Services Ombudsman. If the Commissioner takes the view that the complaint is suitable for conciliation because it does not amount to inadequate professional service or professional misconduct, the Commissioner will write to both parties suggesting that conciliation should take place. The letter to the barrister concerned will make it clear that he/she should initiate the conciliation process. On the other hand, if the Commissioner takes the view that the complaint should be investigated, the barrister concerned will be asked to comment on the allegation(s) made in the complaint form. A copy of the letter sent to the barrister will be sent to the instructing solicitors and to other relevant witnesses who will be asked to submit comments. On receipt of the barrister's response and submissions from other parties, the Commissioner will then re-examine the complaint. Having done so, he/she may decide to dismiss it, giving reasons for the decision to the complainant. If the Commissioner takes the view that the complaint should be taken further, the matter will be referred to the Professional Conduct and Complaints Committee of the Bar Council (known as the PCC).

The PCC comprises a number of barristers who are appointed by the chairperson of the Bar, two lay representatives and the Complaints Commissioner. On considering the complaint the PCC can adopt one of three possible courses of action:

(a) dismiss the complaint, if and only if the two lay representatives agree

(b) decide that the barrister *may* have provided an inadequate professional service

(c) decide that the barrister *may* have engaged in unprofessional misconduct which may or may not amount to a breach of the Code of Conduct.

If the complaint is dismissed the client will be informed of this decision and of the reasons. It is then for the client to decide whether to refer the matter to the Legal Services Ombudsman. Inadequate professional service may range from serious rudeness to the client, delay in dealing with papers, to poor or inadequate work on the case.

If the PCC takes the view that the barrister may have provided inadequate professional service but has not engaged in professional misconduct the complaint will be passed to an adjudication panel that will be chaired by the Complaints Commissioner. He/she will be assisted by two barristers and a member of the Bar Council's panel of lay representatives. The adjudication itself will be conducted on the basis of documents and correspondence received – neither the complainant nor the barrister concerned will appear in person although both will be notified of the date on which the panel is to be convened. If some important matter is raised at the hearing on which the complainant should be given the opportunity to comment, the hearing will be adjourned. At the end of the hearing, if the Panel is satisfied with the barrister's explanation, it can dismiss the complaint provided it gives reasons for its decision. If this should happen the complainant must then decide whether to refer the matter to the Legal Services Ombudsman. On the other hand, should the Adjudication Panel decide that the barrister has provided inadequate professional service, it may require the barrister to apologise to the client, refund or waive all or part of his/her fee or to pay compensation of up to £5,000.

Where the PCC has decided that the barrister may have engaged in professional misconduct or may be in breach of the Code of Conduct it can decide that the matter is dealt with in one of three ways:

(a) refer the matter for an informal hearing

(b) refer the matter for consideration by a Summary Procedure Panel

(c) refer the matter to a disciplinary tribunal.

Informal hearings are conducted by a panel of four comprising a QC (as chairperson) two barristers and a member of the Bar Council's panel of lay representatives. Copies of the relevant papers will be sent to the parties beforehand and the barrister concerned is required to appear before the panel to provide it with an explanation of his/her conduct. At the end of the process, if the panel is satisfied with the barrister's explanation it will dismiss the complaint giving its reasons and it is then for the client to decide whether to refer the matter to the Legal Service's Ombudsman. Alternatively the panel may decide that the barrister has provided inadequate professional service or that the barrister's conduct amounts to professional misconduct. In the event of the former, the sanctions available to the panel are the same as those that were available to the adjudication panel considered earlier. If the finding is one of professional misconduct the panel may 'admonish' the barrister or advise him/her regarding his/her future conduct. Such a finding will go on to the barrister's personal record at the Bar Council and will be disclosed to the Lord Chancellor if he/she ever applies to become a QC or a judge.

The composition of a summary procedure panel is similar to that of the panel for informal hearings. It too may dismiss the complaint if the barrister provides a satisfactory explanation of his/her conduct. The principal difference between the two panels is that the summary procedure panel can impose a number of penalties ranging from 'advice' as to future conduct to suspension from practice for a period of up to three months for professional misconduct. An adverse outcome for the barrister will result in the panel's findings being entered on to his/her record with the same implications as above for his/her future career.

The most serious allegations of professional misconduct will be dealt with by a disciplinary tribunal that will be chaired by a judge. The judge will be assisted by three barristers and a lay representative. Disciplinary tribunals are usually conducted in public and both the complainant and the barrister concerned will be present. Although the tribunal may dismiss the complaint this is less likely to occur than with the procedures already considered. Nevertheless, the tribunal could decide that the barrister's conduct amounts to inadequate professional service rather than professional misconduct. In the event of such a finding, the sanctions will be those that could be imposed under the summary procedure. A finding of professional misconduct will be entered on to the barrister's record and will entitle the tribunal to impose one or more of the following sanctions:

(a) advice as to future conduct

(b) admonishment

(c) reprimand

(d) repayment or reduction of fees

(e) a fine of up to £5,000 payable to the Bar Council

(f) suspension for any period the tribunal considers appropriate

(g) disbarrment.

Disbarrment is the most serious of the sanctions because it means that the barrister can no longer practice as a barrister.

It should be noted that a barrister can appeal a decision made against him/her in the disciplinary process. However, appeal must be made within 28 days of the decision (21 days for decisions of a summary procedure panel or a disciplinary tribunal). An appeal against a finding of inadequate professional service by an adjudication panel or informal panel will go to an appeals panel established by the Bar Council which may reverse the earlier decision or reduce or even increase the award. Appeals against a finding of professional misconduct by a summary panel or disciplinary tribunal are heard by Visitors of the Inns of Court and the appeal tribunal will be chaired by a High Court judge.

16. Legal Services Ombudsman

The Office of the Legal Services Ombudsman (LSO) was created by the Courts and Legal Services Act 1990 s. 21 and the office-holder is appointed by the Lord Chancellor. The role of the LSO is set out in s. 22 which states that he/she is to oversee the way that complaints against lawyers are dealt with chiefly by the General Council of the Bar and the Office for Supervision of Solicitors.

Most of the complaints against lawyers are dealt with to the reasonable satisfaction of the complainants by the agencies established by the professional bodies but, that said, the LSO does receive well over a thousand complaints annually from dissatisfied complainants. A dissatisfied complainant has three months from the date of the final decision of the agency concerned to refer the matter to the office of the LSO which is based in Manchester. There is a simple application form and a leaflet setting out the functions of the LSO. An investigating team will review the way in which the agency of the professional body has dealt with the complaint. Having considered an individual complaint, the LSO can recommend that the lawyer concerned or the professional body pay compensation to the complainant for loss, distress or inconvenience. It may even recommend that the complaint be reconsidered and that the lawyer concerned should be disciplined.

Although the addressee of a recommendation is required to notify the LSO of the proposed action to be taken, a weakness of the scheme has been that the LSO's recommendations are not legally binding even though the Courts and Legal Services Act 1990 does require that those who fail to comply with the recommendations of the LSO publicise their failure and the reasons for it in whatever fashion the LSO may specify. If the LSO takes the view that stronger action is required, the Access to Justice Act 1999 s. 49 now empowers the LSO *to order* the lawyer or the appropriate organisation to take action following an investigation with a view to making amends.

17. Legal Services Complaints Commissioner

Should the Lord Chancellor take the view that the system of self-regulation by the professional bodies is not working properly, the Access to Justice Act 1999 s. 51 enables him to appoint a Legal Services Complaints Commissioner (LSCC). The appointment would be for a term not exceeding three years but there is a possibility for reappointment for a further period. As with the LSO, the person appointed LSCC must not be a professional lawyer. The powers exercisable by the LSCC would be more extensive than those currently exercised by the LSO in that the LSCC may impose penalties on the professional bodies should they fail to put in place adequate systems for the handling of complaints.

18. Is there a case for a unified legal profession?

Over the years arguments have been put forward to the effect that a divided profession and its working practices result in great inefficiencies and inflated costs. Not only are there unnecessary delays, it has also been argued that the present structure reduces users' confidence in the system and makes access to justice too expensive for most individuals unless they have some form of legal insurance. The Bar is against fusion because of its long history and established traditions, but the Law Society is largely in favour. Although some savings might be made by the client in civil litigation, these may not be very great and there might be advantages to the client in retaining the services of both a solicitor and a barrister. In some instances, the self-employed barrister might be able to undertake the advocacy of a case in court at a substantially lower cost than a partner in a firm of solicitors because the overheads of some firms of solicitors are very high, especially those based in London. The high costs of running a large solicitors' practice must be charged to clients on an hourly basis and in many instances the total cost could be higher than the fee charged by a barrister. Moreover, the barrister is likely to be more detached and objective in his/her approach to the case and may be in a better position to advise a client on the likely attitude of a judge to the claim being brought to court. If the government were to force fusion on the profession it is possible that the most successful barristers would be 'head-hunted' by the large London law firms and their services would only be available to those persons who were able to become clients of those firms. The small solicitors' practices, especially those outside London, would no longer be able to compete on equal terms with the very large London law firms. At present they all have equality of access to the same specialist pool of advocates for their clients.

The debate over fusion continues but it is possible that fusion may occur in the future. In its *First Report on Legal Education and Training* the now defunct Lord Chancellor's Advisory Committee on Legal Education called for common vocational training for all would-be lawyers irrespective of whether they intend to practise as barristers or solicitors. If this were to be adopted, it might lead to a situation where all new entrants to the legal profession qualified as solicitors. Those solicitors who wished to specialise in advocacy in the superior courts might then join chambers and become members of a smaller but even more highly specialised independent Bar to offer their services to the public at large.

Progress test

1. How is the legal profession in England and Wales structured?

2. What services might a local firm of solicitors be expected to provide to the local business community?

3. If a non-graduate were to begin as a trainee legal executive, how long would it take him/her to become a fully qualified solicitor?

4. Why would a person determined on a legal career opt to qualify as a barrister?

5. Why do barristers (and some solicitors) apply to become Queen's Counsel?

6. What is the role of the Office for the Supervision of Solicitors? Should all complaints against solicitors be made to the OSS in the first instance?

7. Does the Bar Council operate a complaints system?

8. Why was the Office of Legal Services Ombudsman created?

9. Why might the Lord Chancellor decide to appoint a Legal Services Complaints Commissioner and if he/she did, would the Legal Services Ombudsman be redundant?

10. Are the arguments against a fused legal profession overwhelming?

Further reading

Books

Bailey, S.H. and M.J. Gunn (1996) *The Modern English Legal System* (London: Sweet & Maxwell, chapters 3 and 4).

Cownie, F. and A. Bradney (2000) *The English Legal System in Context* (London: Butterworths, chapter 8).

Slapper, G. and D. Kelly (1999) *The English Legal System* (London: Cavendish Publishing, chapter 11).

Ward, R. (1998) *Walker and Walker's English Legal System* (London: Butterworths, chapter 12).

Articles

Christensen, C. and J. Worthington (2001) 'Complaint handling within chambers', *The New Law Journal* Vol. 151, No. 6968.

Drummond, H. (1996) 'Standards of advocacy revisited', *The New Law Journal* Vol. 146, No. 6742 655.

Kerridge, R. and G. Davis (1999) 'Reform of the legal profession: an alternative way ahead', *Modern Law Review* Vol. 62, No. 6.

Mears, M. (1999) 'The OSS – Congratulations?!' *The New Law Journal* Vol. 149, No. 6889, p. 743.

Useful websites

The official website of the Institute of Legal Executives is www.ilex.org.uk

The website for the Office for the Supervision of Solicitors can be accessed via the website for the Law Society, which is www.lawsociety.org.uk

Information on the barristers' profession can be obtained from www.barcouncil.org.uk

Information on the Inns of Court can be obtained from the following websites:

www.graysinn.org.uk
www.lincolnsinn.org.uk
www.innertemple.org.uk
www.middletemple.org.uk

Further information on the office of Legal Services Ombudsman can be obtained from the website of the Lord Chancellor's Department at www.gtnet.gov.uk

3

Magistrates, judges and the courts

1. Introduction

Those persons who are appointed to carry out a judicial function are closely identified with the courts over which they preside. These courts form a hierarchy with the magistrates' courts and county courts at the base and the House of Lords at the apex, as can be seen from Figure 3.1.

Magistrates' courts and county courts are regarded as inferior or lower courts whilst all the courts above them in the hierarchy are regarded as superior courts. Apart from the fact that the jurisdiction of the county courts is exclusively civil, there is no neat division between civil courts on the one hand and criminal courts on the other.

The Lord Chancellor plays a key role in all judicial appointments. He is appointed by the Queen, but the reality is that the prime minister, on taking

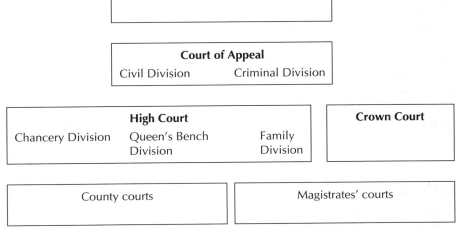

Figure 3.1 Hierarchy of courts.

office after a general election, will choose a distinguished lawyer who is a leading member of his/her political party. As a Cabinet minister, the Lord Chancellor presides over a large Whitehall department for as long as his/her party is in government. The Lord Chancellor's Department closely approximates to what in other countries is recognisable as a ministry of justice. Thus, the Lord Chancellor is not only responsible for the functioning of the legal system in England and Wales but also Speaker of the House of Lords chamber and can sit as a judge of the Judicial Committee of the House of Lords in cases where the government is not a litigant.

2. Magistrates

There are 435 magistrates' courts in England and Wales presided over by more than 30,000 part-time, unpaid magistrates. These courts play a crucial role in the criminal justice system, dealing annually with approximately 98 per cent of all criminal offences. Magistrates, or justices of the peace as they are otherwise known, do not possess professional legal qualifications and are chosen from among members of the local community. Indeed, most adult persons of good character between the ages of 27 and 60 can apply to become magistrates, but persons convicted of a serious criminal offence, bankrupts, serving members of the armed forces, the prison service and police service are not eligible for appointment. It is intended that the composition of the magistracy should, as far as possible, reflect the social and ethnic mix of the locality although this is not always achieved. Even though employers are obliged to release employees to undertake this vital function, they are not obliged to pay them and this may be a factor in the declining number of applications from ordinary working people. All prospective candidates must pass two interviews in order to be recommended by a local advisory committee to the Lord Chancellor for appointment. Appointments in Lancashire, Merseyside and Greater Manchester are made by the Chancellor of the Duchy of Lancaster. On being appointed, all new magistrates must undergo an initial three-month training programme during which they acquire a working knowledge of the law of evidence and an understanding of the principles and purpose of sentencing. A new scheme for the training of magistrates is being implemented nationally which is focused on the acquisition of competences.

All magistrates, whether newly appointed or not, are required to complete a Personal Development Log that is issued by the Magisterial Committee of the Judicial Studies Board. For its part, the Magistrates' Association has established a national scheme for the training of experienced magistrates as mentors who will support all new magistrates in their development during their first two years on the bench. All magistrates must use their Personal

Development Logs as a basis for demonstrating that they have attained the necessary competences which will be assessed through a system of appraisal by mentors.

England and Wales are divided into 'commission areas' and magistrates are appointed to act for particular commission areas. London has six such areas and outside London the commission areas are the respective counties of England and Wales. Magistrates are required to live in or within 15 miles of the particular commission area for which they act. The areas are then subdivided into petty sessional divisions, each of which has its own magistrates' court. Even though magistrates are eligible to sit in any of the courts in their commission area, they are usually assigned to a bench for the division where they either live or work. In court they normally sit as a panel of three comprising an experienced chairperson with two 'wingers'. They try the majority of offences without a jury. Most of these offences are classed as 'summary offences', all of which are defined as such by Act of Parliament. There are other offences that can be tried 'either way', that is, summarily or on indictment at the Crown Court, but many accused persons opt for summary trial when they intend to plead guilty usually in the hope that they will receive a lighter sentence. Lay magistrates can impose fines of up to £5,000 and custodial sentences of up to six months. Apart from trying most criminal cases they also deal with such matters as:

(a) applications for bail from persons charged with offences

(b) the granting of search and arrest warrants

(c) issuing licences for the sale of alcohol by public houses and restaurants and for betting shops and casinos

(d) administering oaths under the Courts and Legal Services Act 1990 s. 56 for the grant of probate or letters of administration

(e) the recovery of civil debts such as unpaid income tax, National Insurance contributions, utility bills and council tax.

Lay magistrates with special training sit as 'youth courts' dealing with juvenile crime and as 'family proceedings courts' dealing with matters such as the finalising of adoptions or access to children on the break-up of a relationship.

In the exercise of its judicial function, a panel of magistrates will be assisted by a court clerk who must be legally qualified as either a barrister or a solicitor. The clerk sits immediately in front of the magistrates in court and advises them on the relevant law that is applicable in the case under consideration. However, it is the magistrates themselves who must decide the outcome – the clerk must not participate in the decision-making nor must he/she attempt to instruct the magistrates on how to decide the case. Apart from the 30,000 or so lay magistrates, there are just under 100 full-time, salaried appointees who were formerly known as stipendiary magistrates but are now known as District Judges of Magistrates' Courts. Prior to their appointment they will have been practising barristers or solicitors having at least seven years' practical experience of advocacy in magistrates' courts. District Judges of Magistrates' Courts are appointed by the Queen on the recommendation of the Lord Chancellor. Both lay magistrates and District Judges of Magistrates' Courts must retire at the age of 70.

3. Circuit judges and district judges

Most full-time judges who sit in the Crown Court are known as circuit judges. The Crown Court is the venue for the trial of all serious criminal offences. The mode of trial is by indictment which specifies each offence as a 'count'. *Archbold*, the leading text on criminal pleadings, evidence and procedure, states that 'a bill of indictment is a written or printed accusation of a crime made at the suit of the Crown against one or more persons'. Where a plea of 'not guilty' has been entered to the count(s) on the indictment, this mode of trial requires a jury to give a verdict either convicting or acquitting the accused person. The most serious offences (e.g. murder, rape, wounding etc.) and the most complex (e.g. fraud) are tried by a High Court judge before a jury. The Crown Court is part of the Supreme Court of Judicature and therefore derives its jurisdiction from the Supreme Court Act 1981. Although it sits in many different locations, the Crown Court is a single court. The locations in which the court sits are classified according to geographical position and to status. In relation to geographical position, every location belongs to one of six circuits: Midlands and Oxford; North Eastern; Northern; Wales and Chester; Western; and South Eastern.

Each circuit is presided over by a High Court judge who has the responsibility for making decisions concerning the administration and distribution of work on the circuit. As regards status, locations are classed either as first, second or third tier. High Court judges sit regularly at first-tier locations but they never sit at third-tier locations. The most famous first-tier location is the Central Criminal Court in London, otherwise known as the Old Bailey. Third-tier locations are presided over by circuit judges or recorders. Apart from trials on indictment, the Crown Court hears appeals from magistrates' courts and deals with proceedings on a committal for sentence from a magistrates' court (see Chapter 11). Although the jurisdiction of the Crown Court is mainly criminal, it does exercise a limited civil jurisdiction mainly in the form of licensing appeals from magistrates' courts. Circuit Judges are appointed by the Queen on the advice of the Lord Chancellor and, as at

January 2000, there were about 560 of them. Fewer than 40 were women and over 90 per cent were practising barristers prior to being appointed. Although some circuit judges are assigned to the county courts, most carry out their duties in the Crown Court where their numbers are supplemented by approximately 900 recorders and 450 assistant recorders, all of whom sit as part-time judges of the Crown Court. In order to qualify for appointment to the rank of circuit judge, the candidate must normally have exercised rights of audience in the Crown Court for at least ten years or have held office as a recorder or assistant recorder for at least three years.

The Lord Chancellor is required to assign at least one circuit judge to each of the 240 county courts whose jurisdiction is exclusively civil. Nevertheless, most of the work in the county courts is done by full time district judges, of whom there were just over 400 as at January 2000. They were assisted by some 750 deputy district judges who serve on a part-time basis. Most district judges were former solicitors with advocacy experience, but both solicitors and barristers must have been practising advocates for seven years to be eligible for appointment.

4. Judges of the High Court

The High Court was created by the Supreme Court of Judicature Act 1873; it is made up of the Court of Appeal, the Crown Court and the Supreme Court of Judicature. In order to facilitate the efficient management of its workload, the High Court is subdivided into three main divisions, these being Chancery, Queen's Bench and Family. Although the Lord Chancellor is the president of the Chancery Division, in practice it is presided over by a senior judge known as the Vice Chancellor because the Lord Chancellor is always otherwise occupied. The Lord Chief Justice is the head of and presides over the Queen's Bench Division, whilst the Family Division is presided over by a senior judge who is known simply as the President. In addition to these 'heads of division', there were approximately 100 High Court judges as at January 2000 but only 8 of them were women. Rather surprisingly, these judges are sometimes referred to as *puisne* judges (pronounced 'pewnee' meaning lesser) although the appointment is very prestigious because male appointees have knighthoods conferred upon them and their female counterparts are made Dames of the British Empire. A High Court judge is referred to either as Mr Justice . . . or Madam Justice . . . when being spoken about but as M'Lord or M'Lady when being addressed in court. In legal textbooks, a High Court judge is referred to by his/her surname with suffix *J* appended, for example: Brown J.

Since only 17 High Court judges were assigned to the Chancery Division and 16 to the Family Division as at January 2000, it is readily apparent that the Queen's Bench Division is the largest of the three divisions. The Lord Chancellor can require any judge to move to another division if and when the volume of work necessitates such a transfer. Even though any division of the High Court can sit anywhere in England and Wales, most of the sittings take place in the building housing the Royal Courts of Justice in the Strand, London. The reason why the workload of the Queen's Bench Division is the largest is because it has both a civil and a criminal jurisdiction, the latter being exclusively appellate. Most of the civil cases reaching the Queen's Bench Division are in the nature of contractual and tort claims and these are tried by a single judge normally sitting without jury. Most of the tort actions take the form of compensation claims for personal injuries sustained through the negligence of others. The Commercial Court, which deals with a wide range of commercial disputes including banking and insurance cases, is attached to this division as is the Admiralty Court which deals mainly with cases concerning shipping law. The appellate jurisdiction of the Queen's Bench Division in civil matters is quite limited in that it deals with appeals from certain administrative tribunals. As was noted above, most of the judges in the Queen's Bench Division spend part of their time in the Crown Court hearing criminal cases.

The Divisional Court of Queen's Bench in London, in which two judges usually sit together, exercises the criminal jurisdiction of the High Court. It hears appeals on points of law by way of 'case stated' from magistrates' courts and from the Crown Court. In a magistrates' court either the prosecution or the defendant may require the magistrates to state a case for the opinion of the Divisional Court of Queen's Bench on the basis that the proceedings in that court were outside its jurisdiction or involved a mistake of law. On considering the case the Divisional Court may confirm, amend or even reverse the decision of the magistrates' court. Applications by way of 'judicial review' of administrative decisions made by government ministers, government departments and local authorities are heard by the Administrative Court. It is usual for such applications to be heard by a single judge when no aspect of the criminal law is involved. When hearing applications for judicial review the Administrative Court exercises what can be best described as a supervisory jurisdiction which enables it to issue the prerogative writ of *habeas corpus* (requiring the release of a person unlawfully detained) and the prerogative orders. These prerogative orders are now known in their new English forms as quashing orders (nullifying administrative decisions), a prohibiting order (preventing inferior tribunals from exceeding their jurisdiction) and mandatory orders requiring a tribunal to rehear a case or, in the case of a government department or minister, to reconsider decisions taken. These prerogative orders are dealt with in far greater detail in the context of judicial review in Chapter 15.

The Chancery Division derives its name from the ancient Court of Chancery that was abolished in 1873. The jurisdiction of this division includes hearing disputes over wills, trusts, the administration of the estates of deceased persons, the affairs of companies and partnerships and matters relating to mortgages of land. A judge from the Chancery Division can sit as a judge of the Court of Protection to supervise the administration of the property and affairs of any adult who has become mentally or in some instances physically incapacitated. There is a Divisional Court of Chancery that can hear certain appeals from county courts on bankruptcy matters and from the Commissioners of Inland Revenue which is a specialist tribunal dealing with appeals against tax assessments.

The Family Division, as the title suggests, is concerned with matters arising from divorce, the custody and welfare of children as well as proceedings under the Children Act 1989. There is also a Family Divisional Court usually comprising two High Court judges which hears appeals from decisions of magistrates' courts in family matters.

5. Eligibility for appointment to the High Court

Advocates must normally have exercised a general right of audience in the High Court for ten years to be eligible for appointment as a High Court judge or have held office as a circuit judge for at least two years. Appointments are made by the Queen on the advice of the Lord Chancellor, and in the past, appointments have been made from members of the Bar who have been in practice for 20 years or more. Most have held the rank of QC. Nowadays, suitably qualified solicitors are eligible for appointment and, in June 1993, Sir Michael Sachs, a former solicitor became the first judge to be appointed to the High Court Bench, but he had been a circuit judge since 1984. As of October 2000, Dr Lawrence Collins QC, a solicitor and highly respected legal scholar, has been appointed to the Chancery Division. He sat as a deputy High Court judge from 1997 to the date of his full-time appointment. The Lord Chancellor appoints deputy High Court judges to assist with the workload of the High Court as well as to assess the competence of the person in the role. Nevertheless, all deputy High Court judges must have the same qualifications as are required for a full-time appointment.

6. Judges of the Court of Appeal

As can be seen from Figure 3.1, the Court of Appeal has two divisions. The Civil Division is presided over by the Master of the Rolls whilst the Criminal Division is presided over by the Lord Chief Justice, but the Vice

Chancellor and President of the Family Division may also sit as judges. In addition to these heads of division, as of January 2000 there were 35 full-time Lord Justices of Appeal – 34 men and 1 woman. In legal textbooks the Lord Justices of Appeal are referred to by their surnames with the suffix *LJ*, for example: May LJ. For the most part, Lord Justices of Appeal are promoted from among the ranks of High Court judges by the Queen on the advice of the prime minister who will take care to consult with the Lord Chancellor. The Lord Chancellor will, for his part, consult with other senior members of the judiciary before advising the prime minister on the suitability of a candidate. Both divisions of the court are kept very busy with civil and criminal appeals throughout the year. Thus in both divisions a number of courts are empanelled to sit and hear appeals. In the Civil Division, a High Court judge is permitted to sit with one or more Lord Justices to constitute a court, and in the Criminal Division it is possible for two High Court judges to sit with one or more Lord Justices of Appeal to hear appeals from the Crown Court.

7. Judges of the House of Lords

The Appellate Jurisdiction Act 1876 reconstituted the House of Lords as an appeal court above the Court of Appeal. It is therefore necessary to distinguish the court from the chamber of the legislature of the same name even though the court sits at the Parliament building at Westminster. The Act provides for the creation of a number of salaried 'life peers' with the official title of Lords of Appeal in Ordinary whose main function it is to hear both civil and criminal appeals usually from the Court of Appeal but occasionally from lower courts. The Lord Chancellor may sit as a judge but is normally too busy to do so. Instead, the work of the court is conducted by the twelve Law Lords sitting either as a court of five or sometimes as a court of seven even though the Act allows for the convening of a court of just three if the Lord Chancellor sits as a judge. A civil appeal to the House of Lords is possible only if either the Court of Appeal or the House of Lords itself gives permission, and in criminal cases there is an additional requirement that the appeal has to focus on a point of law of general public importance. Appointments to the House of Lords are made by the Queen on the advice of the prime minister who will always consult with the Lord Chancellor. In practice, virtually all appointments are made from the ranks of the Lords Justices of Appeal.

Some of the Law Lords also sit from time to time as members of the Judicial Committee of the Privy Council assisted by other judges who are privy counsellors that have held or hold high judicial office including the present and former Lord Chancellors. The origins of the Judicial Committee of the Privy Council as an appellate court can be traced back several centuries but in its modern form it dates from the enactment of the Judicial Committee Act 1833 which established it as special committee of the Monarch's Privy Council to hear appeals from overseas territories of the Crown. With the dissolution of the British Empire and creation of the Commonwealth, the Judicial Committee of the Privy Council still functions as the final court of appeal for New Zealand and certain West Indian states such as Jamaica and Trinidad. Closer to home, it hears final appeals from the Channel Islands and Isle of Man as well as certain domestic tribunals such as the Professional Conduct Committee of the General Medical Council. It is usual for five judges to hear an appeal with the exception of appeals from certain domestic tribunals which are heard by three judges. Permission to appeal is usually required. Most recently, the Judicial Committee of the Privy Council has been given the jurisdiction under the Government of Wales Act 1988, the Scotland Act 1988 and the Northern Ireland Act 1998 to decide issues relating to the competences of the executive authorities and legislative assemblies of Scotland and Northern Ireland established under these statutes.

8. Judicial appointments and tenure

Prior to the general election in 1997, the Labour Party whilst in opposition expressed support for the idea of the creation of a Judicial Appointments Committee that would be completely independent of government. Not long after taking office the Labour government made it clear that it did not intend to make any fundamental changes to the existing system of appointing judges. There are good arguments for removing the system for appointments from any political influence since it is of paramount importance that the judiciary should not only be independent but should also be seen to be independent of government and the legislature. Some commentators have argued that there was too much secrecy surrounding the traditional system of appointments but others have defended the system which is an evolving one. The Lord Chancellor's Department has addressed some of the criticisms by advertising vacancies at the level of the High Court and below on an annual basis making it clear that appointments will always be made on merit regardless of ethnic origin, gender, marital status, political affiliation, sexual orientation, religion or disability. Suitably qualified laypersons are now involved in the shortlisting of candidates for interview as well as in the interviewing process itself. However, the Lord Chancellor has the final say and he retains the discretion to appoint persons who have not made an application. Moreover, appointments to the rank of deputy High Court judge are made on an annual basis by invitation only and a significant number of future full-time appointments to the High Court bench will always be made from among the ranks of deputy High Court judges.

According to the Supreme Court Act 1981, all senior judges at the level of the High Court and above hold office subject to their good behaviour and can only be removed by the Queen as a result of an address by both Houses of Parliament. Nevertheless, one High Court judge did retire in 1998 having been publicly criticised by the Court of Appeal over an inordinate delay in giving judgement in a case. Circuit judges and district judges, on the other hand, can be removed from office because of incompetence or misbehaviour by the Lord Chancellor alone. He can and does remove lay magistrates if there is good cause. The normal retirement age for judges and magistrates is now 70. Many judges retire before reaching this age because, after 20 years of service, a judge can retire on a pension equivalent to half salary. There are nevertheless some serving judges over the age of 70 who were appointed before the retirement age was lowered.

9. The Judicial Studies Board

In 1979 a review was conducted by Lord Justice Bridge of the needs of the judiciary presiding over criminal cases for training and development. As a result, the Judicial Studies Board (JSB) was established as an autonomous non-governmental agency to ensure that judicial independence was not compromised in the training process. Then, in 1985, the remit of the Board was widened to cover the training needs of other members of the judiciary whose jurisdiction was in the various branches of the civil law and family law. The training of magistrates and chairpersons of administrative tribunals was also included. The JSB now has five operational objectives as follows:

(a) To provide high quality training to full and part-time judges in the exercise of their jurisdiction in civil, criminal and family law.

(b) To advise the Lord Chancellor on the policy for, and content of, training for lay magistrates and on the efficiency and effectiveness with which magistrates' courts committees deliver such training.

(c) To advise the Lord Chancellor and government departments on the appropriate standards for, and content of, training for judicial officers of tribunals.

(d) To advise the government on the training requirements of judges, magistrates and judicial officers of tribunals if proposed changes to the law, procedure and court organisation are to be effective and to provide and advise on the content of such training.

(e) To promote closer international cooperation over judicial training.

The Lord Chief Justice is the patron of the Board but it operates through a main Board whose chairperson and members are appointed by the Lord Chancellor, including the chairpersons of its six committees that are responsible for organising the provision of training. Apart from the chairpersons of its six committees, the main Board comprises other members of the judiciary, a lay magistrate, at least one academic, a QC and civil servants from the Lord Chancellor's Department and the Home Office. Appointments to the individual committees are made by the committee chairperson having regard to the Nolan principles. A full-time Director of Studies, who must be a circuit judge and whose remit is to oversee and coordinate the various training programmes, is now appointed by the Board. The pivotal role of the Director of Studies is underlined by the fact that he/she attends all meetings of the JSB and its six committees. The routine day-to-day work of the JSB is carried out by a full-time secretariat of about 30 civil servants who are supervised by the Secretary to the Board.

All part-time judges are required to attend an induction course organised by the JSB before they are allowed to preside judicially and every full-time and part-time judge must attend a refresher seminar every three years in every major area of jurisdiction over which he/she presides. Many of the courses are planned and delivered by practising judges, but the JSB does invite leading academics and practitioners to contribute to the courses that are offered. The range of courses provided and the names of those who have delivered them are set out in the annual report which can be downloaded from the JSB website.

The JSB has links with similar bodies in North America and Europe and each year it receives a number of visitations. The JSB also arranges study trips abroad for members of the judiciary from time to time.

Progress test

1. Although most adult persons between the ages of 27 and 60 can apply to be appointed as magistrates, which classes of persons are not eligible to be appointed?

2. Who is responsible for appointing magistrates in England and Wales?

3. Who appoints circuit judges and on whose advice and recommendation?

4. What are the criteria to be met before a person is eligible to be appointed as a High Court judge?

5. Who presides over (a) the Civil Division of the Court of Appeal, and (b) the Criminal Division of the Court of Appeal?

6. Who appoints the Lord Justices of Appeal and whose advice and recommendations are sought?

7. How are the Lords of Appeal in Ordinary appointed?

8. What role does the Judicial Committee of the Privy Council fulfil nowadays and who is eligible to sit as a judge in Judicial Committee of the Privy Council?

9. What is the normal retirement age for judges and magistrates?

10. Why was the Judicial Studies Board created? How important do you consider its role to be?

Further reading

Books

Bailey, S.H. and M.J. Gunn (1996) *The Modern English Legal System* (London: Sweet & Maxwell, chapter 4).

Cownie, F. and A. Bradney (2000) *The English Legal System in Context* (London: Butterworths, chapter 9).

Griffith, J.A.G. (1997) *The Politics of the Judiciary* (London: Fontana).

Slapper, G. and D. Kelly (1999) *The English Legal System* (London: Cavendish Publishing, chapter 6).

Ward, R. (1998) *Walker and Walker's English Legal System* (London: Butterworths, chapter 12).

Articles

Frazer, C. (2000) 'Judicial independence', *New Law Journal* Vol. 150, No. 6928.

Gladwell, D. (2001) 'Judicial appointments', *New Law Journal* Vol. 151, No. 6984.

Useful websites

The website www.gtnet.gov.uk/ is that of the Lord Chancellor's Department and contains much useful information on the judiciary and magistracy. The website of the Judicial Studies Board is www.jsboard.co.uk/ and that of the Judicial Committee of the Privy Council is www.privy-council.org.uk/

The law-making process

4

The law-making process 1: Case law and law reporting

1. Introduction

Over the centuries the judges have created a vast body of case law, much of which is still applicable in England and Wales to this day. This case law forms the basis of many of the major branches of the civil law. When a judge decides a case (either for the claimant or for the defendant), he/she will issue an order giving effect to his/her decision which will be entered in the court records. The judgement so entered is binding on the parties unless it is overturned on appeal – as lawyers would say, the matter is *res judicata* (settled) because the decision resolves the dispute between the parties. However, the judgement itself will normally be based on the application of one or more legal principles to the facts as established before court and it is this aspect of the case that lawyers refer to as the *ratio decidendi* (or *ratio* pronounced 'rayshio') which is capable of becoming a precedent for the future should another dispute arise involving similar facts. As long ago as 1833, Park CJ said in *Mirehouse* v *Rennell* (1833) that:

Precedent must be adhered to for the sake of developing the law as a science.

Following established precedent has a number of advantages in that there is a degree of consistency and predictability associated with this form of law-making. Also, where it is known that judges are predisposed to follow earlier precedents, lawyers are able to advise their clients with some degree of confidence of the likely outcome to a dispute if there is one or more relevant precedents with broadly similar facts. This in itself may help to save the time and money that might otherwise be spent on unnecessary litigation.

Most of the precedents that have contemporary relevance in the various branches of the civil law (for example, contract and the law of torts) are developments and refinements of earlier precedents created in the old common law courts and indeed, the Court of Chancery. It is important to have a clear understanding of the evolution of case law over the centuries to appreciate the distinction between common law and equity. Therefore, a short historical account has been included at the end of this chapter but the historical dimension need not detain you for the present. A good grasp of modern case law technique and the process of law-making by precedent may be achieved through a case study approach.

2. Case studies

This case study focuses on an important aspect of the law of contract, namely, the precise nature of contractual obligations. Until the second half of the nineteenth century it was widely accepted by the judiciary that contractual obligations were absolute and that unforeseen subsequent events did not provide an excuse for non-performance. After all, if it were possible for one of the parties, having freely entered into the contract, to abandon it simply because he/she regarded his/her obligations as too onerous in the light of some subsequent event, that would undermine the entire concept of the contract as a legally binding agreement. Nevertheless, exceptions had long been acknowledged where performance of the contract had been rendered unlawful because of the application of a rule of law or, in the case of con-tracts for personal services, by the death or permanent incapacity of one of the parties. In all other instances, the judges were of the view that once a party had freely entered into a contract he/she must perform it or pay compensation (damages) to the other party who had suffered because of his/her failure to perform what had been agreed at the outset.

It was against this background that the dispute in the case known as *Taylor* v *Caldwell* (1863) came before the Court of Queen's Bench for resolu-tion. The case was brought by Taylor who was an impresario. The defend-ant, Caldwell, owned a concert venue known as the Surrey Gardens and Music Hall and the two entered into a contract, the basis of which was that Taylor could hire the venue to stage a series of four concerts in the summer months. Taylor agreed to pay Caldwell a substantial sum of money by the standards of the time just prior to each concert. A few days before the first concert was to be given a fire broke out and the music hall was gutted by the blaze. The debris was strewn about the venue so that it could no longer be used as intended. Taylor took the view that Caldwell's obligation to provide the venue was absolute and he therefore sued alleging breach of contract, claiming as damages all the expenses that he had incurred in publicising and organising the concerts. Caldwell's defence was that the fire was not his fault and that it was impossible to carry out the contract as envisaged because the music hall had been destroyed. The judge had to decide whether the obligations arising under the contract were, as a matter of legal principle, at an end or whether the defendant was obliged to pay the damages claimed by Taylor for breach of contract.

Blackburn J in giving his judgement stated:

> In the present case, looking at the whole contract, we find that the parties contracted on the basis of the continued existence of the music hall at the time when the concerts were to be given, that being essential to their performance. We think, therefore, that, the music hall having ceased to exist without fault of either party, both parties are excused, [Taylor] from taking the gardens and paying the money and the defendant from performing their promise to give the use of the hall and gardens, and other things.

The precedent created in *Taylor* v *Caldwell* was applied in the later case of *Appleby Bros* v *Myers* (1867) in which Appleby Bros contracted to supply and erect certain machinery on the defendant's premises and to keep it in good repair for two years. The price agreed for the work and materials was to be paid by the defendant on completion. After part of the work had been completed and whilst other parts were in progress, a fire accidentally broke out which destroyed the premises and all the machinery. It is interesting to note that the judgement of court was given by Blackburn J who invoked the principle he had developed in *Taylor* v *Caldwell*. This precedent was then extended in *Nickoll and Knight* v *Ashton* [1901] to a slightly different set of facts. In this case there was a contract for the sale of a cargo of cotton seed to be shipped from Alexandria to the United Kingdom during January 1900 by the steamship *Orlando*. After the contract had been made, the *Orlando*, which was then in the Baltic, became stranded. As a result, the vessel was badly damaged and the sellers gave notice on 20 December to Nickoll and Knight (the buyers) that it would be impossible for the *Orlando* to load before March. On 28 December, the buyers informed the sellers that as performance of the contract had been rendered impossible, they considered it cancelled. Somewhat surprisingly, this did not stop the buyers suing for damages for breach of contract and the case eventually reached the Court of Appeal. Two of the three judges in the Court of Appeal affirmed the judgement of the lower court and ruled that the precedent established in *Taylor* v *Caldwell* should be applied and as a result, there could be no claim for breach of contract and damages. The principle that was developed in *Taylor* v *Caldwell* has since been developed into the wider doctrine of frustration of contract although that phrase was not used by Blackburn J in any part of his judgement.

3. *Ratio decidendi* and *obiter dicta*

A case may stand as authority for a proposition of law, but not everything that a judge says in delivering his/her judgement will constitute the *ratio decidendi* of a case. A judge may refer to a number of matters in the course of delivering his/her judgement that do not relate directly to the material facts as established in the case. Sometimes a judge may even hypothesise on the outcome if the facts were somewhat different. However, it is only the material facts and the principles of law as applied to those facts which leads to the decision that constitutes the *ratio decidendi*. Everything else said by the judge in the course of delivering his/her judgement is *obiter dicta* (literally, things said by the way). *Obiter dicta* is not precedent and will not therefore be binding on another court.

Extracting the *ratio decidendi* of a case is likely to prove a more straight-forward task where there is just one judgement to consider when a case is initially tried. The process becomes more complex if there is an appeal with the original judgement being overruled unless there is a leading judgement in the Court of Appeal with which the other judges concur. This is because the three judges (occasionally five) have the right to deliver independent judgements and, although they may agree on the outcome, they may adopt different lines of reasoning sometimes invoking different legal principles. There could be a split decision of two to one even though it is the majority decision that will count. These difficulties may be compounded if there is a subsequent appeal to the House of Lords which then overrules the decision of the Court of Appeal because appeals in the House of Lords are heard by five Law Lords each of whom may deliver a full judgement. Nevertheless, some attempt has to be made to extract the *ratio decidendi* although on occasion this may prove to be an impossible task. This impossibility is well illustrated by the House of Lord's decision in the case of *Elder, Dempster & Co. Ltd* v *Paterson, Zochonis & Co. Ltd* [1924]. When considering this case in the later case of *Scruttons Ltd* v *Midland Silicones Ltd* [1962], Lord Reid said:

> It can hardly be denied that the *ratio decidendi* of the Elder, Dempster decision is very obscure . . . when I look for such a principle I cannot find it and the extensive and able arguments of counsel . . . have failed to discover it.

Clearly, isolating the *ratio decidendi* of a case is not the equivalent of isolating a chemical element in an experiment. It is a matter of summarising the relevant part of the judgement but this can often be done at different levels of generalisation or abstraction. A very narrow formulation of the *ratio* in *Taylor* v *Caldwell* would have limited it to the destruction of enter-tainment venues, but Blackburn J evidently did not intend that it should be construed so narrowly. He obviously formulated his *ratio* on the basis that it should be capable of a wider application and applied it in *Appleby Bros* v *Myers* to cover a contract for the installation of equipment when the busi-ness premises were destroyed by fire. Since then, what has become known as the principle of frustration of contract has been applied to contracts where there was no destruction of the subject matter by fire as in *Nickoll and Knight* v *Ashton* and in *Krell* v *Henry* [1903] (to be discussed later). Thus, there is a sense in which the understanding and application of the *ratio decidendi* of an earlier case can be affected by how it comes to be interpreted and applied by subsequent courts.

Although what is deemed to be *obiter dicta* does not form part of the precedent this does not mean that it is of no value whatsoever. The *dicta* of judges in the Court of Appeal and House of Lords may be important for the subsequent evolution of case law. For example, the *obiter dicta* of Lord Denning MR delivered as part of his judgement in the Court of Appeal in *Central London Property Trust Ltd* v *High Trees House Ltd* [1947] signalled an important development in the law of contract in the area of contractual waiver. Moreover, the *obiter dicta* of the Law Lords in *Hedley Byrne Ltd* v *Heller & Partners Ltd* [1964] indicated that there would be an important development in the tort of negligence. Their Lordships stated that in future there should be liability under certain circumstances for negligent misstatements that cause loss.

4. Precedent and the hierarchy of the courts

Since the latter part of the nineteenth century, there has existed a clear hierarchy of courts and the process of law-making by precedent operates through this hierarchical structure (see the diagram in Chapter 3). A precedent established in the High Court is not, strictly speaking, binding in the sense of having to be followed by another High Court judge who is called upon to decide a case with similar facts at a later date. That said, however, it will be strongly persuasive and will usually be followed on the basis that, as a matter of procedural justice, like cases should be treated alike. You will recall that *Taylor* v *Caldwell* was followed in *Appleby Bros* v *Myers* even though it was not a binding precedent. Divisional Courts of the High Court are bound by their previous decisions in both civil and criminal cases but they do not bind Crown Courts. Precedents established in the High Court are binding on all lower courts such as county courts and magistrates' courts in respect of their civil jurisdiction. Since decisions of county court judges are rarely reported, they bind only the parties to the litigation but no other court. All precedents established in the appellate courts are regarded as particularly authoritative if the judges agree on the outcome and have employed similar lines of reasoning. Thus precedents set by the House of Lords bind the Court of Appeal and all lower courts and tribunals, but since 1966 the House of Lords has been free to depart from its own precedents. The Practice Statement [1966] 1 WLR 1234 issued by Lord Gardiner, the then Lord Chancellor, on behalf of the Law Lords stated:

Their Lordships regard the use of precedent as an indispensable foundation upon which to decide what is the law and its application to individual cases. It provides at least some degree of certainty upon which individuals can rely in the conduct of their affairs as well as a basis for orderly development of legal rules. Their Lordships nevertheless recognise that too rigid adherence to precedent may lead to injustice in a particular case and also unduly restrict the proper development of the law. They propose therefore to modify their present practice and, while treating former decisions of this House as normally binding, to depart from a previous decision when it appears right to do so. In this connection they will bear in mind the danger of disturbing retrospectively the basis on which contracts, settlements of property and fiscal arrangements have been entered into and also the special need for certainty as to the criminal law. This announcement is not intended to affect the use of precedent elsewhere than in this house.

The House of Lords first exercised its power to overrule one of its earlier precedents in *Conway* v *Rimmer* [1968] by overruling *Duncan* v *Cammell Laird & Co.* [1942]. In relation to the number of occasions on which the House of Lords has been asked by counsel to overrule one of its established precedents it has exercised this freedom infrequently and with caution. The House did overrule its earlier precedent set in *Robert Addie & Sons (Collieries) Ltd* v *Dumbreck* [1929] in the later case of *British Railways Board* v *Herrington* [1972] ruling that an occupier of premises may incur liability to a trespasser. Although the Court of Appeal (Civil Division) is bound by precedents established by the House of Lords, it is also bound by its own precedents. The exceptions to this state of affairs were set out by Lord Green MR in *Young* v *Bristol Aeroplane Co. Ltd* [1944] and may be summarised as follows:

(a) Where two previous precedents of the Court of Appeal on similar facts are shown to differ, one must be followed and the other rejected.

(b) Where a previous decision of the Court of Appeal is at variance with a later decision of the House of Lords its previous decision cannot be followed even if it was not expressly overruled by the House of Lords.

(c) Where a previous decision of the Court of Appeal can be shown to be given *per incuriam* (literally, through want of care) it should not be followed, but this principle has been interpreted narrowly to apply to instances in which some binding authority or statutory provision has been overlooked by the court.

In relation to (a) above, the Court of Appeal (Civil Division) may one day have to decide whether *Ingram* v *Little* [1961] was wrongly decided and whether *Lewis* v *Avery* [1972] represents the law where a contract is made as a result of a mistake as to the identity of the other party. The latter case is more easily reconciled with the earlier precedent of *Phillips* v *Brooks* [1919] and some doubt over the correctness of *Ingram* v *Little* was expressed in *Lewis* v *Avery* but it was not overruled. The case of *Rakhit* v *Carty* [1990] provides a good example of (c) above. The claimant, who was a landlord, let a furnished flat to the defendant, Mrs Carty, for 364 days at a rent of £450 per month. Neither party was aware that a 'fair rent' of £550 per *annum* had been registered in respect of this flat in 1974 when the flat was unfurnished and was recorded as such in the rent register. When Mrs Carty's contractual tenancy came to an end she remained in occupation as a 'statutory tenant' and so the landlord commenced legal proceedings against her for possession. He argued that he reasonably required the flat as a residence for himself under the Rent Act 1977 Schedule 15, Case 9, and he claimed arrears of rent and expenses. The defendant resisted the claim for possession on the basis that it was not reasonable to make the order and that pursuant to Schedule 15 Part III greater hardship would be caused to her by granting the order than would be caused to the landlord by refusing to grant it. She also counterclaimed for arrears of rent on the basis that, where a fair rent was registered, the rent recoverable for any contractual period of a regulated tenancy was limited to the rent so registered. In a nutshell, she argued that there were no arrears of rent but that she had overpaid the rent for the flat and was entitled to a refund. The county court judge upheld the landlord's claim and dismissed Mrs Carty's counterclaim because he considered himself bound by earlier decisions of the Court of Appeal. Mrs Carty appealed contending, among other matters, that the Court of Appeal's earlier decisions had been given *per incuriam* because they had not considered the Rent Act 1977 s. 67(3). This subsection provided that if there was a change in the condition of the dwelling, terms of the tenancy or the quantity, quality or condition of any furniture provided so as to make the registered rent no longer a fair rent either party could apply for a reregistration. The Court of Appeal held that since its earlier decisions had not referred to s. 67(3) it was justified in treating them as having been given *per incuriam* because they had been given in ignorance of the subsection. Accordingly, Mrs Carty's appeal against the dismissal of her counterclaim was allowed but the Court of Appeal saw no basis for interfering with the county court judge's decision to make a possession order. Thus her appeal against the possession order failed. In giving the judgement of the Court of Appeal, Russell LJ cited part of the judgement of Lord Donaldson's MR in *Ricards* v *Ricards* [1989] when the latter referred to *Young* v *Bristol Aeroplane Co. Ltd* and some later cases. In that case Lord Donaldson MR stated:

> These decisions show that this court is justified in refusing to follow one of its own previous decisions not only where that decision is given in ignorance or forgetfulness of some inconsistent statutory provision or some authority binding on it, but also, in rare and exceptional cases, if it is satisfied that the decision

involved a manifest slip or error. In previous cases the judges of this court have always refrained from defining this exceptional category and I have no intention of departing from that approach save to echo the words of Lord Greene M.R. . . . and to say that they will be of the rarest occurrence.

Since the exceptions set out by Lord Greene MR in *Young* v *Bristol Aeroplane Co. Ltd*, a fourth exception has emerged from *Boys* v *Chaplin* [1968]. It is now clear that the Court of Appeal (Civil Division) is not bound by an interlocutory (interim) order made by two appeal court judges sitting as the Court of Appeal. The Criminal Division of the Court of Appeal is never bound by its previous decisions if it considers the law has been misapplied or misunderstood in an earlier case but it is bound by precedents established by the House of Lords.

It is expressly provided in the Human Rights Act 1998 s. 6(1) that it is unlawful for a public authority (a court or tribunal) to act in a way that is incompatible with a Convention right as contained in Schedule 1. Moreover, s. 2(1) states that a court or tribunal in determining a question that has arisen in connection with a Convention right must take account of any judgement, decision, declaration or advisory opinion of the European Court of Human Rights and any opinion of the Human Rights Commission in a report adopted under Article 31 of the Convention. The effect of all this is that all previous rulings of the European Court of Human Rights become jurisprudence that British courts must at least consider. If an existing precedent, particularly in the sphere of public law, should be shown to be at variance with a ruling of the European Court of Human Rights, it may have to be disregarded. This development will have important implications for the House of Lords and Court of Appeal but it will be interesting to see whether a High Court judge will be prepared to abrogate a precedent well established by appellate courts.

5. Flexibility or rigidity?

Given the way in which law-making by precedent operates through the hierarchical structure of the civil courts, you might ask whether the process places judges in the Court of Appeal and those lower down the hierarchy in something of a straitjacket. The judges do, in fact, have a degree of freedom and flexibility within certain limits. Even at the level of the High Court it is possible for a judge to 'distinguish' a precedent cited by the advocate that the judge has been invited to follow. Such a precedent will be direct authority only if the facts are alike. However, the judge may be able to 'distinguish' the present case *on its facts* by emphasising some important dissimilarity to the facts of the precedent cited by the advocate. Of course, this must be justifiable on the basis of the material facts as established in evidence in the case under review, otherwise a departure from existing precedent would require some other justification. If adopted, this stratagem enables the judge to reach an independent decision and in the process a new precedent may be created.

An example of the process of factual distinguishing may be given by considering its application within the doctrine of frustration of contract by comparing and contrasting two cases. The precedent of *Taylor* v *Caldwell* was applied in the case of *Krell* v *Henry* [1903]. Krell was the tenant of some rooms in Pall Mall, London which overlooked the route that the coronation procession of Edward VIII was destined to take. The litigation arose out of a contract that he made with the defendant, Henry. Under this contract Krell agreed, for a fee, to make the rooms available to the defendant on the days on which the coronation procession was scheduled to pass by so that he could view it from a vantage point. Unfortunately, after the contract had been made and just before the date set for the coronation pageant, the King became very ill and the event was cancelled. This did not inhibit Krell from suing to recover the agreed fee and the case eventually went on appeal to the Court of Appeal. All three judges ruled that the principle enunciated in *Taylor* v *Caldwell* should be applied and so there was no basis for Krell's claim since the contract had been discharged as a matter of law when the coronation pageant was cancelled. At about the same time, the Court of Appeal had to deal with the case of *Herne Bay Steam Boat Co.* v *Hutton* [1903]. The company owned and operated a steamboat and it made a contract with the defendant under which he could hire it to take a party of people to see the naval review by Edward VIII of the British fleet of warships anchored off Spithead. After watching the review it was planned to spend the rest of the time cruising around the fleet that was at anchor. The naval review was officially postponed on 25 June because of the King's illness but the fleet remained at anchor off Spithead. Although the company telegraphed the defendant, no reply was received and he failed to arrive with his party of people on the due date. When he subsequently refused to pay the balance of the hire fee, the company then sued for breach of contract claiming damages. The Court of Appeal declined to apply the precedent of *Taylor* v *Caldwell* and distinguished it from the case under consideration on the basis that the naval review of the fleet by the King was not the sole basis of the contract as it would still have been possible for the defendant and his party to cruise around the fleet anchored off Spithead. Accordingly, there *had* been a breach of contract and the defendant was liable in damages.

There is always a danger that factual distinguishing may be taken too far in order to achieve a difference of outcome from an earlier precedent. This can result in the making of some very fine distinctions of fact which merely serve to make the law on a particular subject unnecessarily complex.

Reference has already been made to the problem of reconciling *Ingram* v *Little* with the earlier precedent of *Phillips* v *Brooks* and with the later case of *Lewis* v *Avery*.

Factual distinguishing is not the only stratagem available to the judges. Another possibility would be to say that the rule or principle of law formulated in the earlier case cited by the advocate was formulated *too widely* and that this was unnecessary to achieve the desired result in that case. This is known as restrictive distinguishing. It is a process by which the judge or judges reduce the scope of the earlier rule or principle so that it no longer extends to and encompasses the facts and circumstances of the case under consideration, thus paving the way for an independent decision.

In order to avoid following a precedent set in the High Court and cited by the advocate as authority to be followed, a judge can say that the previous case was wrongly decided and that therefore the *ratio is faulty*. The previous precedent is then said to be 'disapproved', but this can only be done in practice if there is some consensus that the earlier decision was wrong and that it should no longer be followed. It is not something a judge would do without careful consideration and it is to be noted that one High Court judge cannot overrule another. Disapproving is a technique that can be used by the appellate courts although the Court of Appeal can never disapprove of a precedent set in the House of Lords.

Precedents set in the lower courts can, of course, be overruled by the appellate courts. The House of Lords can overrule a precedent set in the Court of Appeal although the Court of Appeal cannot overrule a precedent established by the House of Lords. Once a precedent has been overruled it may no longer be cited as authority in any court. It is no longer good law.

6. Importance of law reports

Law-making by precedent depends to a very large extent on the accurate reporting of the decisions of the superior courts. It is important that lawyers and judges (as well as law students) are able to refer to the more significant judgements that are delivered in these courts. Indeed, it is difficult to envisage how a system of binding precedent could operate without a reliable system of law reporting. Prior to 1863 this reporting was largely a private, uncoordinated activity although some reports of a very high standard were produced by members of the legal profession and judiciary but this was not invariably so. The Law Reports of Espinasse (1793–1807) in particular are famed for their unreliability. It was only in the second half of the nineteenth century, however, that some leading members of the legal profession started to campaign to have law reporting established on a more systematic basis. In 1863 the Council for Law Reporting for England and Wales was established and this body was formally incorporated in 1870 as the Incorporated Council for Law Reporting for England and Wales whose stated aim remains:

> The preparation and publication in a convenient form, at a moderate price and under gratuitous professional control of Reports of judicial decisions of the superior and appellate courts of England.

The Incorporated Council receives no public funds but functions as a registered charity whose income is derived exclusively from publishing. It now publishes four sets of reports annually known as the Law Reports. The Appeal Cases are decisions of the House of Lords but the set also contains reports of cases heard by the Law Lords sitting as the Judicial Committee of the Privy Council which hears civil and criminal appeals from certain Commonwealth countries. In addition, there is one set of reports for each division of the High Court namely, Queen's Bench, Chancery and Family Division. Decisions of the Court of Appeal do not appear in the Appeal Cases but in the reports for the three divisions of the High Court, the particular volume being determined by the court that heard the case at first instance. In Practice Direction [1999] 1 WLR 1027, the Court of Appeal (Civil Division) made it clear that if a case is published by the Incorporated Council for Law Reporting for England and Wales, this is the version that should be cited in court. The reasons are twofold. Firstly, it is a requirement that the barrister or solicitor responsible for preparing the report must be in court when the judgement is handed down. Secondly, the judges themselves edit their judgements prior to publication and the advocates edit the summaries of their arguments. The Law Reports always appear in bound form many months after the calendar year to which they relate and so, since 1953, the Incorporated Council has published the Weekly Law Reports in paperback parts to ensure that all the more important judgements are available as quickly as possible. The judgements in these reports are not revised by the judges prior to publication but they are still of value to lawyers, academics and law students.

In addition to the law reports produced by the Incorporated Council, there are a number of highly regarded reports produced by commercial publishers. The best known series is the All England Law Reports published by Butterworths which date from 1936 but there are a number of others including Lloyd's Law Reports, Simon's Tax Cases and the Industrial Relations Law Reports.

7. Historical development of common law

Most of the existing precedents of contemporary relevance are developments and refinements of much earlier precedents created in the old courts of common law (Court of Exchequer, Court of Common Pleas and Court of King's/Queen's Bench) and subsequently the Court of Chancery. The common law courts simply developed as offshoots from what legal historians refer to as the *curia regis* (the king's council) which was both an administrative and a judicial body that was very much centred on the medieval kings. Apart from the monarch, the full *curia regis* included the great feudal landowners, important clerics and the great officers of state, but it was convened infrequently. A smaller body comprising the monarch and important officers of state such as the King's Justiciar (chief justice) the Lord Treasurer and Lord Chancellor conducted most of the business of the council. The Court of Exchequer was the first of the common law courts to be established as a separate institution from the *curia regis*. It was followed by the Court of Common Pleas which started as an 'experiment' in the last quarter of the twelfth century and became a permanent institution after Magna Carta 1215. Henry II (1154–89) re-established a basic criminal justice system, and a body of civil law was gradually synthesised partly by royal decree and partly by travelling judicial commissioners. The Norman and later Angevin kings (1066–1216) appointed these judicial commissioners to visit the various counties of England and collect taxes, punish wrongdoing and hear disputes mainly involving land or rights associated with land ownership. In addition to applying law created by royal decree, they sought to develop a system of civil law that could be applied nationwide by adopting some of the older Saxon laws and by adapting reasonable local customs. The system of law that they synthesised came to be known as 'common law' because it was intended to be 'common' to the entire kingdom. It was, however, the foundation of the courts of common law as separate institutions, distinct from the king's council in the twelfth and thirteenth centuries that proved to be the catalyst in the subsequent growth of the common law. These courts gradually evolved their own procedural rules. In the early years there was a degree of flexibility in the way in which they operated but this flexibility gradually disappeared.

Two developments were particularly important in the subsequent growth of the common law. Henry II revived the use of juries in civil cases. Thus the ascertainment of issues of fact became the sole province of a jury of laypersons. The second development was that the presiding judge(s) assumed sole responsibility for deciding issues of legal principle that could not be entrusted to poorly educated laypersons. It was these judges who decided the legal principles that would be applied after the lawyers had pleaded their clients' cases. In time, these judges were creating the early precedents which made up the case law of the early common law.

The ability to litigate civil claims in the courts of common law depended upon the claimant being able to obtain a writ. Legal historians disagree over whether it was the King's Justiciar in the scriptorium (office) of the Court of Exchequer or the Chancellor in the Chancery Office who was responsible for issuing the originating writs. In the Middle Ages a writ was quite specific in that there was a special type of writ for every form of recognised claim that could be brought before the common law courts – the ancient writs were not general-purpose documents. It is likely that the King's Justiciar or the Chancellor and his assistants in the Chancery devised new forms of writ as and when the need arose with a view to permitting the litigation of those claims that were thought to have merit. In any event it is unlikely that novel writs would have been drawn up without there being consultation with the king's council. As a result there came to be a number of specific writs – for example, one for trespass, one for debt (for the recovery of money), another for covenant and so on. The practice of devising novel writs was stopped in 1258 under the Provisions of Oxford when rebel barons forced the king to agree to their changes in the legal system. The ban was partially relaxed in the fourteenth century but, apart from the expansion of the scope of the writ of trespass, there was a general reluctance to create entirely new forms of writ in case there might be a massive increase in the volume of litigation with which the courts would be unable to cope.

8. Deficiencies in common law

Although there were a large number of different writs then in use, there were still many claims that could not be litigated. Some comprised facts that could not be realistically framed within one of the existing writs. For example, it was not possible to litigate a simple breach of an oral contract. In those days contractual agreements had to be made in the form of a deed to be enforceable at common law. A deed had to be in writing and had to be signed and sealed by the party or parties to be bound. The execution of the deed also had to be witnessed by a third party to be regarded as valid in court. Very few defences were allowed to a person being sued who had placed his seal on a document. This in itself could sometimes give rise to injustice. If someone borrowed money and the contract of loan was in the form of a deed, the borrower might sometimes be forced to pay twice in the event that he failed to ensure that the deed was cancelled when he made his repayment. The common law courts would not enforce the arrangement that is today known as a 'trust' whereby land (and other property) was transferred to trustees with instructions that it was to be held for the enjoyment of one or more beneficiaries. The legal title to the land had to be transferred to the trustees and the common law courts would not interfere with their legal rights of ownership. Nor would they allow someone who had mortgaged his land as security for a debt to recover it if he had not paid off the debt with interest by the agreed date. This was often a source of grievance because the value of the land might be worth many times the amount borrowed and this would give the lender a substantial profit because the borrower was not able to repay the debt on the agreed date.

For the above and other reasons, legal historians have described the early common law system as excessively formalised and inflexible. At that time, procedural rules governing the presentation of the case were often as important as what the lawyers refer to as the substantive rules – the actual rules constituting a particular body of law. Of course, this meant that legitimate claims and grievances were lost on mere technical points of procedure. Although a dispossessed landowner could recover his land, the only other remedy available in the common law courts took the form 'damages' and this was often an inadequate remedy especially when an owner of land wanted to prevent a nuisance or a continuing trespass to his land.

9. The development of equity

The defects and deficiencies in the common law system gradually gave rise to a parallel and, for the most part, a complementary system of rules and remedies devised in the court of the Lord High Chancellor. These rules and remedies became known as equity. In the fourteenth century, litigants who were unable to obtain justice by pursuing their claims in one of the common law courts would petition the king in council. They might do this because there was no suitable writ which covered their particular grievance or because they were seeking a remedy other than damages. The medieval kings by their coronation oaths were obliged to see that justice was done to their subjects and many took this duty very seriously. When the sheer volume of these petitions from dissatisfied litigants became so onerous, the task of hearing them was delegated by the king to his chief minister who was known as the Chancellor. The first Chancellors were bishops of the medieval church who were more concerned with upright behaviour and Christian morality rather than legal niceties. They would deal with these petitions in a far less formal way than the judges who sat in the common law courts and endeavoured to arrive at a fair and just solution on a case by case basis.

Lawsuits in the Chancellor's court were commenced by issuing bills of complaint which, from 1422, were drafted in English, not Latin. The Chancellor could compel the attendance of the defendant by writ of subpoena otherwise he would face the prospect of a large fine. Witnesses could be summoned in the same way. In comparison with the courts of common law the process of 'pleading' by which the complainant stated his case was quite informal. There were no formal pleadings as there were in the courts of common law. Evidence could be taken from the parties and from witnesses on oath and the Chancellor could punish those who gave perjured evidence. The fact that there was no jury meant that the Chancellor decided questions of fact as well as the outcome and remedy, if any, to be granted. Prior to 1473 the Chancellor, having heard both sides, would issue a decree in the name of the king in favour of the party he deemed to be in the right according to his notions of right reason and good conscience. In the last quarter of the fifteenth century, Chancellors were issuing decrees in their own name instead of in the name of the king, presumably with his approval. It seems reasonable to date the Court of Chancery as a separate court in its own right from this time. The justice dispensed in the Court of Chancery at this time was very much discretionary and no attempt was made until after 1530 to achieve greater consistency of outcomes by rationalising the principles on which it operated and by establishing criteria for the granting of the special remedies available. Nevertheless, the Court of Chancery was used extensively by litigants and eventually became located in the same building, Westminster Hall, as the courts of common law.

Cardinal Wolsey, who was Chancellor from 1515 to 1529, succeeded in alienating the legal profession and judiciary. They objected to his public disdain for legal learning and to his high-handedness in entertaining claims after they had been settled in the common law courts. Henry VIII was reluctant to confer the office of Chancellor on another cleric after Wolsey and it is likely that he desired to place administration of equity and procedures of the Court of Chancery on a more satisfactory basis and thereby placate the judges. He appointed Thomas More, a prominent intellectual who was a trained lawyer and the son of a common law judge, as Chancellor in 1529. Although More was prepared to issue injunctions to prevent persons from exercising their common law rights when he considered this necessary to prevent injustices being done, he was also concerned that equity should be developed as a rational set of principles to operate alongside, and so complement, the existing common law system. Unfortunately More's Chancellorship was of rather short duration and his reforming zeal was not shared by all his successors. It was only from 1672 that it became a requirement for all subsequent Chancellors to be qualified common lawyers.

10. Common law and equity in conflict

Although equity as a system of rules and remedies had evolved to mitigate the rigidity, harshness and excessive technicality of the common law, tensions and ultimately conflict arose between the two systems towards the end of the Chancellorship of Lord Ellesmere (1596–1617). He encouraged disappointed litigants to pursue claims in the Court of Chancery after judgement had been given in one of the courts of common law. Moreover, he used the injunction as a means of preventing successful litigants from enforcing their common law rights where he considered this was unconscionable. As a result, a large backlog of claims built up in the Court of Chancery. When Sir Edward Coke was appointed Chief Justice of England in 1613 he challenged Lord Ellesmere's right to reopen cases which had been adjudicated in the common law courts and his right to imprison people for not obeying an injunction when they were merely asserting their rights under common law. The imprisonment of successful litigants could be ended by obtaining a writ of *habeas corpus* from the Court of King's Bench, but this rivalry between the two systems was something of a public scandal. Matters came to a head in 1615 and the king, James I, decided to refer this conflict of jurisdictions to a small committee of his advisors presided over by Francis Bacon, a renowned scholar who was also the Attorney General. On the basis of the advice received, James I decreed that whenever there should be a conflict between the principles and rules of equity and common law that equity should prevail over the common law. Thereafter the Court of Chancery and common law courts operated alongside each other in reasonable harmony.

Later Chancellors assumed responsibility for developing the principles of equity and equitable remedies that remain of contemporary relevance. They devised remedies that the beneficiary of a trust could enforce against trustees such as account and indemnity. Trusts were not officially recognised by the common law courts. The analogy of the trust was then used to establish 'fiduciary duties' for persons such as agents (and much later, company directors) who were placed in positions whereby others reposed special trust and confidence in them. They would be obliged to observe certain minimum standards of behaviour and failure to do so would result in claims being brought against them in the Court of Chancery. Another innovation of equity was the acknowledgement of a mortgagor's *equity of redemption* whereby a borrower could recover land given as security for a debt even though the actual date set for repayment had passed. Of course, additional interest would be payable by the borrower until the debt was finally repaid. Other remedies were developed such as the right to disclosure of documents prior to litigation. From 1557 onwards the decisions of the Court of Chancery were reported and subsequently published. Thus, over the centuries, equity gradually became a highly rationalised system of rules and principles in which the system and doctrine of precedent came to play an increasingly important role. Three Lord Chancellors in particular, namely Lord Nottingham (1673–82), Lord Hardwicke (1736–56) and Lord Eldon (1801–27), were instrumental in this process.

11. Nineteenth-century reforms

By the end of the eighteenth century the legal system that had evolved over many centuries was inadequate to respond to the new demands that would be made upon it arising from the social and economic upheavals to be set in train by the ongoing processes of industrialisation and urbanisation. The civil justice system was slow, inefficient and expensive. The defining feature of the system was the dual systems of common law and equity with their separate courts and procedures. It was often necessary for a litigant to commence two lawsuits simultaneously in respect of the same dispute. One would be commenced in the Court of Chancery for an equitable remedy whilst the other would be commenced in one of the courts of common law in order to claim damages. The reason for this was that before 1858 the Court of Chancery did not have the authority to award damages. In some instances a litigant's preferred remedy might be a decree of specific performance for the breach of a contract for the purchase of land. If this was refused in the Court of Chancery, it would then be necessary to consider the advisability of a second lawsuit in a court of common law to recover damages. The novelist Charles Dickens mercilessly exposed to a wider public the excessive delay associated with suits in the Court of Chancery in his novel *Bleak House* which revolves around the fictional case of Jarndyce v Jarndyce. Jeremy Bentham (1752–1832), the philosopher and writer, as a qualified lawyer had been well aware of the urgent need for reform. Through his writings he influenced many prominent lawyers, intellectuals and politicians of his day regarding the necessity for a general overhaul of both the criminal and civil justice systems. Although Bentham's writings were highly influential among the intellectual elite of his day, it was really the great economic and social upheavals of the early nineteenth century together with the needs of expanding commerce that created the momentum for the reforms of existing institutions of government including the law and its administration.

A number of reforms were made possible following the enactment of legislation to reform Parliament in 1832. The most important reform in the civil justice system was the Common Law Procedure Act 1854 which abolished all the old forms of action based on the ancient writs. The Court of Chancery was empowered to decide questions of common law, try issues of fact by jury and award damages where appropriate. The Chancery (Amendment) Act 1858 conferred on the Court of Chancery the discretion to award damages in substitution for, or in addition to, a decree of specific performance to enforce a contract. The courts of common law were permitted to grant injunctions and allow equitable defences to be pleaded. Far-reaching though these reforms were, they did not go far enough to satisfy members of the ruling elite. Thus the entire civil legal system was overhauled between 1873 and 1875 by the Supreme Court of Judicature Acts which abolished the old courts of common law and Court of Chancery. These were replaced by the Supreme Court of Judicature comprising the High Court of Justice and the Court of Appeal. The Supreme Court of Judicature Act 1873 would have abolished the appellate jurisdiction of the House of Lords but before the relevant provision came into effect an incoming Conservative administration enacted the Appellate Jurisdiction Act 1876. This Act conferred on the House of Lords an appellate jurisdiction above that of the Court of Appeal. The administration of the rules of common law and equity were now combined within a single hierarchical court structure (see Figure 3.1 in Chapter 3) and the supremacy of equity was finally put on a statutory basis in the Supreme Court of Judicature Act 1873 s. 25(11) which stated:

> Generally in all matters not herein before particularly mentioned in which there is any conflict or variance between the rules of equity and the rules of common law with reference to the same matter, the rules of equity shall prevail.

This provision has since been re-enacted in the Supreme Court Act 1981 s. 49(1). The Supreme Court of Judicature Act 1875 Schedule 1 contained a new set of rules for the conduct of civil litigation.

12. The modern relationship

Equity continues to operate as a discretionary form of justice and equitable remedies are not available merely on request. The 'maxims of equity' govern the exercise of the court's discretion, the particularly relevant ones being:

(a) He who comes to equity must come with clean hands.

(b) He who seeks equity must do equity.

(c) Delay defeats equity.

The first requires that the claimant must not have behaved harshly or unreasonably towards the other party prior to bringing the action, whereas the second requires that the claimant will accept conscientiously any conditions imposed by the court in relation to the remedy sought as a condition of its being granted. The common law remedy of damages, on the other hand, is available as of right once the claimant has proved his/her case – there is no element of discretion. Both common law and equity now operate as a rationalised, coherent and interrelated system of case law embodied in precedents. This body of case law is still relied upon to resolve a wide variety of disputes that arise nowadays but equity still operates to mitigate the harshness of the common law as is evident from the recent Court of Appeal judgement in *Bank of Credit and Commerce (in liquidation)* v *Ali and others* [2000]. The background to this case was that the House of Lords had previously decided in another case that employees of the bank, which had been managed in a fraudulent manner, should be entitled to 'stigma damages' to compensate them for the difficulty experienced in obtaining alternative employment in the banking and finance sector when the bank collapsed. Approximately one year before the final collapse, in exchange for enhanced redundancy payments a number of employees had signed a form of release in respect of any claims that they might have against the bank. The appellant contended that signing the release did not prevent him and the others who signed from claiming the 'stigma damages'. Although their claim was rejected by the High Court, the Court of Appeal exercising its equitable jurisdiction allowed the appeal on the basis that the release that was signed at the time could not be used as a defence to a claim based on facts known to the bank but not known and concealed from the employees who had signed the release.

13. Equitable remedies in modern litigation

The equitable remedies of injunction, specific performance, rectification and rescission in particular are of importance in modern litigation. A prohibitory injunction is a court order forbidding a person to whom it is addressed from doing some act such as breaking a contract, although it is more usually granted in civil law to prevent someone committing a form of wrong known as a tort. A mandatory injunction, on the other hand, requires the person to whom it is addressed to do a certain act such as to remove an impediment to a right of way over land or an obstruction to a right to light associated with the ownership of premises. An injunction is not only granted as a remedy at the end of legal proceedings. It can also be granted on an *interim* basis if there is a strong likelihood of loss being incurred before the case can be heard in court. Injunctions may also take the form of 'freezing orders' to prevent the removal of assets from the jurisdiction of the court and 'search orders' enabling a claimant to enter premises and search for property.

Specific performance takes the form of a court order requiring a person to complete a contract that he/she has made. Decrees of specific performance are usually reserved for contracts for the sale of land but they may be granted where a contract has been made for the sale of some unique object if damages would not be an adequate remedy for the victim of the breach of contract.

Rectification may be sought where a document was executed under seal but it fails to embody accurately the terms of the agreement reached between the parties owing to some form of clerical error. The error can be corrected by order of the court so that the document accurately records the terms of the agreement arrived at by the parties. It is also possible for a court to order rectification to correct a mistake in a will. In *Wordingham* v *Royal Exchange Trust Co. Ltd* [1992] the court granted a husband rectification of his deceased wife's will under the Administration of Justice Act 1982 s. 20(1)(a) because the solicitor who drew up the will had omitted an essential clause.

Rescission is the cancellation of a contract by a court where the plaintiff has been induced to enter into it because of fraud or misrepresentation. Nevertheless, the remedy may be denied if the person requesting it delays in seeking it or if a third party acquires an interest in the subject matter in good faith having paid money to do so. It may also be denied if it is not possible to restore both parties to their former position.

Progress test

1. What do you consider to be the *ratio decidendi* of *Taylor* v *Caldwell*?

2. In what later cases was the *ratio* in *Taylor* v *Caldwell* applied?

3. What is the basis of the distinction between *ratio decidendi* and *obiter dicta*?

4. Are precedents created by High Court judges binding or persuasive?

5. To what extent is the Court of Appeal bound by its previous decisions?

6. Does the House of Lords follow its previous decisions and is it bound to do so?

7. What do you understand by the phrase 'factual distinguishing'?

8. What do you understand by the phrase 'restrictive distinguishing'?

9. How does the Human Rights Act 1998 affect the operation of law-making by precedent?

10. Why are the *Law Reports* produced by the Incorporated Council for Law Reporting in England and Wales so important to a system of law-making by precedent?

11. What do you understand by the term 'equity' and why did equity emerge as a separate body of case law?

12. Identify four equitable remedies and consider whether these remedies are available as of right to a litigant?

Further reading

General texts

Ingman, T. (2000) *The English Legal Process* (London: Blackstone Press, chapters 9 and 10).

Slapper, G. and D. Kelly (1999) *The English Legal System* (London: Cavendish Publishing, pp. 44–56).

Twining, W. and D. Miers (1999) *How To Do Things With Rules* (London: Butterworths, chapter 8).

Ward, R. (1998) *Walker and Walker's English Legal System* (London: Butterworths, chapter 3).

Zander, M. (1999) *The Law Making Process* (London: Butterworths, chapters 4–7).

Historical texts

Baker, J.H. (1990) *An Introduction to English Legal History* (London: Butterworths, chapters 1–6).

Manchester, A.H. (1980) *Modern Legal History* (London: Butterworths).

Richardson, H.G. and G.O. Sayles (1966) *Law and Legislation from Aethelbert to Magna Carta* (Edinburgh: Edinburgh University Press).

Useful website

www.bailii.org for the British and Irish Legal Information Institute (BAILII) which contains information on UK and Irish legislation and case law.

5

The law-making process 2: Primary legislation

1. Introduction

The Westminster Parliament is the legislature of the United Kingdom and it also functions as a forum for political debate. In the past three hundred years especially, Parliament has been called upon to enact numerous detailed schemes of law to facilitate the political, economic and social evolution of the UK. As a result, enacted law (or statute law or legislation as it is otherwise known) has long since become the predominant form of law-making. By comparison, the ongoing contribution of the judiciary to the law-making process through development of precedent occurs on a relatively modest scale. Law-making by precedent is also an unplanned process because it depends on the randomness of the litigation process. Thus, this chapter focuses on the legislative process, but before doing so it will be necessary to consider some aspects of UK constitutional law. Having dealt with the legislative process, it will then be appropriate to examine the doctrine of parliamentary sovereignty before critiquing the quality of statute law.

2. Constitutional arrangements past and present

The United Kingdom is a relatively modern creation in the history of the British Isles. It came into being in 1707 as a result of a treaty between England and Scotland after which the Scottish parliament in Edinburgh was dissolved. Wales had operated within the same political and legal framework as England since 1536 and was automatically subsumed into the union with Scotland. As a result of another Act of Union in 1800, the whole of Ireland became part of the United Kingdom in 1801 but when the Irish Free State (later to be known as the Republic of Ireland) was created in 1922, only the six northern counties remained within the United Kingdom with England, Wales and Scotland. The Labour government that was elected in 1997 was committed to a programme of constitutional reform through devolution of political power to the regions. As a result, Scotland has been granted a system of devolved government by the Westminster Parliament with a new Scottish Parliament sitting in Edinburgh. The Edinburgh Parliament has the power to enact primary legislation for the whole of Scotland within the limits specified in the Government of Scotland Act 1998. In this respect the Welsh Assembly is different because it does not have the power to enact primary legislation. Northern Ireland was granted a new system of devolved government in the Northern Ireland Act 1998 similar to that for Scotland. Nevertheless, the Westminster parliament retains the power to legislate for the entire UK on a wide range of matters including taxation, defence and foreign relations as well as to incorporate EU directives. Every year the UK Parliament produces in the region of 60–70 statutes known as Acts of Parliament on a very wide range of topics.

3. Composition of the Westminster Parliament

In the constitutional law of the UK the Westminster Parliament comprises the House of Commons, the House of Lords and the Queen in Parliament. The House of Commons is the only elected element, comprising 659 members who represent the various parliamentary constituencies as defined by the Parliamentary Constituencies Act 1986. The House of Lords (which is to be distinguished from the appeal court of the same name) is unelected and at present comprises 92 hereditary peers, 26 bishops of the Church of England and a large number of life peers, many of whom are former politicians. The number of hereditary peers with voting rights was reduced by the House of Lords Act 1999 as part of the Labour government's package of constitutional reforms. Life peers may be created under the Life Peerages Act 1958 and they now outnumber hereditary peers. The Stevenson Commission has been established to oversee the appointment of future life peers. Having taken up references and interviewed applicants, it will recommend the appointment of between eight and ten 'outstanding' persons each year as life peers. Just to complicate matters, the Law Lords who comprise the appellate court known as the House of Lords are life peers. They also have the right to sit and participate in proceedings of the House although they do not usually participate in party political debates. The role of the monarch is largely ceremonial. It is mainly confined to summoning a newly elected Parliament, opening each annual session (during which the Queen's speech is delivered from the throne in the House of Lord's chamber) and dissolving Parliament prior to a general election being called. Although the Labour government plans to modernise the procedure of the House of Commons, it has been reported in the *Financial Times* (30 March 1998) that the prime minister has insisted that the Queen's speech and all aspects of the ceremony surrounding it must be kept. The monarch must, in principle, assent to all new legislation and the reality surrounding the Royal Assent will be considered subsequently.

4. Proposals for new legislation

Some of the government's proposals for new legislation will have derived from specific manifesto pledges on which the government was elected to office. It was a manifesto commitment of the Labour Party in 1997 to devolve power from Westminster and make available the rights enshrined in the European Convention on Human Rights and Fundamental Rights in national law. These commitments were subsequently fulfilled through the enactment of the Human Rights Act 1998 and the devolution legislation mentioned above. Most of the proposals for new legislation, however, derive from within the various Whitehall departments as the civil service endeavours to implement the overall policy objectives of the government.

The government of the day is lobbied from time to time by a variety of pressure groups (for example, the CBI, TUC, Consumers' Association, National Union of Farmers, Child Poverty Action Group). If the government decides to take action in response to pressure group activity, then new legislation may be called for. In addition there are usually proposals for law reform from the Law Commission requiring implementation, and sometimes from a Royal Commission that the government may have established to investigate some particular problem. Ordinary members of the Commons and members of the House of Lords are also lobbied to introduce Private Members' Bills by various interest groups who wish to see changes in the law. In the case of members of the House of Commons this is likely to happen if they secure one of the slots by ballot that enables them to propose new legislation on one of the thirteen occasions in each session allowed for considering such proposals. Unless the government takes an interest in a private member's proposal and allows sufficient parliamentary time, it is unlikely that the proposal will be enacted. For example, Richard Shepherd, a Conservative MP, introduced a Private Member's Bill to protect people who 'blew the whistle' on fraud, crime in general and malpractice in the workplace. The Bill received the support of Ian McCartney, a government minister, and it was subsequently enacted as the Public Interest Disclosure Act 1998. Often government legislation will be preceded by a White Paper that sets out the government's standpoint of a range of issues within the particular area of policy. Sometimes a White Paper is preceded by a Green Paper which sets out proposals for consideration and comment by the public at large.

5. Time pressures

There is no shortage of proposals for new legislation, merely a shortage of parliamentary time for them all to be considered. The maximum duration of 'a Parliament' is five years, but within this timescale there will be annual sessions that usually commence in November in one year and run to the following October interspersed with recesses for vacations. Therefore in an annual session, Parliament sits for only about 30 weeks and the government of the day tends to monopolise its timetable because it wishes to ensure that all its proposed legislation for the session can be debated and enacted.

6. Establishing priorities

Except when there has been a change of government, approximately six weeks into the new session of Parliament (mid-December) the Cabinet Office will ask the various government departments to submit lists of proposed Bills required for the *next* session of Parliament. The departments will be asked to rank these proposals in order of importance and provide an indication when the instructions to the parliamentary draftspersons will be ready. These lists are then submitted to a special Cabinet committee known as the Future Legislation Committee whose members include the leaders of both Houses and the government's chief whip. In the following January, the Cabinet committee will draw up a provisional list of proposed Bills for discussion with the ministers of the departments that put forward the proposals. After discussions with the ministers concerned and the First Parliamentary Counsel from the Office of Parliamentary Counsel to the Treasury, a shortlist will be compiled for the next session of Parliament to be submitted to the full Cabinet. All this may take five months. The order of priority is likely to be altered as a result of discussion in Cabinet, and the list that is finally agreed becomes the government's programme for the next session of Parliament. Since this planning process is forward-looking, the legislation that is mentioned in the Queen's speech at the state opening of Parliament will normally comprise the list that was agreed by the Cabinet during the previous session of Parliament. Control of the government's current legislative programme which is outlined in the Queen's speech passes to the Legislation Committee which also regulates the flow of instructions to the parliamentary draftspersons. However, there has to be a degree of flexibility in the government's current programme to allow for the possibility of emergency legislation which can be slotted in if necessary.

7. Role of Parliamentary Counsel to the Treasury

The Bills that are destined to become Public General Acts of Parliament will be drafted by an elite corps of solicitors and barristers working in the Office of Parliamentary Counsel to the Treasury. They are supervised by the First Parliamentary Counsel. It is a small government department that was established in 1869 and which now comprises a professional staff of about 40 persons based in Whitehall. Once a proposed Bill has been included in the government's current legislative programme, the First Parliamentary Counsel will sometimes receive detailed written instructions from the relevant Whitehall department, but often the policy brief will be partly oral and partly in writing. The First Parliamentary Counsel will usually assign two members of his/her staff to the task of producing an initial draft Bill. The persons so tasked will liaise with the senior civil servants and junior ministers in the relevant department as they prepare this first draft for their consideration. Following the production of the initial draft, there will often be a series of conferences that will give rise to successive redraftings for major pieces of legislation. In all, the process could take several months. Parliamentary Counsel do not function as passive scribes but are able to offer advice on the precise wording of the various provisions to be included in a Bill and on their likely effectiveness. They also have the responsibility for deciding when the Bill is in a final form such that it can be presented to Parliament. The Bill will usually be presented to Parliament by the Cabinet minister whose department has sponsored it. Just prior to this a copy will have been delivered by one of the parliamentary draftspersons to the Public Bill Office of the House where the Bill is to be introduced. Thereafter, the draftspersons will be on hand to assist with the framing of any amendments as the Bill proceeds through its various parliamentary stages.

Although some Bills can be quite short, comprising just a few pages, a Bill on a very important topic might run to 200 or even 300 pages. It will be set out in a schematic fashion, divided into parts so that each part can be identified by a Roman numeral. The rules of law contained therein will be set out in a very precise verbal form and will be identified by numbered clauses and sub-clauses that will subsequently be referred to as 'sections' and 'subsections' once the Bill becomes an Act of Parliament.

8. The process of enactment

If a Bill is to be enacted it must normally have three readings in both Houses before being presented for the Royal Assent. If a Bill is not politically controversial and does not involve the expenditure of public money it can be introduced into the House of Lords before being passed to the House of Commons. The majority of government Bills that are destined to become Public General Acts are introduced in the House of Commons, and all Bills involving the raising of tax and expenditure of public funds must, by constitutional convention, be introduced into the House of Commons first before being passed to the House of Lords. The so-called First Reading is something of a misnomer because it does not entail the recitation of the entire Bill in the Chamber. If a Bill originates in the House of Commons, Standing Order 57(2) requires that it must be 'read for the first time' without discussion, that a date for the Second Reading is fixed and that it shall be ordered to be printed. All these are taken together as a single formal stage in the overall process. The Clerk of the House of Commons reads out the short title of the Bill and the Speaker then calls on the minister or member presenting the Bill to name a day for the Second Reading. The Speaker reiterates this date whereupon the short title is entered into the Journal of the House. The Bill is then ordered to be read a second time on the specified date and it is also ordered to be printed at public expense.

Once the draft of the Bill has been examined it is sent for printing in accordance with the order made by the House so that its contents are available to every MP (and every interested member of the public) prior to second reading. The date for the Second Reading will normally be set two weeks after the date of the First Reading in the case of government Bills. The Human Rights Act 1998 s. 19 provides that before the Second Reading, the minister sponsoring the Bill must make a statement in writing to the effect that in his/her view the provisions of the Bill are compatible with the Convention rights set out in Schedule 1 of the Act. Alternatively, he/she must make a statement to the effect that, although he/she is unable to make such a statement, the government nevertheless wishes the House to proceed with the Bill.

The Second Reading is the crucial stage through which all government and private members' Bills have to pass. The short title appears on the Notice Paper with the other orders of the day and the minister or member in charge of the Bill puts forward a motion 'That the Bill now be read a second time'. It is only at the Second Reading that there will be an opportunity to debate the general principles and merits (or otherwise) of the Bill. However, the debate does not extend to the details of the various clauses comprising the Bill. A Cabinet minister will usually open the debate if the Bill is a government Bill, outlining its principles and summarising the most important clauses. The relevant opposition spokesperson must then respond, and during the debate the views of backbench MPs of all parties will also be heard. At the end of the time allotted, a junior minister will wind up the debate by responding to the points raised. It is not uncommon for the government to limit the amount of time available in the House of Commons for debate and for the other stages of the Bill due to the shortage of parliamentary time. This process is referred to as guillotining the Bill. Opponents of the Bill will often vote against the question put by the Speaker for a Second Reading, but it is also possible for them to put forward a reasoned amendment to the question. There is usually a vote at the end of the Second Reading debate.

After the debate on a question is over, the question must be put to the House. To do this the Speaker rises from his/her chair and puts to the House: 'The question is, That . . .'. He/She then says, 'As many as are of that opinion say, aye, and as many as are of the contrary opinion say, no.' The Speaker does his/her best to judge the respective volumes of each response and expresses his/her opinion by saying: 'I think the ayes (or noes) have it.' If the House accords with this decision, the question is said to be 'agreed to' or 'negatived' as the case may be. Nevertheless, his/her judgement is not final in the matter because those deemed to be in the minority can dispute the Speaker's decision by crying 'no' or 'aye'. If this should happen, the Speaker will then say 'Clear the lobby', so that a physical count of the members for and against can be determined. If there is a vote against the Bill at the end of the Second Reading stage it is 'lost', but this seldom happens to government Bills where the government of the day has a substantial majority of MPs. If a Bill should be lost at the end of the Second Reading it will not be possible to introduce a fresh Bill with the same provisions in that session of Parliament.

As an alternative to a Second Reading on the floor of the House, Standing Order 90 provides that a public Bill can be referred to a Second Reading Committee. The Committee is convened in an upstairs committee room provided a motion to do this is put by a government minister at the commencement of public business on the day in question. It is necessary for him/her to give 10 days' notice of any such motion and it must be put to the House immediately. If at least 20 MPs signify their objection by standing up, the Speaker must declare that the motion is defeated. Under Standing Order 59 all Law Commission Bills are referred to a Second Reading Committee (*see* Chapter 16).

If a public Bill survives its second reading in the House of Commons it must, unless it is exempted by the House, be considered in Committee. Unless the Bill is to be considered by a Committee of the Whole House in the chamber, a standing committee of between 16 and 50 MPs is empanelled to consider the Bill clause by clause, each of which must be approved. Although the committee is referred to as a standing committee, the MPs sit at tables facing each other in one of the upstairs committee rooms in the Palace of Westminster (Parliament Building). Some members of the House of Commons staff will be in attendance together with some staff of Hansard who will record the official version of the proceedings. It is quite normal for parliamentary counsel to be in attendance too with senior civil servants who will be on hand to give advice to ministers. The membership of the Committee itself is weighted to reflect the relative strength of the political parties in the House of Commons so that the government will always have an inbuilt majority, but the Speaker appoints the chairperson and that person is supposed to be impartial. Amendments to the Bill can be included at the committee stage but opposition amendments are unlikely to be included unless they are acceptable to the government. Whilst government MPs are able to call upon the services of parliamentary counsel to draft their amendments, opposition MPs are obliged to seek the assistance of the staff in the Public Bill Office to draft their amendments. At the conclusion of the committee stage, the Bill is 'reported' back to the House. It may be reprinted to take account of all the amendments that have been made at the Committee Stage. If an amendment is carried at the Committee Stage to be incorporated in a government Bill but the amendment is not acceptable to the government, the Bill can be withdrawn and the government can later present a fresh Bill which has the same effect as the original. This second Bill can then be put forward for the Royal Assent provided that it completes all its stages in both Houses.

It is possible for further amendments to be incorporated into the Bill at the Report Stage and some debate may be allowed on the amendments that were made during the Committee Stage. Although the Report Stage must be conducted on the floor of the House, it is usually of short duration. If the Bill was amended during the Report Stage it may be reprinted to take account of these amendments.

The Third Reading follows immediately after the Report Stage. There will be a short review of the content of the Bill and any further debate must normally be confined to its final content but no further amendments are permitted. If a vote did not take place at the end of the Second Reading, a vote may follow at the end of the Third Reading before the official copy of the Bill is endorsed by the Clerk of the House and passed to the House of Lords.

In the House of Lords the Bill will be introduced by a peer who is also a government minister. The procedure in the House of Lords is similar in many respects except that there is no standing committee – the Bill is considered by the entire House. Thus all members of the House of Lords can, in principle, put down amendments to the Bill during its Committee Stage. At the Third Reading there is no debate but only a formal motion that is put to the House to the effect that the Bill should be passed. It often happens that the Bill is amended in the House of Lords and if so, it must go back to the House of Commons for further consideration. If the amendments are acceptable to the government, all will be well. If this should not be the case, a compromise of some kind may be reached but if this proves impossible, the government can invoke the Parliament Acts 1911 and 1949 to ensure that its will prevails. If a Bill is enacted under the Parliaments Acts the enacting formula is varied. It will state:

> Be it enacted by the Queen's most Excellent Majesty, by and with the advice and consent of the Commons in this present Parliament assembled in accordance with the provisions of the Parliament Act 1911 and by the authority of the same as follows.

By virtue of this legislation a Bill can only be delayed by the House of Lords for one year and, in the case of a Bill dealing with taxation or finance, it can only be delayed for a month no matter how much the House of Lords should object to its content. However, the Parliament Acts cannot be invoked in respect of Bills that have been introduced in the House of Lords.

9. Royal Assent

It is necessary for a Bill to receive the Royal Assent in order for it to become an Act of Parliament, but this is almost a formality because by constitutional convention the assent cannot be withheld. The last time that a reigning monarch pronounced the Royal Assent in person was in 1854, and since 1541 it has been possible for the Royal Assent to be given by Commissioners on behalf of the monarch. Bills are not assented to individually and nowadays as a result of the Royal Assent Act 1967 there is a simplified procedure for giving the Assent. The Lord Chancellor, as speaker of the House of Lords, periodically submits a list of Bills requiring the Royal Assent to the monarch. The list is actually compiled by the Clerk to the Parliaments but an advance copy is sent to the Clerk of the Crown, an official of the Lord Chancellor's office, to ensure that he/she includes the relevant Bills in the letters patent that will be executed by the monarch. When the letters patent have been executed by the monarch, the Clerk of the Crown will read the short titles of those Bills requiring the Assent. He does so in the presence of the Lord Chancellor, in his capacity as Speaker of the House of Lords, the Speaker of the House of Commons and the Clerk of the Parliaments (sic) in the House of Lords. The Royal Assent is then pronounced in Norman French on behalf of the monarch by the Clerk of the Parliaments who is empowered to do so under the letters patent. Norman French was the language of government after the conquest in 1066. The assent is then notified to each House separately by its Speaker. Each Speaker merely states: 'I have to notify the House, in accordance with the Royal Assent Act 1967 that the Queen has signified her Royal Assent to the following Acts.' The short titles are then read out.

Although a copy of the Act is prepared for printing and general distribution, about six months after the Royal Assent has been given, two official copies of the Act are prepared on vellum, one of which is filed with the House of Lord's records and the other is held at the Public Records Office. The Royal Assent does sometimes operate to bring the Act into operation immediately but it is quite common for the commencement of all or part of an Act to be suspended to be brought into effect at some future date.

Once a statute has been enacted it does not cease to be operative simply because of the passage of time unless this has been expressly stated. Thus a statute usually has to be expressly repealed by a subsequent statute.

10. Other forms of Public General Act

Legislation may be used occasionally in order to codify a body of case law on a particular topic. The aim is to simplify the law by converting all the established precedents into a single statute or code for the benefit of practitioners and others. Thereafter, it will be the sections of the Act and not the previous case law that will be referred to as the source of various legal rules. This has been done in relation to the law on partnership by the Partnership Act 1890 and to the law on contracts of sale by the Sale of Goods Act 1893 which has been subsequently consolidated with other related statutes into the Sale of Goods Act 1979.

The enactment of a number of statutes on a given topic such as employment law (where later statutes amend the provisions of earlier ones) can make it difficult to ascertain the law on a particular point quickly. Therefore the process of 'consolidation' of statutes is a great help to practitioners and others. The consolidation process entails bringing together in a single statute all the existing statute law contained in several statutes. A good example of this is the Employment Rights Act 1996 which consolidated all the previous legislation relating to individual employment rights. There is a special expedited process for the enactment of consolidated statutes. The Bill must start in the House of Lords but it is then passed to the Joint Consolidation Committee with the comments of the draftsperson explaining those parts that are not a strict consolidation of the existing law. The Consolidation of Enactments (Procedure) Act 1949 makes it possible for corrections and minor improvements to be made in a consolidation statute. The Bill is considered on a clause by clause basis by the Committee with the draftsperson in attendance who is obliged to answer any questions posed by the Committee. When it has done its work it will report to the Lords and Commons and, provided the report is favourable, the Bill can be passed in both Houses without delay. If there is any debate at all it must be confined to alterations that have been made to the earlier legislation. Most of the

71

work on consolidation is undertaken by Parliamentary Counsel seconded to the Law Commission whose work will be considered in Chapter 16.

11. Private Acts of Parliament

Attention has so far focused on Public General Acts of Parliament which are so called because they impinge upon the public and business at large. From time to time, however, Parliament does enact Private Acts that deal with the particular concerns and interests of certain organisations and institutions including local authorities. There is a special procedure for enacting private Bills which varies depending on whether the measure is opposed or unopposed by outside interests. In the past, certain businesses have been incorporated by means of a Private Act of Parliament.

12. Citation

The old method of citing legislation was quite cumbersome. A statute was referred to by reference to the regnal year of the monarch in relation to the session of Parliament in which it was enacted followed by a chapter number. As a result of the enactment of the Acts of Parliament Numbering and Citation Act 1962, all subsequent Acts are referred to by means of the short title and the calendar year of enactment.

13. Supremacy of statute law over case law

The supremacy of statute law over judge made law was finally established in the Revolution Settlement in 1688 when James II (1685–88) was deposed. The Bill of Rights 1689 proclaimed that thenceforward Parliament was superior to the monarch and the courts. Statute law is therefore a higher form of law than case law and statutes have sometimes been enacted to neutralise the effect of judicial decisions that have been politically controversial. Good examples of this are provided in the area of trade union law where judgements such as *Taff Vale Railway Co. Ltd v ASRS* [1901] were neutralised by subsequent legislation. Since 1689 the courts have accepted that they cannot normally question the validity of an Act of Parliament. Difficulties do occasionally arise because there may be an inconsistency between the wording of a provision in an earlier Act and the wording of a later Act that has not expressly repealed the earlier legislation. The courts resolve this by invoking the doctrine of 'implied repeal' by which they assert that the later Act has impliedly repealed the earlier Act to the extent of the inconsistency.

The complete legislative supremacy of the Westminster Parliament is difficult to reconcile with the fact of UK membership of the EU. It was much easier to declare the traditional doctrine of parliamentary sovereignty which asserts that there are no limits to the legislative power of Parliament in an era when the Westminster Parliament was at the hub of a vast colonial empire upon which 'the sun never set'. Once the UK government signed the Treaty of Accession to the Treaty of Rome in 1972 it committed the UK to participate indefinitely in the ongoing process of ever closer European economic and political integration with the other member states. Membership of the EU requires that EU law in the form of Treaty provisions and regulations must override any inconsistent national law of every member state otherwise the process of achieving closer economic and political integration would come to a standstill. Whilst it is true that EU law could only become part of the law of the UK as a result of the enactment of the European Communities Act 1972 and that this statute could be repealed in future, such a repeal is unlikely because of the adverse economic consequences. Thus for as long as the European Communities Act 1972 is part of the statute law of the UK the courts must accord precedence to EU law over national law.

14. Supremacy of EU law over national law

This supremacy of EU law over inconsistent national law was forcefully demonstrated in *Factortame Ltd and others* v *Secretary of State for Transport No. 2* [1991]. In order to understand the background to this important case one needs to be aware that the EC Treaty guarantees the nationals of all member states certain rights. What is now Article 43 EC guarantees the right to set up a business in any other member state, and what is now Article 49 guarantees the right to provide services across borders. Moreover, what is now Article 294 requires that member states must accord nationals of other member states the same rights as their own nationals with regard to the ownership of shares in companies. The claimants were companies formed and registered in England whose directors and shareholders were, for the most part, Spanish nationals. In 1970 the EEC (as it then was) established a common fisheries policy to conserve fish stocks and ensure equality of access for the vessels of member states to fishing grounds and exclude the fishing fleets of non member states except on agreed terms. A special agreement was made by the Community with Spain in 1980 that gave Spanish vessels the right to fish for particular species in designated waters of the member states. Spain did not join the EEC until 1986 but when the UK joined in 1973 it had to comply with the rules of the common fisheries policy. European Regulation 170/83 operative across the European Community set up a system of national quotas in 1983 for total allowable catches. Prior to that, Spain, by Royal decree, had conferred advantages by way of landing rights on those Spanish fishing companies that were registered with another state to enable them to fish in the fishing grounds of that state. The UK government took the view that the Spanish vessels that were registered on the British register in order to have access to the fishing grounds of the UK were exploiting the 1980 agreement between the EEC and Spain. In other words, they were Spanish vessels availing themselves of the British quota and there was considerable domestic political pressure to exclude foreign vessels from fishing under the British quota. Under the Merchant Shipping Act 1988, the Secretary of State was empowered to create a new register of British fishing vessels that would govern the ability of such vessels to fish under the British fishing quota.

The Merchant Shipping Act 1988 s. 14(2) provided that a vessel would qualify for registration if the company owning it was at least 75 per cent owned by British citizens. The claimants did not qualify because most of their directors and shareholders were Spanish nationals living in Spain and they sought to challenge Part II of the Act and Regulations made under it on the basis that they contravened Treaty provisions and thereby deprived them of their legal rights under EU law in relation to freedom of establishment and non-discrimination. Although the action was commenced in the High Court, the case was of such constitutional importance that it eventually reached the House of Lords and the Law Lords were asked to issue an interim injunction suspending the operation of the relevant part of the legislation. The House of Lords considered itself bound by the principle of common law that an injunction could not be issued against the Crown (effectively the government) and declined to do so but referred the matter to the European Court of Justice for a preliminary ruling (see *Factortame Ltd and others* v *Secretary of State for Transport* [1989]). The European Court of Justice ruled in Case C-213/89 *R* v *Secretary of State for Transport ex p. Factortame Ltd and others* [1990] that a national court was obliged to set aside a rule of national law that prevents it from granting interim relief where rights are claimed under EU law. Thereafter, the House of Lords issued an interim injunction against the Crown which prevented the minister from enforcing the relevant provision of the Merchant Shipping Act 1988 and the Regulations. In doing so the House of Lords created an important precedent and made constitutional history.

Thus parliamentarians are now only too well aware, if they were not at the time, that Parliament as an institution must not legislate in a way that is at variance with EU law whilst the UK continues to be a member state of the EU. Failure to observe this fundamental principle is likely to prove expensive. In 1997, a Divisional Court of the Queen's Bench ruled that following the decision of the European Court of Justice in joined Cases C-46/93 and C-48/93 *Brasserie du Pecheur SA* v *Germany* and *R* v *Secretary of State for Transport ex p. Factortame Ltd and others*, the UK was obliged to pay substantial compensation (but not exemplary damages) to the trawler companies owned by the Spanish nationals for a serious breach of EU law by the UK Parliament in approving the legislation. This was subsequently affirmed on appeal by both the Court of Appeal and House of Lords (*see R* v *Secretary of State for Transport ex p. Factortame Ltd and others* [1999]).

Conflicts between EU law and national law do not arise that frequently. Thus, in general, the courts will not be sympathetic to any attempt by an individual or an organisation to challenge the validity of a UK Act of Parliament. In *British Railways Board* v *Pickin* [1974] an attempt to impugn the validity of a Private Act of Parliament by an individual was dismissed as an abuse of the legal process.

15. The effect of the Human Rights Act 1998 on UK law

The government has not permitted the courts to suspend the operation of an Act of Parliament if any of its provisions are found to contravene the Convention rights as embodied in the Human Rights Act 1998 Schedule 1. The Human Rights Act 1998 s. 4(2) merely enables a court to make a declaration of 'incompatibility' and it will be the responsibility of Parliament thereafter to decide whether to repeal the relevant provision(s) or not. If Parliament should fail to do so, s. 3(2)(b) provides that the validity, continuing operation or enforcement of the legislation is not affected just because it is incompatible with the Convention.

16. The clarity of legislation

During the 1960s there was growing concern over the clarity of some of the legislation that was being drafted and enacted by Parliament. It was argued that it was a fundamental civil liberty that citizens who live under the rule of law should be entitled to know what the law is but that very often statute law was unintelligible to the ordinary citizen. This is particularly poignant in the sphere of criminal law where ignorance of the law is no defence. It is just as important that people should be able to arrange their affairs and plan on the basis of being certain as to what the civil law is as it pertains to their lives and business dealings. In the context of the civil law, the nature of the problem may be illustrated by considering the Misrepresentation Act 1967 s. 2(1) which states:

Where a person has entered into a contract after a misrepresentation has been made to him by another party thereto and as a result thereof he has suffered loss, then, if the person making the misrepresentation would be liable to damages in respect thereof had the misrepresentation been made fraudulently, the person shall be so liable notwithstanding that the misrepresentation was not made fraudulently, unless he proves that he had reasonable grounds to believe and did believe up to the time that the contract was made that the facts represented were true.

This is hardly an example of clarity such that the ordinary reader would immediately understand the ideas being expressed. Indeed, in order to understand this provision it would be necessary to undertake a study of the law of contract and in particular the evolution of the law relating to misrepresentation which is not the easiest of concepts to grasp. In 1968, the Statute Law Society was established by a concerned group of lawyers who wished to see improvements in the quality of the legislation that was emanating from Parliament from the standpoint of users. Then in 1973, the government set up the Renton Committee on the Preparation of Legislation. The Committee took evidence and published its report in 1975 comprising some 40 conclusions and 81 recommendations which raised awareness of the shortcomings of the drafting process. It was well received by parliamentarians and by the serious press. Although many of its recommendations have long since been accepted either wholly or in part, a number of issues remain to be tackled. In 1992 another report appeared, namely the Report of the Commission on the Legislative Process sponsored by the Hansard Society. The Commission recommended that Bills should be examined before the Second Reading by a select committee that would receive recommendations on the precise wording from experts, representatives of those affected and from interested members of the public.

Nevertheless, it has to be said that it is not always possible to draft legislation in simple, straightforward language such that it would be immediately intelligible to the average citizen, and there are a number of reasons for this. Firstly, government frequently makes impossible demands on the draftspersons in terms of the time allotted for the drafting process. It is sometimes a choice between a 'quick fix' and a more considered piece of work, with the former sometimes given priority. Secondly, a statute, unlike a White Paper, is a legal text that must be 'justiciable' in the courts. It is the need for precision that is often the main cause of complexity in drafting as the draftsperson seeks to anticipate possible misunderstandings and tries to deal with a variety of situations that may arise. Thirdly, the subject matter may not lend itself to a concise treatment in simple language. This is particularly true of revenue law, although the Inland Revenue is currently engaged in a project to simplify tax law.

Readers interested in the ongoing debate concerning the clarity of drafting and the intelligibility of statute law may wish to refer to the *Statute Law Review* for January 1993. Mr Martin Cutts, who has long campaigned for the use of plain English in commerce and the law, produced a redraft of the Timeshare Act 1992 in plain English which he entitled the Clearer Timeshare Act 1993. His redraft was submitted to the Office of Parliamentary Counsel to the Treasury, and the draftsperson, Euan Sutherland, responded to Mr Cutt's redraft. Euan Sutherland's article appears in the *Statute Law Review* (Vol. 14 (1993) p.163) and it makes interesting reading.

In recent years some statutes have been singled out and praised for their clarity and precision. The Arbitration Act 1996 in particular has been praised as an example of outstanding drafting. Members of the legal profession and judiciary, together with others possessing special expertise, were consulted on the text of the Bill before it was presented to Parliament. In winding up the Second Reading debate in the House of Lords, Lord Fraser of Carmyllie stated:

> My Lords, I reflect somewhat ruefully that when I once had responsibility for the activities of same of the draftsmen, I can never recollect an occasion when drafting of a Bill was approved in such a magnificent form and which secured the approval of so many distinguished judges. Nevertheless, as the departmental Minister responsible for the Bill in your Lordships' House, I am delighted there has been such a universal degree of approval for the fashion in which the Bill has been drafted. I am particularly grateful to the noble and learned Lord, Lord Ackner. A number of people were rightly complimented on their contributions, but it was good of the noble and learned Lord to mention the way in which parliamentary counsel finally drew the Bill together in such an acceptable form. I have no doubt that those who have contributed to the drafting will be particularly flattered that my noble friend Lord Hacking should go so far as to compare it with the great statutes, with which we are all familiar, of the 19th century.

Even though great care was taken with its drafting, an error was subsequently discovered in the Act in the case of *Inco Europe Ltd and others* v *First Choice Distribution and others* [2000] (*see* Chapter 8 on the interpretation of legislation).

Progress test

1. What are the constituent elements of the Westminster Parliament?

2. How easy is it for a backbench MP to propose a new piece of legislation? What is the likelihood that he/she will see it enacted?

3. Who is actually responsible for drafting government Bills and who provides the brief?

4. Who introduces a government Bill to Parliament and must this always be done in the House of Commons?

5. How likely is it that amendments put forward by the opposition in the House of Commons will be incorporated into the Bill?

6. If the House of Lords refuses to pass a Bill that has completed all its stages in the House of Commons can the government still present the Bill for the Royal Assent?

7. Does the Queen assent to legislation in person? Can the Royal Assent be withheld?

8. What do you understand by the phrase a 'consolidated statute'?

9. Can the Human Rights Act 1998 be invoked to successfully challenge the validity of an Act of Parliament in the courts?

10. Can EU law be invoked to successfully challenge the validity of an Act of Parliament in the courts?

Further reading

Books

De Smith, S. and R. Brazier (1998) *Constitutional and Administrative Law* (Harmondsworth: Penguin, chapter 15).

Ingman, T. (2000) *The English Legal Process* (London: Blackstone Press, chapter 5).

Limon, Sir D. and W.R. Mckay (eds) (1997) *Erskine May's Treatise on the Law, Privileges, Proceedings and Usage of Parliament* (London: Butterworths).

Slapper, G. and D. Kelly (1999) *The English Legal System* (London: Cavendish Publishing, chapter 2).

Twining, W. and D. Miers (1999) *How To Do Things With Rules* (London: Butterworths, chapter 9).

Zander, M. (1999) *The Law Making Process* (London: Butterworths, chapters 1 and 2).

Useful websites

The website of the Westminster Parliament is www.parliament.uk/ and texts of recent Acts of Parliament may be accessed on www.hmso.gov.uk/

An easy to access website for alphabetical and chronological lists of Acts is www.infolaw.co.uk

Bills introduced into Parliament can be found at www.parliament.the-stationery-office.co.uk/pa/pabills.htm

6

The law-making process 3: Subordinate legislation

1. Introduction

In addition to the 60–70 statutes enacted by the Westminster parliament each year, some 3,000 pieces of subordinate legislation are created in the form of rules, regulations, orders and directions. Most of this subordinate legislation is made under the authority of a Public General Act of Parliament. Indeed, it was Henry Thring, the first person appointed as Parliamentary Counsel in 1869, who recommended that the fine detail of legislative proposals should not be included in the Bill to be presented to Parliament. Instead, he advocated that the detail should be devised at a later date and be brought into effect through the medium of subordinate legislation. Accordingly, parliamentarians would be able to concentrate on matters of broad principle and would not become enmeshed in matters of abstruse technicality. Since 1945, government has become increasingly involved in all aspects of economic and social life of the nation and this has resulted in the enactment of a vast amount of complex legislation. If every detail of such legislation had to be incorporated into the original Bills, those Bills would have been unwieldy documents and would have absorbed far more parliamentary time than was justified. That said, in recent years, some disquiet has arisen because of a tendency of government to use subordinate legislation as a means of developing policy and not simply as a way of delegating matters of detail.

2. The extent of delegation

The most significant delegation of law-making powers ever made under an Act of Parliament was granted to ministers under the European Communities Act 1972 s. 2(2). The Act empowers government to give effect to the obligations of the UK under Articles 10 and 249 of the EC Treaty by means of subordinate legislation. Apart from central government, other institutions and bodies have also been granted the power to make subordinate legislation. The Welsh Assembly has authority under the Government of Wales Act 1998 s. 44 to create subordinate legislation for those aspects of the government of Wales for which the Assembly has delegated powers. The Northern Ireland Assembly enjoys similar powers under the Northern Ireland Act 1998. Local authorities can make compulsory purchase orders to acquire land under the Acquisition of Land Act 1981, and district local authorities as well as the London boroughs can make bye-laws for their respective areas under a procedure set out in the Local Government Act 1972. Most of these bye-laws must first be sent in draft for approval by the Secretary of State for Environment, Transport and the Regions. Bye-laws can also be made by certain public corporations who have been empowered to do so by Act of Parliament, and they too are normally subject to approval by the relevant government minister. If there is an infringement of a bye-law, the body responsible for making the bye-law can have recourse to criminal proceedings to enforce it. In *Boddington* v *British Transport Police* [1998] the validity of a bye-law imposing a fine for smoking on a train was upheld by the House of Lords. In order to ensure efficient management of the civil courts, the Civil Procedure Rules Committee has the power under the Civil Procedure Act 1997 to make rules for the conduct of litigation and case management.

3. Statutory Instruments Act 1946

Most of the more important pieces of subordinate legislation take the form of statutory instruments. The Statutory Instruments Act 1946 s. 1(1) provides that statutory instruments can take the form of Orders in Council (orders approved by the monarch) as well as orders or regulations made by a government minister where the enabling Act so states. The Act re-enacted provisions of the Rules of Publication Act 1893, and so under s. 1(2) it was expressly provided that the rules of those rule-making authorities who had previously enjoyed delegated law-making powers would also be known as statutory instruments. The bye-laws of local authorities, however, are not statutory instruments nor are compulsory purchase orders made by them. Whether a statutory instruments is to take the form of an Order in Council or simply a regulation made by a minister is determined by the precise wording of the provision in the enabling Act under which delegation is authorised. The Statutory Instruments Act 1946 s. 2(1) provides that immediately after an instrument has been made it must be sent to the Queen's printer, numbered in accordance with the scheme devised by the Statutory Publications Office and put on sale. The Queen's printer is the Controller of HM Stationery Office. Statutory instruments dealing with purely local matters are exempted from the requirements of printing and sale.

4. Drafting of statutory instruments

Most statutory instruments are drafted within the various government departments by civil servants who are legally qualified either as solicitors or barristers. If a particular department does not have a legal section, the drafting can be done by the Treasury Solicitor's Department. Although care is needed, many statutory instruments are relatively straightforward because they just increase financial thresholds and levels of benefit or amounts of compensation payable to allow for the effect of inflation. As previously stated, it is also quite common to use statutory instruments to bring parts of Acts of Parliament that have received the Royal Assent into operation, and these are known as commencement orders. These will simply mention the sections of the Act to be made operative. If, however, a statutory instrument is likely to assume special importance, perhaps because it transposes an EU directive or because it deals with complex subject matter, the department concerned may call on the expertise of a parliamentary draftsperson from the Office of Parliamentary Counsel to the Treasury.

5. Citation

It is usual to cite statutory instruments by giving the title first. After the title comes the year in which the instrument was made, followed by the number given to the instrument. Consider these examples: The Institute of Legal Executives Order 1998 (No. 1077), and Maternity and Parental Leave Etc. Regulations 1999 (SI 1999 No. 3312). The first was an Order in Council made under the authority of the Courts and Legal Services Act 1990 whereas the second was a ministerial order made under the Employment Rights Act 1996.

6. Parliamentary awareness

Not all statutory instruments must be drawn to the attention of Parliament and this is particularly true of those instruments that are of purely local concern but it may also apply to instruments of minor significance where the enabling Act does not require it. For those instruments that must be brought to the attention of Parliament, the enabling Act will specify that an instrument must be laid before Parliament either in draft or in final form. The official copies must be certified as facsimiles of the original document that is retained by the government department responsible for creating the instrument. An instrument cannot normally become operative until it is filed with the Office of Votes and Proceedings in the House of Commons, but in the event of some great urgency the instrument may become operative immediately provided notification and a proper explanation is given at the time to the Lord Chancellor and the Speaker of the House of Commons. Usually an instrument that must be laid before Parliament will be filed with the Office of Votes and Proceedings at least 21 days before it comes into effect. A list of all statutory instruments received at Westminster is published weekly in the House of Commons for the benefit of members.

Most of the statutory instruments that are required to be laid before Parliament will be subject to the negative resolution procedure which means that unless there is an objection by either House the instruments will become law by default. In principle, any member of the Lords or Commons can move a 'prayer' (a motion) that an instrument be annulled or, if it was laid in draft, that it is not made in final form. The Statutory Instruments Act 1946 provides that this must happen within 40 business days of the date of the instrument being laid before Parliament. In the House of Commons such a motion takes the form of an early day motion, which is usually submitted to the Table Office on a specially printed form. Normally there is very little prospect of this motion ever being debated unless it is put down by the official Opposition or another opposition party usually in the name of its leader. Early day motions put down in the name of the official Opposition are more likely to be debated but not on the floor of the House. Standing Order 118(4) provides that where a motion has been put down that a statutory instrument be annulled, a minister may put a motion at the commencement of business that the instrument should be referred to a standing committee on delegated legislation. Only if 20 or more members rise immediately to object will this motion be defeated and if there is no such objection the instrument will be passed to a standing committee for consideration. This procedure was invoked for the Transnational Information and Consultation of Employees Regulations 1999 (SI 1999 No. 3323) which were made under the European Communities Act 1972 s. 2(2) to implement Directive 97/74 EC which extended to the UK the directive on establishing European works councils or information and consultation procedures for employees. The previous Conservative government had negotiated an 'opt out' from the Social Policy Protocol and Social Policy Agreement of the Treaty of European Union but this had been reversed shortly after the Labour Party had won the general election in 1997. The statutory instrument in question was made on 12 December 1999 and laid before Parliament on 14 December; subject to a negative resolution, it was due to come into force on 15 January 2000. It was hardly surprising therefore that the leader of the Opposition put down an early day motion, EDM 293, that the instrument and the regulations it contained should be annulled. The instrument was considered and debated by the Seventh Standing Committee on Delegated Legislation on 3 February for just over two hours and the Committee then voted 9:3 in favour of the measure. Such an outcome is hardly surprising bearing in mind that the composition of the standing committee reflects the relative strengths of the political parties in the House of Commons.

An alternative to the negative resolution procedure is the affirmative resolution procedure which can take one of three forms. An instrument can be made by the appropriate government department and take immediate effect with the proviso in the enabling Act that it will lapse if it is not approved by one or both Houses within a period of 28–40 days. This procedure is often used for instruments dealing with taxation. An alternative would be for the enabling Act to require the instrument to be laid in draft form before one or both Houses with the proviso that it is not to be made final and brought into effect unless one or both Houses present an address asking for this to be done. The third and simplest alternative is for the enabling Act to require the minister to lay the instrument in final form with the proviso that it will come into effect only after a resolution by one or both Houses has been passed.

Standing Order No. 118(3) of the House of Commons requires initially that all instruments that have to be approved by an affirmative resolution must be referred to a standing committee on delegated legislation. Following a debate in committee, which should not exceed 90 minutes, a motion to approve the instrument is put to the House. During the debate the instrument cannot be amended and must be withdrawn if a majority vote cannot eventually be secured in its favour. In the House of Lords the motion for an affirmative resolution cannot be put until a report is received from the Joint Committee on Statutory Instruments. The affirmative resolution procedure is often incorporated into primary legislation for the creation of subordinate legislation that is considered to need greater scrutiny by Parliament because of its importance, but this is not invariably the case.

7. Deregulation orders

The Deregulation and Contracting Out Act 1994 permits a government minister by statutory instrument to *amend or repeal* provisions in *other statutes* enacted prior to the end of the 1993/94 session of Parliament if he/she considers they impose a burden on persons carrying out trade, business or other professions. These powers have been used quite extensively to date. Each House has established its own select committee to report on proposals and on the draft instruments to be made under the Act. Having consulted with the interested parties, if a minister takes the view that a deregulation order should be made, he/she is obliged to lay his/her proposal before Parliament in the form of an explanatory memorandum describing:

(a) the burden to be relieved

(b) the financial and other benefits of the proposed change

(c) how any necessary protection is to be continued

(d) details of the consultation process undertaken

(e) the changes, if any, that he/she has made in view of the responses received from the consultation process.

The period of 60 days for Parliamentary consideration begins to run from the date that the proposals have been laid before Parliament but only normal business days are counted. The process is more than a mere formality because the House of Commons Deregulation Committee has to report that a draft order should be laid before the House on the basis of the terms contained in the memorandum. Alternatively, it may report that the proposal should be amended before a draft order is prepared and laid before Parliament or that the order-making power should not be used in this instance. The Committee has indeed recommended on a few occasions that the order-making power should not be used. The minister is required to take account of the report of the Deregulation Committee and the report of the Delegated Powers and Deregulation Committee of the House of Lords as well as representations received from interested parties within the 60-day period referred to above. At the expiration of the 60-day period the minister can prepare his/her draft order and lay it before Parliament with a statement that gives details of the reports made by the Committees of both Houses together with any other representations received describing any changes that have been made to the proposal in the light of them. Standing Order 141 requires that the draft order must be referred to the Deregulation Committee but at this stage the Committee cannot put forward any amendments to the order. Within 15 business days following the laying of the order before Parliament, the Committee must report its recommendation whether the draft order should be approved. Although the minister is not obliged to wait for the Committee's report before asking the House to approve the order, he/she will wait for the report to be compiled. If the Committee recommends approval of the draft order without a need for a division on the report, the motion to approve the draft must be put to the House straight away. If the approval of the draft order came about only after a division on the report, further debate on the motion can continue on the floor of the House but for no longer than 90 minutes. As soon as the time allowed for debate has elapsed, a motion to approve the draft must be put to the House. In the event that the Committee reports that the draft order should *not* be approved, the House must firstly consider a motion whether to disagree with the Committee's report. Such a debate must not exceed three hours and, should the House resolve to disagree with the report at the conclusion of the debate, the motion to approve the draft order must be put straight away. The procedure adopted in the House of Lords is similar but not identical.

8. Remedial orders

The Human Rights Act 1998 s. 10 has made it possible for a minister to amend primary legislation by statutory instrument where it has been declared by a superior court to be incompatible with the Convention rights contained in Schedule 1 of the Act. The minister may also decide to amend other legislation in the light of the court's declaration other than the statute that contains the incompatible provision. Where a minister decides to exercise his/her power under s. 10 to make a 'remedial order' one of two procedures is available depending on the urgency of the matter. If there is no great urgency, the normal procedure as set out in Schedule 2 requires the minister to lay before Parliament the 'required information' comprising an explanation of the incompatibility which the proposed order seeks to remove, including details of the relevant declaration and a statement of the reasons for proceeding under s. 10. The minister also has to explain in his/her statement the reasons for making the draft order in the terms in which it has been drafted. The information and the draft order must be laid before Parliament for a period of 60 business days. If the minister receives representations from lobby groups and others during this period, a summary of these representations and any changes to the draft order arising from these representations must be incorporated into a statement to accompany the order in its final form which must also be laid before Parliament. At the end of a subsequent 60-day period the order must be approved by a resolution of each House.

If the matter should be urgent the minister can use the emergency procedure set out in Schedule 2 para. 2(b) which enables him/her to make the order in final form before laying it before Parliament in draft. The order must state that the normal procedure is being by-passed because of the urgency of the matter. Nevertheless, the order must still be laid before Parliament after it has been made, together with the 'required information' specified above. As with the normal procedure, if the minister receives representations from lobby groups and others within 60 days of the making of the order, he/she must present to Parliament a statement containing a summary of these representations and any changes he/she considers it appropriate to make to the original order in the light of these representations. In any event, the original order must be replaced by a second remedial order at the end of the 60-day period which must be laid before Parliament for a further 60 days. If a resolution approving the order has not been passed by each House at the end of a period of 120 business days beginning with the date on which the original order was made, it will cease to have legal effect. This does not, however, invalidate anything done whilst the order was in force. It is likely that the government will do its utmost to ensure that the necessary resolutions are passed in each House to validate the order.

9. Orders in Council

The procedure for giving effect to Orders in Council is a little different from that governing the bringing into effect of ministerial orders and regulations. Orders in Council are so called because they are approved at a meeting of the Privy Council even though the authority for their creation derived from an Act of Parliament. There are in excess of 400 members of the Council and so it never meets with the monarch in its entirety. All Cabinet ministers must be duly sworn as Privy Counsellors and it is they who attend the meetings for the approval of Orders in Council which are usually held at Buckingham Palace or Windsor Castle. Once Orders in Council have been drafted they are laid before Parliament, and if a challenge is made in either House a motion will be passed that the Order is not submitted to HM the Queen. Those that are unchallenged will be listed for approval at a scheduled meeting of the Privy Council. At the meeting the Queen stands surrounded by her ministers who also stand in her presence. As the titles of the various Orders are read aloud by the Lord President, the Queen, who does not see the Orders in advance, merely utters the word 'agreed' at the end of the title of each Order. The Orders then become operative from the date specified in the instrument.

10. The case for scrutiny of statutory instruments

A number of modern statutes contain what are known as Henry VIII clauses, which are so called because the Statute of Proclamations 1539 conferred sweeping powers on the Tudor monarch to govern by Royal decree. It may be argued that the conferring of very wide-ranging powers on the government, exercisable through the creation of subordinate legislation, merits careful scrutiny. As indicated above, there are special parliamentary procedures for dealing with deregulation orders made under the Deregulation and Contracting Out Act 1994 and remedial orders under the Human Rights Act 1998. Nevertheless, there are a number of statutes that grant wide-ranging powers to ministers that are not subject to special procedures.

An example of such a statute is the International Transport Conventions Act 1983. Sections 8 and 9 permit the Act to be *amended* by means of statutory instrument. The Transport Act 1985 s. 46 confers even wider powers because it provides that Part II of the Act can be *repealed* by statutory instrument. Thus it is readily apparent that statutory instruments can be used by government to bring about important legislative changes without recourse to the normal parliamentary process for enacting primary legislation. A strong case can therefore be made for effective scrutiny by Parliament of these instruments as well as others that are complex or produce important changes in the working environments of citizens.

11. Joint Committee on Statutory Instruments

For the most part, the task of scrutiny is entrusted to the Joint Committee on Statutory Instruments comprising seven members from each House. The chairperson is always an opposition MP, and although there are 14 members it can function with a quorum as low as two. It is assisted in its task by Counsel to the Speaker and Counsel to the Lord Chairman of Committees as well as by other members of the parliamentary staff. Under the Committee's terms of reference it is required to decide whether it ought to draw the attention of both Houses to a particular statutory instrument for any of the following nine reasons:

(a) That it imposes a tax or a charge on the citizen or upon the public revenue.

(b) That it is made under primary legislation which expressly excludes the instrument from being challenged in the courts.

(c) That it appears to have retrospective effect whereas the enabling Act does not provide for this.

(d) That there appears to be an unjustifiable delay in publishing the instrument or in laying it before Parliament.

(e) That the instrument has come into operation prior to being laid before Parliament and there seems to have been an unjustifiable delay in sending notification as required by the Statutory Instruments Act 1946 s. 4(1).

(f) That it appears doubtful that the instrument is drafted within the powers conferred by the enabling Act or it seems to make some unusual or unexpected use of the powers conferred by the enabling Act.

(g) That the form or purport of the instrument requires clarification.

(h) That the drafting of the instrument seems to be defective in some important respect.

(i) Any other substantial reason other than one which impinges on the merits of the instrument or the policy behind it.

The Committee meets only for a few hours one afternoon a week, usually when Parliament is in session, which means it sits no more than about 30 times in each session. The chairperson is not always in attendance and other members attend as and when they can. This hardly amounts to close scrutiny of subordinate legislation. Moreover, when the Committee does report, there is no requirement that its views and recommendations are acted upon. Even if it does decide to draw the attention of Parliament to one or more statutory instruments, it is obliged first to give the department concerned the opportunity to explain itself either orally or in writing. Because of the special arrangements for dealing with deregulation orders made under the Deregulation and Contracting Out Act 1994, the Joint Committee on Statutory Instruments does not spend time scrutinising them.

In the 1973/74 session an attempt was made to increase the time available for the scrutiny of certain types of statutory instrument. The government decided that in future those statutory instruments that required only an affirmative resolution of the House of Commons (mainly those dealing with taxation) could be referred to a standing committee comprising 17 MPs. The referral can only be made by a minister and the proposal can be defeated if 20 MPs in the chamber object. The consensus of opinion is that although this procedure has been invoked, it has not been a particularly successful innovation.

Under the Government of Wales Act 1998 s. 58, a scrutiny committee has been established to examine subordinate legislation for the ministerial functions that have been transferred to the Welsh Assembly and similar arrangements exist under the Northern Ireland Act 1998.

12. The validity of subordinate legislation

Although by constitutional convention the courts cannot normally question the validity of primary legislation it is possible for them to consider the validity of subordinate legislation if it is challenged. In *Hoffman La Roche* v *Secretary of State for Trade* [1975] the House of Lords considered an application by the Secretary of State for an injunction restraining certain pharmaceutical companies from charging prices for drugs above those specified in a statutory instrument. Lords Diplock and Cross indicated that the courts have jurisdiction to declare an order in the form of a statutory instrument invalid even where it has been the subject of an affirmative resolution procedure in both Houses. A challenge can be either direct or indirect. An indirect challenge occurs when it is argued as a defence in the course of enforcement proceedings that the instrument is *ultra vires*, that is, beyond the scope of the powers that were delegated by the enabling Act. If this should prove to be so, the court can declare the instrument invalid either completely or in part. A direct challenge would occur if an individual or organisation set out to challenge the validity of an instrument in a claim for judicial review. The aim would be to obtain a declaratory judgement that the instrument is invalid. This procedure is considered in detail in Chapter 15.

Challenges may be mounted on the basis that the instrument is procedurally *ultra vires* because the specified procedures have not been followed. Although it is often difficult to be sure how a court will interpret the procedural requirements, if certain procedural requirements are specified as mandatory and these have not been followed, then non-compliance will almost certainly render the instrument invalid. If there is an element of discretion regarding a consultation process, a failure to consult will not usually affect the validity of the instrument. On the other hand, a challenge on substantive grounds relates to the precise content of the instrument concerned and the allegation would be that all, or part, of the instrument exceeds the powers that were originally delegated by Parliament.

An example of substantive *ultra vires* is provided by the case of *Hotel and Catering Industry Training Board* v *Automotive Proprietary Ltd* [1969]. The Industrial Training Act 1964 s. 1 authorised the minister to establish industrial training boards for persons employed 'in any activities of industry or commerce' and s. 4 empowered the boards to impose training levies on employers in the relevant industries. The Hotel and Catering Board was then established under the provisions of a statutory instrument, and Schedule 1 para. 1(a) of the instrument specified that the activities of the hotel and catering industry included the supply of food and drink, in the course of any business, to persons for immediate consumption. Paragraph 3(c) of the same Schedule defined 'business' as including the activities of any person or body of persons in the management or operation of a club. The Board then sought to impose a levy on a private members' club. The House of Lords affirmed the decision of the Court of Appeal to the effect that the words 'in any activities of industry or commerce' should be given their ordinary meaning. Thus the instrument was declared to be invalid to the extent that it extended to private members' clubs. A challenge based on an infringement of fundamental rights is provided by *R* v *Lord Chancellor ex p. Witham* [1997]. The Lord Chancellor made the Supreme Court Fees (Amendment) Order 1996 under powers conferred on him by the Supreme Court Act 1981. Article 6 of this order amended the Supreme Court Fees Order 1980 in that it provided for a minimum fee of £120 for issuing a writ for claims of £10,000 or less and for a fee of £500 for issuing a writ where no monetary limit was specified. Article 3 of the same order nullified provisions in the 1980 order which excused 'litigants in person' who were in receipt of income support, from the obligation to pay fees and permitted the Lord Chancellor to reduce or waive the fee in any particular case on grounds of undue financial hardship in exceptional circumstances. The applicant wanted to bring proceedings for defamation as a 'litigant in person' but he was unemployed, had no savings and was in receipt of income support of just under £60 a week. Since legal aid was not available for defamation actions he was effectively prevented from bringing his action and so he sought to challenge the validity of Article 3 of the order on the basis that it was *ultra vires* the Supreme Court Act 1981 s. 130. The basis of his argument was that it deprived him of his common law constitutional right of access to the courts. The Divisional Court of Queen's Bench held that the applicant's common law right could only be abrogated by specific statutory provision or by regulations made pursuant to legislation that specifically conferred the power to abrogate that right. There was no provision in the Supreme Court Act 1981 s. 130 that conferred such a power on the Lord Chancellor to prescribe a level of fees that would preclude persons from having access to the courts. Moreover Article 3 operated to bar many persons from seeking justice in the courts. Accordingly Article 3 was held to be *ultra vires* s. 130 and unlawful.

A court may declare that all or part of a statutory instrument is 'incompatible' with the Human Rights Act 1998 if it has not been possible to interpret it according to the Convention rights contained in Schedule 1 and it may disapply it unless the primary legislation prevents the removal of the incompatibility. If the primary legislation does prevent the removal of the incompatibility, then the instrument will remain operative unless and until a minister changes the parent Act by remedial order as described above. Although a remedial order can have retrospective effect this will not benefit either of the parties to the original proceedings. A freestanding piece of subordinate legislation that is not made under the authority of primary legislation (a comparatively rare occurrence) may be declared invalid and be disapplied if it is incompatible with a Convention right.

Progress test

1. Is subordinate legislation really necessary?

2. What are the principal forms of subordinate legislation?

3. Who is responsible for drafting subordinate legislation?

4. What do you understand by the negative resolution procedure?

5. What do you understand by the positive resolution procedure?

6. Does all subordinate legislation have to be brought to the attention of Parliament?

7. How does an Order in Council differ from other statutory instruments?

8. What is the role of the Joint Committee on Statutory Instruments? How effective is it?

9. How effective have standing committees in the House of Commons been in the scrutiny of statutory instruments?

10. How does the Human Rights Act 1998 affect statutory instruments?

Further reading

Books

De Smith, S. and R. Brazier (1998) *Constitutional and Administrative Law* (Harmondsworth: Penguin, chapter 18).
Ingman, T. (2000) *The English Legal Process* (London: Blackstone Press, chapter 5).
Parpworth, N. (2000) *Constitutional and Administrative Law* (London: Butterworths, pp. 164–72).
Slapper, G. and D. Kelly (1999) *The English Legal System* (London: Cavendish Publishing, pp. 40–4).
Twining, W. and D. Miers (1999) *How To Do Things With Rules* (London: Butterworths, chapter 9).
Zander, M. (1999) *The Law Making Process* (London: Butterworths, pp. 91–103).

Useful website

Copies of new statutory instruments can be accessed on the website www.hmso.gov.uk

7

The impact of the European dimension

1. Introduction

A proper account of the modern English legal system cannot be given without considering the legal implications arising from UK membership of the European Union. The EU is the result of an evolutionary process that can be traced back to 1951. It is a complex entity that was brought into being by the Treaty of European Union 1992 and it continues to evolve. Article A of the Treaty of European Union declares that the Union is founded upon three existing supra national organisations which were themselves created by international treaty together with two distinct intergovernmental agreements. These supra national organisations are the European Coal and Steel Community (ECSC), the European Community and the European Atomic Energy Community (Euratom). Some commentators have used the metaphor of an ancient Greek temple, the portico of which is supported by three pillars, to describe the structure of the Union. The first (central) pillar comprises the three existing communities referred to above. The second pillar is the agreement relating to the development of a common foreign and security policy, whilst the third pillar is the agreement governing cooperation in the spheres of police, judicial and criminal matters. At the time of writing, the EU consists of 15 member states, but if and when the Treaty of Nice is ratified by the member states it will pave the way for a Union of 27 member states. The EU is a political entity. It does not have a legal personality and it is not a state, and certainly not a super-state as some have asserted. Thus it does not have a constitution resembling that of a modern nation state. It does, nevertheless, have what has been described as a 'constitutional charter' that is derived from the various treaties that create its constituent elements and establish its policy and decision-making institutions. These institutions are:

(a) the Council of the European Union

(b) the European Commission

(c) the European Parliament

(d) the European Court of Justice

(e) the Court of Auditors.

These institutions are vital to the functioning of the EU and to the law-making process in particular and so an account must be given of their respective roles. This chapter, then, focuses on the European Community which lies at the core of the EU before proceeding to examine the various sources of EU law and the processes to enacting secondary legislation. Since the 'constitutional charter' of the EU is based on the rule of law, due consideration must also be given to a number of important concepts arising from the jurisprudence of the European Court of Justice (ECJ). Finally, the chapter deals with the issue of fundamental rights in the EU as developed by the ECJ through its general principles of law.

THE INSTITUTIONS

2. The Council of the European Union

At the outset, it is important to differentiate between the European Council and the Council of the European Union. The European Council comprises the heads of states and President of the Commission. It usually meets at least twice a year to establish broad political guidelines. Its meetings are held in the territory of the member state holding the presidency of the Council at that time. The Council of the European Union, on the other hand, meets several times a month at the Council building in Brussels and is both a legislative and a decision-making body. It has greater political legitimacy than the Commission because its members are all ministers of democratically elected governments who must be authorised to commit their respective states in the decision-making process. They are accustomed to act in the interests of their national governments and so the decision-making at the highest level in the EU tends to reflect the interests of the governments of the member states. General Council meetings are attended by the respective foreign ministers of the member states but specialist meetings are attended by the appropriate government ministers in relation to the business under discussion. So, if the Council is discussing agriculture, it will be constituted by the ministers for agriculture of the various member states. The powers of the Council are set out in Article 202 of the EC Treaty in the following terms:

To ensure that the objectives set out in this Treaty are attained, the Council shall in accordance with the provisions of the Treaty:

(a) ensure co-ordination of the general economic policies of the Member States;

(b) have powers to take decisions;

(c) confer on the Commission, in the acts which the Council adopts, powers for the implementation of the rules which the Council lays down.

The presidency of the Council is held by each member state in turn at six monthly intervals and meetings are usually convened at the request of the president but they can be convened at the request of the Commission or any member state. The office of president has become increasingly important in recent years and a member state will use its occupancy of the office to promote issues that it deems of importance.

Since the Council of Ministers is not a fixed grouping, it is vital that there should be a body to ensure that there is continuity in its work. This is achieved through an entity known as COREPER (an acronym after its French title). The legal basis for the existence of COREPER is found in Article 4 of the Merger Treaty 1965 which provides that a Committee consisting of the permanent representatives of the member states shall be responsible for preparing the work of the Council and for carrying out the tasks assigned to it by the Council. COREPER also serves an important function as a permanent liaison body for the exchange of information between national governments and the Community institutions. It is in fact subdivided into two equal committees, namely COREPER I and COREPER II. The former is composed of deputy permanent representatives (deputy ambassadors) and the latter by the permanent representatives (ambassadors). The Council also has its own full-time secretariat based at the Council building in Brussels that has an important role in coordinating the work of the Council.

3. The European Commission

The Commission is a unique institution that has administrative, executive, quasi-judicial as well as some delegated legislative functions. It has been likened to a national civil service but this analogy should not be taken too far. Its central concern is to facilitate the ongoing process of European integration. Its base of operation is in Brussels and its officials function under the political control of a College of Commissioners. The College currently comprises 20 Commissioners, and even if the accession negotiations for all the applicant states are successful after 2004, it is possible that the number of commissioners will remain at 20 and so a system of rotation that is fair to all member states will have to be devised. The Commissioners are nominated by the governments of the member states. Currently, the five largest member states: Germany, France, Italy, the UK and Spain nominate two Commissioners each, whilst the remaining member states nominate one each. However, if and when the Treaty of Nice is ratified, the Commission will comprise just one Commissioner from each member state from 2005. The governments of the member states have been required to reach a unanimous decision on the person they wish to nominate as President of the Commission. The governments then, by common accord, nominate those they wish to serve as Commissioners but these persons must be acceptable to the nominated president too. The European Parliament must then approve the appointment of the President and the members of the Commission as a whole in a single vote. Once this has been done, each Commissioner is formally appointed by his/her own government. If and when the Treaty of comes into force, the Council acting by a qualified majority vote (*see* **13**) will nominate the person it intends to appoint as President of the Commission and the nomination must then be approved by the European Parliament. Thereafter, the Council acting by qualified majority and by common accord with the nominee for President will nominate a list of other persons that it intends to appoint as Commissioners in accordance with the proposals made by each member state. Once the approval of the European Parliament is obtained, the president and other commissioners will be appointed by the Council by qualified majority vote.

On taking office, each Commissioner is required to give a solemn undertaking in a special session of the ECJ to perform his/her duties as specified in the EC Treaty. Under the EC Treaty they are required to act in the general interests of the Community and be completely independent of their national governments in the performance of their duties. The normal term of office is five years but this may be extended. Until now the members of the Commission have been allocated their different portfolios (areas of responsibility and interest) by the President on the basis of preliminary informal discussions even though the final allocation must be ratified by the Commission as a whole. The prestige of the Commission has suffered somewhat since the resignation of the Commission presided over by Jacques Santer following the publication of a damning report by a committee of independent experts.

If the Treaty of Nice comes into operation, the position of the President will be strengthened. Under the new Article 217 EC the Commission must work under the political guidance of its President who will decide its internal organisation in order to ensure that it acts consistently and effectively. The President will be able to reallocate portfolios during the Commission's term of office and he/she may require a member of the Commission to resign provided that the approval of the rest of the Commission is obtained. The Commission meets in private and all decisions are taken on the basis of simple majority vote. These decisions are of the Commission as a whole for which there is collective responsibility.

Every Commissioner has his/her own personal staff of approximately six officials which is known as his/her cabinet. The Commission also has a permanent secretariat of some 21,000 full-time officials that support the work undertaken by the various Commissioners. These are organised into 24 directorates-general (see the Europa website at www.europa.eu.int/). Each directorate-general is under the overall supervision of its own director-general. Since every directorate-general comprises a number of separate directorates, each directorate is supervised by a director who reports to the director-general. In addition to the directorates-general, there are a number of service units such as the Legal Service and Statistical Office that provide services across the Commission.

4. The European Parliament

The European Parliament has been directly elected ever since 1979. Its function is to represent the peoples of the EU and it acts as co-legislator with the Council in most policy areas. Unfortunately, its proceedings are under-reported in the British media but the Europa website is an excellent source of up-to-date information. The committee work of the Parliament is carried out at the Parliament building in Luxembourg but the actual decision-taking is reserved for the monthly meetings that are held at Strasbourg. All 626 MEPs sit in groupings corresponding to their political alignments when the Parliament meets in full plenary session each month at Strasbourg. Until the elections in 1999 the largest grouping was that of the European Socialists but this has now changed with the emergence of a centre-right majority. Germany, as the largest member state, has the largest number of MEPs at 99, whilst France, Italy and the UK each have 87. Spain has 64 and the Netherlands has 31. Other member states each have 25 or fewer MEPs, with Luxembourg electing a mere 6. The prospect of enlargement of the EU after 2002 has necessitated some adjustment in the number of seats allocated to each country. Under the Treaty of Nice the number of seats allocated to the existing member states has been scaled back to 535, and by 2009, if all applicant states join, there will eventually be 732 MEPs. Although the European Parliament must approve the Community budget, it cannot enact legislation by itself and it has no tax-raising powers; yet its involvement in the law-making process has increased steadily since the mid-1980s. If and when the Treaty of Nice is ratified, the Parliament's contribution to law-making will be enlarged under the co-decision process and it will be called upon to state its opinion should the European Council wish to declare the existence of a serious and persistent breach of fundamental rights by a member state.

5. The European Court of Justice

The European Court of Justice (ECJ) comprises 15 judges – one from each member state – and is based in Luxembourg. It is assisted by eight advocates-general but they are not members of the Court as such. They provide reasoned submissions to the Court on every case that it hears. The Court is not bound by these submissions and will sometimes decide the outcome of a particular case contrary to the submissions of the advocate-general. These submissions of the advocate-general are, nevertheless, useful in considering the issues that the Court has had to grapple with in the course of its deliberations because it only produces a single judgement – there are no dissenting judgements. The 15 judges are grouped together in 'chambers' of three or five, and most cases brought before the Court are heard by a 'chamber' of three or five judges rather than by the entire Court. Nevertheless, when a member state or an institution makes a formal request, the Court must sit in plenary session with all 15 judges present. The Court is the supreme authority on all matters relating to Community law and its jurisdiction and powers are set out in Articles 220 to 245 of the EC Treaty. It draws upon the legal principles and traditions of all member states in the formulation of its own procedures and principles. It is therefore heavily influenced by the Continental civil law model which is quite distinct from the English tradition. The working language of the Court is French and so all documents must be translated into French, and it delivers all its judgements in French which must then be translated. Since September 1989, the ECJ has been assisted by a Court of First Instance. Its jurisdiction was mainly confined to cases involving competition law excluding Article 234 references. It judicially reviews all Commission decisions in the sphere of competition law and deals with employment law disputes between the staff of the EU and its institutions. Under the Treaty of European Union, the Court of First Instance (CFI) was given jurisdiction to hear all action brought by parties other than member states or Community institutions including anti-dumping cases. If the Treaty of Nice is ratified there will be changes once it comes into operation. The ECJ will continue to be composed of one judge from each member state, but as new member states join possibly after 2004 the number of judges will gradually increase to 27 assuming that all accession negotiations are successful. The Treaty of Nice introduces the concept of the grand chamber which will comprise 11 judges including the President of the Court together with the presidents of the existing five judge chambers. The grand chamber will hear those cases that are currently heard by a plenary session of the Court. After 2004 (assuming ratification), the number of judges comprising the CFI may also gradually rise, but immediately following ratification, COREPER has agreed to an increase of six in the number of judges. Following the ratification of the Treaty there will be a new distribution of responsibilities between the ECJ and the CFI so that, subject to certain exceptions, the latter will deal with all direct actions under Articles 230, 232 and 235.

6. The Court of Auditors

The Court of Auditors is not a court as such but an institution whose function is to oversee the financial management of the EU and in particular to assist the Parliament and the Council with the implementation of the Budget.

THE EUROPEAN COMMUNITY

7. The Community and the Union

The most significant supra national organisation comprising the EU is the European Community which has evolved from the European Economic Community that was created in 1958. Thus the treaty provisions referred to in this chapter are those of the EC Treaty unless otherwise stated. The European Community (EC), unlike the EU, is a legal entity. The general aims of the EC, as distinct from the ECSC and Euratom, are set out in the consolidated version of the Treaty in Article 2 which provides:

> The Community shall have as its task, by establishing a common market and an economic and monetary union and by implementing common policies or activities referred to in Articles 3 and 4, to promote throughout the Community a harmonious and balanced development of economic activities, a high level of employment and of social protection, equality between men and women, sustainable and non-inflationary growth, a high degree of competitiveness and convergence of economic performance, a high level of protection and improvement of the quality of the environment, the raising of the standard of living and quality of life, and economic and social cohesion and solidarity among member states.

This is highly aspirational language and it is readily apparent that the aims of the EC, as a constituent element of the EU, extend far beyond the economic sphere to include social and environmental protection. These general aims are to be achieved through the means set out in Articles 3 and 4. The nature of the European Community and its relationship with its member states was declared by the ECJ in Case 26/62 *NV Algemene Transporten-Expeditie Onderneming Van Gend en Loos* v *Nederlandse*

Administratie der Belastingen [1963] long before the UK became a member state when it stated:

> the Community constitutes a new legal order of international law for the benefit of which the states have limited their sovereign rights, albeit within limited fields, and the subjects of which comprise not only Member States but also their nationals. Independently of the legislation of Member States, Community law therefore not only imposes obligations on individuals but is also intended to confer upon them rights which become part of their legal heritage. These rights arise not only where they are expressly granted by the Treaty, but also by reason of obligations which the Treaty imposes in a clearly defined way upon individuals as well as upon the Member States and upon the institutions of the Community.

In Case 294/83 *Les Vert-Parti Ecologiste* v *Parliament* [1986] the ECJ stated that the EC 'is a Community based on the rule of law'. The principal sources of EU law are:

(a) the EC Treaty and subsequent treaties amending this treaty

(b) the secondary legislation created by the institutions

(c) the case law (jurisprudence) of the European Court of Justice.

These will be considered in turn. The fact that EU law has any impact on UK law at all is attributable to the fact that the Westminster Parliament enacted the European Communities Act 1972 soon after the government of the day had signed the Treaty of Accession. This was essential because the UK is a 'dualist' state for the purposes of international law rather than a 'monist' state. Thus, international law does not become part of the law of the UK unless and until it is specifically incorporated by Act of Parliament. The crucial provision of the European Communities Act 1972 is s. 2(1) which provides:

> All such rights, powers, liabilities, obligations and restrictions from time to time created or arising by or under the Treaties, and all such remedies and procedures from time to time provided for by or under the Treaties, as in accordance with the Treaties are without further enactment to be given legal effect or used in the United Kingdom shall be recognised and available in law, and be enforced, allowed and followed accordingly; and the expression 'enforceable Community right' and similar expressions shall be read as referring to one to which this subsection applies.

The legal effect of this somewhat convoluted provision was and is to make what is now referred to as EU law, part of the law of the UK. Not only is it part of UK law it is superior to it should there be a conflict of legal rules as was seen in Chapter 5 when the *Factortame* litigation was discussed in relation to parliamentary sovereignty.

SOURCES OF EU LAW

8. The EC Treaty

It was obvious that the EC Treaty imposed obligations on the member states that signed it, but, as indicated in the judgement of the ECJ in Case 26/62 *NV Algemene Transporten-Expeditie Onderneming Van Gend en Loos* v *Nederlandse Administratie der Belastingen* above, it is clear that the Treaty can also confer rights and obligations on private legal persons. In this case the ECJ devised the doctrine of direct effect whereby certain Treaty provisions could be operative in the national legal system of all member states without having to be individually enacted. The Court's initial motives for devising this legal doctrine was to give momentum to the process of economic integration and to directly engage the national courts of the member states in implementing EC law. It is significant that this concept was not explicitly stated in the EC Treaty and it is an early example of what commentators have referred to as 'judicial activism' on the part of the ECJ. The Treaty provision in question (now Article 25 EC) prohibited the creation of new customs duties and charges having equivalent effect and a Dutch company sought to enforce this Treaty provision against the Dutch government in respect of chemicals that it had imported from Germany. The advocate-general in his submissions to the ECJ argued that the Treaty only imposed obligations on member states – it did not create rights that other legal persons could enforce. As indicated above, the ECJ rejected the advocate-general's submissions. The Court subsequently set out the criteria that must be satisfied before a Treaty provision can have direct effect, the elements of which are:

(a) the right in question must be clear, precise and it must be unconditional,

(b) it must not require implementing measures by a member state or an EC institution, and

(c) it must not leave scope for the exercise of discretion by a member state or an EC institution.

Thus not all EC Treaty Articles have direct effect but the ECJ has ruled in many subsequent cases that a considerable number do operate in this way, especially those dealing with free movement of goods and persons. The doctrine of direct effect has important practical applications in this regard. Imagine the plight of a British exporter who wishes to sell his products to a German importer but the goods are refused entry by the German authorities. Article 28 EC provides that qualitative restrictions on imports and all measures having equivalent effect are prohibited between member states.

There would be little point in the British exporter suing the German author-ities in the British courts because they have no jurisdiction in Germany. It is vital that the exporter can sue the German authorities in the German courts and this is what the doctrine of direct effect makes possible. The German judiciary, being fully conversant with EC law, can make the appro-priate order against the relevant government agency in Germany that has blocked the entry of the goods contrary to Article 28 EC. Similarly, it is vitally important that a German national who has exercised his/her rights to free movement under Article 39 EC and who encounters discrimination in employment in England should be able to sue in the English courts relying on the protection afforded by Article 39 EC.

The prohibition against discrimination in relation to 'pay' on the basis of gender was declared to have direct effect by the ECJ in Case 43/75 *Defrenne* v *SABENA* [1976] and so women have the right to insist on equal pay for work of equal value throughout the EU. The main provisions on competi-tion law, namely Articles 81 and 82 EC, also have direct effect so that action can be taken in national courts where infringements arise. In relation to Treaty Articles, the doctrine of direct effect operates vertically and horizont-ally. This means that a Treaty Article can be enforced against the government of the state or some agency of the state (vertically) as well as another pri-vate legal person (horizontally) such as a company. However, the doctrine of direct effect does not apply to any part of the intergovernmental agreement on a common foreign and security policy nor to the agreement on police and judicial cooperation in criminal matters.

9. Supremacy of EC Law

Not long after the ECJ devised the doctrine of direct effect, it ruled in Case 6/64 *Costa* v *ENEL* [1964] that EC law took precedence over national law. It declared:

> The integration into the law of each Member State of provisions which derive from the Community, and more generally the terms and the spirit of the Treaty, make it impossible for the State, as a corollary, to accord precedence to a unilat-eral and subsequent measure over a legal system accepted by them on a basis of reciprocity. Such a measure cannot therefore be inconsistent with that legal sys-tem. The executive force of Community law cannot vary from one state to another in deference to subsequent domestic laws, without jeopardising the attainment of the objectives of the Treaty set out in Article 5(2) and giving rise to the discrimina-tion prohibited by Article 7.
>
> . . .
>
> The precedence of Community law is confirmed by Article 189 [now Article 249], whereby a regulation 'shall be binding' and 'directly applicable in all Member

States'. This provision, which is subject to no reservation, would be quite meaningless if a State could unilaterally nullify its effects by means of a legislative measure which could prevail over Community law.

In Case 11/70 *Internationale Handelsgesellschaft GmbH* v *Einfur-und Vorratstelle für Getreide und Futtermittel* [1970] the ECJ declared:

> [The] validity of a Community measure or its effect within a Member State cannot be affected by allegations that it runs counter to either fundamental rights as formulated by the constitution of the State or the principles of a national constitutional structure.

The principle of the supremacy of Community law over inconsistent national law was even more clearly set out in Case 106/77 *Amministrazione delle Finanze dello Stato* v *Simmenthal* [1978] because the case dealt with legislation enacted prior to the coming into force of the Treaty as well as subsequent legislation. The ECJ declared:

> Furthermore, in accordance with the principle of the precedence of Community law, the relationship between the provisions of the Treaty and directly applicable measures of the institutions on the one hand and the national law of the Member States on the other is such that those provisions and measures not only by their entry into force render automatically inapplicable any conflicting provision of current national law but – in so far as they are an integral part of, and take precedence in, the legal order applicable in the territory of each of the Member States – also preclude the valid adoption of new national legislative measures to the extent to which they would be incompatible with Community provisions.

Clearly, if national law could override EC law, the ongoing process of integration would become stalled as the doctrine of direct effect would be rendered futile.

10. Secondary legislation

At the inception of the European Community, it was realised that the Treaty would be incapable of providing a complete code of law for the evolving needs of the Community. Thus express provision was made in the Treaty for the creation of new legislation by the institutions as and when necessary. Due consideration must therefore be given to the role of the Commission in proposing new legislation and to the involvement of the Council and the European Parliament in formally adopting it. There is no general legislative power that is conferred on the Community institutions by the EC Treaty. Instead, individual Treaty Articles confer the power to create legislation in particular areas and the same Treaty Articles also prescribe the legislative process to be adopted. Thus every piece of secondary legislation must have a legal base in the Treaty and this must actually be stated in the text of the instrument that is to be adopted. The Commission usually initiates the legislative process but the Council does not have to wait for a Commission proposal. It may ask the Commission to undertake a study and submit appropriate proposals to achieve any of the objectives set out in the EC Treaty. The European Parliament now has a similar power under Article 192 EC if a majority of its members so request, but the Commission in both cases retains the discretion regarding the content and the timing of any proposals it makes to the Council.

The law-making powers of the institutions are set out in Article 249 EC which provides that:

> In order to carry out their task and in accordance with the provisions of this Treaty, the European Parliament acting jointly with the Council, the Council and the Commission shall make Regulations and issue Directives, take Decisions, make Recommendations or deliver Opinions.

11. Secondary legislation and subsidiarity

In the negotiations leading to the signing of the Treaty of European Union, some member states were concerned that power to initiate legislation that had long been exercised by national parliaments was being assumed by the Commission and that legislative decision-making was becoming over-centralised in Brussels. Thus the subsidiarity provision was inserted into the EC Treaty. The concept of subsidiarity requires that decision-making should take place at the lowest possible level to the people affected by the decision. The subsidiarity provision became Article 5 which is as follows:

> The Community shall act within the limits of the powers conferred upon it by this Treaty and of the objectives assigned to it therein. In areas which do not fall within its exclusive competence, the Community shall take action in accordance with the principle of subsidiarity, only if and in so far as the objectives of the proposed action cannot be sufficiently achieved by the Member States and can therefore, by reason of the scale or effects of the proposed action, be better achieved by the Community.
>
> Any action by the Community shall not go beyond what is necessary to achieve the objectives of this Treaty.

The Community has reserved exclusive competence for itself to make law in those areas where it has legislated already. These areas include free movement of goods, services, persons and capital together with freedom of establishment. Thus there is no scope for member states to enact their own legislation in these areas unless it is to implement legislation that has been adopted by the Council. However, there are areas where the Community has not yet claimed exclusive competence, for example, social policy, consumer protection, and environment. If new legislative action is proposed in these areas to achieve some objective or purpose it is then that the principle of subsidiarity comes into play. It is necessary for the Commission to consider initially whether the action would be better taken at national level or whether the matter demands action at Community level for the sake of overall effectiveness. In bringing forward a legislative proposal at Community level, the Commission must provide an explanatory memorandum justifying the necessity of Community action to satisfy the subsidiarity principle. Article 253 EC states:

> Regulations, directives and decisions adopted jointly by the European Parliament and the Council, and such acts adopted by the Council or the Commission, shall state the reasons on which they are based and shall refer to any proposals or opinions which were required to be obtained pursuant to this Treaty.

In a Protocol to the Treaty of Amsterdam 1997 it is expressly stipulated that the Commission must provide copies of legislative proposals in 'good time' so that national parliaments have an opportunity to consider them. National parliaments will, of course, wish to pass on their comments to the Commission having given due consideration to a proposal.

Although the legislative process is usually initiated by the Commission, the Council is empowered to legislate in some areas without having received a proposal from the Commission and without even consulting with the European Parliament. Nevertheless, the Parliament has become increasingly involved in the legislative process since 1979 mainly through the devising of new legislative procedures with successive revisions of the Treaty after intergovernmental conferences. There are four distinct procedures that require consideration: (1) the consultation procedure (2) the co-decision procedure (3) the cooperation procedure and (4) the assent procedure.

12. Consultation procedure

The consultation procedure is so called because of the requirement imposed on the Council to consult with the Parliament. In the past it was the most frequently used of the four procedures. A proposal, usually in the form of a draft regulation or directive, is put forward by the Commission. The requirement for consultation must be strictly complied with and the proposal will normally be considered by a committee of the Parliament. Failure to consult the Parliament amounts to the infringement of an essential procedural requirement and the measure can be annulled in proceedings before the Court of Justice as in Case 138/79 *Roquette Frères* v *Council* [1980] where the ECJ annulled a regulation. If the original proposal is subsequently amended by either the Council or the Commission there must normally be a further round of consultation with the Parliament. Although the Parliament must be consulted, it is the Council of Ministers that takes the final decision and it is not bound by the views of the Parliament. As a result of the Treaty of Amsterdam, the Council is now required to consult the European Parliament in respect of measures to be adopted under Title VI of the EC Treaty concerning police and cooperation in judicial and criminal matters.

13. Co-decision procedure

The co-decision procedure was created under the Treaty of European Union 1992 in response to demands from the Parliament for a much greater say in the legislative process. It is now contained in Article 251 EC of the Treaty having been modified slightly by the Treaty of Amsterdam 1997. As a result of the Treaty of Amsterdam, the power of the Parliament has been considerably enhanced because the list of policy areas to which the co-decision procedure applies has been increased from 15 to 38. Some of the new areas that come under the co-decision procedure are transport, environment, research, overseas aid, transparency and access to information, regional policy implementing decisions, customs cooperation, equal pay and some aspects of employment policy. If the Treaty of Nice is ratified, another seven policy areas (under Articles 13, 62, 63, 65, 157, 159 and 191 EC) will be dealt with under co-decision. Thus, if the Treaty is ratified most of the legislative measures that require the Council to act by qualified majority will be decided under the co-decision procedure. However, co-decision has not been extended to all legislative measures which already require qualified majority voting in the Council such as agricultural policy and trade policy.

The Commission is required to submit its draft regulation or directive to the Parliament and the Council. The Council must seek the opinion of the Parliament but need not adopt a 'common position' thereafter. If the Parliament does not put forward any amendments the Council can adopt the measure by a qualified majority vote and it may do the same if the amendments proposed by the Parliament are acceptable to it and are incorporated. If the Parliament does suggest amendments that are controversial, the Council must adopt a common position and communicate it to the Parliament together with the reasons which led it to adopt the common position. The Commission must also inform the Parliament of its own position. There is then a 'window' of three months within which the Parliament may approve the common position so that the Council can adopt the measure by qualified majority vote. If the Parliament does not respond within the three months, the Council can also adopt the measure at the expiry of this time. If the Parliament rejects the common position by majority vote, the measure cannot be adopted by the Council. On the other hand, if the Parliament puts forward amendments to the common position by majority vote, the amended text must be forwarded to the Council and to the Commission. The Commission must then deliver an opinion on the amendments. The Council can, acting by qualified majority, approve all the amendments and adopt the measure provided that these amendments are acceptable to the Commission. If not, the amendments can only be incorporated into the draft legislation if the Council can muster a unanimous vote. Nevertheless, the Parliament can still exercise a veto if it disapproves of the proposed measure.

14. Cooperation procedure

The cooperation procedure was introduced under the Single European Act 1986 in order to give the Parliament a little more input into the legislative process than it had under the consultation procedure. This procedure is now set out in Article 252 but the entire procedure has now been marginalised under the Treaty of Amsterdam 1997. It has been retained only for the monetary policy provisions of the EC Treaty.

15. Assent procedure

The assent procedure was introduced by the Single European Act 1986 and is used to approve (or not, as the case may be) applications for membership from states wishing to join the European Union. It also applies to measures conferring tasks on the European Central Bank in relation to supervision of financial institutions apart from insurance companies; the amendment of certain Articles of the Statute on European System of Central Banks; defining the tasks, objectives and organisation of the structural funds; and proposals on procedures for elections to the European Parliament.

16. Voting in the Council

Most legislation must pass a vote in Council. Article 205(1) provides that unless otherwise stipulated in the Treaty, the voting in Council is to be by simple majority, but in most instances the Treaty does specify that the voting must be either by unanimous vote or by qualified majority. Measures of a constitutional nature usually require a unanimous vote but abstentions by member states will not prevent the adoption of an Act by the Council where unanimous voting is required. Even if the Treaty of Nice is ratified by the member states, unanimous voting is still required for proposals relating to: taxation, culture, coordination of social security schemes, foreign and security policy together with police and judicial cooperation in criminal matters.

Qualified majority voting was first introduced under the Single European Act 1986 as it was essential to ensure the completion of the legislative programme for the single market by the end of December 1992. It was extended to cover many other areas under the Treaty of European Union 1992. Decisions taken on the basis of a qualified majority vote are binding on all member states, not just those who voted in favour. It is a system of weighted voting detailed in Article 205 whereby member states have a certain number of votes to cast according to their size and population. At present a total of 87 votes are allocated to the 15 member states. A qualified majority requires 62 votes in favour and would require a minimum of 8 of the 15 member states to vote in favour. A total of 26 votes can form a blocking minority that would prevent a resolution being passed or a legislative measure being adopted. The Treaty of Nice, in seeking to pave the way for enlargement, will alter the allocation of votes in the Council but at the time of writing the precise figure needed to achieve a qualified majority is not easy to establish. According to a declaration on enlargement, in a Union of 27 member states, a total of 345 votes will exist and a qualified majority would require 258 votes. On this basis, a blocking minority would require 88 votes. Elsewhere, the figures are put at 255 votes and 91 for a blocking minority. Assuming that no new member states have joined by 1 January 2005, the existing member states will have a total of 237 votes, and on this figure a qualified majority would rise to 170 votes. In addition, the votes in favour of any measure initiated by the Commission must be cast by a majority of member states and a single member state will be able to prevent a decision being adopted by showing that the qualified majority does not represent 62 per cent or more of the total population of the EU.

Careful consideration is given to all legislative proposals by the Council's own working parties and COREPER before the Council meets in formal session. Thus many votes can be taken in the Council without much discussion beforehand. The Council does, from time to time, confer delegated law-making powers on the Commission which the latter must be careful to exercise within the scope of the authority that has been granted. If the Commission should exceed the scope of the authority that has been granted in the way that it drafts the instrument, its validity may be challenged before the ECJ.

17. Application of secondary legislation

The status of these forms of secondary legislation is further elaborated upon in Article 249 EC which provides that a regulation shall have general application and shall be binding in its entirety and directly applicable in all member states. Thus, the provisions that make up a regulation are directly applicable and are capable of having direct effect both vertically and horizontally where the criteria for direct effect are satisfied. No action is necessary on the part of the UK government as a member state to give effect to a regulation. It becomes operative in its legal systems from the date specified in the *Official Journal* or, if no date is specified, 20 days after its publication. Although derogation (i.e. withdrawal by a member state) may be provided for, all regulations are presumed valid until declared otherwise by the ECJ. A directive is to be binding upon member states to whom it is addressed as to the result to be achieved but it is for the national authorities to choose the form and methods for implementation. Directives must be notified to all member states and normally indicate a time limit for their implementation. As indicated previously, a directive may be implemented in the UK by means of primary legislation (for example, the Data Protection Act 1998) or by means of subordinate legislation. A general power to create subordinate legislation to implement directives is contained in the European Communities Act 1972 s. 2(2). If a directive is not implemented, or not properly implemented within the time limit specified, the member state in question will be in breach of Article 10 EC and the Commission can invoke enforcement proceedings under Article 226. A decision of the Council or Commission shall be binding in its entirety upon those to whom it is addressed and may have direct effect. Decisions of the Council and Commission become effective on their notification to the relevant addressees but their validity can be challenged by the parties before the ECJ. Recommendations and opinions have no binding force but they do have an influential role in EC policy-making as a form of soft law. For example, the Commission Recommendation 92/131/EEC on the Protection of the Dignity of Women and Men at Work has proved to be influential with employment tribunals in the UK when dealing with claims of sexual harassment.

18. Jurisdiction and jurisprudence of the ECJ

The jurisprudence of the ECJ derives from its extensive jurisdiction which is firmly rooted in particular Treaty provisions. It has jurisdiction to hear infringement proceedings brought by the Commission under Article 226 against member states in which the Commission alleges that a member state has failed to comply with its obligations under Article 10 the text of which is as follows:

> Member States shall take all appropriate measures, whether general or particular, to ensure fulfilment of the obligations arising out of this Treaty or resulting from action taken by the institutions of the Community. They shall facilitate the achievement of the Community's tasks.
>
> They shall abstain from any measure which could jeopardise the attainment of the objectives of this Treaty.

Article 226 contains a lengthy procedure, comprising a number of stages, which is aimed at gaining compliance without the necessity of a hearing before the ECJ. Only if the Commission has been unable to secure compliance will the ECJ be required to adjudicate over a member state's alleged failure to comply. Over the years, the Commission has been obliged to institute infringement proceedings against most of the member states, and the UK has been brought before the Court on at least 14 occasions. Infringement actions may also be brought before the Court by another member state under Article 227. There is only one reported instance of this, in Case C-141/78 *France* v *UK* [1979] where the ECJ ruled that UK measures on mesh sizes for fishing net did not conform with Community law. Although most infringement actions are decided in favour of the Commission, some are decided in favour of the member states concerned. The judgement of the ECJ in infringement actions is only declaratory and the Court has no powers to enforce its judgements by levying penalties. As a result of an amendment to the EC Treaty, Article 228(2) provides that proceedings can now be brought by the Commission after the initial hearing under Article 226 for payment of a lump sum or penalty payment by the member state for non-compliance with the judgement of the Court. However, the time-scale set by the Commission for compliance must have elapsed. This power has recently been exercised in Case C-387/97 *Commission* v *Hellenic Republic* when Greece failed to fulfil it obligations under Directives 75/442/EEC and 78/319/EEC in relation to its failure to draw up plans for the disposal of toxic waste. Having failed to comply with the judgement arising from the infringement action within the time limit that had been set, the ECJ imposed a penalty payment, in this case of €20,000 for each day that Greece failed to comply with the judgement.

Under Article 230, the ECJ is able to review all acts of the Council, the Commission, the European Parliament and the European Central Bank other than recommendations or opinions. The grounds for challenging a measure are limited to lack of legal competence, infringement of an essential procedural requirement, infringement of the Treaty or any rule of law relating to its application or misuse of powers. The member states, together with the Council and Commission are 'privileged applicants' in proceedings under Article 230 so that they are automatically entitled to bring an action before the ECJ. In order to protect their particular interests, the European Parliament, the Court of Auditors and the European Central Bank are also permitted to instigate actions for annulment. Private legal persons, on the other hand, are 'non-privileged applicants'. They must show either that a decision is addressed to them or that it is of direct and individual concern in order to challenge it. This latter requirement was established by the ECJ in Case 25/62 *Plaumann & Co.* v *Commission* [1963]. If an action under

Article 230 is held to be well founded, the ECJ will declare the measure to be void. In Case C-295/90 *European Parliament* v *Council* [1992], Directive 90/366, dealing with the right of residence of students, was annulled because it was adopted under Article 235 (now Article 308 EC) rather than Article 6(2) (now Article 12(2)). The UK government sought to use Article 230 in Case C-84/94 *UK* v *Council* [1996] to challenge the legal base of Directive 93/104 on the regulation of working time but did not succeed. Article 232 EC complements Article 230 EC to ensure that the European Parliament, the Council and Commission do act on the powers conferred on them when there is a clear legal duty to act under the Treaty. Thus, the ECJ will hear applications from member states, the institutions and other interested parties over a failure to act when there is a clear obligation to do so.

Under Articles 235 and 288(2) the ECJ has jurisdiction to hear disputes relating to the non-contractual liability of the institutions of the EU where private legal persons have suffered loss. The ECJ may award damages to compensate persons who have suffered loss as a direct result of action taken by an institution. In Case 5/71 *Zuckerfabrik Schoppenstedt* v *Council* [1971] the ECJ formulated a test for determining liability for acts where the institutions are involved in economic policy choices, which was restated in Cases 83, 94/76; 4, 15, 40/77 *Bayerische HNL Vermehrungsbetriebe GmbH & Co. KG* v *Council and Commission* [1978] when the Court declared:

> the Community does not incur liability on account of a legislative measure which involves choices of economic policy unless a sufficiently serious breach of a superior rule of law for the protection of the individual has occurred.

The concept of a superior rule of law has not been restrictively interpreted and applies to some of the general principles of law adopted by the ECJ to be considered later. However, in the above case the 'sufficiently serious' requirement was expressed in terms of the Community institution having 'manifestly and gravely' disregarded the limits on the exercise of its powers. The requirement tends to make the recovery of compensation quite difficult where this adversely affects individual interests because it operates to protect the institutions when exercising legislative power.

A relatively recent aspect of the jurisdiction of the ECJ relates to the hearing of appeals on points of law from the Court of First Instance. According to Article 51 of the Statute of the Court, an appeal may be based on lack of competence of the CFI, a breach of procedure that adversely affects the interests of the appellant or the infringement of Community law by the CFI.

19. Jurisdiction under Article 234

Important though these aspects of the Court's jurisdiction are, it is its jurisdiction under what is now Article 234 (formerly Article 177) that has been the main means by which the ECJ has been able to develop its jurisprudence. In order to ensure the uniform application of Community law in all member states, the ECJ is empowered by the Treaty to give preliminary rulings on matters of interpretation referred to it by national courts and tribunals concerning Community law. Under Article 234, the ECJ has the power to give preliminary rulings on questions of EU law submitted by the courts and tribunals of member states who are required to decide cases pending before them that involve the application of EU law. Such preliminary rulings are binding on the national courts and this provision has been of great importance for the development of some of the key concepts of EC law. References have already been made to Case 26/62 *NV Algemene Transporten-Expeditie Onderneming Van Gend en Loos v Nederlandse Administratie der Belastingen* in which the ECJ devised the doctrine of direct effect and to Case 6/64 *Costa v ENEL* in which it pronounced the supremacy of EC law over inconsistent national law. Given the reluctance on the part of member states to take legal action against each other under Article 227, one can only praise the wisdom and foresight of the ECJ in devising the doctrine of direct effect whereby private legal persons can enforce treaty provisions through national courts. The jurisdiction of the ECJ is not confined to the EC Treaty and extends to all EU legislation.

20. Expansion of the doctrine of direct effect

As was stated earlier, the ECJ ruled that certain Treaty Articles were capable of having direct effect if they satisfied the stipulated criteria. It then sought to expand the scope of the doctrine through its case law when the opportunity presented itself. In Case 9/70 *Grad v Finanzamt Traunstein* [1970] a Munich tax tribunal asked for a preliminary ruling on whether an Article of a decision in conjunction with an Article in a directive produced direct effect between member states and those under their jurisdiction. The tribunal was also asking whether the provisions referred to created rights for individuals that national courts had to protect. The ECJ stated:

> However, although it is true that by virtue of Article [249], regulations are directly applicable and therefore by virtue of their nature capable of producing direct effects, it does not follow from this that other categories of legal measures mentioned in that Article can never produce similar effects. In particular, the provision according to which decisions are binding in their entirety on those to whom they are addressed enables the question to be put whether the obligation created by the decision can only be invoked by the community institutions against the addressee or whether such a right may possibly be exercised by all those who have an interest in the fulfilment of this obligation. It would be incompatible with the binding effect attributed to decisions by Article [249] to exclude in principle

111

the possibility that persons affected may invoke the obligation imposed by a decision. Particularly in cases where, for example, the Community authorities by means of a decision have imposed an obligation on a Member State or all the Member States to act in a certain way, the effectiveness (*l'effet utile*) of such a measure would be weakened if the national of that State could not invoke it in the courts and the national courts could not take it into consideration as part of Community law.

Subsequently, in Case 41/74 *Van Duyn* v *Home Office* [1974] the ECJ had to decide whether Directive 64/221 would be invoked against the UK government when it had not transposed it into its national law. The directive defined the 'public policy' exceptions whereby a member state could refuse entry to a national from another member state who was otherwise guaranteed free movement under Article 48 (now Article 39 EC). A Dutch national was refused permission to enter the UK to take up employment with an organisation known as the Church of Scientology because the UK government considered this organisation to be socially undesirable. When this was challenged in the High Court, it applied for a preliminary ruling under Article 177 (now Article 234 EC) to the ECJ. Having confirmed that Article 48 had direct effect, the ECJ virtually repeated its ruling in *Grad* v *Finanzamt Traunstein* and added:

> In particular, where the Community authorities have, by Directive, imposed in Member States the obligation to pursue a particular course of conduct, the useful effect of such an act would be weakened if individuals were prevented from relying on it before their national courts and if the latter were prevented from taking it into consideration as an element of Community Law.

The elements of the criteria for the 'direct effect' of a Treaty Article apply to a directive but there is the additional requirement which is that the time limit specified for implementation of the directive must have expired. If the directive has been defectively implemented, an individual may also invoke it before the national court provided, of course, that the date for implementation has passed. Initially the ECJ relied on the principle of effectiveness to justify its ruling that directives could have direct effect, but in Case 148/78 *Pubblico Ministero* v *Ratti* [1979] it also justified its ruling on the principle that a member state should not be able to rely on its own default in not implementing a directive as a defence. In these early cases the ECJ was dealing with the direct effect of a directive as against the government of the state (vertical direct effect). However, the ECJ subsequently expanded the boundaries of its concept of 'the state' in Case 152/84 *Marshall* v *Southampton and South West Hampshire Area Health Authority (Teaching)* [1986]. Helen Marshall was a dietician who worked for the health authority for some 14 years but she was dismissed in 1980 because she had passed the normal retirement age for women under the authority's employment policy. Female employees were supposed to retire at the age of 60 but male employees could work on to the age of 65. Under the existing national legislation, women became eligible to receive the state pension at the age of 60 but men did not become eligible until the age of 65. This did not impose any obligation on women under national law to retire at the age of 60 because payment of the state pension could be deferred to the date of actual retirement. Helen Marshall, who was in good health, did not wish to retire before the age of 65 because she wished to go on making contributions to the NHS pension fund. On this basis, when she did retire at 65 she would be able to draw an enhanced pension. When she was obliged to retire she felt that she had been discriminated against because of her sex – if she were a man there would have been no problem about her working to age 65. At that time the Sex Discrimination Act 1975 exempted all arrangements relating to retirement from the ambit of the legislation and so consequently she could not challenge the area health authority's retirement policy as sex discrimination under national law. She therefore based her case on Directive 76/207 – the equal treatment directive – which required that national governments should amend their national law to ensure that men and women received equality of treatment in employment. Her case eventually worked its way from an industrial tribunal to the Court of Appeal which referred the question to the ECJ asking whether she could rely on the provisions of the directive notwithstanding the apparent inconsistencies between it and the Sex Discrimination Act 1975.

The ECJ ruled that the directive could have direct effect since the date for implementing it had passed. If the Court had permitted the directive to be enforced against a private legal person this would be what lawyers refer to as horizontal direct effect; but on a strict interpretation of what is now Article 249, the ECJ would not permit this. Thus it was fortunate that Helen Marshall worked in the public sector (for the NHS). Had she worked in the private sector (e.g. for a Nuffield Hospital) she would not have been able to rely on the directive at that time to contest the legality of her employer's decision to retire her before the age of 65. The Sex Discrimination Act 1975 was amended as a result of this ruling by the Court of Justice when the Westminster Parliament enacted the Sex Discrimination (Amendment) Act 1986.

In giving its judgement in *Marshall* v *Southampton and South West Hampshire Area Health Authority (Teaching)*, the ECJ stated:

> With regard to the argument that a directive may not be relied upon against an individual, it must be emphasised that according to Article 189 of the EEC Treaty, [now 249 EC] the binding nature of a Directive, which constitutes the basis for the possibility of relying on the Directive before the national court, exists only in relation to 'each Member State to which it is addressed'. It follows that a Directive

may not of itself impose obligations on an individual and that a provision of a Directive may not be relied upon as such against such a person'. It must therefore be examined whether, in this case, the respondent must be regarded as having acted as an individual.

In that respect it must be pointed out that where a person involved in legal proceedings is able to rely on a Directive as against the State he may do so regardless of the capacity in which the latter is acting, whether employer or public authority. In either case it is necessary to prevent the State from taking advantage of its own failure to comply with Community Law.

In Case 222/84 *Johnston* v *Chief Constable of the Royal Ulster Constabulary* [1986] the ECJ ruled that the police could be regarded as part of the state, and in Case C-188/89 *Foster* v *British* Gas [1990] it indicated in paragraph 20 of its judgement that the concept of the state could extend to

a body, whatever its legal form, which has been made responsible, pursuant to a measure adopted by the State for providing a public service under the control of the State and has for that purpose special powers beyond those which result from the normal rules applicable in relations between individuals, is included in any event among the bodies against which the provisions of a Directive capable of having direct effect may be relied upon.

Weatherill and Beaumont (*EU Law*, 3rd edition) have suggested that the ECJ in an earlier part of its judgement has created the possibility that directives may be invoked by individuals against a legal entity that is not itself under state control. The final part of paragraph 18 of the Court's judgement can be interpreted in this way. Support for this view is provided by paragraph 47 of the judgement of the Court in Joined Cases C-253/96 and C-258/96 *Kampelmann* v *Landschaftsverband Westfalen-Lippe* [1997] in which employees were allowed to rely on Article 2(2)(c) of Directive 91/533 as against their employer, a municipally owned utility company. In the event, the House of Lords interpreted the guidelines provided by the ECJ in *Foster* v *British Gas* and held that the provisions of Directive 76/207 could be invoked against British Gas which at the relevant time was a nationalised industry under state control even though it had been subsequently privatised. Following this ruling, Blackburne J in *Griffin* v *South West Water Services Ltd* [1995] decided that a privatised water company was an emanation of the state on the basis that it was under the control of the state. Then the Court of Appeal in *NUT and others* v *Governing Body of St Mary's Church of England (Aided) Junior School* [1997] held that although the governors of a voluntary aided school were not under the direct control of the state, once the school obtained voluntary aided status it became part of the state education system. At that point the governors became a public body responsible for providing a public service, subject to statutory powers exercisable by the local education authority. It could therefore be regarded as an emanation of the state and the teachers could rely on the provisions of Directive 77/187 against the governing body. It does now seem that a directive may be enforced against entities that are not directly connected to state.

In Case 14/83 *Von Colson and Kamann* v *Land Nordrhein-Westfalen* [1984] and Case 79/83 *Harz* v *Deutsche Tradax* [1984] the ECJ had stated that all national authorities, including courts, had an obligation to interpret their national law in such a way that the aims of a directive were achieved. This principle was subsequently restated by the ECJ in Case C-106/89 *Marleasing SA* v *La Comercial Internacional de Alimentacion SA* [1990] but the ECJ added the rider that the obligation arose only where it was possible to do so. Nevertheless, this could result in a national court imposing liability on private legal persons in some instances which would be tantamount to giving horizontal direct effect to directives. Having expanded the scope of the doctrine of direct effect by expanding the concept of the state, it was predictable that the ECJ would eventually be asked to go one step further and rule that a directive could have horizontal direct effect. This was implicit in the reference that was made in Case C-91/92 *Faccini Dori* v *Recreb Srl* [1994]. The case was not without merit in that Ms Dori had made a contract at Milan station for the purchase of an English language correspondence course. Had Italy implemented Directive 85/577 which was intended to harmonise national law in respect of contracts negotiated away from business premises to provide a 'cooling-off period', she would have been able to withdraw from the contract during this period. She sought to rely on the directive as a defence to a claim brought by the other contracting party to enforce the contract and the Italian court applied for a preliminary ruling under Article 177 (now Article 234). The ECJ refused to ignore the very clear wording of Article 249 and stated that a directive could not impose obligations on private legal persons. Persons in Ms Dori's situation are no longer without a remedy because they can now sue the government of the state concerned and obtain reparation for its failure to implement a directive.

21. State liability

In the period prior to the completion of the single market, the ECJ was particularly concerned over the non-implementation or defective implementation of directives by some member states despite their obligations under what are now Articles 10 and 249. Non-implementation meant that Community law was not uniform across the Community, and if it were to happen on a wide enough scale it could seriously retard the process of integration. The problem was highlighted by Cases 6 and 9/90 *Francovich and Bonifaci* v *Italian State* [1991]. In 1980, the Council had adopted Directive 80/987 on the protection of employees in the event of the insolvency of their employer. The directive provided that member states must ensure that an institution was established to guarantee payment of employees' outstanding claims for pay and redundancy compensation. Italy had failed to implement this directive by the date set and the Commission had already brought a successful infringement action against Italy in 1987 in Case 22/87 *Commission v Italy* [1989]. Despite a clear ruling against the Italian state, the Italian government had still not implemented the directive at the time this case was brought by Francovich and Bonifaci. The Court held that the Italian state was in breach of its obligations under Article 5 [now Article 10] of the Treaty. Although the ECJ stated that the directive in question was not sufficiently precise to give rise to direct effect, the Court went on to rule that a state had a duty to compensate individuals for loss suffered as a result of its failure to implement the directive by the specified deadline. However, the ECJ made it clear that this obligation on the part of member states would only arise when the following criteria were met:

(a) the directive conferred rights on individuals

(b) the content of those rights could be identified from the terms of the directive

(c) there is causation (a clear link) between the member state's failure to implement and the loss/damage suffered by the individual.

The ECJ then went on to declare that it was a matter for each member state to designate the competent courts and to establish detailed procedural rules for the necessary legal proceedings aimed at safeguarding the rights that individuals derive from Community law. It then added that the rules for reparation in national law must not be less favourable than those relating to similar domestic claims and not be framed in such a way as to make it virtually impossible or excessively difficult to obtain reparation. Where individuals are able to claim against their own national governments for failure to implement directives, the distinction between horizontal and vertical direct effect is no longer of importance because the individuals concerned will be claiming against the state and not against a private employer or some other private legal person. Moreover, numerous claims for compensation against the government of a member state may have the desired result of inducing them to be more conscientious in future about implementing directives within the timescale permitted.

In the later Joined Cases C-46/93 and 48/93 *Brasserie du Pecheur SA v Germany* and *R v Secretary of State for Transport ex p. Factortame Ltd and others* [1996] the ECJ extended the scope for reparation against member states beyond the failure to implement directives to other breaches of EC law.

Factortame Ltd and others sought compensation following the ruling that the UK was in breach of EC law and the Divisional Court of the High Court made a preliminary reference to establish whether the UK was liable to compensate the company and, if it was, what consideration should be taken into account in the assessment of claims for damages. The company's claim was joined with a similar reference made by a German court in respect of a claim by a French company against the German government for the infringement of a Treaty provision on the free movement of goods. The ECJ ruled that EC law conferred a right to reparation under three conditions:

(a) the rule of law infringed must be intended to confer rights on individuals

(b) the breach must be sufficiently serious

(c) there must be a direct causal link between the breach of the obligation resting on the state and the damage sustained by the injured parties.

There was no difficulty with the first element of the criteria because both Articles 6 and 52 (*Factortame Ltd*) and Article 30 (*Brasserie du Pecheur*) had long ago been declared to have direct effect. In relation to the second element, the ECJ endeavoured to provide guidance when it stated in paragraphs 56 and 57:

> The factors which a competent court may take into consideration include the clarity and precision of the rule breached, the measure of discretion left by that rule to the national or Community authorities, whether the infringement and the damage caused was intentional or involuntary, whether any error of law excusable or inexcusable, the fact that the position taken by a Community institution may have contributed towards the omission, and the adoption or retention of national measures or practices contrary to Community Law.
>
> On any view, a breach of Community Law will be sufficiently serious if it has persisted despite a judgement finding the infringement in question to be established or a preliminary ruling or settled case law of the Court on the matter from which it is clear that the conduct in question constituted an infringement.

In relation to the third element of the above criteria, the ECJ stated in paragraph 58 that it was for national courts to decide whether there was a direct causal link between the breach of the obligation by the state and the damage suffered. Thus national courts must not only decide whether there has been a sufficiently serious breach, they must also decide the issue of the causal link within which they must consider the application of a duty to mitigate loss through the prompt taking of legal action and the application of any contributory negligence. National rules on the limitation of actions also apply to such claims. The caveats provided by the ECJ are that national remedies must be effective and non-discriminatory in that Community rights must not receive less favourable treatment than similar national claims.

From a UK perspective, this was novel because there was no existing principle of law of state liability for legislative acts.

The principle of state liability has been developed further through a series of subsequent cases:

(a) Case C-392/93 *HM Treasury* v *British Telecommunications Plc* [1996]

(b) Case C-5/94 *R* v *Ministry of Agriculture, Fisheries and Food ex p. Hedley Lomas* [1996]

(c) Joined Cases C-178/94, C-179/94, C-188/94, C-189/94 and C-190/94 *Dillenkofer and others* v *Germany* [1996]

(d) Joined Cases C-283/94, C-291 and C-292/94 *Denkavit International BV* v *Bundesamt für Finanzen* [1996].

However, there continues to be a degree of uncertainty over the nature of the breach necessary to give rise to liability. The ECJ has attempted to align the liability of member states to that of the non-contractual liability of EU institutions under Article 288(2) although the two are not strictly comparable in practice. Consequently, where a member state acts in an area where it has wide discretion, the ECJ is likely to take a less strict approach to the question of liability. The government and/or national authorities will only be liable if they have manifestly and gravely disregarded the limits of their discretion. If the member state has either no discretion in implementing EU law or no discretion to act in a way that is at variance with EU law, the infringement may be sufficient to establish the existence of a sufficiently serious breach. This is particularly so where there is a clear and inexcusable violation of a precise obligation.

The UK government was able to avoid the imposition of liability in *HM Treasury* v *British Telecommunications Plc* on the basis of the very clear guidance provided by the ECJ to the national court. The ECJ was firmly of the view that the provision of the directive in question lacked clarity and that the UK was acting in an area of wide discretion. Moreover the Commission had not objected to the text of the UK regulations implementing Directive 90/531, a copy of which was sent to it. On the other hand, in *R* v *Ministry of Agriculture, Fisheries and Food ex p. Hedley Lomas*, the ECJ took the view that the UK had little or no discretion in the granting of a licence and was not called upon to make legislative choices. On this basis there could be liability for breaching Article 34 (now Article 29) on free movement of goods. In *Dillenkofer and others* v *Germany*, liability could be imposed for the failure to transpose Directive 90/314 conferring consumer protection in the sphere of holiday travel by the specified deadline even though there had been no prior infringement action against Germany. On the other hand, in *Denkavit International BV* v *Bundesamt für Finanzen*, the ECJ applied the criteria set out in paragraph 56 of its judgement in *Brasserie du Pecheur SA* and held that the breach was not sufficiently serious because of the uncertainty surrounding Article 3(2) of Directive 90/435 on an aspect of company taxation. Other member states, having discussed the directive with the Council, had adopted the same faulty interpretation of the directive as Germany.

FUNDAMENTAL RIGHTS IN EU LAW

22. Fundamental human rights

The European Convention on Human Rights and Fundamental Freedoms (hereafter ECHR) was drafted in 1950 by the Council of Europe. The Council of Europe was established in 1949 as a political forum to foster political cooperation at the European level in the aftermath of the Second World War. It therefore predated the establishment of any of the European Communities referred to at the beginning of the chapter and is quite distinct from them. The Council of Europe drafted the ECHR in the form of a treaty to safeguard against the possibility of a political group similar to the Nazi party ever securing power in western Europe again. It was signed by those European countries that were members of the Council of Europe at the time (including the UK) and other European states have since acceded. The ECHR comprises a number of civil and political rights and was inspired by the International Covenant on Civil and Political Rights which forms part of the UN Universal Declaration of Human Rights, but unlike the UN declaration, it has its own enforcement mechanisms. The Convention was not incorporated into the original EEC Treaty in 1957 probably because, in the beginning, the aims the Community were purely economic and it was not considered that the individual rights of private legal persons were likely to be infringed. When the implications of the Court's declaration of the supremacy of Community law over inconsistent national law had been completely absorbed, it began to be appreciated that Community law might override constitutional guarantees of fundamental rights. This was the basis of the application to the ECJ in Case 11/70 *Internationale Handelsgesellschaft GmbH* v *Einfur-und Vorratstelle für Getreide and Futtermittel* [1970] in which the ECJ declared in paragraph 3 of its judgement that 'respect for fundamental rights forms an integral part of the general principles of Community law protected by the Court of Justice'. However, this was qualified in the next sentence in which the Court stated: 'The protection of such rights, whilst inspired by the constitutional traditions common to the Member States, must be ensured within the framework of the structure and objectives of the Community'.

Having considered the grounds for the alleged infringement, the ECJ decided that there had been no infringement of the right claimed. This was because the restriction on the freedom to trade in the form of a deposit payable for the export of maize meal was not disproportionate to the general interest that the deposit system sought to achieve. However, when the case returned to the German Constitutional Court, a contrary conclusion was reached. In Case 4/73 *Nold* v *Commission* [1974] the ECJ enlarged on its earlier declaration stating:

> fundamental rights form an integral part of the general principles of law, the observance of which it ensures.
>
> In safeguarding these rights, the Court is bound to draw inspiration from constitutional traditions common to the Member States, and it cannot therefore uphold measures which are incompatible with fundamental rights recognised and protected by the Constitutions of those States.
>
> Similarly, international treaties for the protection of human rights on which the Member States have collaborated or which they are signatories, can supply guidelines which should be followed within the framework of Community Law.

This indirect reference to the ECHR was made explicit in Case 222/84 *Johnston* v *Chief Constable of the RUC* [1986]. On numerous occasions, private legal persons have attempted to challenge the validity of Community legislation on the basis that it infringed fundamental human rights. In most instances the ECJ has decided on the facts that the legislation does not breach any fundamental human right as it interprets that right. A notable exception arose in Case 63/83 *R* v *Kent Kirk* [1985] where a Danish fisherman was able to avoid criminal liability for fishing in UK territorial waters by successfully pleading that UK legislation retroactively validated by a Community measure violated Article 7 of the Convention.

The ECJ has since developed its case law in Case 249/86 *Commission* v *Germany* [1989] to the point where member states are required to respect fundamental human rights when implementing Community law. This case concerned a violation of Article 7 of ECHR by Germany in implementing Article 10 of Regulation 1612/68 on free movement of persons. The German authorities had refused to renew the residence permits of certain migrant workers and threatened to expel them to their country of origin. They had complained to the Commission over the implementation of Regulation 1612/68 by the German authorities. Nevertheless, the ECJ has stated in its Opinion 2/94 that the EC does not have the legal competence to accede to the Convention and that an amendment to the Treaty would be necessary if this was to be achieved. If this were to happen, it would mean that the ECJ would not have the final say on the application of fundamental human rights in the EC because it would have to defer to the European Court of Human Rights.

23. General principles of EU law

The ECJ was only too well aware that the EC Treaty did not specifically safeguard fundamental human rights. It therefore gradually formulated a number of general principles of law which form part of its case law by drawing on legal principles operative on the various member states. In this way it was able to 'square the circle'. It could maintain the supremacy of Community law over inconsistent national law but refute any allegation that it had judicially incorporated the ECHR into Community law. At the same time, by drawing on the ECHR as a source of inspiration it was able to assert that there was a consensus among the member states regarding the foundations of the general legal principles of Community law, or EU law as they should now be known. These principles are:

(a) proportionality

(b) equality

(c) legal certainty

(d) procedural justice.

24. Proportionality

The principle of proportionality is a borrowing from German administrative law and is applicable within a number of areas of EU law including the guaranteed rights in relation to free movement and freedom of establishment as well as the Common Agricultural Policy. It is used to test the legality of action taken in the context of EU law by the institutions as well as by member states. The application of the principle requires a balancing of means and ends so that the precise means chosen to achieve a particular end or outcome should be no more than is necessary to do so. Some weight or value must, of course, be assigned to the particular end to make a balancing process possible. A good example of the operation of this principle is provided by Case 114/76 *Bela-Muhle Josef Bergmann KG* v *Grows-Farm GmbH & Co. KG* [1977]. The Council adopted Regulation 563/76 on the compulsory purchase of skimmed milk powder. The intervention agencies had accumulated very large stocks of skimmed milk powder and these were still increasing. The regulation aimed to reduce these stocks. The protein contained in the milk powder was to be used in processed animal feed. A provision in the regulation made the grant of aid provided for certain vegetable protein products together with the free circulation in the Community of certain imported animal feed products subject to the obligation to purchase specified quantities of the treated milk powder. The purchase

121

price imposed for the purchase of the treated milk powder was almost three times more expensive than the alternative feed made from soya. The defendant contested the validity of the regulation on the basis that it conflicted with the objective of the Common Agriculture Policy and the principle of proportionality. The ECJ ruled that the compulsory purchase price imposed a disproportionate burden on importers and users of animal feed which could not be justified in terms of the objectives of the Common Agricultural Policy and declared the regulation devoid of legal effect. Proportionality was also used to test the legality of member state action in Case 120/78 which is widely known as the *Cassis de Dijon* case.

25. Equality

The principle of equality is expressed in Article 12 in terms of a prohibition on discrimination based on nationality, in Articles 39, 43 and 49–50 in relation to free movement and in Article 141 (formerly Article 119) with regard to equality of treatment as between men and women in relation to pay. In the context of the Common Agriculture Policy, Article 34(2) provides that there shall be no discrimination as between producers and consumers. In EU law the principle of equality, however, has a much wider application. The first stage in deciding whether a breach of the principle has taken place where two persons are similarly situated is to identify the difference in treatment. Having done so, the next stage is to decide whether the difference is justified in the particular circumstances or whether it is not permissible.

26. Legal certainty

Legal certainty requires that the law should, as far as possible, be available to whom it applies so that they can order their affairs and make necessary plans. In the context of this overarching principle there are three related principles: legitimate expectations, non-retroactivity and vested rights. The principle of legitimate expectations may be invoked to prevent an EU institution from going back on an undertaking that has been given. In order to invoke this principle, a private legal person must be able to show three things:

(a) the legitimate expectation was properly raised by the action of an institution – normally the Council or Commission,

(b) that reliance was placed on this action, and

(c) loss has been or would be suffered.

The ECJ has permitted the principle of legitimate expectations to be invoked to challenge the validity of a legislative act or decision. Infringement of the principle may also provide the basis for a claim for compensation under Article 288(2). The principle of non-retroactivity is a presumption and not an absolute rule. It is simply a presumption against the retrospective effect of legislative acts and decisions. In Case 88/76 *Exportation des Sucres* v *Commission* [1977], the ECJ ruled that the application of this principle prevented a regulation from taking effect *before* it was published in the *Official Journal*. However, in Case 98/78 *Racke* v *Hauptzollamt Mainz* [1979] the ECJ upheld the validity of two retrospective measures stating that

> Although in general the principle of legal certainty precludes a Community measure from taking effect from a point in time before its publication, it may exceptionally be otherwise where the purpose to be achieved so demands and where the legitimate expectations of those concerned are duly respected.

The principle that criminal legal provisions may not have retroactive effect is one that is common to the legal systems of all member states. Thus, in *R* v *Kent Kirk* (referred to in **22** above) the ECJ ruled that the retroactive nature of Regulation 170/83 could not be regarded as validating a national measure imposing criminal penalties. The retroactive application of a measure may be accepted by the Court in a non-criminal context where an important Community objective is being pursued and where legitimate expectations are properly respected. The principle of vested rights is linked to the principle of non-retroactivity in that rights acquired by private legal persons may be extinguished only if there are compelling reasons.

27. Procedural justice

The principle of procedural justice is a borrowing from English, Irish and Scots law and is nothing more than the applications of the principles of natural justice. In Case 17/74 *Transocean Marine Paint Association* v *Commission* [1974] the Association had obtained from the Commission an exemption in respect of Article 85(3) (now Article 81(3)) for an agreement which was binding on its members, some of whom were within the EEC but others were not. When the Association applied to renew the agreement, the Commission imposed a condition relating to the provision of new information and the Association argued that it had not been given the opportunity to make its objection concerning this condition to the Commission before a final decision was made. In giving its judgement the ECJ stated in paragraph 15:

> It is clear [that the relevant regulation implementing Regulation 17/62] applies the general rule that a person whose interests are perceptibly affected by a decision

taken by a public authority must be given the opportunity to make his point of view known. This rule requires that an undertaking be clearly informed, in good time, of the essence of conditions to which the Commission intends to subject an exemption and it must have the opportunity to submit its observations to the Commission. This is especially so in the case of conditions to which, as in this case, impose considerable obligations having far-reaching effects.

Another aspect to the principle of procedural justice is the requirement to give reasons for any decision that is taken so that it may be reviewed to ensure that it has not been formulated on an arbitrary basis.

Although these general principles have been derived from the legal systems of the member states, their adoption by the ECJ has resulted in their becoming somewhat detached and independent of specific principles within the constitutional and legal systems of the member states which originally inspired them.

The commitment to fundamental human rights has since been strengthened by Article 6 (paragraphs 1 and 2) of the Consolidated Text of the Treaty of European Union which provides that

> The Union is founded on the principles of liberty, democracy, respect for human rights and fundamental freedoms, and the rule of law, principles which are common to the Member States.
>
> The Union shall respect fundamental rights, as guaranteed by the European Convention for the Protection of Human Rights and Fundamental Freedoms signed in Rome on 4 November, 1950 and as they result from the constitutional traditions common to the Member States, as general principles of Community Law.

Since Article 6 has not been incorporated into the EC Treaty, it is only binding on member states. The Treaty of Amsterdam 1997, nevertheless, makes this Article justiciable before the ECJ. Thus a private legal person cannot bring a case to the European Court of Human Rights alleging that there has been an infringement of the Convention by an EU institution.

A European Charter of Fundamental Rights was finalised in October 2000 and was adopted by a proclamation of the Council, Parliament and the Commission at the European Council meeting in December 2000. The authors of the Charter intended that people in the EU should be better informed about their rights, and it is possible that in time this Charter may be incorporated into the EC Treaty. This Charter is a fusion of the rights taken from the ECHR, decisions of the ECJ, together with other EU charters including the EU Charter on the Fundamental Rights of Workers. It also contained some totally new rights relating to the protection of personal data and rights in the sphere of bioethics. Although it was decided that this charter should not be legally binding, EU citizens can refer to it when challenging any decision taken by the institutions and by member states when implementing EU law.

Since the ECHR has not been incorporated into EU law (nor UK law) as such, a more detailed discussion of fundamental human rights as set out in the Convention has been deferred to Chapter 8 which deals with the interpretation of UK and EU law.

28. A note on citizenship of the EU

The Treaty of European Union established the concept of EU citizenship and Article 17 provides that everyone who holds the nationality of a member state is a citizen of the EU. This gives rise to certain rights in that every EU citizen is able to move and reside freely within the territory of any member state subject to the limitations specified in the EC Treaty. Having exercised this right, every EU citizen has the right to vote and stand as a candidate in municipal elections and elections to the European Parliament where he/she resides, under the same conditions as a national of that state (Article 19). Under Article 20 there is a right to the protection from diplomatic missions of other member states in countries where the citizen's own state is not represented. In addition, Article 21 provides that every EU citizen has the right to petition the European Parliament in accordance with Article 194 and to address complaints of maladministration to the Ombudsman under Article 195.

Progress test

1. By what means did European Community law become part of the law of the UK?

2. What is the status of EC law in the UK in relation to national law? How crucial is this to the process of economic integration?

3. Which institution is responsible for drafting regulations and directives?

4. Which institutions are involved in enacting secondary legislation?

5. Which of the legislative processes confers least power on the European Parliament?

6. How much power does the co-decision procedure confer on the European Parliament?

7. What powers does the European Parliament exercise over the European Commission?

8. Why is it necessary to have a Court of Justice? What is the jurisdiction of the Court of Justice?

9. Why should national courts wish to make references to the ECJ under Article 234?

10. What is the jurisdiction of the Court of First Instance and which aspect of its work do you consider is the most important for the maintenance of the single market?

11. Why is it important that Treaty Articles and the provisions of some secondary legislation should be accorded 'direct effect'?

12. What is the essential difference between a regulation and a directive?

13. Distinguish between vertical direct effect and horizontal direct effect?

14. What criteria must be met before a directive can have vertical direct effect?

15. Under what circumstances can a member state be held liable to compensate an individual over the failure to implement a directive?

Further reading

Books

Craig, P. and G. de Burca (1999) *EU Law: Text and materials* (Oxford: Oxford University Press).

Kapteyn, P.J.G. and P. VerLoren van Themaat (1998) *Introduction to the Law of the European Communities* (London: Kluwer Law International).

Steiner, J. and L. Woods (1999) *Textbook on EC Law* (London: Blackstone Press).

Weatherill, S. and P. Beaumont (1999) *EU Law* (Harmondsworth: Penguin).

Articles

Anagnostaras, G. (2001) 'The allocation of responsibility in state liability actions for breach of Community law: a modern Gordian knot?', *European Law Review* Vol. 26, No. 2.

Piris, J-C. (1999) 'Does the European Union have a constitution? Does it need one?', *European Law Review* Vol. 24, No. 6.

Steiner, J. (1998) 'The limits of state liability for breach of European community law', *European Public Law* Vol. 4, No. 1.

Wilson, C. and Downes, T. (1999) 'Making sense of rights. Community rights in EC law', *European Law Review* Vol. 24, No. 2.

Useful websites

For general information on the EU visit www.europa.eu.int/. For the Court of Justice visit www.curia.eu.int/

8

Interpretation of UK and EU legislation

1. Introduction

It is not only lawyers and judges that find themselves in situations where they have to interpret primary and subordinate legislation. Tax inspectors must interpret tax legislation when making tax assessments and civil servants working at the Benefits Agency must interpret social security legislation in order to assess benefit entitlements. In addition, there is a vast array of legislation that impacts directly on business in areas such as health and safety, environmental protection, consumer protection and employment. Managers must become conversant with this legislation in so far as it pertains to their responsibilities so that they can ensure compliance by their respective organisations. It comes as a surprise, therefore, to many people to learn that there is no Act of Parliament that lays down a clear set of principles that must be followed by anyone engaged in the task of statutory interpretation. Moreover, a leading practitioners' text on the subject, *Maxwell – On the Interpretation of Statutes* does not provide anything by way of a coherent body of principles for guidance. The preface to *Maxwell* states:

> it is, I trust, not taking too cynical a view of statutory interpretation in general, and this work in particular, to express the hope that counsel putting forward diverse interpretations of some statutory provision will each be able to find in *Maxwell* dicta and illustrations in support of his case.

This chapter considers firstly the interpretation of national law before moving on to consider the impact of the Human Rights Act 1998. There will then be a consideration of the principles underlying the interpretation of EU law.

2. The normal rule

How should the numerous statutory provisions enacted by the Westminster Parliament be interpreted by managers and others? In view of the fact that a relatively small number of provisions ever give rise to disputed meanings, the only reasonable answer and one that has overwhelming judicial support is that the words used must be interpreted according to their normal grammatical meaning in context. For example, the Arbitration Act 1996 s. 26(1) states that: 'The authority of an arbitrator is personal and ceases on his death.' The meaning of this provision is straightforward. It is clear that if an arbitrator dies in the course of the proceedings, it will be necessary for a new arbitrator to be appointed if the arbitration is to continue. Where the words comprising the provision are clear and unambiguous, giving them their normal grammatical meaning will be consonant with the purpose behind the legislation because the draftsperson will have drafted the legislation with its readers and users in mind. Where technical terms are used, these should be given their technical meaning and the draftsperson may have helped by including an 'interpretation' section that defines technical or special terms that have been used.

Nevertheless, statutory provisions do vary in their degree of complexity and not all are as straightforward as the Arbitration Act 1996 s. 26(1). The Misrepresentation Act 1967 s. 2(1) has been previously cited as an example of complexity, but consider the Sale of Goods Act 1979 s. 11(3):

> Whether a stipulation in a contract of sale is a condition, the breach of which may give rise to a right to treat the contract as repudiated, or a warranty, the breach of which may give rise to a claim for damages but not to a right to reject the goods and treat the contract as repudiated, depends in each case on the construction of the contract; and a stipulation may be a condition, though called a warranty in the contract.

A certain amount of legal learning has to be brought to bear in order to interpret this provision. It is not immediately clear how a condition is to be differentiated from a warranty and it might be necessary to have recourse to a solicitor unless the reader has made a detailed study of the law of contract.

In the English legal system, judges are called upon to provide authoritative interpretations of statutory provisions if the meaning is disputed because the words used are ambiguous or obscure. Sitting as a court, one or more judges may have to decide whether an infringement of the criminal law has occurred under conditions of doubt. In the context of the civil law, where the wording of a provision is ambiguous or is obscure and forms the basis of a dispute between two or more parties, it will be necessary for the court to arrive at an authoritative interpretation to resolve the dispute. The remainder of this chapter will therefore be devoted to the approach taken by the judiciary to resolve such difficult issues of interpretation.

3. Case study

Giving statutory words their normal grammatical meaning and, if technical terms are used, their normal technical meaning, will often produce a satisfactory result. Occasionally, though, this approach may produce an unsatisfactory result that is arguably at odds with the purpose of the legislation or it may produce a manifestly unjust outcome. In such situations the court is likely to consider other possible meanings but this has not always happened in the past as is well illustrated by the case of *Carrington and others* v *Therm-A-Stor Ltd* [1983]. The Court of Appeal had to consider certain provisions which have since been re-enacted (without changes) in ss 152 and 153 of the Trade Union and Labour Relations (Consolidation) Act 1992. Section 153 states that

> Where the reason or principal reason for . . . dismissal of an employee was that he was redundant but it is shown that the reason . . . why he was selected for dismissal was one of those specified in section 152(1), the dismissal shall be regarded as unfair . . .

Section 152(1)(a) states:

> the dismissal of an employee shall be regarded as unfair if the reason for it . . . was that the employee was, or proposed to become a member of an independent trade union . . .

The dispute arose because the management of the company had dismissed 20 of its employees because virtually all of the employees at the company's newly opened factory had either joined or had applied for membership of the TGWU or were actively considering doing so. The senior management was antipathetic to the activities of trade unions and when the district secretary of the union applied for 'official recognition' of the TGWU for the purpose of collective bargaining, the management instructed supervisors to select 20 employees for dismissal on the ostensible basis that they were redundant (i.e. surplus to requirements). Obviously the senior management wished to signal its disapproval with a view to inducing its workforce to abandon any trade union involvement. Most of those dismissed were trade unionists. When they presented a petition to a tribunal claiming that they had been dismissed contrary to their statutory right *not to be unfairly dismissed* because of their trade union membership, the tribunal rejected their claim because the supervisors, in selecting the employees for dismissal, did not, at the time of dismissal, take into account actual or proposed trade union membership. They dismissed the employees on a random basis. The Employment Appeal Tribunal reversed the tribunal's decision but the company then appealed to the Court of Appeal which restored the original decision of the tribunal. The leading judgement in the Court of Appeal was given by Sir John Donaldson MR He stated:

> As I read this section it is concerned solely with the dismissal of an employee and provides that it shall be regarded as unfair if the reason was that the employee had done or proposed to do one or more specified things. The reason why each of the employees was dismissed had nothing to do with anything which the employee concerned had personally done or proposed to do. The section therefore has no application.

Sir John Donaldson MR then went on to state that the reason why the dismissals had occurred was attributable to the response of management to the union's plea for recognition. As you can see, this was not a contingency *specifically* provided for in the legislation cited and therefore the men were not protected by the statutory provisions even though they were trade unionists and, but for their joining the TGWU, their dismissals would probably not have happened. Counsel representing the dismissed men argued that what is now s. 153 of the Trade Union and Labour Relations (Consolidation) Act 1992 should be interpreted to mean that the men were collectively dismissed for their trade union membership – a more purposive approach to the interpretation of the legislation. However, in his judgement, Sir John Donaldson went on to say:

> it is the duty of the court to give effect to the intention of parliament. However, the concept that 'parliament must have intended a particular result' is not without its dangers. If regard is had solely to the apparent mischief and the need for a remedy, it is only too easy for a judge to persuade himself that parliament must have intended to provide a remedy which he would himself have decreed if he had legislative power. In fact, parliament may not have taken the same view of what is a mischief, [it] may have decided as a matter of policy not to legislate for a legal remedy or [it] may simply have failed to realise that the situation could ever arise.

You may consider that this very narrow, rather literal approach has little to commend it because it resulted in an unjust outcome for the men involved. They could not be reinstated in their jobs (a possible remedy) nor were they entitled to any compensation. It is possible that a similar case might be decided differently today. The Human Rights Act 1998 can impose obligations on private legal persons and it is difficult to reconcile such a narrow interpretation of the provisions in question with the spirit of the Convention rights as contained in the Act which is to be considered later. One of the fundamental rights guaranteed is freedom of association which translates into the right to be a member of a trade union. However, the provisions in question were clearly drafted in terms of individual employee rights. Lord Millett, a Lord of Appeal in Ordinary, writing in *Statute Law Review 1999* Vol. 20 stated:

we are all purposive constructionists now; but there are limits to what even purposive construction can achieve. The language of the statute is sometimes just too plain or too closely articulated to give any room for manoeuvre.

It could be that the High Court might regard itself as bound by the ruling in *Carrington and others* v *Therm-A-Stor Ltd* as might the Court of Appeal itself. A future court could make a declaration of 'incompatibility' but this would not produce a difference of interpretation or outcome unless and until Parliament alters the wording of the provisions. A case with facts similar to those of *Carrington and others* v *Therm-A-Stor Ltd* is unlikely to arise whilst the statutory recognition provisions favouring trade unions contained in the Employment Relations Act 1999 are in force, but an incoming Conservative government could repeal these provisions.

If the meaning of a particular statutory provision is not readily apparent to a court and it wishes to consider possible alternative interpretations it can have recourse to the recognised intrinsic and extrinsic aids to construction.

4. Intrinsic aids

Judge(s) who are in doubt over the precise meaning of a provision can read the whole of the statute including the long and short titles, cross-headings and schedules. Unfortunately, the short title (e.g. The Employment Rights Act 1996) is just descriptive and is rarely of much assistance, but the long title which appears at the beginning of the enactment may be read to resolve ambiguity because it sets out the purpose of the legislation. Modern statutes rarely have preambles that commence with the word 'whereas', but when the statute does have a preamble the judge(s) can refer to it for assistance. The Schedules that appear on the end of an Act of Parliament may also be examined in cases of uncertainty, and punctuation may be relied upon in some instances to resolve ambiguity. Although the marginal notes that appear in a modern statute are not discussed in the passage of a Bill through Parliament, they may sometimes be used as an aid to interpretation. In addition to these intrinsic aids, there are three well established conventions of English usage that may be invoked by the judge(s) which can be stated as follows:

(a) General words such as 'or other' appearing at the end of a list of more particular words to save giving further examples take their meaning from the preceding list of *particular* words. This is often referred to as the *ejusdem generis* rule (meaning, of the same kind) and operates to confine the scope of the general words. In this context, see for example the case *DPP* v *Jordan* [1977].

(b) Words can be 'coloured' by their context. This is sometimes referred to as the *noscitur a sociis* rule and means simply that the meaning of a word can depend on the context in which it is used and should not be taken out of context. An example of this may be seen in the case *Pengelly* v *Bell Punch Co. Ltd* [1964].

(c) Express mention of one member of a class by implication excludes other members of the same class. This is sometimes referred to in Latin as *expressio unius exclusio alterius* which normally operates to confine the scope of a statutory provision. For an example of this see *Johnson* v *Moreton* [1980].

5. Extrinsic aids

A court may have recourse to a number of extrinsic aids. Their order of appearance should not be taken as an indication of an order of precedence. They are as follows:

(a) Authoritative evidence of the general historical climate at the time when the Act was passed.

(b) Practitioners' textbooks and dictionaries, but dictionaries must be used with care because they tend to reflect changes in usage over time.

(c) Related statutes dealing with the same subject matter can be referred to provided they were enacted prior to the statute under consideration.

(d) Statutory instruments made under the statute in question.

(e) Reports of the Law Commission or a Royal Commission may be referred to in order to identify some defect or deficiency in the pre-existing state of the common law where legislation has been enacted to deal with it.

(f) Where a statute incorporates an international treaty, the treaty itself and the historical background may be referred to as an aid to interpretation.

The Court of Appeal in *Yaxley* v *Golls* [1999] stated that where a statute has been enacted as a result of recommendations of a Law Commission report (*see* Chapter 16) it was both appropriate and permissible to consider the recommendations of that report in order to identify both the 'mischief' the Act was meant to cure and the public policy underpinning it. In *Mandla* v *Dowell Lee* [1983] the International Convention on the Elimination of All Forms of Discrimination was referred to in the House of Lords to support an interpretation of the word 'ethnic' so that it could be applied to a Sikh. The use of one or more of these intrinsic and extrinsic aids may resolve the ambiguity or obscurity, but if not, it will be necessary to consider the purpose behind the legislation in so far as it has a single or dominant purpose.

The new Civil Procedure Rules (CPR) made under the authority of the Civil Procedure Act 1997 have not been drafted with the same precision as the old Rules of the Supreme Court that they have replaced. Nevertheless, the requirement that the courts give effect to the overriding objective of the of the CPR (to deal with cases justly) means that the courts must give these rules a purposive interpretation. For multipurpose statutes such as the Trade Union and Labour Relations (Consolidation) Act 1992 or Companies Act 1985 it will only be possible to consider the purpose behind particular parts of the Act.

6. Search for the underlying purpose

Where the words used are ambiguous or altogether obscure, it will be impossible to declare a single ordinary grammatical meaning and it is therefore necessary to consider a permissible secondary meaning that accords with the purpose behind the statutory provision. In the past it has not been possible for courts to refer to the parliamentary history of legislation as the Bill was being debated in Parliament. This has often prevented the courts from adopting a purposive approach. Referring to the parliamentary history entails reading Hansard (an edited version of the proceedings in both chambers of the legislature) and committee reports with a view to ascertaining the underlying intention behind the legislation. In *Pepper (HM inspector of Taxes) v Hart* [1993], the House of Lords finally abrogated this self-denying ordinance and courts may now refer to Hansard if a statutory provision is ambiguous or otherwise obscure.

The appeal to the House of Lords in this case was made by the Inspector of Taxes who wished to tax a number of teachers and the bursar of an independent school under the Finance Act 1976 s. 61(1) on the basis that they had received a benefit in kind in respect of having the full fees waived for their children who were attending the school. Although the school was not full, the 20 per cent of normal fees paid by the teachers did cover the additional cost to the school of educating their children. According to the Finance Act 1976 s. 63, the parents in question should be taxed on the 'cash equivalent' of the benefit which was 'an amount equal to the cost of the benefit'. This cost was 'the amount of any expense incurred in or in connection with its provision'. Whilst the Inspector of Taxes argued that they should pay an amount in tax related to the full fees normally payable, the parents argued that their tax liability should be linked to the additional cost to the school of educating their children which was met by the fees actually paid. Since the fees paid covered the costs incurred, it was argued that 'the cash equivalent of the benefit' was zero as was their tax liability in this regard. Six of the seven Law Lords considered that the Finance Act 1976 s. 63

was ambiguous in that the 'expense incurred in or in connection with' could be interpreted either as being the additional cost to the school of providing the benefit to the parents in question or a proportion of the total cost incurred in providing education at the school for all children. By referring to the parliamentary history of the Bill it was apparent that the Financial Secretary to the Treasury during the committee stage of the Bill had made it clear that ss 61 and 63 should be interpreted on the basis that in-house benefits, particularly concessionary education for the children of teachers, should be assessed on the additional cost to the employer and not on the proportion of the total cost of providing education at the school for all children. Thus the parents had no tax liability to meet on this benefit because on the interpretation adopted it was equivalent to zero.

Six of the seven Law Lords ruled that parliamentary materials could be referred to where:

(a) the legislation was ambiguous or obscure or the literal meaning led to absurdity

(b) the material relied upon consisted of statements by a minister or other promoter of the Bill which led to the enactment of the legislation together, if necessary, with such other parliamentary material as was necessary to understand such statements and their effect

(c) the statements relied on were clear.

This approach was subsequently taken by the House of Lords in *Warwickshire C.C.* v *Johnson* [1993] where the manager of a high street electrical appliance store was charged with an offence under the Consumer Protection Act 1987 s. 20(1). This involved the giving of a misleading indication of price. The issue to be resolved by the House of Lords was whether the manager, as distinct from the company of which he was an employee, could be prosecuted for the offence. Section 20(2) stated:

> a person shall be guilty of an offence if – (a) in the course of any business of his, he has given an indication to any consumers which, after it was given, has become misleading as mentioned in subsection (1) above . . .

In giving the leading judgement in the House of Lords, Lord Roskill referred to the official record of the proceedings on the Bill in Lord's chamber in which it was noted that there was no intention to prosecute employees for misleading price indications so that the words 'any business of his' were interpreted to refer to the employer, not an employee.

The material which may be relied upon is specified in a Supreme Court Practice Note of 20 December 1994 reported in [1995] 1 All ER 234 as parliamentary proceedings recorded in the official reports of either House of Parliament as they appear in Hansard. Other reports of parliamentary proceedings may not be relied upon. According to the Note, any party intending to refer to any extract from Hansard in support of any such argument as is permitted by the decisions in *Pepper (Inspector of Taxes) v Hart* and the earlier case of *Pickstone v Freemans Plc* [1982] must, unless the judge otherwise directs, serve upon all other parties and the court copies of any such extract together with a brief summary of the argument intended to be based upon such an extract. Subsequently, in *McKay v Northern Ireland Public Service Alliance* [1995] it was indicated that White Papers may be referred to in order to identify any 'mischief' that a statute was enacted to cure where this can be demonstrated to be the case.

7. Adding words to the text

Judges may add to the words of a statute in order to prevent a provision from having a result that is clearly contrary to the underlying intention of the legislation. This may be illustrated in relation to a series of cases which have focused on the interpretation of the Race Relations Act 1976 ss 1(1)(a) and 4(2)(c). The former provides that

> A person discriminates against another in any circumstances relevant for the purpose of any provision of this Act if –
> (a) on racial grounds he treats that other person less favourably than he treats or would treat other persons;

and the latter that

> It is unlawful for a person, in the case of a person employed by him at an establishment in Great Britain to discriminate against that employee –
> (c) by dismissing him, or subjecting him to any other detriment.

The overriding objective of this statute is to make it unlawful for a person to engage in racial discrimination in the employment sphere and elsewhere. In *Zarczynska v Levy* [1979] the complainant was dismissed for serving a black customer contrary to her employer's express instructions. She had not been employed long enough to be able to make a claim for unfair dismissal under the relevant legislation so she was obliged to bring her claim under the Race Relations Act 1976. The tribunal that initially heard the complaint adopted a literal interpretation of the Act and decided that there was no racial discrimination because she was not dismissed because of *her own colour*. The Employment Appeal Tribunal declined to take such a narrow literal interpretation of the statutory provisions and decided that racial discrimination could include treating a person less favourably on the grounds of *another's colour*. In the later case of *Showboat Entertainment Centre Ltd v Owens* [1984] a white employee was dismissed for refusing to carry out an instruction from the employer to exclude young blacks from an entertainment centre. Although such an instruction was unlawful under the Race Relations Act 1976 s. 30, only the Commission for Racial Equality is empowered to take enforcement action of that section. Following its decision in *Zarczynska* v *Levy* the Employment Appeal Tribunal decided that Parliament could not have intended to leave an employee without a remedy in such a situation – the phrase 'on racial grounds' in s. 1(1)(a) was interpreted as including discrimination on the grounds of another's race, colour etc. A similar approach was taken in *Weathersfield Ltd* v *Sargent* [1998] when a receptionist felt impelled to resign because she could not bring herself to comply with instructions from her employer to discriminate against black customers. This was deemed unlawful discrimination on the grounds of customers' race which had caused the necessary 'detriment' in the form of constructive dismissal.

Apart from being able to add some words to a statute, the House of Lords has recently restated the right of the judiciary to correct drafting errors in *Inco Europe Ltd and others* v *First Choice Distribution and others* [2000]. Lord Nicholls in giving judgement, with which all four of the other Law Lords concurred, said:

> the courts exercise considerable caution before adding or omitting or substituting words. Before interpreting a statute in this way the court must be abundantly sure of three matters: (1) the intended purpose of the statute or provision in question; (2) that by inadvertence the draftsman and Parliament failed to give effect to that purpose in the provision in question; and (3) the substance of the provision Parliament would have made, although not necessarily the precise words Parliament would have used, had the error in the Bill been noticed.

He stated that the third condition was of crucial importance otherwise any attempt to determine the meaning of the statutory provision in question would cross the boundary between construction (interpretation) and judicial legislation which would not be permissible. In the particular circumstances of the case, Lord Nicholls ruled that the three conditions were fulfilled and the House of Lords then proceeded to correct a drafting error in the Arbitration Act 1996 Schedule 3 para. 37(2). He also indicated that even where the above criteria are satisfied, a court may on occasion feel unable to alter the precise wording of the statute, especially one in the sphere of the criminal law where a strict interpretation is more usual. Once a court does give an authoritative pronouncement of the meaning of a statutory provision it takes the form of a precedent and if the pronouncement is made in the House of Lords it will be binding on all lower courts. Nevertheless, some existing precedents will require reconsideration in the light of the Human Rights Act 1998.

8. Human Rights Act 1998

The European Convention on Human Rights and Fundamental Freedoms has not been incorporated into UK law as such and so there is nothing equivalent to the doctrine of direct effect that operates in relation to EU law. The legislation imposes human rights obligations mainly on public authorities. Persons who consider that their Convention rights have been infringed by a public authority can rely on these rights embodied in the Human Rights Act 1998 Schedule 1 as a defence in criminal or other public law proceedings or as a basis for an appeal. Alternatively, they may seek judicial review. The term 'public authority' against whom these rights may be enforced includes government departments, executive agencies, police, immigration officers, quangos, local authorities as well as courts and tribunals. It is expressly provided that Parliament is not a public authority for the purposes of the Act but the House of Lords in its judicial capacity is a public authority. The basic idea is that a victim or potential victim can invoke the Convention rights to prevent the misuse of power. It is likely that a public company that is exercising a public function, for example a company operating a remand centre or prison, could be subject to the provisions of the Act. Moreover, employees of the bodies indicated above should be able to enforce a number of Convention rights against their employers if their employers can be regarded as emanations of the state and if the employees concerned can establish that they are victims as required by s. 7(1). The term 'victim' is defined by s. 7(7).

Article 1 of the Convention requires that member states must ensure that everyone within their jurisdiction can enjoy the rights and freedoms contained within it. The UK has fulfilled this requirement by simply enacting the Human Rights Act 1998. The rights and freedoms set out in Schedule 1 are shown in full in the appendix to this chapter but are merely outlined below to facilitate discussion:

- Article 2   The right to life
- Article 3   A prohibition of torture, inhuman or degrading treatment or punishment
- Article 4   A prohibition of slavery or forced labour
- Article 5   The right to liberty and security
- Article 6   The right to a fair trial
- Article 7   The right not to be punished unless it is sanctioned by law and prohibition
- Article 8   The right to respect for private life and family life, the home and correspondence
- Article 9   The right to freedom of thought, conscience and religion

- Article 10 The right to freedom of expression including the right to receive information
- Article 11 The right to freedom of assembly and freedom of association including the right to form and join a trade union
- Article 12 The right to marry and found a family
- Article 13 The requirement of an effective remedy for victims. (This has not been specifically incorporated into Schedule 1 as such)
- Article 14 The prohibition of discrimination in relation to the enjoyment of the rights and freedoms guaranteed by the Convention.

Section 1(2) of the Act provides that the above Articles have effect subject to any designated derogation (opt out) or reservation as defined in ss 14 and 15 as well as Schedule 3. Article 13 of the Convention is given effect through s. 7 of the Act, whereby Convention rights can be raised and argued before national courts by a victim, and s. 8 whereby the judges may grant whatever relief or remedy they consider 'just and appropriate'. Articles 2, 3, 4(1) and 7 as contained in Schedule 1 are absolute and cannot be qualified in any circumstances, but Articles 4(2) and 4(3), 5 and 6 are capable of derogation but they are not to be otherwise balanced against the wider public interest. Articles 8, 9, 10 and 11 are qualified rights and can be balanced against the wider public interest as specified. In addition to the above Articles, there are rights under Protocols to the Convention that the UK has ratified. Under the First Protocol, Articles 1–3, there is the right to peaceful enjoyment of one's possessions, the right to education and a right to free elections. Under the Sixth Protocol, Articles 1–2, there is a prohibition on the death penalty in the absence of war.

As indicated already, the Convention operates primarily, albeit not exclusively, in the sphere of public law. According to s. 6(1) it is unlawful for a public authority to act in a way that is at variance with the rights designated as Convention rights. However, this is immediately qualified by s. 6(2) which provides that s. 6(1) does not apply if, as a result of one or more provisions of primary legislation, the authority could not have acted differently. There is a similar provision in the case of subordinate legislation which cannot be given effect in a way that is compatible with the Convention rights. On a literal interpretation, those through whom a public authority acts (its employees and agents) do not incur personal liability under s. 6(1). Thus the liability of a public authority under the Act is incurred directly and not vicariously. Section 6(1) forms the basis of the so-called interpretative obligation which is supplemented by ss 2 and 3. Section 3(1) of the Act requires that all primary and secondary legislation is to be read and given effect in a way that is compatible with the Convention *in so far as it is possible to do so*. It does not matter whether the legislation in question was passed before or after the Act and the general stipulation regarding interpretation applies to any agency administering the legislation and not just the courts. The House of Lords held in *R* v *A* [2001] that the Youth Justice and Criminal Evidence Act 1999 s. 41 should be interpreted so that it is compatible with Article 6(1) even though a literal interpretation would indicate that complainants must be protected from questioning in court concerning their sexual history when they allege rape. Section 2 of the Act requires all courts and tribunals that are called upon to decide a question that involves the application of a Convention right to take account of the jurisprudence of the European Court of Human Rights, the opinions of the European Commission of Human Rights (now defunct) and the decisions of the Committee of Ministers. This requirement does not, however, oblige the national courts to follow this jurisprudence.

It should be possible for a court to interpret the national legislation in question according to the particular Convention right(s) in issue where a minister has made a statement of compatibility prior to the Second Reading of the Bill under s. 19. Such a statement is not definitive, however, as the minister has merely given an honest opinion albeit with the benefit of legal advice. The difficulties are more likely to arise with older legislation. If the wording of a provision is quite clearly at variance with the right(s) in Schedule 1, then the provision must be interpreted according to its wording. Although s. 4 enables the court to make a declaration of incompatibility, according to s. 4(6) this does not affect the validity of the provision which must continue to be applied unless and until it is changed by Parliament. Nor will it affect the outcome of the case. Section 5(2) provides that the appropriate minister is entitled to be joined as a party to the proceedings if a court is contemplating making a declaration of incompatibility under s. 4(2) so that he/she can put the government's case. If the proceedings are criminal, where government has been made a party to the proceedings, it may appeal to the House of Lords against a declaration of incompatibility. In *Wilson* v *First County Trust Ltd* [2001] the Court of Appeal made a declaration of incompatibility in relation to the Consumer Credit Act 1974 s. 127(3) on the basis that it was not compatible with the rights guaranteed under Article 6(1) of the Convention and Article 1 of the First Protocol as set out in the Human Rights Act 1998. The House of Lords in *R (on the application of Alconbury Developments Ltd)* v *Secretary of State for the Environment, Transport and the Regions* [2001] overturned a declaration of incompatibility made by the Divisional Court of Queen's Bench in relation to the minister's refusal to grant planning permission. The House of Lords took the view that the exercise by the minister of his powers under various statues was not incompatible with Article 6(1).

The Convention itself is a 'living text' and the European Court of Human Rights does not therefore follow a system of binding precedent as the English courts do and which was explained in Chapter 4. In interpreting the Convention, European Court of Human Rights follows the Vienna Convention on the Law of Treaties 1969. Accordingly, divergences could occur between the interpretation of the Convention by the European Court of Human Rights in Strasbourg and the application of Convention rights by courts in the UK.

9. European law

It is clear from the ruling of the European Court of Justice in Case 26/62 *NV Algemene Transporten-Expeditie Onderneming Van Gend en Loos* v *Nederlandse Administratie der Belastingen* [1963] that national courts must apply all directly effective EU law. It is vital to the functioning of the EU that all EU legal provisions are interpreted uniformly so that there are no significant variations in the application of the law between the various member states. The authors of the EC Treaty were aware of the potential problem and what is now Article 234 (formally Article 177) is intended to harmonise the way in which member states ultimately apply EU law. It provides:

> The Court of Justice shall have jurisdiction to give preliminary rulings concerning:
> (a) the interpretation of this Treaty;
> (b) the validity and interpretation of acts of the institutions of the Community and;
> (c) the interpretation of the statutes of bodies established by an act of the Council.
> Where such a question is raised before any court or tribunal of a Member State, that court or tribunal may, if it considers that a decision on the question is necessary to enable it to give judgement, request the Court of Justice to give a ruling thereon.
>
> Where any such question is raised in a case pending before a court or tribunal of a Member State against whose decisions there is no judicial remedy under national law, that court or tribunal shall bring the matter before the Court of Justice.

It is clear that the ECJ may give authoritative interpretations of EU law whether in the form of Treaty provisions or legislative acts of the institutions as set out in Article 249 EC. Yet, the national court is to be the sole judge of whether a preliminary reference under Article 234 EC is required and the ECJ will not review the exercise of this discretion. According to the second paragraph of Article 234 EC, courts and tribunals whose decisions give rise to a remedy in national law have a discretion in deciding whether or not to request a preliminary ruling on points of EU law they are called upon to apply. Bingham J. (as he then was) in *Commissioners of Customs and*

Excise v *Samex Ap S* [1983] highlighted the advantages of seeking a ruling from the ECJ when trying to interpret the 'guidelines' that had been laid down by Lord Denning MR in the earlier case of *H.P. Bulmer Ltd* v *J. Bollinger SA* [1974]. He said:

> Sitting as a judge in a national court, asked to decide questions of Community law, I am very conscious of the advantages enjoyed by the Court of Justice. It has a panoramic view of the Community and its institutions, a detailed knowledge of the Treaties and of much subordinate legislation made under them, and an intimate familiarity with the functioning of the Community market which no national judge denied the collective experience of the Court of Justice could hope to achieve. Where questions of administrative intention and practice arise the Court of Justice can receive submissions from the Community institutions, as also where relations between the Community and non-Member States are in issue. Where the interests of Member States are affected they can intervene to make their views known . . . Where comparison falls to be made between Community texts in different languages, all texts being equally authentic, the multinational Court of Justice is equipped to carry out the task in a way which no national judge, whatever his linguistic skills, could rival. The interpretation of Community instruments involves very often not the process familiar to common lawyers of laboriously extracting the meaning from words used but the more creative process of applying flesh to a spare and loosely constructed skeleton. The choice between alternative submissions may turn not on purely legal considerations, but on a broader view of what the orderly development of the Community requires. These are matters which the Court of Justice is very much better placed to assess and determine than a national court.

Bingham J then referred the issues of EU law in question to the ECJ for a preliminary ruling. An application under Article 234 EC can be made by both civil and criminal courts and in the case of the latter, a reference is likely to be made because a provision of EU law has been raised as a defence in criminal proceedings. However, the mere fact that a party asserts that the resolution of the case necessitates the interpretation of EU law does not of itself mean that a court or tribunal is compelled to consider that a question has been raised within Article 234 EC. This is a matter for the national court to determine. It is clear, nevertheless, from the third paragraph of Article 234 EC that where a matter of EU law is raised in a case pending before a national court or tribunal against whose decision there is no remedy in national law, that court or tribunal is supposed to refer the question(s) to the ECJ. This does not mean that only the House of Lords is obliged to make a reference because the ECJ in Case 6/64 *Costa* v *ENEL* [1964] was prepared to accept a reference from a *guidice conciliatore* in Milan. This was because the sum of money involved being so small, the magistrate had final jurisdiction in the particular case. Thus paragraph 3 applies to any court or tribunal from whose decision there is no appeal such as the

National Insurance Commissioners. Balcombe LJ set out the approach that would be taken by the Court of Appeal in *Chiron Corporation* v *Murex Diagnostics Ltd* [1995] when he said:

> Except in those cases . . . where the Court of Appeal is the court of last resort, the Court of Appeal is not obliged to make a reference to the ECJ . . . If the Court of Appeal does not make a reference to the ECJ, and gives its final judgement on the appeal, then the House of Lords becomes the court of last resort. If either the Court of Appeal or the House of Lords grants leave to appeal, then there is no problem. If the Court of Appeal refuses leave to appeal, and the House of Lords is presented with an application for leave to appeal, before it refuses leave it should consider whether an issue of Community law arises which is necessary for its decision (whether to grant or refuse leave) and is not *acte clair*. If it considers that a reference is requisite, it will take such action as it may consider appropriate in the particular case.

The above statement would have been influenced by the ruling of the ECJ in Case 283/81 *CILFIT* v *Ministro della Sanità* [1982]. In that case the ECJ ruled that even courts of final resort are not obliged to request a preliminary reference where the answer to the question(s) on EU law cannot affect the outcome of the case. The question(s) raised must be central to the disposal of the case. Even where the questions of EU law are essential to disposing of the case, the ECJ ruled that courts of final resort are under no obligation to refer if

(a) the point has already been decided in a previous ruling by the ECJ irrespective of the form of the proceedings and even if the questions raised were not completely identical, or

(b) the correct application of EU law is so obvious as to leave no scope for any reasonable doubt as to the manner in which the question raised is to be resolved.

In relation to (a) above, since the ECJ is not absolutely bound by its previous decisions, a UK court is free to refer a point of law if it wishes the ECJ to reconsider its earlier ruling. The ECJ may, of course, merely restate its earlier ruling, but it may not. Previous rulings therefore have some value as precedents and there is now a considerable body of such case law to guide national courts. Before a UK court can take upon itself the responsibility under (b) above it must be convinced that the matter is equally obvious to the courts of other member states and to the ECJ. The Court made it clear in Case 283/81 *CILFIT* v *Ministro della Sanità* that if a national court were to assume responsibility for interpreting EU law it should bear in mind the specific characteristics of EU law, the particular difficulties to which its interpretation gives rise and the risk of divergences in judicial decisions within the EU. Bearing in mind what was said in *Commissioners of Customs and Excise* v *Samex Ap S* it might seem that UK courts would have to be very confident indeed to assume responsibility for interpreting a provision of EU law in the absence of an earlier ruling by the ECJ. However, UK courts make fewer references under Article 234 EC than some smaller member states.

The national proceedings must be suspended pending the outcome of the reference under Article 234 EC which will normally be couched in terms of a set of general questions of law. In responding, the ECJ cannot rule on the facts of the case or on the validity of national law as such. Its ruling will focus on the interpretation of EU law only and it is then for the UK court to apply the ruling to the case under consideration. As was indicated in Chapter 7, the Article 234 EC procedure has been responsible for the extensive development of the jurisprudence of the ECJ.

The ECJ is far more flexible in its approach to the interpretation of EU legislation than UK courts are in relation to national legislation. The ECJ is not always over-concerned with the precise wording of a provision. Under conditions of doubt it will usually look to the aims of the Community as set in Article 2 of the EC Treaty and consider the general context and purpose of the legislation. The treaties in particular are drafted in quite general terms. The ECJ has therefore felt the need to engage in a certain amount of 'judicial activism' in order to fill gaps in the Treaty, drawing its inspiration from the general aims of the Community and from the general principles of law that it has adopted from the legal systems of various member states. This has already been considered in Chapter 7 in relation to the doctrine of direct effect, supremacy and state liability.

10. Case study

The approach of the ECJ to the specific problem of interpretation may be examined by looking at its jurisprudence in the area of sex discrimination as a case study. Having ruled in Case 43/75 *Defrenne* v *SABENA* [1976] that Article 119 EC (now Article 141) had direct effect, it has been concerned to eradicate differences between men and women in relation to 'pay'. The original wording of Article 119 was as follows:

> Each Member State shall . . . ensure and subsequently maintain the application of the principle that men and women should receive equal pay for equal work.
>
> For the purpose of this Article, 'pay' means the ordinary basic or minimum wage or salary and any other consideration, whether in cash or in kind, which the worker receives, directly or indirectly, in respect of his employment from his employer.
>
> Equal pay without discrimination based on sex means:
> (a) that pay for the same work at piece rates shall be calculated on the basis of the same unit of measurement;
> (b) that pay for work at the same rates shall be the same for the same type of job.

Although the concept of 'pay' was quite widely defined in Article 119 EC, the Court was prepared to give it an even wider meaning. In Case 69/80 *Worringham* v *Lloyds Bank* [1981], a female employee contested the legality of supplementary payments made by the employer to male members of staff under the age of 25 for the purpose of compensating them for having to make contributions to the employer's occupational pension scheme. The ECJ ruled that these payments were 'pay' and since they had not been made to female staff there had been an infringement of Article 119. In Case 12/81 *Garland* v *British Rail Engineering* [1982] the ECJ ruled that the term 'pay' could extend to special travel facilities granted to ex-employees after retirement even though they were not based on a contractual entitlement. In Case 170/84 *Bilka-Kaufhaus GmbH* v *Weber von Hartz* [1986] the company operated a non-contributory pension scheme but part-time employees were only eligible to join after they had worked for the company for at least 15 years. This restriction was not imposed on full-time employees, but because most of the part-time employees were women, the complainant alleged that the scheme was discriminatory. Since the pension scheme was contractual, the ECJ ruled that it came within Article 119 so the difference in treatment, as it affected part-timers, was contrary to Article 119. In Case 171/88 *Rinner-Kuhn* v *FWW* [1989] the ECJ ruled that German legislation excluding part-time workers (most of whom were women) from an entitlement to sick pay was contrary to Article 119 unless objectively justified (a matter for the national court) because the continued payment of wages to workers during sickness came within Article 119. In Case C-262/88 *Barber* v *Guardian Royal Exchange Assurance Group* [1990] the ECJ not only ruled that differential retirement ages for men and women under an occupational pension scheme that operated to the disadvantage of men by way of their having to wait for pension benefits was unlawful, it also ruled that redundancy payments constituted 'pay' within the meaning of Article 119.

11. Transposed legislation

Interpreting subordinate legislation drafted to incorporate a directive according to the ordinary grammatical meaning of the words used will often be unsatisfactory especially where this does not accord with the way in which Community law is developing. The extensive preamble to a directive may be particularly useful as an aid to interpretation of such subordinate legislation where there is uncertainty, but the UK courts must follow the relevant case law of ECJ. The House of Lords has usually adopted a purposive approach to the interpretation of subordinate legislation that has been enacted to incorporate a directive. In *Litster* v *Forth Dry Dock and Engineering Co. Ltd* [1989] their Lordships gave a purposive interpretation to Regulation 5(3) of the Transfer of Undertakings (Protection of Employment) Regulations 1981 which were made to implement Directive 77/187/EEC. The directive makes possible the automatic transfer of the contracts of employment of workers, with all their existing rights and obligations preserved, when a business is transferred to a new owner. It also protects workers from dismissal by the seller or new owner of the business unless the dismissals are permitted by the limited exceptions specified in the directive. Their Lordships added the words *'or would have been so employed if he had not been unfairly dismissed in the circumstances described in Regulation 8(1)'* to the relevant statutory instrument. They did this so that the employees of an insolvent company who were dismissed because a business is sold to a new purchaser would have their employment transferred automatically to the new purchaser. Their Lordships' aim was to defeat the then widespread practice in the UK of dismissing employees prior to the transfer of the business leaving the new buyer to take on as many (or as few) of the workers as were needed on whatever terms that were thought suitable at the time. These would usually be much inferior to those previously enjoyed. Thus their Lordships actually read words into the statutory instrument so that it would be in conformity with the developing case law of the ECJ.

As has been mentioned previously, the ECJ has ruled in Case C-106/89 *Marleasing SA* v *La Commercial Internacional de Alimentacion SA* [1990] that national courts should interpret their national legislation whenever possible in such a way as to ensure that the objectives of EU law are achieved. The emphasis is on the phrase 'whenever possible' and, of course, there are significant parts of UK national law that are untouched and therefore unaffected by EU law. Nevertheless, the obligation imposed on national courts by the ECJ is particularly relevant to the interpretation of subordinate legislation made to incorporate an EU directive.

Appendix

Human Rights Act 1998

Schedule 1
THE ARTICLES

PART 1
THE CONVENTION
RIGHTS AND FREEDOMS

ARTICLE 2
RIGHT TO LIFE

1. Everyone's right to life shall be protected by law. No one shall be deprived of his life intentionally save in the execution of a sentence of a court following his conviction of a crime for which this penalty is provided by law.

2. Deprivation of life shall not be regarded as inflicted in contravention of this Article when it results from the use of force which is no more than absolutely necessary:

(a) in defence of any person from unlawful violence;
(b) in order to effect a lawful arrest or to prevent the escape of a person lawfully detained;
(c) in action lawfully taken for the purpose of quelling a riot or insurrection.

ARTICLE 3
PROHIBITION OF TORTURE

No one shall be subjected to torture or to inhuman or degrading treatment or punishment.

ARTICLE 4
PROHIBITION OF SLAVERY AND FORCED LABOUR

1. No one shall be held in slavery or servitude.
2. No one shall be required to perform forced or compulsory labour.
3. For the purpose of this Article the term 'forced or compulsory labour' shall not include:

(a) any work required to be done in the ordinary course of detention imposed according to the provisions of Article 5 of this Convention or during conditional release from such detention;
(b) any service of a military character or, in case of conscientious objectors in countries where they are recognised, service exacted instead of compulsory military service;
(c) any service exacted in case of an emergency or calamity threatening the life or well-being of the community;
(d) any work or service which forms part of normal civic obligations.

ARTICLE 5
RIGHT TO LIBERTY AND SECURITY

1. Everyone has the right to liberty and security of person. No one shall be deprived of his liberty save in the following cases and in accordance with a procedure prescribed by law:

(a) the lawful detention of a person after conviction by a competent court;
(b) the lawful arrest or detention of a person for non-compliance with the lawful order of a court or in order to secure the fulfilment of any obligation prescribed by law;
(c) the lawful arrest or detention of a person effected for the purpose of bringing him before the competent legal authority on reasonable suspicion of having committed an offence or when it is reasonably considered necessary to prevent his committing an offence or fleeing after having done so;
(d) the detention of a minor by lawful order for the purpose of educational supervision or his lawful detention for the purpose of bringing him before the competent legal authority;
(e) the lawful detention of persons for the prevention of the spreading of infectious diseases, of persons of unsound mind, alcoholics or drug addicts or vagrants;

146

(f) the lawful arrest or detention of a person to prevent his effecting an unauthorised entry into the country or of a person against whom action is being taken with a view to deportation or extradition.

2. Everyone who is arrested shall be informed promptly, in a language which he understands, of the reasons for his arrest and of any charge against him.

3. Everyone arrested or detained in accordance with the provisions of paragraph 1(c) of this Article shall be brought promptly before a judge or other officer authorised by law to exercise judicial power and shall be entitled to trial within a reasonable time or to release pending trial. Release may be conditioned by guarantees to appear for trial.

4. Everyone who is deprived of his liberty by arrest or detention shall be entitled to take proceedings by which the lawfulness of his detention shall be decided speedily by a court and his release ordered if the detention is not lawful.

5. Everyone who has been the victim of arrest or detention in contravention of the provisions of this Article shall have an enforceable right to compensation.

ARTICLE 6
RIGHT TO A FAIR TRIAL

1. In the determination of his civil rights and obligations or of any criminal charge against him, everyone is entitled to a fair and public hearing within a reasonable time by an independent and impartial tribunal established by law. Judgement shall be pronounced publicly but the press and public may be excluded from all or part of the trial in the interest of morals, public order or national security in a democratic society, where the interests of juveniles or the protection of the private life of the parties so require, or to the extent strictly necessary in the opinion of the court in special circumstances where publicity would prejudice the interests of justice.

2. Everyone charged with a criminal offence shall be presumed innocent until proved guilty according to law.

3. Everyone charged with a criminal offence has the following minimum rights:

(a) to be informed promptly, in a language which he understands and in detail, of the nature and cause of the accusation against him;

(b) to have adequate time and facilities for the preparation of his defence;

(c) to defend himself in person or through legal assistance of his own choosing or, if he has not sufficient means to pay for legal assistance, to be given it free when the interests of justice so require;

(d) to examine or have examined witnesses against him and to obtain the attendance and examination of witnesses on his behalf under the same conditions as witnesses against him;

(e) to have the free assistance of an interpreter if he cannot understand or speak the language used in court.

ARTICLE 7
NO PUNISHMENT WITHOUT LAW

1. No one shall be held guilty of any criminal offence on account of any act or omission which did not constitute a criminal offence under national or international law at the time when it was committed. Nor shall a heavier penalty be imposed than the one that was applicable at the time the criminal offence was committed.

2. This Article shall not prejudice the trial and punishment of any person for any act or omission which, at the time when it was committed, was criminal according to the general principles of law recognised by civilised nations.

ARTICLE 8
RIGHT TO RESPECT FOR PRIVATE AND FAMILY LIFE

1. Everyone has the right to respect for his private and family life, his home and his correspondence.
2. There shall be no interference by a public authority with the exercise of this right except such as is in accordance with the law and is necessary in a democratic society in the interests of national security, public safety or the economic well-being of the country, for the prevention of disorder or crime, for the protection of health or morals, or for the protection of the rights and freedoms of others.

ARTICLE 9
FREEDOM OF THOUGHT, CONSCIENCE AND RELIGION

1. Everyone has the right to freedom of thought, conscience and religion; this right includes freedom to change his religion or belief and freedom either alone or in community with others and in public or private, to manifest his religion or belief, in worship, teaching, practice and observance.
2. Freedom to manifest one's religion or beliefs shall be subject only to such limitations as are prescribed by law and are necessary in a democratic society in the interests of public safety, for the protection of public order, health or morals, or for the protection of the rights and freedoms of others.

ARTICLE 10
FREEDOM OF EXPRESSION

1. Everyone has the right to freedom of expression. This right shall include freedom to hold opinions and to receive and impart information and ideas without interference by public authority and regardless of frontiers. This Article shall not prevent States from requiring the licensing of broadcasting, television or cinema enterprises.
2. The exercise of these freedoms, since it carries with it duties and responsibilities, may be subject to such formalities, conditions, restrictions or penalties as are prescribed by law and are necessary in a democratic society, in the interests of national security, territorial integrity or public safety, for the prevention of disorder or crime, for the protection of health or morals, for the protection of the reputation or rights of others, for preventing the disclosure of information received in confidence, or for maintaining the authority and impartiality of the judiciary.

ARTICLE 11
FREEDOM OF ASSEMBLY AND ASSOCIATION

1. Everyone has the right to freedom of peaceful assembly and to freedom of association with others, including the right to form and to join trade unions for the protection of his interests.
2. No restrictions shall be placed on the exercise of these rights other than such as are prescribed by law and are necessary in a democratic society in the interests

of national security or public safety, for the prevention of disorder or crime, for the protection of health or morals or for the protection of the rights and freedoms of others. This Article shall not prevent the imposition of lawful restrictions on the exercise of these rights by members of the armed forces, of the police or of the administration of the State.

ARTICLE 12
RIGHT TO MARRY

Men and women of marriageable age have the right to marry and to found family, according to the national laws governing the exercise of this right.

ARTICLE 14
PROHIBITION OF DISCRIMINATION

The enjoyment of the rights and freedoms set forth in this Convention shall be secured without discrimination on any ground such as sex, race, colour, language, religion, political or other opinion, national or social origin, association with a national minority, property, birth or other status.

ARTICLE 16
RESTRICTIONS ON POLITICAL ACTIVITY OF ALIENS

Nothing in Articles 10, 11 and 14 shall be regarded as preventing the High Contracting Parties from imposing restrictions on the political activity of aliens.

ARTICLE 17
PROHIBITION OF ABUSE OF RIGHTS

Nothing in this Convention may be interpreted as implying for any State, group or person any right to engage in any activity or perform any act aimed at the destruction of any of the rights and freedoms set forth herein or at their limitation to a greater extent than is provided for in the Convention.

ARTICLE 18
LIMITATION ON USE OF RESTRICTIONS ON RIGHTS

The restrictions permitted under this Convention to the said rights and freedoms shall not be applied for any purpose other than those for which they have been prescribed.

Progress test

1. Are the meanings of statutory provisions always self-evident? What sense can you make of the Misrepresentation Act 1967 s. 2(1) and the Sale of Goods Act 1979 s. 11(3)?

2. Could an interpretation that focuses merely on the ordinary meaning of the words used in an Act of Parliament be regarded as a purposive approach?

3. Do you see anything wrong with the way in which the Court of Appeal interpreted the provisions from what is now the Trade Union and Labour Relations (Consolidation) Act 1992 in *Carrington* v *Therm-A-Stor*?

4. Did the Employment Appeal Tribunal adopt a purposive approach in *Zarczynska* v *Levy*? If so, why? If not, why not?

5. Identify the 'intrinsic aids' to interpretation.

6. What do you understand by the term 'extrinsic aids' to interpretation? Give examples.

7. What obligation is imposed on UK courts by the Human Rights Act 1998 with regard to the interpretation of legislation?

8. If the Act had been in operation at the time that the Court of Appeal considered *Carrington* v *Therm-A-Stor*, do you think that it might have affected the outcome?

9. If the provisions of a UK statute are clearly contrary to the Human Rights Act 1998 do the UK courts have the power to disapply it?

10. How does the ECJ approach the task of interpreting EU law in general?

11. If a court or tribunal in the UK is unsure about the interpretation of EU law, what can and should it do?

12. When is a court or tribunal in the UK bound to refer a question of the interpretation under Article 234 EC?

Further reading

Books

Adams, J.N. and R. Brownsword (1999) *Understanding Law* (London: Fontana, pp. 80–106).

Bell, J. and G. Engle (1995) *Cross on Statutory Interpretation* (London: Butterworths).

Craig, P. and G. de Burca (1998) *EU Law: Text and materials* (Oxford: Oxford University Press, chapter 10).

Langan, P. St J. (1980) *Maxwell on the Interpretation of Statutes* (Bombay: Tripathi).

Twining, W. and D. Miers (1999) *How To Do Things With Rules* (London: Butterworths, chapter 10).

Zander, M. (1999) *The Law Making Process* (London: Butterworths, chapter 3).

Articles

Bennion, F. (2000) 'What interpretation is "possible" under section 3(1) of the Human Rights Act 1998?', *Public Law* Spring.

Hartley, T. (1996) 'The European Court, judicial objectivity and the constitution of the European Union', *The Law Quarterly Review* Vol. 95, January.

Millett, Lord (2000) 'Construing statutes', *Statute Law Review* Vol. 20, No. 2.
Morris, D. (2000) 'The Human Rights Act 1998: too many loose ends?', *Statute Law Review* Vol. 21, No. 2.
Wade, Sir W. (2000) 'Horizons of horizontality', *The Law Quarterly Review* Vol. 116, April.

Useful website

Information on the European Convention on Human Rights and Fundamental Freedoms and on the European Court of Human Rights can be found at www.echr.coe.int/

PART THREE

Law in action

9

Resourcing legal services

1. Introduction

Since the 1950s, successive governments have made funding available from general taxation to assist persons of limited financial means to ensure that they have been able to obtain legal advice. Funding has also been made available from the public purse to enable such persons to bring and defend civil claims and to defend themselves if charged with criminal offences. Over the years, public spending on what became known as 'legal aid' grew massively and governments tried, without much success, to control this expenditure. Shortly after taking office in 1997, the Labour government, in the person of the Lord Chancellor, appointed Sir Peter Middleton to conduct a review of civil legal aid in the context of an overall review of the civil justice system and then in 1998, the government produced its White Paper entitled *Modernising Justice*. In the section dealing with civil legal aid, the government stated that it did not believe that the existing system was capable of meeting its objectives and priorities. The White paper drew the following conclusions:

(a) Legal aid is too heavily biased towards expensive, court-based solutions to people's problems. Because the scheme is open-ended it is impossible to focus resources on priority areas, or the most efficient and effective way of dealing with a particular problem. Legal aid is spent almost entirely on lawyers' services. In practice, it is lawyers who determine where and how the money is spent.

(b) Legal aid is sometimes criticised for backing cases of insufficient merit and for allowing people to pursue cases unreasonably, forcing their opponents to agree unfair settlements.

(c) The scheme provides few effective means or incentives for improving value for money. Because any lawyer can take a legal aid case there is little control over quality and no scope for competition to keep prices down. Lawyers' fees are calculated after the event, based on the amount of work done so there is little incentive to work more efficiently. In recent years,

155

higher spending has supported fewer cases. The number of full civil legal aid cases started each year has fallen by 31 per cent from 419,861 in 1992/93 to 319,432 in 1997/98.

(d) It is not possible to control expenditure effectively. The few means of control available, for example cutting financial eligibility, are crude and inflexible. Spending on all forms of civil and family legal aid has risen rapidly from £586 million in 1992/93 to £793 million in 1997/98. This level of growth in expenditure – 35 per cent compared with general inflation of 13 per cent – cannot be sustained.

In Chapter 6 of the White Paper, the government articulated its dissatis-faction with the way in which legal aid was operating within the criminal justice system as well as with its spiralling costs. As a result, the White Paper contained proposals for the abolition of the legal aid scheme in both the spheres of civil and criminal justice and its replacement with an entirely new system. These proposals and others contained in the White Paper ulti-mately found expression in a Bill that was presented to Parliament which was enacted as the Access to Justice Act 1999. A completely new entity in the form of the Legal Services Commission (LSC) has been created by s. 1(1) to replace the Legal Aid Board from April 2000. The LSC has its headquar-ters at Gray's Inn Road in London and it also operates from thirteen regional office throughout England and Wales. According to s. 1(2) of the Act, the Commission has important functions relating to its two sub-entities: the Community Legal Service and the Criminal Defence Service.

The former is concerned with the provision of advice and legal services in the sphere of the civil law whilst the latter, as is clearly indicated by its title, is concerned exclusively with the provision of legal services to those being investigated and those charged by the police with criminal offences. Section 4 of the Act permits the Lord Chancellor, subject to parliamentary approval, to split the Legal Services Commission into two separate bodies. One would be responsible for the Community Legal Service whilst the other would be responsible for the Criminal Defence Service, but this is unlikely to happen in the near future. The powers of the LSC are set out in general terms in s. 3, but this chapter focuses on the role of its two subordinate bodies before examining other forms of resource provision for legal services.

2. The Community Legal Service

The Access to Justice Act 1999 s. 4(1) required that the LSC establish, maintain and develop a Community Legal Service thereby fulfilling a commitment that appeared in the Labour Party manifesto for the 1997 election. The work of this Community Legal Service is funded through a Community Legal

Service Fund that was established by the Legal Services Commission in accordance with the Access to Justice Act 1999 s. 5(1). In the annual public expenditure planning process, the Lord Chancellor sets an annual budget for the Community Legal Service. This takes account of the anticipated contributions and payments to be made by those who have recourse to the fund, but the bulk of the funding for the service comes via the Lord Chancellor's Department from the money voted by Parliament when it approves the annual Finance Act. Although s. 5(3) of the Act requires the Lord Chancellor to take account of the assessment of need made by the Legal Services Commission in accordance with s. 4(6), it is the Lord Chancellor who determines how much will be paid into the Community Legal Service Fund. The amount for 2000/01 was £749 million. Under s. 5(6) he has power to direct the Legal Services Commission to allocate parts of the fund to provide particular types of service to ensure that resources are allocated according to the government's priorities.

The responsibilities of the Community Legal Service are set out in the Access to Justice Act 1999 s. 4(2) and are as follows:

(a) The provision of general information about the law and legal system and the availability of legal services.

(b) The provision of help by the giving of advice as to how the law applies in particular circumstances.

(c) The provision of help in preventing, or settling or otherwise resolving disputes about legal rights and duties.

(d) The provision of help in enforcing decisions by which such disputes are resolved.

(e) The provision of help in relation to legal proceedings not relating to disputes.

The development of the Community Legal Service has entailed the formation and development of Community Legal Services Partnerships within every local government area. Despite the use of the term 'partnership' they are not partnerships as legally defined but rather schemes for local cooperation established between the funding bodies and the various service providers. The funding bodies are mainly the regional offices of the Legal Services Commission and various local authorities but there may also be local private funding bodies in the form of charities. The providing bodies, such as the local Law Society (representing solicitors) Citizens' Advice Bureaux and law centres work with the funding bodies to plan and coordinate financing of local advice and legal services to ensure that, as far as possible, they meet local needs. Having identified local needs for legal services and having assessed the extent to which they are met by the existing provision, the participants in the Community Legal Service partnership can then devise a strategy. It is hoped that this will result in a closer match between local provision and local need. It is anticipated that these local plans and strategies will be kept under review so that it will be possible to incorporate future developments in the provision of legal services. If current plans are realised, it is intended that at least 90 per cent of the population of England and Wales will be served by Community Legal Service Partnerships by 2002. These local partnerships are supported by the Community Legal Service website (www.justask.org.uk) and the *Community Legal Service Directory*. The directory, which is in 13 parts, covers the various Community Legal Service regions in England and Wales and gives details of organisations and other providers of legal services. An electronic version of the directory is provided on the website where users can search to locate service providers who can deal with their queries. Apart from providing online legal information and advice, the website also contains information about Community Legal Service projects together with details of research so that there can be a debate about the functioning of aspects of the service. Links are provided to the websites of individual Community Legal Service Partnerships. The information is available in minority ethnic languages and the site has been constructed so that it can be used by persons with disabilities.

Service providers, who may be firms of solicitors, specialist or general advice agencies or law centres, who wish to be part of the local Community Legal Service Partnership must demonstrate that they meet the required standard for the service or services that they offer. In this scheme there are three categories: information services, general help and specialist help.

The Community Legal Service Quality Task Force has devised a 'quality mark' accreditation system bearing the CLS logo for the three main categories of service on offer. Service providers that meet the requirements will display the appropriate CLS logo so that users can have confidence that the service provided meets the minimum standard laid down. Within the information service there are two tiers: self-help information and assisted information. The former requires that service providers are merely able to supply leaflets, provide access to directories and to the website. At this level, the amount of interaction with users is minimal. This service is available from information points in local council offices. Those providing assisted information at the second level must ensure that staff are on hand to help users with accessing and interpreting information as well as being capable of ascertaining when further information or advice is needed. They must also be able to identify the most appropriate source of information and advice. This service is available at Community Information Service outlets and main public libraries. There are also two tiers of general help.

Service providers at the first level (normally Citizens' Advice Bureaux) must be capable of diagnosing a problem and, if it is a legal one, be able to explain the available options and give appropriate information. In addition, they must be capable of identifying any further action that needs to be taken by users and be able to give assistance with the completion of simple forms and with the drafting of letters. The second level comprises general help with casework which requires that service providers apply for this standard in the designated categories such as welfare benefits, housing, employment, immigration and nationality. Casework entails negotiation with third parties either face to face, on the telephone or by letter on behalf of a client and low-level advocacy before certain tribunals. Those providing the third category, 'specialist help', such as firms of solicitors, law centres and specialist advice agencies will provide legal advice and assistance including representation for clients with more complex problems. Only those solicitors' firms, specialist advice agencies and law centres that have been accredited by the Community Legal Service are able to display the CLS Specialist Help logo. They must also have contracts with the Legal Services Commission. However, these service providers are able to undertake publicly funded civil legal work only in those areas of law for which they have been approved by a process of audit to ensure that they meet the quality standards.

Operating within the context of each Community Legal Service Partnership, the Legal Services Commission Funding Code establishes six levels of service in civil matters, namely:

(a) Legal Help

(b) Help at Court

(c) Approved Family Help

(d) Family Mediation

(e) Legal Representation

(f) Support Funding.

The first and most basic level of service covers work that was previously done under the old legal aid 'green form' scheme by way of advice and assistance with any civil legal problem. Help at Court merely extends to providing a person to speak on the client's behalf in certain court hearings but without the person in question acting as an advocate for the entire proceedings. In this way the cost to the Community Legal Service Fund can be kept to a minimum. Approved Family Help includes the services covered by Legal Help and comes in two forms: help with family mediation and general family help where no mediation is in progress. In the latter form, it includes representation in proceedings where this is necessary to obtain disclosure of information from another party. The Legal Services Commission provides funding for the mediation of family disputes for those couples who qualify financially with a view to reaching a mutually acceptable solution. The fifth level of service is available in two forms, namely investigative help to ascertain the strength of a claim and then full representation which may be granted to assist with the bringing or defending of a claim in court. It is possible for the first to be granted, but even if the claim is a strong one, full representation may be refused if it is considered that the case could be funded under a conditional fee agreement (*see* 6). Support funding is the partial funding by the Community Legal Service Fund of very expensive cases. The aim is to assist with the cost of an investigation in order to establish the strength of a claim with a view to then financing the case itself on a conditional fee basis or alternatively as litigation support. This latter form of assistance would extend to partial funding of a very expensive case under a conditional fee agreement so that the cost is borne partly by the lawyers concerned and partly by the Community Legal Service Fund because the lawyers are unwilling to take the case entirely on the basis of conditional fee arrangement. Applications for litigation support must be submitted to the Legal Services Commission Special Cases Unit with a costed plan and it may be approved only where the costs of the case (excluding disbursements) are likely to exceed £15,000. In addition to these six levels of service prescribed by the Funding Code, the Lord Chancellor may offer other services by making a specific order or direction.

Financial assistance from the Community Legal Service is available only to individuals, and by virtue of Schedule 2 of the Access to Justice Act 1999 some forms of claim and service are excluded. These are:

(a) claims in respect of personal injury or death (with the exception of clinical negligence claims) and claims for damage to property

(b) the transfer of the legal title to houses/flats, known as conveyancing

(c) boundary disputes affecting land

(d) the making of wills

(e) matters relating to the law of trusts

(f) defamation claims and claims for malicious falsehood

(g) matters relating to partnership and company law

(h) matters arising out of the operation of a business.

3. Eligibility for assistance

Financial assistance from the Community Legal Service Fund is available where there is genuine need. This means that persons whose income and capital do not exceed the thresholds currently in operation will not be asked to pay any contribution out of income or capital towards the cost of the services provided. Different thresholds are set for the various levels of service and they are set out in the booklet *A Practical Guide to Community Legal Service Funding* which is available from the Legal Services Commission and the offices of solicitors and law centres. Persons whose income and capital do exceed the thresholds set so that they are not entitled to an entirely free service may still be eligible for some financial assistance on a graduated scale provided that their income and capital do not exceed the upper limits that have been set. However, this will be contingent upon their paying a contribution before receiving support from the Community Legal Service Fund. Solicitors and workers in advice agencies who are participants in the Community Legal Service scheme have the latest information to hand enabling them to undertake assessments of applicants' means. An assessment has to be made of both income and capital. This is done to ascertain whether financial support can be granted with or without contributions from individuals pursuing claims before mental health review tribunals, immigration adjudicators, the immigration appeal tribunal and in a limited range of family cases in magistrates' courts. Most other cases are assessed by assessment officers at the regional offices of the LSC, but for complex cases there is a Special Investigations Unit. If the matter has been dealt with by one of the regional offices of the LSC and it has been decided that the case satisfies the merits criteria and the applicant qualifies on financial grounds, it will issue a certificate where no contribution is required. Those persons in receipt of income support or income-based job seeker's allowance are automatically eligible for the granting of a certificate. If a contribution is required, an 'offer' of a certificate is sent and if the applicant accepts it the contribution from savings has to be paid immediately whereas any contribution from income is paid by monthly instalments. The first contribution from income must be paid when the offer is accepted. Usually, solicitors must report to the LSC when they have reached a certain stage in their work for a client or have spent a predetermined amount.

Where Community Legal Service funding is made available and the person aided is successful, the solicitor (and barrister, if one was engaged) will expect to be paid his/her taxed costs. The amount that the applicant pays depends on whether:

(a) the other side is ordered to pay the costs of the action and does so, and

161

(b) the applicant is awarded any money or property by the court or under an agreement with the other side.

If the other side pays the applicant's costs in full, the applicant can expect to completely recover the amount of any contribution that was paid. If the other side does not pay the applicant's costs in full, the regional office of the LSC must deduct from any money ordered to be paid by the court or agreed with the other side as much as may be necessary to cover the costs. This deduction is referred to as the 'statutory charge'. It will attach to property received by or preserved by the applicant in the case whether as a result of a court order or as a result of a settlement or compromise of the case. It does not attach to maintenance payments or to the first £2,500 recovered in divorce and family proceedings. There is a leaflet entitled *Paying Back the Legal Services Commission – The Statutory Charge* which gives further details of when the statutory charge has to be paid. If the applicant should lose the case, the most that he/she will be required to pay towards the solicitor's costs (and the barrister's fee, if applicable) will be the amount, if any, that was payable under the certificate that was granted.

Well in excess of 300,000 certificates are granted annually to enable individuals to take or defend court proceedings. Occasionally, the other party to the proceedings (or some third party) will contact the LSC alleging that the case does not really merit subsidised assistance and therefore should not be allowed to proceed on that basis. Alternatively, an allegation might take the form that the person aided is not financially eligible perhaps because he/she has not disclosed all his/her assets or income. The LSC will usually send a copy of an objection in relation to the merits of the case to the solicitor acting for the aided person with a request for comments on the allegation(s) raised. An allegation relating to the aided person's means will be referred to an assessment unit for investigation. The LSC can and does from time to time revoke a certificate, but if it does so, the person affected can ask for a review of the decision by an independent funding review committee, the members of which are unconnected with the LSC. As a result of such a review, a certificate could be reinstated but if it is not, the person concerned will normally be obliged to refund all the money paid by the LSC.

4. The Criminal Defence Service

The Access to Justice Act 1999 s. 12(1) required the LSC to establish, maintain and develop the Criminal Defence Service. It operates from offices at six locations in England and Wales that are wholly separate from the existing regional offices of the LSC. Its aim is to ensure that individuals involved in criminal investigations or criminal proceedings have access to the necessary advice, assistance and representation that the interests of justice require. Criminal proceedings are not simply confined to criminal trials because the definition contained in s. 12(2) extends to appeals and sentencing hearings, extradition hearings, binding-over proceedings, appeals on behalf of a convicted person who has died and to proceedings for contempt in the face of the court. A person who needs advice at the police station can call upon the duty solicitor or any solicitor in the area who has a contract for criminal work with the Legal Services Commission to provide advice free of charge. Contracts are awarded only to those firms of solicitors who are able to demonstrate to the LSC that their members and staff who provide services under the scheme meet the standards set. Not only must they have the requisite legal knowledge but they must also be able demonstrate that they possess the skills and experience to advise suspects and conduct criminal cases. Those firms of solicitors who secure contracts from the LSC are expected to compete with one another for the available work to ensure that best value is obtained for the services provided.

Once a suspect is charged, that solicitor's firm will continue to represent him/her for the duration of the case unless the Criminal Defence Service agrees that there is a valid reason for a change. The Criminal Defence Service employs its own 'salaried defenders' so that persons charged with criminal offences requiring financial assistance with the cost of representation may choose between solicitors in private practice whose firms have contracts with the LSC or lawyers employed by the Criminal Defence Service in its Public Defender Service. In accordance with the Access to Justice Act 1999 s. 16 the LSC has drawn up a code of conduct to be observed by its salaried defenders as they carry out their duties. The government hopes that the service will fill gaps in the provision in parts of the country where there are just a few solicitors' firms and barristers' chambers participating in the new scheme. It also intends to use cost data from the salaried service to assess whether the prices charged by lawyers in private practice are reasonable.

5. Eligibility for financial assistance

Where an individual has been charged with an offence at a police station and appears before magistrates either on bail or from custody, there is no means test to be satisfied before assistance is granted for representation. The same applies to persons appearing before a youth court and to the early administrative hearings under the Crime and Disorder Act 1998 s. 50 – no contribution whatever is payable towards the cost of representation. However, this does not apply to persons charged with indictable offences (those triable by jury at the Crown Court) or any other offence for which an individual is 'sent' to the Crown Court for trial under the Crime and Disorder

Act 1998 s. 51. Such persons will continue to be subject to a means test but this will only be conducted if the person is convicted. If it emerges during the trial that the defendant has substantial assets, the judge can make an order when passing sentence regarding the contribution required towards the costs of representation. In other cases, the judges will ask the Criminal Defence Service to investigate the defendant's means and they will then make an order as to the amount of the contribution at a later date.

6. Contingency and conditional fee agreements

The upper limits for financial assistance set by the Legal Aid Board, the forerunner of the Legal Services Commission, to meet the cost of commencing a civil action were quite low. This has meant that many people on modest incomes have frequently been deterred from pursuing valid claims by the costs of litigation – not just their own costs but also the risk of having to pay the costs of the other party if the claim is unsuccessful. It has long been possible in the USA for civil claimants to enter into an agreement with a lawyer, the essence of which is that the lawyer will take the case on a 'no win, no fee' basis. If the lawyer wins the case for his/her client, the lawyer will be entitled, under the terms of the agreement, to receive a percentage of the damages recovered or another specified sum. This obviously compensates lawyers for taking on those cases where the client loses. Awards of damages in the USA tend to be much higher than in the UK perhaps because juries and judges are aware of the existence of conditional fee agreements. Consequently, lawyers in the USA often receive very large payments under these contingency fee agreements.

Having restricted eligibility for legal aid in its Legal Aid Act 1988 as part of a general strategy to control public expenditure, the Conservative government sought other ways of widening access to justice. In its Courts and Legal Services Act 1990 s. 58 it therefore made it lawful, in principle, for certain types of litigation to be conducted under a variant of the contingency fee agreement known as a 'conditional fee agreement'. The hallmark of such an agreement is that the fee uplift is not based on the level of damages awarded but on the lawyer's actual fee for the work done. These agreements were considered to be less open to exploitation than the simple contingency fee agreement. In 1995, the Lord Chancellor made a statutory instrument under the Courts and Legal Services Act 1990 which permitted conditional fee agreements to be entered into for personal injury claims, insolvency cases and cases before the European Commission of Human Rights.

As part of its agenda for modernising the civil justice system, the Labour government sought to broaden the coverage of conditional fee agreements but found itself constrained by the wording of the Courts and Legal Services

Act 1990. It had been responsible for the Conditional Fee Agreements Order 1998 (SI 1998 No. 1860) which extended the range of proceedings in which conditional fee agreements were permissible. Then, in the Access to Justice Act 1999 s. 27, the original s. 58 of the Courts and Legal Services Act 1990 was replaced with two new sections. The new s. 58(1) requires that all conditional fee agreements must conform to s. 58(3) if they are to be legally enforceable and this has been reinforced by the Conditional Fee Agreements Regulations 2000 (SI 2000 No. 692). A new s. 58A(1) extends the coverage of conditional fee agreements by providing that only criminal proceedings (with the exception of those under the Environmental Protection Act 1990 s. 82) and family proceedings as set out in s. 58A(2) cannot be conducted under a valid conditional fee agreement and this is reiterated in the Conditional Fee Agreements Order 2000 (SI 2000 No. 823). Consequently, persons wishing to pursue civil claims (with the exception of family proceedings) and who do not qualify for assistance from the Community Legal Service Fund are able to negotiate conditional fee agreements for most civil claims with solicitors offering this service. As from April 2000, conditional fee agreements replaced subsidised legal assistance from the public purse for most personal injury cases. Moreover, the Access to Justice Act 1999 makes it lawful for the LSC to refuse subsidised legal assistance where a conditional fee agreement would be appropriate and both solicitors and barristers are able under their rules of professional conduct to enter into conditional fee agreements with clients. Solicitors are subject to controls on the advertising that they can put out when offering to conduct litigation under conditional fee agreements. In recognition of the fact that there is a potential conflict of interests, the Law Society's *Guide to the Professional Conduct of Solicitors 1999*, Principle 12.09, indicates that in deciding whether a conditional fee agreement would be appropriate in the circumstances of a particular case, a solicitor should be careful to ensure that his/her own financial interests are not placed above the general interests of the client. Disciplinary action can be taken against a solicitor who overcharges a client.

Under a conditional fee agreement, the client will usually be required to take out an insurance policy to cover the eventuality of an unsuccessful claim and the associated risk of having to pay the costs of the other side. Those firms of solicitors who have partners or employed solicitors who are members of the Law Society's Personal Injury Panel are able to arrange insurance cover on behalf of clients making personal injury claims up to £15,000 for a premium in the region of £300. However, insurance to cover the risk of having to pay the costs of the other side in a high-value medical negligence claim could be in the region of £8,000 although the premium would be payable in stages as the claim proceeds. Unless it is agreed to the contrary, the client will be responsible for paying expenses other than his/her own solicitor's fee until the outcome of the case is known. Some insurance products may cover essential disbursements (fees payable for expert witnesses, medical and police reports) in the event of an unsuccessful outcome. If the solicitor wins the case for the client, he/she is able to charge a 'success fee' which may not exceed 100 per cent of the firm's costs, which means that the solicitor could recover a maximum of double his/her normal fee. The Law Society has asked its members to cap the success fee at 25 per cent of the amount recovered and the Bar Council has asked barristers to observe a cap of 10 per cent in all personal injury cases.

A worked example will help to clarify the basic principles of a conditional fee agreement. Suppose that a solicitors' firm has won a case for a client on a conditional fee basis and the client was awarded and recovered £7,500 in damages. You should also assume that the solicitor represented the client throughout and so there is no barrister's fee. If the costs incurred by the firm in pursuing the case were £8,000 but, of this, £6,000 was recovered from the other side after the process known as 'taxation of costs', there would be a shortfall of £2,000 to be paid by the client to his/her solicitor. A claim could not be made under the insurance policy because the client was successful. If a 'success fee' of 100 per cent were allowed, this would normally be calculated on the firm's costs and would entitle the firm to recover an additional £8,000, but if the cap of 25 per cent applied this would only entitle the firm to recover £1,875 (£7,500 × 0.25) as a success fee. The Access to Justice Act 1999 provides that the success fee and the insurance premium can be recovered from the party who has lost the action, and so the successful claimant will receive the damages awarded less the £2,000 shortfall referred to above, the amount being £5,500. This sum will be supplemented by the amount of the insurance premium that is recovered. The award of damages will not, however, be reduced any further because the success fee is payable by the unsuccessful defendant in the action who must find an additional £1,875 to the costs and damages awarded.

The claimant is obliged to notify the court and the defendant at the start of the claim of the existence of a conditional fee agreement although there is no necessity at this stage to disclose the amount of the agreed success fee. It is also necessary for the claimant to inform the defendant about the existence of the insurance policy. An unsuccessful defendant can challenge the amount of the success fee on the basis that it is unreasonable when the court assesses the costs at the end of the litigation, and the amount of the insurance premium can be challenged too. If the defendant's challenge of the fee uplift is successful, the solicitor will not be able to recover the resulting shortfall in the success fee unless he/she applies to the court justifying the higher level of uplift. At the time of writing, it is not altogether clear whether the solicitor is precluded from recovering this sum from the client. The government hopes that conditional fee agreements will become an attractive means of pursuing civil claims where a remedy other than damages is being sought now that the success fee, and indeed the insurance premium, can be recovered from the unsuccessful defendant. In practice, the amount of the success fee will always vary with the degree of risk associated with pursuing the claim but it will be comparatively rare for the percentage to be set at 100 per cent. Nevertheless, at the time of writing, there is no compulsory training for solicitors in risk assessment.

In its Consultation Paper *Access to Justice with Conditional Fees* published in 1998 the Lord Chancellor's Department noted that a study had shown that success fees were being set at 50 per cent or less, with an average figure of 43 per cent. It also noted that in 90 per cent of cases the Law Society's voluntary cap of 25 per cent was observed. The report of the working party of the Society for Advanced Legal Studies, London entitled *The Ethics of Conditional Fee Arrangements* (January 2001) which examined some 40 such agreements stated in its executive summary:

> Conditional Fee Arrangements (CFAs) raise inevitable and serious conflicts of interests between clients and lawyers, and between lawyers' financial interests and their duties to the courts. The existence of lawyers' major financial interests in the outcome of cases, as a result of CFAs, will heighten pre-existing tensions in the lawyer–client relationship, and create new conflicts of interest. Furthermore, and crucially, the financial interests of insurance companies which will now occupy a central role on both sides in legal actions, will have a profound impact on access to justice and the ethics of practice.

Amongst its many recommendations, the working party advocated that:

> A compulsory 'period of contemplation' should be required between the explana-
> tion of a draft CFA and the client being asked to sign, except in cases of urgency.
> The benefit of such a period could be strengthened by lending the client a video
> (prepared by the Community Legal Service) explaining the ins and outs of CFAs.

The working party took the view that judges should play an appropriate part in maintaining and raising the ethical standards in the legal profession. Conditional fee agreements are obviously less objectionable in commercial litigation as corporations seek to negotiate a sharing of risks relating to litigation with firms of solicitors. Companies often have their own in-house lawyers who are able to negotiate on equal terms with the large law firms.

7. Contingency fee agreements

Although contingency fee agreements are not permitted in contentious proceedings to finance litigation under the Solicitors' Practice Rules 1990, they may be used as a means of financing non-contentious work. Non-contentious business is defined by the Solicitors Act 1974 s. 87(1) as any business done as a solicitor which is not contentious business which in general terms means work that does not involve proceedings begun before a court in England and Wales or an arbitrator. This would extend to all tribunal work (with the exception of the Lands Tribunal and Employment Appeal Tribunal) and for work undertaken in relation to Criminal Injuries Compensation Authority claims and to planning or public inquiries.

8. *Pro bono publico*

The phrase *pro bono publico* translates as 'for the public good' and has long been used to describe work done by lawyers free of charge mainly, although not exclusively, in the sphere of litigation for those unable to obtain funding under the state scheme. Solicitors interested in promoting *pro bono* work have formed a special Pro Bono Group. The Bar, too, has its own *pro bono* unit which has been set up specifically to offer free legal advice and representation in deserving cases where financial assistance from the state has not been available or where the person concerned simply cannot afford the full cost of these services.

Unlike the situation that obtains in the USA, where the American Bar Association has a clear recommendation in its code of conduct to the effect that lawyers should perform in the region of 40 hours of free work each year, the professional bodies in the UK have not gone that far. For the time being they have left it to individual solicitors and barristers to decide how much, if any, free work they undertake. However, pressure is growing for solicitors' firms to draw up *pro bono* policies where they are prepared to consider direct approaches from members of the public. Such policy statements need to reflect the size of the firm and its areas of expertise. Ideally they should make it clear that *pro bono* work is not treated differently from other paid work in that the procedures followed and standards observed are the same. Members of some firms of solicitors already undertake *pro bono* work with Citizens' Advice Bureaux and neighbourhood law centres and may make it clear in their publicity material that they will not deal with requests for help directly from the public.

On 2 June 2000, the Law Centres' Federation and the Solicitors' Pro Bono Group launched a new initiative to be known as Law Works which is aimed at improving legal services in the major cities by matching volunteers with front-line agencies and by organising training in social welfare law for volunteer lawyers from the large commercial firms. In an attempt to stimulate interest in *pro bono* work among young lawyers, the College of Law announced in March 2000 that it was offering a *pro bono* service whereby supervised *pro bono* 'clinics' would be integrated into the teaching programme and law students would be able to obtain credit for the work that they do.

Progress test

1. What are the responsibilities of the Community Legal Service as set out in the Access to Justice Act 1999 s. 4(2)?

2. What is the main idea behind Community Legal Service Partnerships?

3. What are the six levels of service established under the Legal Services Funding Code?

4. What are the salient features of the Criminal Defence Service?

5. What is the difference between a contingency fee agreement and a conditional fee agreement?

6. Are there circumstances in which a solicitor is able to work under a contingency fee agreement?

Further reading

Books

Sime, S. (2000) *A Practical Approach to Civil Procedure* (London: Blackstone Press, chapter 4).
Society for Advanced Legal Studies (2001) *The Ethics of Conditional Fee Agreements*, Research Paper (London: Society for Advanced Legal Studies).
Underwood, K. (1999) *No Win No Fee – No Worries* (Welwyn Garden City: CLT Professional Publishing).

Articles

Bawdon, F. (2001) 'Conditional fee agreements', *New Law Journal* Vol. 151, No. 6972.
Moorhead, R. and A. Sherr (2001) 'Midnight in the garden of the CFA people', *New Law Journal* Vol. 151, No. 6972.
Wignall, G. (2001) 'CFA and the Bar', *New Law Journal* Vol. 151, No. 6972.

Useful websites

The Legal Services Commission can be located at www.legalservices.gov.uk/ and the Community Legal Service at www.justask.org.uk/. Information on conditional fee agreements can be obtained from the Law Society website at www.lawsociety.org.uk/

10

Criminal justice system 1

1. Introduction

The criminal justice system can be conceptualised as comprising the police, the Crown Prosecution Service, the courts, the probation service and the prison service. Thus, the area of study is as fascinating as it is vast. However, a book of this size can do no more than provide an overview of parts of the system, in anticipation that the reader will strive to deepen his/her understanding by reading the more specialist texts indicated at the end of this and the next chapters and by studying the various journal articles. The criminal justice system is seldom out of the news and miscarriages of justice continue to receive much media attention. These, together with serious errors and malpractice on the part of individual police and prison officers, have operated to erode public confidence in the system in recent years. The publication of the MacPherson Report in 1999 drawing attention to racist attitudes among some serving police officers has merely heightened public concern over the functioning of the police service in the context of a society that is both multiracial and multicultural. Clearly, much remains to be done to restore public confidence in the police and in other parts of the criminal justice system in the twenty-first century.

This chapter focuses initially on the powers of the police to stop, search, detain and arrest suspects. Consideration will then be given to the rights of suspects in police detention before dealing with the charging and decision to prosecute.

2. The regulatory framework

The Royal Commission on Criminal Procedure (the Phillips Commission) was set up in 1991 as a response to widespread concern over the rising rate of crime. Some groups, including some high-ranking police officers, thought that the police were being hampered in the effective investigation of crime by the restraints imposed by existing police procedure. Others, particularly civil liberties groups, felt that the police were abusing the powers that they already had. The Royal Commission's terms of reference were to review the criminal process from the start of an investigation to the point of trial. In its report, the Royal Commission stressed the need to achieve a balance between the interests of society in ensuring that the guilty were brought to justice and the right of individuals not to have their civil liberties infringed unnecessarily by the police. The Commission's report was largely responsible for the enactment of the Police and Criminal Evidence Act 1984 (PACE) and the establishment of the Crown Prosecution Service (CPS).

Although the police play a very important part in uncovering crime, the fact remains that the majority of offences on which they take action are reported to them. If the police are to prevent crime as well as take action to apprehend suspects, they must be endowed with adequate powers by the state. The Police and Criminal Evidence Act 1984 (and other legislation) confers on the police extensive powers of stop and search, seizure of property, arrest and detention of persons. PACE is supplemented by codes of practice issued by the Home Secretary under the authority conferred by s. 67(1) to regulate particular aspects of police powers and procedure. The codes themselves are not statutory instruments but they were brought into operation by a statutory instrument made by the Home Secretary under s. 67(4). An infringement of the codes may not necessarily amount to a criminal offence or, for that matter, a civil wrong. However, courts are obliged to take into account breaches of the codes especially in relation to the admissibility of evidence. There are sanctions to prevent infringements of PACE and the codes by the police as follows:

(a) If the infringement amounts to a criminal offence, the police officer(s) can be prosecuted.

(b) If the infringement amounts to a civil wrong, the victim can sue the officer(s) concerned but usually the chief constable who is vicariously liable.

(c) Infringements may be a disciplinary offence covered under the police disciplinary regulations and the officer(s) could face dismissal.

(d) Evidence that is obtained as a result of an infringement of PACE or the codes may be inadmissible.

(e) Confessions obtained as a result of an infringement of PACE or the codes may also be inadmissible.

Successful prosecutions against serving police officers are rare events. The existing system for investigating complaints against the police and police disciplinary procedures is to be found in PACE ss 83–106. If misconduct is established at a disciplinary hearing, the most usual sanction is a fine though dismissals do occur from time to time. Often, police officers will be subjected to the less formal disciplinary measure known as 'giving words of advice'. This is a formal admonishment of the officer(s) concerned and will be recorded. Such admonishments may affect future promotion prospects.

3. Stop and search

The police have wide powers conferred by PACE s. 1 to stop and search persons and vehicles in a public place or a place where the public has access if a constable has reasonable grounds for suspecting that he/she will find stolen or prohibited articles. It is a power to stop and search and not a general power to ask questions. If the police constable is not in uniform he/she must produce a warrant card as identification.

Prior to commencing a search, the constable should disclose his/her name to the suspect and the name of the police station where he/she is attached, the object of the search, the grounds on which it is being made and the right of the person to have a copy of the record of the search. Under PACE s. 2(9)(a), the most that a constable carrying out the search can request a suspect to do in public is to remove an outer coat, jacket or gloves, but he/she can take a suspect to a nearby police van or indeed to a nearby police station in order to conduct a more thorough search away from public view. If in the course of a search a constable/officer discovers an article which he/she has reasonable grounds for suspecting to be stolen or is a prohibited article, he/she may seize it. For the purposes of PACE, an article is prohibited if it is an offensive weapon or an article made or adapted in the course of or in connection with an offence. The offences to which s. 1(7)(b)(i) applies are burglary, theft and offences under the Theft Act 1968.

Although powers to stop and search may not be exercised in a dwelling house they may be exercised in the garden or yard of a house where this is not the yard or garden of the occupier. If the need arises, the police can use reasonable force to detain and search, but PACE ss 2 and 3 regulate the conduct of these searches. Failure to observe these provisions may transform an otherwise lawful search into a trespass and thereby deprive police officers who face resistance of the protection afforded by the offence of assaulting a constable acting in the execution of his/her duty.

Under ss 1(2) and 1(3) a police constable/officer may only search a person or a vehicle if he/she has reasonable grounds for suspecting that he/she will find stolen or prohibited articles. Code A paras 1.6, 1.6A, 1.7, 1.7A and 1.7AA give detailed guidance on what amounts to reasonable suspicion justifying a stop and search. According to para. 1.7:

reasonable suspicion can never be supported on the basis of personal factors alone without supporting intelligence or information. For example, a person's colour, age, hairstyle or manner of dress, or the fact that he is known to have a previous conviction for the possession of an unlawful article, cannot be used alone or in combination with each other as the sole basis on which to search that person. Nor may it be founded on the basis of stereotyped images of certain persons or groups more likely to be committing offences.

The requirement in PACE s. 1 that a constable/officer has 'reasonable grounds for suspecting' is an attempt to strike a balance between effective policing and safeguarding individual liberties. Only approximately 10 per cent of stop and searches under PACE result in arrests.

In addition to powers conferred by PACE, the police are allowed by virtue of other legislation to conduct searches. For example, under the Misuse of Drugs Act 1971 s. 23 a police officer can search for illegal drugs but he/she must have objective reasons for doing so and he/she may also search for firearms under the Firearms Act 1968 s. 47. The Criminal Justice and Public Order Act 1994 s. 60 empowers the police to stop and search in anticipation of violence if the authorisation is given by an officer above the rank of inspector (normally a superintendent) who reasonably believes that incidents of serious violence may take place in his/her police area. The powers of stop and search under s. 60 of the Act may be exercised by a constable even though he/she has no grounds for suspecting that the person or the vehicle is carrying weapons or dangerous instruments. It is enough that the person concerned is within the geographical area in which the powers have been invoked. Under s. 60(6) a constable may seize any item which he/she has reasonable grounds for suspecting to be an offensive weapon.

The Terrorism Act 2000 confers exceptional powers of stop and search on the police. Section 43(1) provides that a constable may stop and search a person anywhere in the UK whom he/she reasonably suspects to be a terrorist in order to discover whether he/she has anything in his/her possession that may constitute evidence that he/she is a terrorist, but the search must be conducted by someone of the same sex. The constable is then empowered by s. 43(4) of the Act to seize and retain anything found during the search provided that he/she reasonably suspects that the article may constitute evidence that the person is a terrorist. The power to stop and search a person is extended by s. 116(2) to include a vehicle.

Apart from the statutory powers of stop and search considered above and the statutory power to conduct road checks under PACE s. 4(1), the police are permitted under common law to set up road checks to prevent a breach of the peace. Provided a police officer honestly and reasonably forms the opinion that there is a real risk of a breach of the peace, then he/she may take reasonable preventative action.

173

If it can be established that a person has been deprived of his/her liberty as opposed to enduring a mere restriction of movement, he/she could raise the matter as an infringement of Article 5 of Schedule 1 of the Human Rights Act 1998. There might even be a claim under Article 8 under which everyone has the right to be accorded respect for his/her private and family life, although this is not an absolute right.

4. Search under warrant

PACE s. 8 enacts that a constable may apply to a justice of the peace who may issue a warrant authorising the constable to enter and search premises as well as any vehicle, vessel or aircraft if the magistrate has reasonable grounds for believing all of the following:

(a) a serious arrestable offence has been committed,

(b) that there is material on the premises specified which is likely to be of substantial value to the investigation of the offence, and

(c) that the material is likely to be relevant evidence.

The material must not include items subject to legal privilege (lawyer–client communications as defined by s. 10(1)), excluded material (as defined by PACE s. 11(1)) or special procedure material (journalistic material except excluded material and other material coming under PACE s. 14). The warrant is granted to search premises and not to search for evidence against individuals or companies. A magistrate is not barred from issuing a search warrant just because there may be special procedure or excluded material on the premises. The issue of a warrant would only be barred if the material falls into these categories and is, or forms part of, the subject matter of such an application.

Code B para. 2.4 makes it clear that an application for a search warrant should only be made on the authority of an officer of at least the rank of inspector, but where an officer of this rank is not on duty, the senior officer on duty can authorise the application. Moreover, PACE s. 8(3) provides that a search warrant must not be issued unless one of the following conditions is satisfied:

(a) it is not practicable to communicate with any person entitled to grant entry to the premises, or

(b) if it is, that it is not practicable to communicate with any person entitled to grant access to the evidence, or

(c) that entry to the premises will not be granted unless a warrant is produced, or

(d) that the purpose of the search may be frustrated or seriously prejudiced unless a constable arriving at the premises can secure immediate entry to them.

Under s. 8(2) a constable may seize and retain anything for which a search has been authorised under the search warrant.

The Human Rights Act 1998 Schedule 1 Article 8(2) creates a right to privacy enforceable against the state, and interference with this right requires justification. Thus the requirement for independent judicial scrutiny under PACE is important when considering whether the conditions of Article 8(2) have been satisfied. A violation of Article 8(2) is more likely to arise as in *McLeod* v *UK* [1998] where the police seek entry to premises in exercise of common law powers without judicial sanction.

5. Helping police with inquiries

It is not always necessary to arrest someone to obtain further information about a crime because the police can invite a person with his/her agreement to come to the police station so that he/she can be questioned more conveniently. Such a person has not been formally arrested but is just 'helping the police with their inquiries'. It is undoubtedly the case that frequently persons in this situation believe that if they do not go voluntarily, they will be arrested. Thus Code C para. 10.2 states that when a person is officially cautioned at the police station, he/she must be told that he/she is not under arrest and is not required to remain with the police officer. During his/her time there he/she is entitled to free legal advice from the duty solicitor and is entitled to communicate with anyone outside the police station. Moreover, PACE s. 29 makes it clear that a person is free to leave a police station at any time unless placed under arrest, but the police are not under a statutory obligation to tell someone that they may leave. The premises of a person helping police with their enquiries can be searched with his/her consent provided the constable informs the person that he/she is not obliged to consent. Of course, it is possible that someone who starts out helping police with their enquiries may be subsequently arrested if there is sufficient evidence against him/her, but they must be cautioned prior to the arrest.

6. The alternative to arrest and charge

In order to commence a prosecution it is not absolutely necessary for the police to arrest the suspect and take him/her to a police station to charge him/her with the offence. It is possible for anyone, including the police, to

175

lay 'an information' before a magistrate alleging that the person accused in the information has committed one or more specified offences. A summons can then be served on the accused requiring him/her to attend a magistrates' court on a particular day to answer the allegation. In more serious cases, however, it is usual for the police to arrest and then charge a suspect.

7. Arrest

Arrest is not defined in PACE but is a common law concept. In *R* v *Brosch* [1988] the Court of Appeal confirmed that PACE follows the common law as set out in *Alderson* v *Booth* [1969] and that it was unnecessary to use the exact words 'you are under arrest'. An arrest clearly involves a deprivation of liberty although not every deprivation of liberty is an arrest. A deprivation of liberty may amount to the tort of false imprisonment unless it is lawful, and for an arrest to be lawful either it must be made under a warrant or, if it is made without a warrant, it must be lawful either at common law or by statute. Thus, in arresting a person, a police constable must be able to justify his/her actions by reference to lawful authority whether that be common law or statute.

An application can be made to a justice of the peace by the police for an arrest warrant under the Magistrates' Courts Act 1980 s. 1. Under s. 1 a magistrate may issue an arrest warrant on the basis of a written information substantiated on oath if he/she decides not to issue a summons. If an arrest warrant is issued, it may or may not be endorsed for bail but if it is, the warrant may specify the amounts for which any sureties are to be bound. A surety is a person who undertakes to pay the court a specified amount of money should the accused fail to surrender to custody. If bail is to be granted with sureties, the police must release the offender once sureties approved by the police officer have entered into the necessary undertakings. These undertakings are known as recognisances. Thereafter the person bailed is bound to appear before a magistrates' court at a time and place stated in the recognisance. The power of a magistrates' court to issue an arrest warrant is restricted by s. 1(4) which requires that the offence must be triable on indictment or be punishable by imprisonment or the person's address must be insufficiently established for a summons to be subsequently served upon him/her. If the offence is serious enough to justify the issuing of an arrest warrant by a magistrate it is quite likely that the police will be able to arrest without a warrant. The Supreme Court Act 1981 s. 80(2) provides that where an indictment has been signed but the person charged has not been committed for trial, the Crown Court may issue a summons requiring that person to appear before the court or it may issue a warrant for his/her arrest. Under the Magistrates' Courts Act 1980

s. 125, an arrest warrant issued by a justice of the peace may be executed anywhere in England and Wales by any police constable within his/her police area. The effect of this provision taken together with the Police Act 1996 s. 30 is to enable a constable to execute such a warrant anywhere in England and Wales. A constable who arrests a person under warrant must inform the person that he/she is acting under a warrant and the reason for the arrest.

8. Arrest without a warrant

In practice, most arrests are made by the police without a warrant under the general powers conferred by PACE ss 24 and 25. Section 24(6) provides

> Where a constable has reasonable grounds for suspecting that an arrestable offence has been committed, he may arrest without warrant anyone whom he has reasonable grounds for suspecting to be guilty of the offence.

Section 24(7) provides that

> A constable may arrest without a warrant –
> (a) anyone who is about to commit an arrestable offence;
> (b) anyone whom he has reasonable grounds for suspecting to be about to commit an arrestable offence.

These powers of arrest do not just apply to the offence in question but extend to conspiracy, attempt to commit, inciting, aiding and abetting as well as counselling or procuring the commission of an arrestable offence. Section 24(4) gives private citizens a power to arrest that is not as extensive as that given to the police because it provides only that

> Any person may arrest without warrant
> (a) anyone who is in the act of committing an arrestable offence;
> (b) anyone whom he has reasonable grounds for suspecting to be committing such an offence.

Private citizens have no power to arrest on the basis that an offence is about to be committed, and if they do arrest on the basis of reasonable suspicion that a person is committing an arrestable offence they must show that someone committed the offence suspected. Where a private citizen arrests a suspect without a warrant they will usually hand the suspect over to the police with a view to preferring (submitting) a charge.

Apart from some offences that are specifically classed as arrestable offences, the term is normally applied to those offences that are punishable with a prison term of five years or more. Section 25 empowers the police (but not private citizens) to arrest on reasonable suspicion that a non-arrestable offence has been or is being committed by the person concerned and the service of a summons is impracticable or inappropriate. Nevertheless, an arrest should only be made if a number of 'general arrest conditions' are satisfied. These powers of arrest do not extend to those persons who are suspected of being about to commit an offence or to those whose involvement takes the form of conspiracy to commit the offence or inciting, aiding or abetting. The conditions include the person refusing to give his/her name and address or giving details that the officer reasonably doubts are correct. An arrest may also be justified under s. 25 if it is necessary to prevent the person from harming himself/herself or others or to prevent him/her from damaging property or committing an offence against public decency or obstructing the highway. The powers conferred under s. 25 are discretionary and a police officer will consider whether an arrest is necessary. An arrest may be justified under common law where a breach of the peace has been committed and there are grounds for believing that it will be continued or renewed.

Many of the statutory powers conferred on the police in relation to arrest without a warrant are based on a constable having reasonable cause to believe that the suspect has committed, is committing or is about to commit an offence. In this context, reasonable cause relates to the existence of facts and not to the state of the law and what the constable knew and perceived at the time of the arrest. He/she may rely upon hearsay provided that it is reasonable and that the constable believes it. Accordingly he/she could rely upon a radio message or even an anonymous telephone call provided the person arrested corresponds to the person described in the message. However, just because the arresting officer has been instructed to effect an arrest by a superior cannot give rise to reasonable grounds for suspecting that the arrested person committed the offence. Failure to make inquiries before making an arrest could show that there were insufficient grounds for the arrest but an officer need not wait until he/she has sufficient evidence that would render a conviction more likely than not.

PACE s. 17(1) confers a power of entry on a police constable/officer to enter premises to arrest any person for an arrestable offence provided he/she has reasonable grounds for believing that the person is on the premises.

Apart from PACE Schedule 2 which preserves various diverse powers of arrest under particular statutes, the Public Order Act 1986 and the Criminal Justice and Public Order Act 1994 confer powers of arrest without warrant on the police. A constable may arrest without warrant anyone he/she reasonably suspects of committing an offence under the Public Order Act 1986 s. 4(1). There are two offences: (a) threatening, abusive or insulting words or behaviour, or (b) distributing to another person any writing, sign or other visible representation which is threatening abusive or insulting with intent to cause a person to believe that immediate unlawful violence will be used against him/her or another person or to provoke the immediate use of unlawful violence. Under s. 5(4), an arrest without warrant may be made in relation to harassment, causing alarm or distress by disorderly behaviour. However, s. 5(4) provides that the constable must first warn the offender to stop the offensive conduct and may only arrest if the person engages in further offensive conduct. The constable must reasonably believe that the offensive conduct constitutes an offence under the section although the conduct and further conduct need not be the same. The Act also confers powers to arrest without warrant under ss 12(4)–(6), 13(10), 14(4) and 18(3). The Criminal Justice and Public Order Act 1994 s. 61 gives a constable in uniform who reasonably suspects that a person is committing an offence under that section, power to arrest him/her without warrant. Moreover, s. 62 enables a constable to seize and remove any vehicle which a person failed to remove having been required to do so. A police constable in uniform has similar power under s. 63(8) to arrest without warrant in the case of unlicensed 'raves'.

9. Making an arrest

It must be made clear to the person arrested that he/she has been arrested and is not free to leave as well as the reason for the arrest. If it is impractical for the reason for the arrest to be given at the time, because the person is violently resisting or is incapable because of alcohol or drugs, it must be conveyed to him/her as soon as practicable afterwards and it may be given by a colleague of the arresting officer. Unless the reason for the arrest is given, the arrest is not lawful. If force has to be used to achieve the arrest, it must be reasonable force. A court, in deciding what force was reasonable, will take account of the nature and degree of force used, the gravity of the offence, the harm that would follow from the use of force against the suspect and the possibility of effecting the arrest or preventing the harm by other means. Suspects should not be handcuffed unless this is reasonably necessary to prevent an escape or to prevent a violent breach of the peace on the part of the suspect. A caution in the following terms may be given prior to the arrest:

> You do not have to say anything. But it may harm your defence if you do not mention when questioned something which you later rely on in court. Anything you do say may be given in evidence.

According to Code C para. 10.3, if the caution was not given upon arrest, it must be given on making the arrest unless this is impracticable because of the suspect's violent behaviour. There is no need to give a caution if the suspect has already been cautioned immediately prior to arrest.

10. Role of the custody officer

The role of the custody officer was a creation of PACE. It is the duty of a police constable under s. 36(1) to appoint one custody officer for each designated police station. He/she will usually be an officer from the uniform branch who holds at least the rank of sergeant. It is a very responsible position and may at times be quite onerous.

According to PACE s. 36(5), none of the functions of the custody officer can be performed by an officer engaged in the investigation of the particular offence for which the suspect was arrested. When the suspect is presented to the custody officer, the latter is entitled to assume that the arrest was lawful. Code C para. 2.1 makes it clear that the custody officer must open a custody record on the suspect who may have been brought to the police station under arrest or who is arrested there having previously arrived voluntarily. Paragraph 2.3 states that the custody officer is responsible for the accuracy and completeness of the custody record and for ensuring that the record or a copy of the record accompanies a suspect if he/she is transferred to another police station.

Whether the suspect was arrested prior to arrival or was arrested at the police station having initially attended voluntarily, the custody officer must inform him/her of his/her rights and that these are of a continuing nature and may be exercised at any time. These rights are as follows:

(a) The right to have someone informed of his/her arrest.

(b) The right to consult a solicitor in private and the fact that independent legal advice is available free of charge.

(c) The right to consult the codes of practice.

The custody officer is required to give the suspect a written notice containing all the rights set out above and the right to a copy of the custody record. He/she must also caution the suspect in the words set out in **8** above. The notice must also explain the arrangement for obtaining legal advice. An additional written notice must be given to the suspect which sets out his/her general entitlements (food and rest) if held for a lengthy period. Having done so, the custody officer will ask the suspect to sign the custody record to acknowledge the receipt of all these notices and a refusal to sign must be noted on the custody record. If the arrested suspect does not understand English or appears to be deaf, the custody officer must call in an interpreter and ask that person to convey the necessary information. If the arrested suspect is a juvenile, the custody officer must, if practicable, ascertain the identity of a person responsible for his/her welfare and inform that person that the juvenile has been arrested and the reason why he/she is being detained. In addition, where a juvenile is being detained, the custody officer must ask an 'appropriate adult' to come to the police station. It is important to note that a solicitor who is attending the police station on a suspect's behalf is not deemed to be an 'appropriate adult' for this purpose. The phrase 'appropriate adult' is likely to be a parent, but the phrase extends to include a guardian or, if the juvenile is in care, it would be a social worker from the local authority or relevant voluntary organisation. A juvenile detainee should be informed that the appropriate adult is there to advise him/her and that a private consultation is possible at any time. Similar considerations apply when the police are dealing with suspects who are suffering from mental illness or mental handicap. Under PACE s. 37(1), the custody officer is able to detain an arrested person for such a period as is necessary to enable him/her to decide whether there is enough evidence to charge him/her for the offence for which he/she has been arrested. According to *Blackstone on Criminal Practice*, a period of not more than six hours will be considered acceptable and most instances of police detention last less than this.

11. The power of search after arrest

A police constable who arrests someone at a place other than at a designated police station is permitted by PACE s. 32(1) to search that person if he/she has reason to believe that the person may present a danger to himself/herself or to others. Moreover, the constable may seize and retain any object that the person may use to injure himself/herself or others. If the constable has reasonable cause to believe that the person has material on his/her person that could be used to escape from lawful custody or which might be evidence in relation to an offence, the constable/officer may require the arrested person, pursuant to s. 32(4), to submit to a search. The person concerned may be required to remove an outer coat, jacket and gloves where the search takes place in public and, in addition, the constable/officer may even search the person's mouth.

Searches by a constable at a police station following arrest are to be conducted under the provisions of PACE ss 54 and 55, but by no means every suspect is searched. If a suspect is likely to be detained for a short time only and is not placed in a cell, the custody officer may decide that a search is unnecessary. The legislation makes a distinction between non-intimate and intimate searches. Section 54(1) requires that the custody officer ascertains and records everything that a suspect has with him/her when he/she is brought to the police station on being arrested (or committed to police custody by order of the court). The rationale for the search is that the custody officer must ascertain what property the suspect may have acquired for an unlawful or harmful purpose whilst in custody. If the custody officer considers it necessary in the performance of his/her statutory obligations, he/she may, under s. 54(6), order that the suspect be searched. Paragraph 4.1 of Code C makes it clear that it is for the custody officer to decide in his/her discretion how extensive the search should be. The custody officer may seize and retain anything in the possession of the detained suspect except any personal effects and the custody officer remains responsible for the property taken and retained. Items may only be seized if the custody officer believes that the suspect may use them to cause physical harm to himself/herself or another, to damage property, to interfere with evidence or to escape. If the custody officer has reasonable grounds for believing that clothes or personal effects may be evidence relating to an offence, these too may be seized and retained. Unless a detained suspect is violent (or likely to become so) or is incapable of understanding what is said to him/her, the custody officer must inform the suspect of the reason for the seizure and retention of any article. Paragraph 10 of Annexe A to Code C makes it clear that strip searching may take place only where the custody officer thinks that it is necessary to remove an item that the suspect would not be allowed to keep. A strip search can only be conducted by a constable of the same sex as the person being searched and must be conducted in an area where the person being searched cannot be seen by anyone who does not need to be present or by a member of the opposite sex. Unless there is a risk of serious harm to the person concerned, where a strip search would involve exposure of intimate parts of the body, two officers of the same sex must be present whilst the search is carried out. Persons who are searched in this way should not normally be asked to remove all their clothes at the same time and no physical contact should be made with any body orifice by those carrying out such a search.

Section 55 provides that under certain circumstances an arrested suspect in police detention may be subjected to an intimate search. An intimate search entails an examination of the body orifices other than the mouth and the case of R v *Hughes The Times* 12 November 1993 makes it clear that to qualify as an intimate search there must be some intrusion into a bodily orifice. According to Code C Annexe A para. 2, the reasons why an intimate search is deemed necessary must be explained to the person before the search takes place. In any event, PACE s. 55(1)(a) provides that for an intimate search to be authorised, an officer of at least the rank of superintendent must have reasonable grounds to believe that the suspect has concealed on him/her an article that he/she could cause injury to himself/herself or others and which he/she might use whilst in police detention or in the custody of a court. There is a similar provision in s. 55(1)(b) in relation to Class A drugs. A detained suspect is afforded a degree of statutory protection in that the officer must have reasonable grounds for believing that the article(s) in question cannot be found unless the suspect is searched intimately. Intimate searches may only be conducted by a registered medical practitioner or a registered nurse and are comparatively rare events. Special protection is afforded juveniles, mentally ill and handicapped persons in that intimate searches may only be carried out if the appropriate adult of the same sex is present. Intimate searches may be carried out at a police station or on medical premises except in cases of a Class A drug search. These searches must be carried out at a hospital or a doctor's surgery or at another place used for medical purposes. Where an intimate search is conducted this has to be entered into the custody record which must also indicate what parts of the body were searched. Any items seized as a result of such a search can be retained by the police.

12. Search of premises following arrest

Apart from searching a suspect, a police constable has the power under PACE s. 32(2)(b) to enter and search any premises where the person was at the time of, or immediately before, arrest, and this power extends to the search of vehicles. The constable must have reasonable grounds but the power is not confined to arrestable offences. In order to comply with s. 18(4), an officer of at least the rank of inspector must authorise the search. If the premises should consist of two or more dwellings, the power is limited to the dwelling where the arrest took place or where the person arrested was immediately before the arrest and the communal areas. The constable/officer must have reasonable grounds for believing that there is material on the premises that relates to the offence that could be used as evidence.

Where property is seized lawfully it may be retained by the police until trial provided that the police consider, in good faith, that it will be required as evidence. In addition, police may retain allegedly stolen goods with a view to returning them to their rightful owner.

13. Detention without charge

Just because someone has been arrested it does not necessarily follow that he/she will be charged with an offence. Someone who is arrested must be taken to a police station pursuant to s. 30(1) as soon as practicable, whether arrested by a constable or taken into custody by a constable having been arrested by some other person. If it is necessary for the person to be kept in police detention for more than six hours, a constable must normally take the suspect to a designated police station where he/she may be detained without charge for questioning. A designated police station is defined by s. 35 as one used for the purpose of detaining arrested persons.

The notion of balance put forward by the Royal Commission on Criminal Procedure is reflected in the drafting of PACE because a detained suspect has his/her rights safeguarded in principle by the provisions of the Act and the codes. However, at the same time, the police are allowed to continue with their investigations without undue interference. They can hold a detained suspect for up to 24 hours without charging him/her, but where a serious arrestable offence has been committed, a suspect may be detained for up to 36 hours on the authority of a superintendent.

PACE s. 34(1) provides that a person who has been arrested can be kept in police custody in accordance with the provisions of Part IV of the Act. PACE and Code of Practice C set out the requirements relating to the supervision of police detention and the other conditions that apply to it. Where a person is arrested without a warrant or under a warrant that is not endorsed for bail, the person must be delivered up by the arresting officer to the custody officer.

14. Decision-making by the custody officer

According to s. 34(1), a person arrested for an offence is not to be kept in police detention except in accordance with the provision of Part IV of the Act. If at any time the custody officer decides that the grounds for the detention cease to apply and is not aware of any other grounds on which continued detention could be justified, it is the duty of the custody officer under s. 34(2)(b) to order the person's immediate release from custody. If the custody officer decides to release the person arrested then according to s. 32(5) he/she must be released without bail unless the custody officer takes the view that there is need for further investigation of any matter for which he/she was detained or that proceedings may be taken against him/her in respect of any such matter. If either of these conditions apply, the person detained is to be released on bail as required by s. 34(5)(b). Although the police can grant bail unconditionally, under the Bail Act 1976 s. 3A(5) conditions can be imposed in certain circumstances. Where the custody officer is of the view that there are good grounds for detaining the suspect but does not have sufficient evidence to sustain a charge, the custody officer must under s. 37(2) release him/her with or without bail unless he/she reasonably believes that detention of the suspect is necessary to secure or preserve evidence relating to an offence for which he is under arrest or to obtain evidence by questioning him/her. In *R v Davidson* [1988] a finding by the court that the detention of a suspect was in breach of s. 34 was a factor in the judge's decision to exclude evidence on the grounds of oppression.

A custody officer may authorise the detention of a suspect in police custody under s. 37(2) if:

(a) he/she considers it necessary to detain a suspect without charge to secure or to preserve evidence relating to an offence for which the suspect is under arrest, or

(b) to obtain such evidence by further questioning.

Where this is so, the custody officer must make a written record of the grounds for the detention as soon as practicable in the presence of the person arrested, who must be informed of the grounds for the further detention at that time or before he/she is questioned further about the offence. If at the time the suspect is incapable of understanding what is being said to him/her or is violent or likely to become violent or is in need of urgent medical attention, the written record need not be made in the presence of the suspect.

If and when the custody officer decides that there is sufficient evidence to charge the suspect with the offence for which he/she was arrested then he/she must either be charged or be released with or without charge either with or without police bail. If the suspect is released at a time when a decision whether to prosecute for the offence for which he/she was arrested has not been made, the custody officer must inform him/her of that fact. Persons who are not in a fit state to be charged or released can be kept in police custody pursuant to s. 37(7)(a) until such time as they are fit. Apart from those instances where a suspect is arrested for a serious arrestable offence, as defined in PACE, a suspect may not be held in police detention without charge for more than 24 hours. If after 24 hours have elapsed the person has not been charged he/she must be released on bail or without bail.

15. Review of detention

PACE requires that reviews of the detention of suspects who have not been charged as well as those who have, are conducted as required by s. 40. The detention of suspects arrested but not charged is reviewed by an officer of at least the rank of inspector who has not been directly involved in the investigation. For those suspects who have been charged, the review is conducted by the custody officer. In both cases, the first review should be conducted no later than six hours after detention was first authorised and the second review should be conducted no later than nine hours after the first, with subsequent reviews carried out at intervals of no more than nine hours. Nevertheless, a review may be postponed if it is impracticable to carry it out at the latest time specified. Such a postponement may be justified if the reviewing officer is satisfied that a review would interrupt questioning then in progress and would thereby prejudice the investigation. It may also be postponed if no review officer is readily available at the time. However, a postponed review must be carried out as soon after the latest period as practicable and the review officer must record the reason for the postponement on the custody record.

Where a person is being held without charge, the reviewing officer must decide whether to charge him/her, release the person with or without bail or detain him/her further. Prior to conducting the review, the reviewing officer must ensure that the suspect in detention is reminded of his/her entitlement to free independent legal advice from the duty solicitor. The reviewing officer should also give the detained suspect or the solicitor representing him/her at the time of the review an opportunity to make representations concerning further detention before a decision is made on this matter. A violent or abusive suspect may not be given a hearing because the reviewing officer is not obliged to receive representations from a suspect who is considered unfit to make representations because of his/her condition or behaviour under PACE s. 40(13).

As previously mentioned, a suspect cannot be detained at a police station without charge for more than 24 hours from the commencement of detention, but the period of detention may be extended up to 36 hours if the conditions specified in s. 42(1) are satisfied. These are:

(a) that a police officer of the rank of superintendent or above who is responsible for the police station at which the person is detained has reasonable grounds for believing that such detention is necessary to secure or preserve evidence relating to an offence for which the person is under arrest or to obtain such evidence by questioning him/her;

(b) that the offence for which he/she is under arrest is a serious arrestable offence;

(c) that the investigation is being conducted diligently and swiftly.

No order for extended detention can be made before the second review of detention, that is 15 hours after the commencement of detention. If extended detention is authorised, the suspect, and/or his/her solicitor must be afforded the opportunity to make representations. When the period of extended detention elapses, the suspect must be released from detention either with or without bail unless he/she has been charged with an offence or further detention has been authorised by a magistrates' court under s. 42(10). A suspect who has been released may not be arrested for the same offence unless new evidence is uncovered that would justify his/her being re-arrested. Detention extending to a maximum of 96 hours from the commencement of detention may be ordered by a magistrates' court under s. 44(1) through the issue of a warrant on the application of a constable, but this is resorted to infrequently.

A highly informative extract from the book *Safeguarding the Rights of Suspects in Police Custody* (1990) by Dixon *et al.* appears in the book *Criminal Justice, Text and Materials* (1999) by Wasik *et al.* at page 266.

16. Questioning of suspects

The questioning of suspects is not an activity that can only be undertaken by the police. It may, for example, be undertaken by store detectives and by a representative of the management of a store. Anyone undertaking the questioning of suspects must work within a regulatory framework that is partly common law, partly statute law (PACE) and partly subordinate legislation in the form of Code C. The infringement of Code C may result in some important evidence being excluded in the event of a prosecution. Code C para. 11.1 states that following a decision to arrest a suspect, the suspect must not be 'interviewed' about the relevant offence except at a police station or other authorised place of detention unless the delay would be likely to:

(a) lead to interference with or harm to evidence connected with an offence or interference with or physical harm to other people, or

(b) lead to the alerting of other people suspected of having committed an offence but not yet arrested for it, or

(c) hinder the recovery of property obtained in consequence of the commission of an offence.

Interviewing in any of the circumstances specified in (a) to (c) above must cease once the relevant risk has been averted or the necessary questions have been asked to attempt to avert that risk. Code C para. 12.1 states that the custody officer is responsible for deciding whether to deliver the suspect into the custody of a police officer who wishes to interview or conduct inquiries that require the presence of the suspect. Interviewing is defined in general terms in para. 11.1A as the questioning of a person regarding his/her involvement or suspected involvement in a criminal offence(s) which, by virtue of para. 10.1, is required to be conducted under caution. If the caution is omitted, the evidence obtained may be ruled inadmissible. The procedures undertaken pursuant to the Road Traffic Act 1988 s. 7 (the provision of specimens for analysis) do not amount to interviewing for the purposes of PACE and as specified in Code C. Nor does the questioning of a person only to establish his/her identity, or the ownership of a vehicle or to obtain information in accordance with any relevant statutory requirement. Moreover, questioning that is confined to the proper and effective conduct of a search does not constitute an interview, nor does an informal conversation that does not relate to the circumstances of an offence that the police are investigating. Questions asked of a person designed to secure admissions do, however, constitute an interview, as do questions intended to elicit an explanation of the circumstances that appear to amount to the commission of a criminal offence. The test for deciding whether questioning at the time of the arrest is an interview is whether the questions asked are directed at obtaining admissions on a vital part of the case against the person arrested. Thus an extensive conversation in a police car on the way to the police station could constitute an interview.

If the suspect has requested legal advice he/she may not be interviewed without this advice being provided unless he/she is being lawfully held incommunicado under PACE s. 58 or an officer of the rank of superintendent or above has reasonable grounds to believe that the delay will involve an immediate risk of harm to persons or a serious loss of, or damage to property. The suspect may also be interviewed without the benefit of legal advice where a solicitor has been contacted and agreed to attend but awaiting his/her arrival would cause unreasonable delay to the process of investigation or where attendance of the solicitor nominated by the suspect cannot be obtained and the suspect does not wish to avail himself/herself of the services of a duty solicitor. In this latter situation, or where the suspect has waived his/her right to legal advice, the interview can start without delay.

A suspect will normally have been cautioned on being arrested unless his/her condition or behaviour rendered this impracticable at the time. If this should have been the case, he/she must be cautioned before any questions relating to the offence (or further questions, if his/her previous answers have provided grounds for suspicion) are put to him/her with a view to obtaining evidence that may be given in court. Deaf persons and those who do not understand English very well (or at all) may require an interpreter, although this right can be waived by the suspect. All interviews must take place in rooms that are lighted, adequately heated and ventilated.

Since any significant statement made by the suspect may be used in evidence against him/her, the interviewing officer must put this to the suspect at the start of an interview carried out at a police station. If a suspect is being questioned about a serious offence, the police officer must inform him/her of the offence of which he/she is suspected, lest the suspect should make admissions unaware of the gravity of the offence. If the interview is suspended and then recommenced, the interviewing officer must remind the suspect of his/her entitlement to free legal advice immediately prior to the recommencement of the interview. Paragraph 11.5 of Code C states that an accurate record must be made of all interviews whether or not the interview takes place at a police station. Most interviews at police stations are routinely tape-recorded on a special recording machine to prevent subsequent tampering. The tape recording of interviews is regulated by Code E. However, the Crown Prosecution Service tends to rely on a written summary of the tape-recorded interview and these summaries often vary in their quality and accuracy. The tape itself is only likely to be used if there is some subsequent dispute over the way in which the interview was conducted.

According to para. 3.4 of the code of practice issued under the Criminal Procedure and Investigations Act 1996 in conducting an investigation, the investigating officer should pursue all reasonable lines of inquiry whether these point towards or away from the suspect. It is quite proper for police officers to pursue their interrogation of the suspect to obtain admissions even where he/she denies any involvement in the offence or simply declines to answer. However, questioning that is carried on after repeated denials or refusals to answer questions may become oppressive. A solicitor who is present should intervene if he/she considers that the police officer's questioning has become oppressive because the officer may not realise that he/she has crossed the boundary between what is permitted and what is not. There is a body of research evidence that indicates in the recent past that solicitors and accredited non-solicitor advisors tended to remain silent and when they did intervene it was to help the police rather than their clients. Under the Human Rights Act 1998 Schedule 1 Article 3 there is a right not to be subjected to inhuman and degrading treatment. Verbal bullying by the police could constitute such treatment and so police officers must be careful not to overstep the mark between what is permitted and what is not. Unless the suspect asks the officer directly, the officer must not indicate the action the police will take if he/she answers or refuses to answer questions or make a statement. In the event of a direct question from the suspect, the interviewing officer may inform him/her of the proposed action but Code C para. 11.3 makes it clear that the proposed action must be both proper and warranted. If the interviewing officer decides to take a break in questioning under caution, he/she must ensure that the suspect is aware that the caution is still operative and, in case of doubt, the caution should be given once more. When dealing with juveniles, mentally disordered and handicapped persons, the caution must be repeated in the presence of the appropriate adult. It is essential that the person cautioned should be clear about the significance of the caution, and the interviewing officer should, if necessary, explain it in words that the suspect can understand. Irrespective of whether they are suspected or are merely helping police with their enquiries, juveniles, mentally disordered and handicapped persons must not be asked to provide a signed written statement in the absence of the appropriate adult unless circumstances are such as to give rise to, or pose an immediate danger to persons or serious damage to property. According to Code C para. 12.3, a suspect who is unfit because of the effect of alcohol or drugs may not be questioned except in accordance with Annexe C of Code C. The police surgeon can give advice on whether such a person is fit to be interviewed. Code C para. 10.5C makes it clear that a suspect should not be left in any doubt that persistent silence may result in continued detention for interrogation.

17. The right to remain silent

The right to remain silent whilst in police detention remains but it was significantly undermined by the Criminal Justice and Public Order Act 1994 ss 34–37 because the courts may draw inferences from a suspect's failure to mention facts in an interview that he/she later seeks to rely upon as a defence. In *Condron* v *UK* [2000], two men were accused of drug dealing. Their solicitor believed that they were unfit to answer police questions even though there was medical evidence to the contrary, but both men refused to answer questions. They had been cautioned by the police and confirmed that they understood the implications of the warning regarding the inference that might be drawn by the jury arising from their exercise of their right to remain silent. The trial judge, when summing up, omitted to remind the jury that they could draw an adverse inference from the accused's silence only if that silence could be sensibly attributed to their being either no answer or none that would stand up to cross-examination in court. Having stated that the jury was not properly directed, the European Court of Human Rights ruled that the Court of Appeal could not adopt the role of the jury or second guess the outcome of jury deliberations if there was a misdirection by the trial judge. The Court went on to state, 'any other conclusion would be at variance with the fundamental importance of the right to silence, a right which, as observed earlier, lies at the heart of the notion of a fair procedure guaranteed by Article 6 of the Convention'.

18. The decision to charge

In the investigation of a crime, the decision to charge a suspect may be seen as the final stage in a three stage process. These stages are:

(a) gathering information

(b) the creation of suspicion in the mind of the interviewing officer

(c) the interviewing officer arrives at the stage where he/she considers that there is sufficient evidence to justify a charge against the suspect.

Alternatively, it may be that the suspect simply confesses to the offence within a short time of being arrested. Indeed, there is research that indicates that the police obtain confessions in approximately 60 per cent of cases either prior to or during an interview, but it has to be remembered that people do sometimes confess to crimes that they did not commit. Once a police officer decides that a point has been reached where he/she has enough evidence to charge the suspect, giving the suspect an opportunity to say anything more will form part of the interview. If anything more is said it must be recorded as part of the interview.

Code C states that once a police officer arrives at the belief that a prosecution should be instigated against the suspect, that there is sufficient evidence for it to succeed and that the suspect has said all that he/she wishes to say about the offence(s), the interviewing officer must bring the suspect before the custody officer without delay. If, however, the person detained is suspected of more than one offence, it is permissible to defer this until he/she has been questioned about these other offences. The custody officer is responsible for deciding whether or not the suspect should be charged with one or more offences. It is necessary to caution a person who is charged. He/she must be provided with a written notice containing the caution but also indicating the particulars of the offence(s) and information relating to the police officer and the police station concerned. Code C para. 16.5 is quite explicit when it states that questions relating to an offence may not normally be put to a person after he/she has been charged with the offence or informed that he/she may be prosecuted for it. Paragraph 16.5 does, however, permit further questions to be put if they are necessary for the purpose of preventing or minimising harm or loss to some other person or to the public or for clearing up an ambiguity in a previous answer or statement. Further questions may also be put where it is in the interests of justice that the suspect should have these put to him/her and have an opportunity to comment on information concerning the offence which has come to light after he/she was charged or informed that he/she might be prosecuted. Although the suspect does not have to say anything, he/she must be warned that anything he/she does say may be given in evidence and he/she must be reminded of his/her right to free independent legal advice. Apart from the exceptions allowed for under para. 16.5 there are two other exceptions where further questioning is permitted after a suspect has been charged. These are:

(a) if a police officer wishes to bring to the notice of the accused a written statement made or the content of an interview with another person;

191

(b) where the director of the Serious Fraud Office can require the production of documents under the Criminal Justice Act 1987 s. 2 and an explanation of them.

19. Police discretion

In *R* v *Metropolitan Police Commissioner ex p. Blackburn* [1968] Lord Denning MR said (at p. 136):

> I hold it to be the duty of the Commissioner of Police of the Metropolis, as it is of every chief constable, to enforce the law of the land . . . He must decide whether or no suspected persons are to be prosecuted . . . But [in this] he is not the servant of anyone, save of the law itself. No Minister of the Crown can tell him . . . that he must, or must not, prosecute this man or that one. Nor can any police authority tell him so. The responsibility for law enforcement lies on him. He is answerable to the law and the law alone.

Although this discretion lies with the chief officer of the police force in question, it is normally exercised by the officers to whom he delegates his authority. The police may therefore release a suspect without charge if the suspect was arrested for an offence. If a suspect was not arrested but warned instead that he/she might be prosecuted, the police may send him/her a notice that no summons will be issued. In such cases the police may give the suspect an informal warning with regard to his/her future behaviour. In addition to such informal warnings the police have discretion to issue a formal caution to adult offenders. These do not count as convictions but they are recorded and the records are kept for five years. In the event that a person who has been formally cautioned should be convicted of an offence in the future, the caution could be cited at the sentencing stage although it would not appear on the same form as the list of previous convictions. A formal caution is usually administered by a police officer of at least the rank of inspector at a police station, but if a person is elderly it may be administered at the person's home at the discretion of the police. Three conditions must be satisfied before the police can administer a formal caution. These are:

(a) the evidence obtained must be sufficient to warrant a prosecution,

(b) the offender must have admitted his/her guilt, and

(c) the person being cautioned agrees to the matter being disposed of in this way bearing in mind that the caution could be cited in court.

An adult offender should sign an acknowledgement signifying his/her agreement to the caution and admit the offence for which it is given. A court may declare invalid a caution where no admission of guilt has been obtained. However, a caution does not preclude a private prosecution being undertaken, but a defendant may be able to apply for a court order that the prosecution should be stayed. In *Hayter* v *L and another* [1998] the defendants were arrested for offences under the Public Order Act 1986 and the Offences against the Person Act 1861 when they attacked another young man. As the defendants were aged 16 at the time and were of previous good character, they received a formal caution from the police, having received legal advice. The victim's father, who was a solicitor, laid informations before magistrates but the defendants then contended that for the magistrates to hear these informations preferred by the father would be an abuse of the process of the court. A youth court concluded that the private prosecution brought by the victim's father was an abuse of process and ordered that the proceedings be stayed. When the victim's father appealed to the Divisional Court of Queen's Bench by way of case stated, the court held that it was not an abuse of process to prosecute a defendant after he/she had been cautioned by the police unless the particular circumstances of the case disclosed an abuse. On this basis, the court ruled that there was no proper basis for the magistrates to have ordered a stay of proceedings.

The Crime and Disorder Act 1988 ss 65 and 66 introduced a procedure for the reprimanding and warning of children and young persons who have committed offences. These apply where:

(a) a constable has sufficient evidence for there to be a reasonable prospect of the child or young person being convicted of an offence,

(b) the offender admits the offence and has not been convicted of any offence, and

(c) the constable is satisfied that it would not be in the public interest for the offender to be prosecuted.

A constable may reprimand an offender who has not previously been reprimanded or warned. Alternatively, the constable may take the graver step of warning an offender who has not been warned previously. If the offence has been committed more than two years after a previous warning and is not so serious as to require a charge to be brought, the constable may issue a further warning. All reprimands and warnings must be given in a police station and, where an offender is aged under 17, it must be given in the presence of an appropriate adult. A person who receives a warning will be referred to a youth offending team and arrangements will be made for him/her to participate in a rehabilitation programme. Failure on the part of the offender to participate in the rehabilitation scheme may be cited in criminal proceedings in the same circumstances as may a reprimand or warning.

20. The role of the Crown Prosecution Service

The Crown Prosecution Service (CPS) was created under the Prosecution of Offences Act 1985 s. 1. Although it is headed by the Director of Public Prosecutions (DPP) the service is organised into 42 regions that almost match the different police authorities. Each regional office is headed by a Chief Crown Prosecutor who is responsible to the DPP for the CPS in his/her area. Each Chief Crown Prosecutor is assisted by a staff of qualified lawyers, who act as Crown Prosecutors, and a support staff. The Prosecution of Offences Act 1985 s. 3(2) requires the DPP to take over the conduct of all criminal proceedings instituted by the police (with the exception of a number of minor road traffic offences). Since the DPP acts through the agency of the CPS it has an unfettered discretion under s. 23 to discontinue any proceedings and withdraw a summons. A case must be reviewed by a CPS lawyer before it is accepted for continued prosecution by the CPS. He/she will serve a notice of discontinuance (or simply offer no evidence in court) if he/she takes the view that proceedings should not have been brought. The CPS lawyer is obliged to follow the guidance given by the DPP in arriving at his/her decision. In principle, a police prosecution should only go ahead if both the police officer(s) responsible and the CPS lawyer to whom it is sent agree that proceedings are appropriate. Nevertheless, there is research to show that despite the creation of the CPS many weak cases are still prosecuted with predictable results.

21. The decision to prosecute

No matter how serious the offence, a prosecution should not go ahead if it does not pass the evidential test as set out in para. 4.1 of the Code for Crown Prosecutors. The Crown Prosecutor must be satisfied that there is enough evidence for there to be a realistic prospect of conviction against the defendant. According to para. 5.2 this is an objective test meaning that a jury or bench of magistrates properly directed, in accordance with the law, is more likely than not to convict the defendant of the charge alleged. In deciding whether the evidence is reliable and can be used, Crown Prosecutors should consider the matters set out in para. 5.3(b) to (c). Paragraph 5.4 states that Crown Prosecutors should not ignore evidence because they are not sure that it can be used or is reliable but they should look at it closely when deciding whether there is a realistic prospect of a conviction.

If there is enough evidence to justify a prosecution, the Crown Prosecutor must consider whether a prosecution would be in the public interest. The Code for Crown Prosecutors in para. 6.4 sets out the factors that indicate that proceedings may be required, whilst para. 6.5 sets out the factors tending against a prosecution. Paragraph 6.6 of the Code states that Crown Prosecutors should not add up the number of factors on each side. Rather, they should carry out an evaluation exercise to form an overview of the case. They should have regard to the interests of the victim (or the victim's family) but it does not follow that a prosecution must be stopped merely because the victim (or the victim's family) desires this. Crown prosecutors must also consider the interests of young offenders when deciding whether it is in the public interest to prosecute but should not avoid a prosecution merely because of the age of the person concerned. Paragraph 6.9 makes it clear that it is the seriousness of the offence and/or the youth's past behaviour that is important in deciding whether to prosecute or not.

According to para. 6.12, Crown Prosecutors should consider alternatives to prosecution, which could include a formal police caution, and should inform the police if they consider that this is more appropriate than a prosecution. If the police do not wish to offer a caution then the Crown Prosecutor can consider the case again.

A decision not to prosecute is capable of judicial review. Even though the DPP is not obliged to give reasons for a decision not to prosecute, failure to provide a sufficient explanation in certain circumstances may give rise to a claim for judicial review. In *R v DPP ex p. Manning* [2000] the applicant's brother had died of asphyxia whilst under restraint following an intense argument with two prison officers whilst on remand for a violent offence. The death was investigated by the police and the papers were ultimately sent to the CPS. At a coroner's inquest the evidence indicated that the death had resulted from the manner in which the deceased's head had been held by an officer during the incident and the jury returned a verdict of unlawful killing. A specialist senior caseworker at the CPS undertook a detailed examination of all the available evidence, including that produced at the inquest, and in his review note he recorded his investigations, his conclusion and the reasoning on which they were based. Although the caseworker referred to the weaknesses and inconsistencies of the prison officers' evidence, he rejected alternative potential charges and considered that in respect of 'unlawful act manslaughter' that it was only the fatal force to the deceased's neck which should be characterised as excessive so that the only potential defendant was the officer identified as holding the deceased's head. He concluded that there was a *prima facie* case but no realistic prospect of the prosecution being able to establish that excessive force had been used deliberately as opposed to an attempt to effect a proper restraint that had been frustrated by the struggle with the deceased. When he communicated his decision not to prosecute, the caseworker stated that there was insufficient evidence to justify any criminal prosecution. Moreover, he was not satisfied that the available evidence would provide a realistic prospect of convicting either of the officers of an offence arising from the death. Having unsuccessfully requested full reasons for that decision, the applicant sought judicial review to challenge the lawfulness of the decision and in so doing the caseworker's review note was served on him. The Divisional Court of Queen's Bench held that there was no absolute obligation imposed on the DPP to give reasons for a decision not to prosecute. However, the court stated that the right to life was the most fundamental of all the rights under the European Convention on Human Rights and Fundamental Freedoms and it allowed limited scope for derogation. Therefore, since the death of a person in the state's custody resulting from violence inflicted by its agents necessarily aroused concern, the DPP would be expected to give reasons for such a decision where an inquest jury had returned a verdict of unlawful killing implicating an identifiable person. Accordingly, the court quashed the DPP's decision.

22. Other prosecuting agencies

The police and the CPS are not the only agencies that are involved in criminal prosecutions. There are a range of other prosecuting authorities including the Trading Standards Officers, Inland Revenue, HM Customs and Excise, the DHSS, the Post Office, RSPCA and the Factory Inspectorate. In addition, victims and their relatives may bring private prosecutions although in some instances they may need official permission as explained below.

23. Jurisdiction of the criminal courts

In general, English and Welsh courts normally decline to accept jurisdiction over offences that were committed outside their territorial jurisdiction. Nevertheless, there are some important exceptions to this general rule. The Criminal Justice (Terrorism and Conspiracy) Act 1998 ss 5–8 confer on English and Welsh courts the jurisdiction to try conspiracies to commit offences abroad if the qualifying conditions are met. The Criminal Justice Act 1993 Part I ss 1–6 confers jurisdiction on English and Welsh courts in respect of certain offences of fraud and dishonesty (and the inchoate offences linked with them) provided that any of the relevant events occurred in England and Wales. Widespread disgust over the phenomenon known as 'sex tourism' led to the enactment of the Sexual Offences (Conspiracy and Incitement) Act 1996 which confers jurisdiction on British courts in respect of certain acts of incitement to commit sexual acts against children abroad. All offences committed in British territorial waters are triable by the British courts, and under the Merchant Shipping Act 1995 s. 282, a crime committed ashore or afloat by a person who was employed as a master or seaman of a British ship is triable in Britain regardless of where it is committed. The Civil Aviation Act 1982 makes offences committed on British-controlled aircraft in flight elsewhere than over the UK, triable in Britain.

Having made the decision to prosecute, the Crown Prosecutor should select those charges that reflect the seriousness of the offending that give the court adequate sentencing powers and which enable the case to be presented in a clear and uncomplicated fashion. Nevertheless, the Crown Prosecutor need not necessarily continue with the most serious charge available where there is a choice and should not continue with more charges than is necessary. Nor should he/she go ahead with a more serious charge just to encourage the defendant to plead guilty to a less serious one.

24. Charge bargaining

Paragraph 9.1 of the Code for Crown Prosecutors states that they should accept a plea arrangement put forward by the defendant (or his/her legal advisor) only if they think that the court would be able to pass a sentence that matches the gravity of the offending especially where there are aggravating features. Paragraph 9.1 makes it clear that Crown Prosecutors must never accept a guilty plea just because it is convenient, and para. 9.2 states that particular care must be observed when considering pleas that would enable the defendant to avoid a mandatory minimum sentence.

25. Consent for a prosecution

It is necessary to obtain the consent of either the Attorney General or the DPP as a precondition for the prosecution of certain types of offence. The Attorney General's consent is required where issues of public policy, national security and relations with foreign countries may affect the decision to prosecute. Examples of such offences include those under the Official Secrets Act 1911, offences stirring up racial hatred contrary to the Public Order Act 1986 and the Law Reform (Year and a Day) Act 1996 for prosecutions of a homicide where the victim dies after three years have elapsed from the event causing death or if the accused has already been convicted for the event that caused the death. The consent of the DPP is required for a diverse range of offences under the Theft Act 1968, the Criminal Law Act 1967, the Sexual Offences Act 1956, the Suicide Act 1961, the Public Order Act 1986 and the War Crimes Act 1991. However, the consent of the DPP may be given a Crown Prosecutor under the Prosecution of Offences Act 1985 s. 1(7) who must consider the propriety or otherwise of an offence before proceedings are commenced.

26. Immunity from prosecution

Before commencing any proceedings, the CPS must consider whether an offender has personal immunity from prosecution. Children under 10 years of age are irrebuttably presumed to be incapable of committing a crime, and for children between the ages of 10 and 13, the prosecutor must consider whether the evidence is strong enough to rebut the presumption that the child is incapable of forming the necessary criminal intent. In addition, foreign sovereigns or heads of state, their families and servants all have immunity under the State Immunity Act 1978 s. 20, as do diplomats, members of staff of diplomatic missions and their families under the Diplomatic Privileges Act 1964.

Progress test

1. Why is it provided in PACE that a constable/officer must have 'reasonable grounds for suspecting' before he/she can stop and search persons or vehicles?

2. How does the power to stop and search under the Criminal Justice and Public Order Act 1994 s. 60 differ from the power granted under PACE s. 1?

3. In what circumstances may a magistrates' court issue an arrest warrant?

4. How does the power conferred on a private citizen to make an arrest under PACE s. 24(4) differ from the powers conferred on the police under s. 24(6) and s. 24(7)?

5. What rights does a suspect who is arrested have once he/she has been brought to a police station?

6. What powers does a police constable have to search a suspect following an arrest?

7. What is the role of the custody officer?

8. When must the custody officer release a suspect unconditionally?

9. What alternatives might the police adopt if they should decide that a prosecution is not warranted where the suspect has been arrested?

10. What considerations should a Crown Prosecutor bear in mind when deciding whether to prosecute or not?

11. In what circumstances might a decision not to prosecute be amenable to judicial review?

Further reading

Books

Cousens, M. and R. Blair (2000) *Butterworths Police and Criminal Evidence Act Cases* (London: Butterworths).

Cownie, F. and A. Bradney (2000) *The English Legal System in Context* (London: Butterworths, chapters 12–14).

Murphy, P. (ed.) (2001) *Blackstone's Criminal Practice* (London: Blackstone Press).

Sprack, J. (2000) *Emmins on Criminal Procedure* (London: Blackstone Press).

Wasik, M., T. Gibbons and M. Redmayne (1999) *Criminal Justice: Text and materials* (London: Longman).

Article

Raine, J.W. and M.J. Wilson (1997) 'Police bail with conditions: perspectives on the use, misuse and consequences of a new police power', *British Journal of Criminology*, Vol. 37, No. 4.

Useful websites

The website of the Lord Chancellor's Department can be accessed on www.gtnet.gov.uk/ and contains much useful information on the magistracy and criminal justice system. Another useful source of up-to-date information is the website of the Home Office which can be accessed on www.homeoffice.gov.uk/

The annual report of the Metropolitan Police can be accessed on www.met.police.uk/ and in the appendices will be found statistics on stop and search, indicating the number of arrests made. These statistics are very revealing and clearly show that most stop and search operations are conducted under powers conferred by PACE.

The website of the Crown Prosecution Service can be accessed on www.cps.gov.uk/

11

Criminal justice system 2

1. Introduction

Almost all criminal cases begin in magistrates' courts even if they do not end there. The *Criminal Statistics for England and Wales* for 1999, which was not an atypical year, show that magistrates' courts dealt with approximately 1.88 million cases. Accused persons sometimes appear before a magistrates' court because they are responding to a summons to answer one or more allegations contained in an information that has been laid by a police officer or a member of the public before a magistrate (or a magistrates' clerk). Rather than issue a summons when an information is laid, a magistrate can issue a warrant under the Magistrates' Courts Act 1980 s. 1(1) so that an accused person can be arrested and subsequently brought before a court. More often, however, accused persons will appear before a magistrates' court following their release from police custody on bail, having been arrested and charged with one or more offences. Alternatively, they may appear having been arrested and charged with one or more offences to answer these charges, having been held in police custody because they were not granted bail, usually because of the seriousness of the offence(s). Indeed, PACE s. 46(2) requires that any person who has been charged with an offence and who has been kept in police detention must be brought before a magistrates' court (for the petty session area in which the police station is situated) as soon as practicable. It is unusual for a case to be completely disposed of on a first appearance in court unless the accused pleads guilty to a relatively minor offence and the court considers that it does not need a pre-sentence report before passing sentence. The Magistrates' Courts Act 1980 ss 5 and 10 confers on a court a general discretion to adjourn a case at any stage. The accused person will often seek an adjournment to see a solicitor, to apply for financial assistance from the LSC (Legal Services Commission, formerly Legal Aid) and to have time to prepare a defence. The Crown Prosecution Service (CPS) will also need time to prepare for a trial and to ensure that the necessary witnesses are available.

This chapter firstly considers the classification of criminal offences before dealing with summary trial procedure for adults. Thereafter, the matter of remand will be considered with the related issue of bail. It will then be appropriate to consider trial on indictment and the process of sentencing. The chapter concludes with an explanation of the system of appeals.

2. Classification of offences

Criminal offences are commonly classified according to their mode of trial. The Criminal Law Act 1977 s. 14 states that there are three types of offence, namely:

(a) summary offences

(b) indictable only offences (serious offences triable only at the Crown Court)

(c) offences that are triable either way, that is summarily or on indictment.

Summary offences are classified as such by the statutes that define them but, in addition, a number of offences which, before the enactment of the Criminal Law Act 1977, were not classified as summary offences are now classed as such. These offences are generally regarded as the least serious and with few exceptions are always tried in a magistrates' court. The jurisdiction of a magistrates' court to try summary offences in its commission area is set out in the Magistrates' Courts Act 1980 s. 2. According to the *Criminal Statistics for England and Wales* for 1999, approximately 73 per cent of all the cases tried in magistrates' courts were summary offences.

SUMMARY TRIAL FOR ADULTS

3. Conduct of the trial

At the outset, the accused is asked by the court clerk to plead in relation to a written charge known as 'the information'. This comes into existence as a result of either:

(a) the prosecution laying an information before a magistrate (or magistrates' clerk) to obtain a summons or an arrest warrant, or

(b) the accused being charged at a police station.

It is a convention that the charge sheet completed at a police station is regarded as 'the information'. As with a count on an indictment, an information may allege only one offence. There may, nevertheless, be more than one information. One may allege a more serious offence and the other a lesser offence. Where the accused does not wish to contest the charge and also does not wish to attend court in order to plead guilty, he/she may plead guilty by post under the provision of the Magistrates' Courts Act 1980 s. 12. This procedure applies to proceedings by way of summons in an adult magistrates' court for motoring offences carrying no more than three months' imprisonment. If, however, the sentence would result in the accused having twelve or more points endorsed on his/her licence, a court appearance will be necessary if there is to be a disqualification from driving. Ultimately, offering the option of pleading by post is at the discretion of the prosecution, and if permitted, the CPS will inform the clerk of the court that the summons has been served. The defendant must then notify the clerk in writing if he/she desires to plead guilty without attending the court.

The only pleas that can be entered in response to the information are guilty or not guilty. If the accused pleads guilty (as the majority do), the court will usually convict him/her without hearing the evidence. Before sentence is passed, the court will hear a summary of the facts from the prosecution advocate and it will hear a plea in mitigation from the defence. The court may adjourn prior to sentencing so that a pre-sentence report can be prepared on the offender.

A not guilty plea to the information will usually be entered by the defendant in person, after which the court will proceed to hear the evidence for the prosecution. If the defence has objected to an item of prosecution evidence (e.g. a confession or other evidence which it is alleged was obtained illegally) the magistrates must consider its admissibility as a preliminary issue before the evidence for the prosecution is given. They have a limited discretion when dealing with an objection to prosecution evidence since they must abide by the rules of evidence.

The advocate for the prosecution has the right to make a short opening speech outlining the prosecution case, but in a trial of minor road traffic offences he/she may decide to dispense with an opening address. In all probability the defence will have obtained copies of the statements of the prosecution witnesses and a case summary in advance of the trial. Thus the advocate for the defence will be in a position to cross-examine the prosecution witnesses after they have been called and have given their testimony for the prosecution. Oral testimony is given on oath or by affirmation where the witness declines to take the oath. Young children give their evidence without taking an oath and the statements of those witnesses whose evidence is not disputed can simply be read into evidence. At the close of the prosecution case, the defence advocate may submit that there is 'no case to answer'.

4. A submission of 'no case'

The test to be applied by magistrates when such a submission is made is to be found in Practice Direction (Submission of No Case) [1962] 1 WLR 227 which states that the submission may be properly made and upheld when:

(a) no evidence has been produced to prove an essential element in the alleged offence, or

(b) the evidence adduced by the prosecution has been so discredited as a result of cross-examination or is so manifestly unreliable that no reasonable tribunal could safely convict upon it.

Where the submission is made, the clerk, in guiding the court on matters of law, should draw the attention of the magistrates to the Practice Direction. If the magistrates do decide to uphold the submission, the accused is discharged; otherwise the trial will continue.

5. The defence

According to the Magistrates' Courts Rules 1981 r. 13 paras 2–6, the defence advocate is entitled to call evidence and make a speech after calling all the evidence for the defence. If the defence advocate calls evidence, the prosecution may call evidence to rebut that evidence. The accused may give evidence on his/her own behalf but cannot be compelled to do so and the prosecution may cross-examine an accused who gives evidence. Although the prosecution advocate has no right to make a closing speech, he/she will normally be permitted to address the court on any point of law raised in the speech for the defence. If the prosecution is permitted to make a second speech, the defence advocate must be permitted to making a closing speech thereby giving the defence the final word.

An accused who is unrepresented on his/her arrival at court can avail himself/herself of the services of the duty solicitor but the latter cannot act as an advocate for him/her. The court clerk may be able to help an unrepresented accused by giving advice on the presentation of the case for the defence but the clerk should not permit himself/herself to become an advocate for the accused. At the conclusion of the evidence for the prosecution, the accused may address the court in person irrespective of whether he/she subsequently calls evidence.

6. The verdict

Lay magistrates will usually retire to consider their verdict but they do so without the court clerk. The result of the magistrates' deliberations need not be unanimous but they may never return a verdict of guilty of a lesser charge where there is only one information. Thus they must either convict or acquit the accused of the offence charged in the information. However, under the Road Traffic Offenders Act 1988 s. 24, magistrates may return an alternative verdict and thus acquit on the offence charged but convict of another, lesser offence. Where the verdict is guilty, the magistrates will then sentence the offender but may adjourn the case for a pre-sentence report and/or a medical report. District judges of magistrates' courts tend to deliver their verdict at the conclusion of the case for the defence. Since the coming into operation of the Human Rights Act 1998, both magistrates and district judges must give reasons for their decisions.

7. Remanding the accused

If the offence is a summary one and the magistrates' court grants an adjournment before trial, the court has discretion to adjourn without remanding the accused. A remand would occur where the court adjourns the case and either bails the accused for the duration of the adjournment or commits him/her to custody to be brought before the court on the adjournment date. If the offence is triable either way and the accused has not been remanded previously and appears in answer to a summons, the court has discretion not to remand when adjourning. In all other cases, namely:

(a) offences triable only on indictment,

(b) offences triable either way where the prosecution was commenced by way of charge, and

(c) adjournment for reports following a summary conviction,

the magistrates must remand the accused by granting him/her bail or remanding him/her in custody. The difference between adjourning without remand and adjourning by granting bail is that, in the former, no adverse consequences follow from failing to appear on the adjournment date except that it is likely that the offence will be proved in his/her absence. In the latter instance, the accused is under a legal obligation to appear and will commit an offence in the event that he/she fails to appear. It is only in the least serious cases that magistrates adjourn without remanding the accused. The decision of the Divisional Court in R v *Nottingham Justices ex p. Davies* [1981] received statutory confirmation in the Bail Act 1976 Schedule 1 para. 11A. The result is that the defence is allowed a maximum of two argued bail applications before magistrates unless there has been a change in the circumstances of the accused. Following an amendment to the Magistrates' Courts Act 1980 s. 128, the accused can consent to being remanded in custody for up to 28 days without attending court, but in any event s. 128A provides that a magistrates' court can remand an accused person for up to 28 days whether he/she consents or not. If the court remands an accused following a conviction in order to have reports prepared on him/her, the period of the remand must not exceed three weeks in custody or four weeks on bail. Under s. 128A, an accused may be remanded in custody for up to 28 days if he/she is already serving a custodial sentence for some other offence.

The Bail Act 1976 confers a right to bail except in specified circumstances. Thus an accused person may be granted bail unconditionally in which case he/she is obliged only to surrender to custody at the specified time and place. However, a person may be refused bail in the circumstances set out in Schedule 1 Part II paras 2–6. The usual grounds that are relied upon when bail is refused are:

- the risk that further offences will be committed
- the risk of non attendance at trial
- the risk of interference with witnesses.

In so far as they are necessary to reduce these risks, conditions may be attached to the granting of bail such as:

- residence at a home address or bail hostel, and/or
- reporting to an identified police station on specific dates and at specified times, or
- prohibitions on the contact with witnesses, or visiting certain places.

In addition to the above, a deposit of security or sureties may sometimes be required to guarantee attendance at court on pain of paying the forfeiture of a specific sum of money. If a person is remanded in custody, the Prosecution of Offences Act 1985 s. 22 sets limits on the amount of time an accused may be held in custody before the commencement of his/her trial. These periods vary depending on the classification of the offence.

If no application for bail is made, the court will tend to assume that there are sufficient reasons for remanding the accused in custody. The CPS can oppose an application for bail but reasons must be given. These could include the seriousness of the charge, that the accused's previous record make it likely that he/she will receive a custodial sentence if convicted, and/or that he/she is appearing before the courts on other charges and the present offence was committed whilst on bail. The advocate representing the defendant may then attempt to counter the objections put forward by the CPS. Having heard the arguments for and against and the evidence, if any, the court will announce its decision giving reasons. In most cases an accused person who has been refused bail by a magistrates' court can make a further application to the Crown Court or High Court, but only a High Court judge can vary the terms on which magistrates have made the grant of bail conditional. For a more detailed treatment of the law relating to bail applications see *Emmins on Criminal Procedure*, chapter 6.

EITHER WAY OFFENCES

8. Mode of trial

If the Criminal Justice (Mode of Trial) Bill is reintroduced into Parliament and becomes law, it will abolish the accused's right of election to trial by jury and the magistrates will decide on the mode of trial. At present, the Magistrates' Courts Act 1980 ss 17A–21 sets out the method for determining the mode of trial when adults are charged with offences that are triable either way. Where the charge is one of criminal damage, s. 22 special rules apply. In general, if the damage to the property does not exceed £5,000, the magistrates are obliged to try the offence summarily. If it exceeds this sum then they are required to determine the mode of trial according to the Magistrates' Courts Act 1980 ss 19–21.

The standard procedure for establishing the mode of trial when an adult accused appears before the court in response to a summons (or as a condition of bail having previously been arrested under warrant) or as a result of a charge having been preferred against him/her at a police station is contained in s. 17A. The procedure has to be complied with before any evidence is called for and it should normally take place in the presence of the accused. It is as follows:

(a) The charge is read out to the accused.

(b) The court explains to the accused that he/she may *indicate* whether he/she would plead guilty or not guilty if the offence proceeded to trial.

(c) The court then asks the accused whether (if the offence went to trial) he/she would plead guilty or not guilty.

In relation to (b) above, before asking the accused to plead, the court should explain that if the he/she pleads guilty, the proceedings will be treated as a trial of a summary offence at which a guilty plea has been tendered. Furthermore, the court must explain that he/she might be committed for sentence to the Crown Court if the court takes the view that its powers of sentencing are inadequate. If the accused pleads guilty the court will, of course, proceed as if he/she had pleaded guilty at summary trial. On the other hand, if the accused indicates that he/she would plead not guilty the court is required by s. 19 to have regard to representations from the prosecutor or the accused on the most suitable mode of trial. It will then make a decision taking into account the nature and seriousness of the offence and whether the punishment that a magistrates' court could impose would be adequate. A final decision on the mode of trial should not, however, be made until the court has considered the circumstances of the case. Magistrates must consider whether the circumstances of the offence render it of a particularly serious character or whether there are any other circumstances which appear to the court to make it more suitable for the offence to be tried one way rather than another. National Mode of Trial Guidelines exist (revised in 1995) that set out the issues to be considered by magistrates when applying s. 19. These are to be found in section 3D of *Blackstone's Criminal Practice*. If it appears to the court that a summary trial is more appropriate, it is required by s. 20(2) to explain in ordinary language to the accused (usually via the court clerk) that:

(a) this is the court's view and that he/she can either consent to be tried summarily or if, he/she wishes, be tried by a jury, and

(b) if he/she is tried summarily and convicted, he/she may be committed to the Crown Court for sentencing if the magistrates take the view that a greater punishment should be inflicted than they have the power to impose.

Depending on the accused's answer, the court proceeds to summary trial or to committal proceedings. According to the *Criminal Statistics for England and Wales*, either way offences constituted 27 per cent of the cases tried in magistrates' courts in 1999. There is some evidence to show that accused persons opt to be tried in a magistrates' court for these offences in anticipation that they will receive a lighter sentence, following a guilty plea. Magistrates do have the option of committing the offender to the Crown Court for sentencing, but when imposing custodial sentences they are subject to the criteria for determining the length of sentence set out in the Powers of the Criminal Courts (Sentencing) Act 2000.

9. Committal proceedings

If it appears to the court that trial on indictment is more appropriate, the Magistrates' Courts Act 1980 s. 21 requires that the court inform the accused of that decision. It will then inquire into the information that formed the basis of the summons and the magistrates assume the role of examining justices in exercise of their jurisdiction under s. 2. In doing so they follow the Magistrates' Courts Rules 1981 r. 7. The prosecution advocate will outline the case for the prosecution and explain any relevant points of law before presenting the evidence which is all documentary. With the permission of the court, the evidence may be summarised and the magistrates may view any original exhibits. Although no evidence can be called for the defence, the accused, or his/her advocate, can make a submission of 'no case to answer'. If he/she does, or if the court is hesitant about committing the accused for trial, the prosecution advocate is entitled to respond. The magistrates then reach their decision whether or not to commit for trial on the basis of the test laid down in the Magistrates' Courts Act 1980 s. 6(1), namely they must commit if they are of the opinion that there is sufficient evidence to put the accused on trial by jury for any indictable offence. If the test is not satisfied, they must discharge the accused. The Magistrates' Courts Act 1980 s. 6(2) makes it possible for magistrates to commit the accused for trial at the Crown Court without any consideration of the evidence provided certain conditions are satisfied. The necessary conditions are:

(a) The evidence before the court must consist entirely of written statements tendered under s. 5(3) of the 1980 Act.

(b) The accused must have a solicitor acting for him although the solicitor need not be in court.

(c) The barrister/solicitor acting for the accused must not have requested the magistrates to consider a submission that the statements disclose insufficient evidence to put the accused on trial by jury for the offence in question.

As a result of the coming into effect of the Crime and Disorder Act 1998 s. 51, committal proceedings are no longer held for offences triable only on indictment. These are sent immediately to the Crown Court following a very brief preliminary hearing in a magistrates' court.

TRIAL ON INDICTMENT

10. Pre-trial disclosure of information

Irrespective of whether the trial of the defendant is summary or on indictment, the prosecution have a statutory obligation under the Criminal Procedure and Investigations Act 1996 (as supplemented by a Code of Practice) of disclosure to the defence. Guidelines on Disclosure of Information in Criminal Proceedings issued by the Attorney General are also relevant in this context. The aim of the Act is to ensure a fair trial. There are two aspects to the statutory obligation, namely:

(a) a duty to notify the defence of the evidence upon which the prosecution intend to rely, and

(b) a duty to make available to the defence any relevant material upon which they do not intend to rely.

In relation to (a) above, the obligation is more limited where there is a summary trial of an offence triable either way but more extensive when the trial is on indictment. Where there is a summary trial of an offence triable either way, the obligation on the prosecution is qualified by the Magistrates' Court (Advance Information) Rules 1985 (SI 1985 No. 601) r. 5 but the prosecution may be required to provide copies of all written statements as to the facts and a summary of the facts and matters the prosecution intend to produce as evidence in the proceedings. When the trial is on indictment, most of the prosecution evidence in the form of statements or depositions will have been disclosed by the prosecution to the defence prior to the committal proceedings or will have been served with a notice of transfer where there was no committal. If, however, the prosecution wish to call evidence that they did not use at the committal stage, they are under an obligation to serve notice of additional evidence on the defence.

In relation to (b) above, the prosecution is required by the Criminal Procedure and Investigations Act 1996 s. 3 to disclose information that was previously undisclosed which will not form part of their case (known as unused material) if in the opinion of the prosecutor it might undermine the case for the prosecution. This form of disclosure is known as primary prosecution disclosure and must be made as soon as practicable. Nevertheless, material must not be disclosed under this provision if a court has decided that it is not in the public interest that it be disclosed. The prosecution will see the judge privately for the purpose of obtaining authority not to disclose relevant material to the defence when the public interest requires that it should remain undisclosed. Where there is no such material, a written statement must be issued to this effect and given to the advocate for the accused. Once primary prosecution disclosure has taken place and the case is committed/sent to the Crown Court for trial, the advocate for the accused must give a defence statement to the prosecution and the court. This statement must set out the nature of the defence case in general terms and those matters on which the accused takes issue with the prosecution, giving the reasons. If this statement disclosed an alibi, details must be given of the name and address of an alibi witness where this is known. Once the defence statement has been served, the prosecution is required by s. 7 to disclose to the advocate for the accused any previously undisclosed prosecution material that might reasonably be expected to assist the accused's defence as disclosed in the defence statement. This is referred to as secondary prosecution disclosure and must be made as soon as practicable.

The Crown Court (Advance Notice of Expert Evidence) Rules 1987 r. 3(1)(a) requires that, as soon as practicable after committal (or transfer), any party intending to rely on expert evidence must, unless he/she has already done so, provide the other parties with a written statement of any findings or opinion which he/she proposes to produce by way of evidence. There is an obligation under r. 3(1)(b) to provide a copy of the written record on request or allow a reasonable opportunity for the examination of such a record. If, however, there are reasonable grounds for believing that compliance with these rules would result in intimidation of witnesses or interfere with the course of justice, disclosure need not be made but notice must be served on the other parties that the evidence is being withheld and the reasons for this. Failure to comply will mean that expert evidence will be admissible only at trial and only with the permission of the judge.

11. Plea bargaining prior to trial

It is by no means unusual for the prosecution and defence to reach agreement outside court prior to the trial. The essence of such an agreement is likely to be that if the accused pleads guilty to some of the counts on the indictment or if he/she pleads guilty to a lesser offence, as permitted by the Criminal Law Act 1967 s. 6, the Crown will not seek to prove him/her guilty as charged in the indictment. Where the accused has agreed to plead guilty to some of the counts but not guilty to other counts, the prosecution will adopt one of two courses of action. Either, the prosecution will offer no evidence on the latter counts in which case a formal verdict of not guilty will be entered on the judge's order. Alternatively, the prosecution will ask the judge to leave these latter counts on the file, marked 'not to be proceeded with' without the permission of the court or Court of Appeal. Leaving those counts on the file to which the accused has pleaded not guilty avoids the need for an expensive trial and also avoids actually acquitting the accused in respect of those counts. Ultimately, it is for the prosecution to decide what pleas are acceptable although the views of the trial judge will frequently be sought. If the judge disapproves, the prosecution will undoubtedly wish to reconsider its position. This reconsideration will take place in the knowledge that the judge may decline to proceed with the case unless and until the prosecution consults with the Director of Public Prosecutions (DPP) on whether to proceed in the light of the judge's comments. If a plea of 'guilty' to a lesser offence is acceptable, no evidence will be presented by the prosecution on the more serious charge and the defendant will stand acquitted of this offence and the court will proceed to sentencing him/her for the lesser offence once he/she enters a guilty plea.

12. Meetings between advocates and judge

Subject to the judge's agreement, the advocates for the parties may see the judge privately in his/her room before (or during) the trial on a matter relating to the case. The most usual reasons for such a meeting are to obtain guidance about the appropriate pleas and the likely sentence, but it is possible that the advocate for the defence may wish to see the judge to discuss other relevant matters that, in the interests of justice, should not be dealt with in open court.

Since such meetings can give rise to misunderstandings and may occasionally be open to abuse, the Court of Appeal in R v *Turner* [1970] laid down certain guidelines for such private meetings. Although the Court of Appeal confirmed that there must be freedom of access between the defence advocate and the judge, any discussion that takes place must be between the judge and both advocates (prosecution and defence). Moreover, the advocate for the defence should ask to see the judge privately only when he/she considers that this is really necessary. For his/her part, the judge should not indicate in private that he/she would be likely to impose one sentence following a guilty plea but that on conviction following a not guilty plea he/she would impose a severer sentence. Were this to happen, this could put the accused under pressure to plead guilty and effectively deprive him/her of his/her essential freedom of choice over the pleas to be entered to the count(s) on the indictment. By way of exception to this rule, a judge may indicate that irrespective of whether the accused pleads guilty or not guilty the sentence will, or will not, take a particular form. If it is made clear to the accused that he/she will not face a custodial sentence, this may encourage him/her to plead guilty and avoid the expense of a jury trial. If the judge does give an indication of the sentence that he/she will impose, he/she cannot later change his/her mind and seek to impose a different sentence.

13. The indictment

An indictment is a document containing the charges against the accused which always follows a standard layout. The word 'indictment' always appears as a heading. Since most prosecutions on indictment are stated to be in the person of the Crown, this is signified by the letter R (denoting the person of the monarch using the Latin *Regina*) followed by the letter v (in lower case) after which the name or names of the accused appear. An example might be as follows: *R v Algernon Fortescue Green and Ernest Claude Pink.* The person or persons who are named at the beginning of the indictment are named again in that part of the document known as the 'presentment' in which it is stated that they 'are charged as follows:-'. The 'count' or 'counts' then appear, which are the offences alleged against the accused, but each count can allege only one offence. A count comprises the statement of the offence followed by the basic details including the date on which the offence is alleged to have been committed. An indictment may contain two or more counts against the accused.

The Administration of Justice (Miscellaneous Provisions) Act 1933 s. 2(1) states that an indictment must be signed by a proper officer of the Crown Court who shall sign it only if he/she is satisfied that the requirements of s. 2(2) of the Act have been complied with. This subsection enacts that no bill of indictment may be preferred unless the accused has been committed for trial or a notice of transfer has been given to the relevant magistrates' court or a High Court judge has directed or consented to the preferment of a voluntary bill of indictment or the Court of Appeal has ordered a retrial.

The ultimate responsibility for the drafting of the indictment resides with the prosecution who are required to ensure that it is in its proper form prior to the arraignment of the accused. As well as being able to indict the accused for those offences for which he/she has been committed for trial and other indictable offences disclosed by the evidence, the drafter of the indictment can, under the Criminal Justice Act 1988 s. 40(1) include counts for certain summary offences. Summary offences such as common assault, driving whilst disqualified and taking a motor vehicle without the owner's consent may be based on the same facts as those for an offence for which the accused has been committed for trial for an indictable offence. If this should be so, then the CPS may, at its discretion, include as a count on the indictment, a summary offence.

For a more detailed treatment of the counts that can be included on an indictment, see *Blackstone's Criminal Practice* section D9. Specimen counts for all common indictable offences are to be found in Parts B and C.

14. Pre-trial and preparatory hearings

Sections 39 and 40 of the Criminal Procedure and Investigations Act 1996 aim to promote the efficient conduct of trials on indictment. These sections consolidate and supplement the rules for Plea and Directions Hearings (PDH) that were set out in Practice Direction: Crown Court (Plea and Directions Hearings) [1995] 1 WLR 1318. According to para 2:

The purpose of the PDH will be to ensure that all necessary steps have been taken in preparation for trial and to provide sufficient information for a trial date to be arranged. It is expected that the advocate briefed to appear in the case will appear at the PDH wherever practicable.

The Practice Direction applies to all cases except serious fraud. A PDH is usually fixed for 28 days from committal, but for cases that are sent to the Crown Court under the Crime and Disorder Act 1998 s. 51, the date is fixed eight days after the case is sent by the magistrates. If the defendant intends to plead guilty to all or part of the indictment, the defence advocate must notify the probation service, the prosecution and the court as soon as this is known.

Prior to the commencement of a PDH, a detailed questionnaire as set out in the Practice Direction para. 10(a)–(r) has to be completed (as far as possible with the agreement of the advocates for both sides) and sent to the court. The defence must supply the court and prosecution with a full list of the prosecution witnesses they require to attend the trial at least 14 days before the PDH where the defendant intends to plead not guilty to some or all of the counts on the indictment. For all class 1 offences and for lengthy and complex cases, the prosecution should prepare a case summary for use by the judge at the PDH. In addition, the Practice Direction requires that the prosecution should scrutinise all class 2 offences to decide whether a case summary should also be provided for the judge at the PDH.

The PDH will be held in open court and can be conducted by a judge who will not be the eventual trial judge. It is normal for the arraignment of the defendant to take place at the PDH and it is therefore essential that the defendant is present for the arraignment to take place. If the defendant is absent, the judge will adjourn the proceedings and will issue a bench warrant for his/her arrest under the Bail Act 1976 s. 7 unless the reason for absence is illness. If the defendant has been remanded in custody, he/she will be brought to court for the arraignment.

The procedure commences with the clerk reading out to the defendant the counts on the indictment, asking him/her whether he/she pleads guilty or not guilty. Should there be a number of counts on the indictment, a plea must be taken on each one separately as soon as it is read out in court. If it is known that the accused intends to plead guilty to one of two alternative counts, that count should be put to him/her first, irrespective of whether it is first on the indictment. Where there is a joint indictment against several accused, it is usual to arraign them together, and separate pleas must be obtained from each of those named in a joint count. Where an accused who is not under a mental or physical disability remains wilfully silent on arraignment or fails to give a direct answer to the charge, the court will enter a plea of not guilty on his/her behalf.

If the defendant pleads guilty, the Practice Direction para. 9 states that the judge should proceed to sentencing whenever possible. If two persons are charged in a single indictment but one pleads guilty whilst the other pleads not guilty, it is usual for the judge to adjourn the case of the person who has pleaded guilty. He/she will be remanded either in custody or on bail until the conclusion of the trial of his/her co-accused. If, however, the judge considers that he/she has enough information available on the accused who has pleaded guilty, the judge may sentence him/her straight away following the guilty plea.

Where the defendant pleads not guilty (or where part or alternative pleas have not been accepted) the prosecution and defence must inform the court of the matters set out in the Practice Direction para. 10(a)–(r) as contained in the completed questionnaire that has been filed. These relate to matters such as the issues in the case, the number of witnesses, details of any alibi defence and points of law that it is anticipated will arise at the trial. The advocate for the defence should have warned the prosecution of any evidence to which the defence intends to object being called. This is usually, but by no means always, disputed confessions evidence. At the PDH the judge can make rulings on questions such as the admissibility of such evidence or on questions of law relating to the case. Although he/she may do so of his/her own motion, such rulings are usually made on the application of the advocates for the parties. Once such a ruling is made it has binding effect but it may subsequently be varied or discharged if it is in the interests of justice to do so.

Apart from the PDH referred to above, the Criminal Procedure and Investigations Act 1996 ss 28–38 allows for preparatory hearings in long and complex cases. The Criminal Procedure and Investigations Act 1996 (Preparatory Hearings) Rules 1997 set out deadlines for both defence and prosecution to apply for a preparatory hearing and establish the procedure for determining any such application. If a preparatory hearing has been convened in a serious fraud case, the defence may be ordered to supply a written statement setting out the nature of the defence with an indication of the principal matters on which they propose to take issue with the prosecution. There is no obligation, however, to disclose the names of the witnesses that they will be calling.

15. Empanelling the jury

If the accused pleads not guilty to some or all of the counts on the indictment, a jury panel (comprising twenty or more potential jurors) will be brought into court by the usher.

The names of the jury panel are selected at random from the electoral roll by computer and are contained on cards that are given to the clerk of the court. The clerk calls the names of the first twelve persons who enter the jury box as their names are called. They take the oath individually or may elect to affirm that they will faithfully try the defendant and give a true verdict on the evidence presented. Just before each juror takes the oath or affirms, he/she can be challenged by the prosecution or defence under the provisions of the Juries Act 1974 s. 12(1)(b). Both prosecution and defence are able to challenge as many jurors as they wish provided they have good cause because certain classes of person are either disqualified or ineligible for jury service, but this right is rarely used nowadays. In addition, the prosecution (but not the defence) can ask any juror to 'stand by' without being required to give a reason to the judge.

Once twelve jurors have been sworn (or have affirmed), the trial of the accused commences. Once the trial is under way, the judge has discretion to discharge up to three jurors whilst allowing the trial to continue with the remaining jurors giving their verdict at the end. A plea of not guilty requires that the prosecution (usually the CPS) satisfies the jury beyond a reasonable doubt that the accused has committed the *actus reus* of the offence (or aided, abetted, counselled or procured its commission). The *actus reus* is the criminal act and, in addition to establishing this, the prosecution must normally establish beyond a reasonable doubt that the accused has the necessary 'intent' or state of mind required for the commission of the particular criminal act at the time, which is known as *mens rea*. There are, however, some offences of strict liability where there is no need for the prosecution to prove *mens rea*. Most of these offences are statutory and many arise in the context of the regulatory framework for the sale of food and drink. In addition, the prosecution is released from the obligation to prove each element of the offence (*actus reus* and *mens rea*) if the defence has made a formal admission under the Criminal Justice Act 1967 s. 10 or where a particular fact is either presumed or 'judicially noticed'.

16. Conduct of the trial

The prosecution must be legally represented and the prosecution advocate puts the case for the Crown. Although a trial on indictment is an adversarial affair, the advocate for the prosecution should not strive for a conviction, come what may. Instead, he/she should regard himself/herself as a minister of justice whose principal task is to assist the court with the administration of justice. The accused will usually be legally represented and the advocate for the defence is entitled to use all his/her legal skills to obtain an acquittal. Thus he/she is not obliged to point out any flaw in the indictment or errors that would adversely affect the prosecution case that could easily be rectified. Nevertheless, he/she must not deceive or mislead the court.

215

The judge's task is to remain above the fray and ensure that the necessary conditions prevail whereby the respective advocates can fulfil their duties fairly and properly. If the judge intervenes excessively and shows partiality towards the prosecution, the accused would be unlikely to receive a fair trial and the Court of Appeal would almost certainly quash a resulting conviction. However, a judge can intervene to prevent unnecessary repetition, to exclude irrelevant matter and to prevent the oppression of witnesses by either advocate. Although it is the jury who decide all issues of fact and the ultimate guilt or innocence of the accused, the judge determines all issues of law as they arise in the course of the trial.

17. The prosecution case

Once the clerk of the court has placed the accused in the jury's charge, the prosecution advocate will present an overview of the case for the Crown to the members of the jury. He/she will normally specify the charges against the accused and then explain any relevant points of law with which they are unlikely to be familiar. He/she must be careful to indicate that what is said in relation to points of law is intended only as a guide because it is for the judge to decide and rule on matters of law. The advocate will also inform the members of the jury that the prosecution must prove their case and that they, the jury, must be sure of the defendant's guilt. It must be made clear to them that if they are unsure whether the accused is guilty, they must acquit. Having done this, the prosecution advocate proceeds to summarise the evidence that he/she intends to call and, on the basis of the documentary evidence tendered at the committal proceedings, he/she will tell the jury the principal facts that he/she anticipates the prosecution witnesses will prove. In addition, he/she will attempt to show how the items of evidence link together to demonstrate beyond a reasonable doubt that the accused committed the offence(s) charged.

Where the advocate for the defence has informed the prosecution that he/she intends to object to certain pieces of evidence, then that evidence must not be included in the prosecution's opening address to the jury unless the objection has been overruled at the PDH. The advocate for the prosecution will then call the witnesses whose names are said to appear on the reverse of the indictment and who will give oral testimony for the Crown.

18. Evidence and admissibility

The reader should refer to *Blackstone's Criminal Practice* for a detailed treatment of the law of evidence because a book of this size cannot cover this important subject in any depth. Certain aspects of the law of evidence are mentioned here because they are essential to an understanding of trial procedure.

Irrespective of whether they are appearing for the prosecution or defence, witnesses appearing in person should normally give their evidence orally in open court so that the jury can not only hear but can see the persons concerned and thereby decide from their general demeanour and body language how credible they are. However, the Criminal Procedure and Investigations Act 1996 Schedule 2 enables the prosecution to read in evidence undisputed statements tendered at the committal stage and the Magistrates' Courts Act 1980 s. 97A has an identical provision in relation to depositions tendered in evidence at the committal stage. Although the defence can object within 14 days of committal to the reading of a statement, under para. 1(4) of Schedule 2, the trial judge may overrule the objection if he/she considers it to be in the interests of justice to do so. Under the Children and Young Persons Act 1933 s. 42 a deposition taken out of court from a child or young person who was the victim of certain sexual or violent offences is admissible in evidence in a trial on indictment. The court must be satisfied on the basis of medical evidence that attendance before the court would involve serious danger to the child's life or health and the deposition is admissible only if the accused was given notice of the intention to take it. In addition the accused must be in a position to cross-examine the child or young person. When children give evidence it is usually via a video link in the court building and their evidence in chief may be given by playing a video recording of their initial interview by the police.

The admissibility of written statements other than in committal proceedings is provided for by the Criminal Justice Act 1967 s. 9. If a statement is to be admissible it must be signed and contain a declaration that it is true to the best of the knowledge and belief of its maker. Thus, properly attested statements can be read to the jury as evidence so that there is no need to call a witness in person provided these statements are uncontroversial. Nevertheless, such statements are admissible only if there is no objection from either side, but even then the trial judge could require the maker of the statement to attend court. Where a witness is too ill to attend court or is outside the UK and is unable to return, the Criminal Justice Act 1988 s. 23 provides that a statement in a document shall be admissible in evidence of any fact which the maker could give as direct oral testimony. This section also extends to death bed declarations and confessions. The provisions of s. 23 are, however, subject to s. 25 which enables the trial judge to exclude such evidence.

As indicated above, the judge may have ruled on the admissibility of evidence to which the defence has objected at the PDH but it may not have been possible to resolve all issues of admissibility at the PDH stage. Once the prosecution has called all the evidence that is not the subject of an outstanding objection by the defence, the defence advocate will usually invite the judge to request that the jury to leave the courtroom. After the jury has left, the defence advocate will make his/her objections to the prosecution evidence known to the judge and the prosecution advocate will reply. The judge will then make his/her ruling on admissibility. This procedure is referred to as a trial on the *voir dire* when it relates to admissibility of a confession and where the issue of admissibility cannot be decided without making prior determinations of fact. If the evidence is ruled inadmissible, the jury will not hear it, but if it is ruled admissible, it will be called as soon as the jury returns. The advocate for the defence will wish to cross-examine all those prosecution witnesses who have given oral testimony, and in so doing, he/she is free to ask any question provided it is relevant and provided the question will not elicit inadmissible material and non-expert opinion. A defence barrister must also observe the Bar Council's Code of Conduct, especially para. 5.10(e), (g) and (h) in cross-examining. Solicitor advocates must observe the corresponding rules in the Law Society's Code for Advocacy.

19. Submission of 'no case to answer'

Once the prosecution evidence has been heard, the prosecution advocate will indicate to the jury that the prosecution case is complete. At that point, the advocate for the defence may submit that there is 'no case to answer'. A submission of no case to answer will succeed if there is no evidence to prove an essential element of the offence. If there is some evidence which establishes each essential element of the offence, the case should be left to the jury, but the judge does have a residual duty to consider whether the evidence is inherently weak or tenuous. If it is, such that no reasonable jury properly directed could convict on it, the submission of no case to answer should be upheld. Although the question of whether a witness is lying is one for the jury, according to *Blackstone* there may be exceptional cases where the inconsistencies in that person's evidence or between that person's evidence and other prosecution witnesses' are so great that any reasonable tribunal would be forced to the conclusion that the witness is untruthful. Thus, in the absence of other evidence that is capable of founding a case, the judge should withdraw the case from the jury when the members of the jury return to the courtroom.

If the submission of no case to answer has been successful, the judge will briefly explain to the jury what has happened in their absence. One of them is asked to stand as foreman. On the judge's direction, he/she formally returns a verdict of not guilty to each count on the indictment and the accused is free to leave the court. If the defence's submission is unsuccessful, the jury are not informed of what transpired in their absence and the case continues with the advocate for the defence presenting the defence case. If the submission has been partly successful in that the judge decides that there is a case to answer on some counts, he/she will inform the jury that he/she will be directing them to return a verdict of not guilty in respect those counts on which the submission was successful and that for the remainder of the trial they should concentrate on the other counts.

20. The case for the defence

The advocate for the defence has a right to make an opening speech only if he/she proposes to call evidence other than testimony from the accused. If he/she does intend to call witnesses other than the defendant, the advocate for the defence may give an overview of the defence case in terms of the testimony to be given by the witnesses and he/she may even criticise the evidence given for the prosecution. Although the defence should have given advance notice to the prosecution in the 'defence statement' at the disclosure stage relating to the defence of alibi, a failure to do so does not prevent the accused from relying on this defence. The defence of alibi is now governed by the Criminal Procedure and Investigations Act 1996 and is effectively defined by s. 5(8) which makes it clear that the evidence of alibi must be such that it establishes that the accused was at a place other than the place where the offence was committed. However, the accused must give the name and address of any witness who is believed to be able to give evidence to support the defence of alibi. Nevertheless, the advocate for the defence is required to consult with the accused before deciding to call alibi evidence, and failure to do so will amount to a material irregularity which may result in a conviction being quashed on appeal.

The accused is not obliged to give evidence on his/her own behalf but if he/she chooses to do so, he/she is liable to be cross-examined by the advocate for the prosecution. If the accused is to give evidence, he/she will normally be called before any of the other defence witnesses. As a result of the Criminal Justice and Public Order Act 1994 s. 35 it is important that the accused should be advised whether or not to give evidence. If the accused decides not to give evidence he/she must be warned in public by the judge in the presence of the jury. The jury may then draw adverse conclusions from his/her failure to give evidence. Where the accused decides not to go into the witness box, the advocate for the defence should insist that the accused signs a statement on the brief to the effect that (a) he/she decided on his/her own accord not to testify and (b) that he/she made that decision bearing in mind the advice received, regardless of what it was; otherwise this could provide the basis for an appeal against conviction.

Once all the evidence has been given, it is usual for the jury to be escorted from the courtroom and for the judge to indicate his/her intentions as to summing up. The advocates then have the opportunity to address him/her on any matter which may be important to their closing speeches. When the jury return, the prosecution is able to make a closing speech, after which the defence will make a closing speech.

In the rare event that the accused is not legally represented, the court will seek to assist him/her in conducting his/her defence and will explain his/her right to cross-examine witnesses and to give evidence himself/herself as well as call witnesses in his/her defence. Failure to do so may result in any conviction being quashed. There are, however, certain statutory restrictions on the right of an unrepresented accused to cross-examine witnesses. Unrepresented adult male defendants may not cross-examine children and women when accused of certain sexual offences against them.

21. The judge's summing up

The judge will remind the jury of the judge's role and their role, and for this reason the summing up is in two stages. Firstly, there is a direction on the law and secondly a summary of the evidence. Whilst the jury must accept what the judge says in relation to the law, it is they who are the judges of the facts as presented in evidence and they may disregard anything that the judge may say in relation to the evidence. In every summing up, the judge must direct the jury regarding the burden of proof (which resides with the prosecution) and the standard of proof (beyond a reasonable doubt) as well as the elements of the offence or offences (*actus reus* and *mens rea*) on the indictment. If the summing up takes some time and does not finish until late in the day, the jury should not be asked to consider their verdict until the following day.

22. Retirement of jury and verdict

At the end of the judge's summing up, the jury bailiff takes an oath to escort the jury to some 'private and convenient place' where he/she will not 'suffer anybody to speak to them about the trial this day, nor will he/she speak to them without leave of the court except it be to ask them if they are agreed upon their verdict'. The jury must not leave the jury room without the consent of the trial judge, but they will be sent home to return the next day if they have not reached a verdict by the late afternoon. During their retirement, the jury are permitted to ask questions of the judge by passing a note to the jury bailiff, but the reply must be read out in open court in the presence of the advocates so that they are aware of the question and the answer.

Prior to commencing their deliberations the jury will have appointed one of their number to act as foreman. Members of the jury are allowed at least two hours and ten minutes before being told that their verdict need not be unanimous. When they have reached a verdict on which they are all agreed (or a majority verdict where permitted by the Juries Act 1974) they will inform the jury bailiff who will escort them back to the courtroom. The foreman is then asked by the clerk what the jury's verdict is on each count on the indictment. If the jury is unable to agree (even on a majority verdict), the judge will discharge the jurors and the accused may be tried subsequently by a different jury. If the jury find the accused not guilty he/she is acquitted and is free to leave the court.

23. Sentencing – some introductory remarks

Sentencing is a subject in itself. The section in *Blackstone's Criminal Practice* dealing with the subject covers over 170 pages and so only the briefest summary of the subject matter can be given in a book of this size. Readers are recommended to read one of the specialist texts on Sentencing to deepen their knowledge of this important, albeit rather complex, subject.

24. Sentencing procedure

If the jury have found the accused guilty or if the accused has pleaded guilty, the court will proceed to sentence him/her. Sentencing procedure is similar in both the Crown Court and in magistrates' courts except that in the latter it is not quite so formal. Having just dealt with trial on indictment, what follows relates more specifically to sentencing procedure in the Crown Court.

If the offender has been convicted by the jury having pleaded not guilty, the judge will be only too well aware of the facts surrounding the offence(s), but if the offender pleaded guilty the advocate for the prosecution is required to summarise the facts, especially those that point to the gravity of the offending. In doing so he/she will make use of the copies of the statements of the prosecution witnesses made for the committal proceedings. The prosecution advocate must still regard himself/herself as a minister of justice and must not suggest a particularly severe sentence because the victim has suffered, but he/she may draw attention to the suffering of the victim through the presentation of a 'victim impact statement'. The prosecution advocate may also apply for a compensation order for the victim. Confiscations and forfeiture orders can also be applied for where appropriate, and orders may be made for the destruction of firearms, offensive weapons and drugs.

During the prosecution's summary of the facts of the offence, the court will be informed of any other offences that the offender wishes to have taken into account. It is usual for a signed list to be given to the judge who will seek the offender's confirmation that he/she wishes these to be taken into account. In his/her capacity as a minister of justice, it is for the advocate for the prosecution to draw the attention of the judge to any limits on the sentencing powers of the court to ensure that it does not exceed its powers which could give rise to an appeal.

Even where the offender has entered a guilty plea, there can still be a dispute between the prosecution and the defence over the immediate circumstances of the offence(s) in relation to its gravity. If this divergence of view is substantial in that it is likely to affect the sentence, the judge must either accept the defence account (in so far as this is possible) or, more usually, give both sides the opportunity to call evidence on disputed matters before deciding what the facts surrounding the offence were. The judge should never just simply side with the prosecution's version of the facts without hearing evidence. Such a hearing is known as a *Newton* hearing after the statement of Lord Lane CJ in *R v Newton* (1982). Since its initial formulation the basic propositions set out in *R v Newton* have been developed and refined. Once a judge has decreed that there should be a *Newton* hearing, it will be conducted on adversarial lines on the issues in dispute but without a jury. Therefore the judge will decide issues of fact whilst bearing in mind the types of direction that he/she would give to a jury for guidance. The prosecution is obliged to prove its version of the facts beyond a reasonable doubt.

25. Evidence of character and antecedents

After the prosecution's summary of the facts following a guilty plea or immediately after a guilty verdict, the prosecution is obliged to produce evidence of the offender's character and antecedents. The antecedents should contain information relating to the offender's age, education, past and present employment, his/her domestic circumstances and income, the date of his/her arrest, whether he/she was remanded in custody or on bail and the date of his/her last release from prison or other custodial institution if applicable. Where the offender has previous convictions, these will also be listed in the antecedents. These will be obtained in the form of a printout of the offender's record from the police national computer. Convictions that are regarded as 'spent' under the Rehabilitation of Offenders Act 1974 must be listed as well.

26. Reports on the offender

Having considered the offender's antecedents, the court will proceed to consider any reports that have been prepared on him/her. These may take the form of pre-sentence reports compiled by probation officers, medical and psychiatric reports and assessments of suitability for community punishment. The pre-sentence reports are presented to the court by the advocate for the defence. Although the Powers of the Criminal Courts (Sentencing) Act 2000 s. 81 states that the court shall obtain and consider a pre-sentence report in deciding whether a custodial sentence should be imposed, this is not obligatory where the offender is over 18 years of age and the court is of the opinion that it is unnecessary.

27. Mitigation of sentence

The plea in mitigation of sentence by the defence advocate is made before the sentence is passed to ensure that it is appropriate and not too severe. The advocate may, at his/her discretion, call witnesses to testify to the offender's previous good character or to explain why (in his/her view) the offender acted as he/she did if this lessens the gravity of the offending. The general principle governing pleas in mitigation were stated by the Divisional Court in *Gross* v *O'Toole* (1982). From what was stated, it is clear the court can reject matters put forward in mitigation even if the offender or other defence witnesses testify in support of those facts and contrary evidence is produced by the prosecution. However, in *R* v *Guppy* [1994] the Court of Appeal (Criminal Division) stated that, in most cases, magistrates or a judge would readily accept the accuracy of the statements made by the defence advocate. Nevertheless, where the advocate for the defence delivers a plea in mitigation following a guilty verdict, it will be quite unrealistic to assert his/her client's innocence and ask the court for forbearance.

28. Types of sentence

Apart from those offences where the sentence is prescribed by statute, the criminal courts are usually able to decide the appropriate sentence from a number of options, although in any particular case the range of options may be narrower owing to the circumstances of the offence. In increasing order of gravity these options include:

223

(a) an absolute discharge

(b) a conditional discharge

(c) a drug treatment and testing order

(d) a drug abstinence order

(e) a supervision order

(f) an attendance order

(g) an exclusion order

(h) a curfew order

(i) a community rehabilitation order (formerly a probation order)

(j) a community punishment order (formerly a community service order)

(k) a suspended custodial sentence

(l) an immediate custodial sentence.

Apart from the sentences listed above, the most usual sentence imposed for summary offences and for those that are triable either way is a fine. The maximum fine that magistrates can impose is £5,000 but there is no limit to the fine that can be imposed by the Crown Court on an offender who has been tried on indictment and convicted or who has been committed for sentence by magistrates. Where the court imposes a fine, it will usually fix a term of imprisonment or detention to be served if the offender fails to pay the fine, but those offenders aged under 21 cannot be committed to prison for non-payment. For relatively minor road traffic offences that are tried summarily, penalty points may be endorsed on the offender's driving licence in addition to any fine imposed by the magistrates. If the offender accumulates 12 or more penalty points he/she will normally be disqualified from driving for a period unless there are special reasons for not doing so.

The maximum custodial sentences for indictable offences and for offences triable either way are usually contained in the statutes creating those offences. However, the maximum is seldom imposed except for the most serious examples of the offence. If a person is convicted on indictment and is liable to be sentenced to imprisonment but the sentence is not limited to a specified term (or life) by statute, the maximum term that can be imposed is two years. Where an offender is over 21, the court may suspend a custodial sentence but the sentence itself must not exceed two years, as a sentence of more than this duration cannot be suspended.

29. Concurrent and consecutive sentences

Where an offender is convicted on more than one count on the indictment, the court should impose separate sentences in respect of each count. Prison sentences may run concurrently (together from the same point in time) or consecutively, but there may be a mix of concurrent and consecutive sentences. The judge must therefore decide whether the sentences are to run concurrently or consecutively, but if he/she fails to do so, there is a presumption that they are to run concurrently.

30. Statutory criteria and custodial sentences

The Powers of the Criminal Courts (Sentencing) Act 2000 contains statutory criteria for determining the imposition and length of custodial sentences. For a person aged 21 or over, the phrase 'custodial sentence' means a sentence of imprisonment including a suspended sentence but does not include a committal for contempt of court. For a person under 21, it means a sentence of detention in a youth offender institution. Section 79(2) limits to some extent the powers of the Crown Court and magistrates' courts to impose a custodial sentence although the Act does not apply to those offences with a custodial sentence that is fixed by law (e.g. murder) or one falling to be imposed under ss 109(2), 110(2) or 111(2) of the Act. The essence of the provision is that (subject to subsection 3) the court should not pass a custodial sentence on the offender unless it is of the opinion either:

(a) that the offence (or any combination of the offence and one or more offences associated with it) was so serious that only such a sentence can be justified for the offence, or

(b) where the offence is a violent or sexual offence, that only such a sentence would be adequate to protect the public from serious harm from the perpetrator.

Subsection 3 makes is clear that nothing is to prevent the court from passing a custodial sentence on the offender if the offender fails to express his willingness to comply with:

(a) a requirement which is proposed by the court to be included in a community rehabilitation order or supervision order and which requires an expression of such willingness, or

(b) a requirement which is proposed by the court to be included in a drug treatment and testing order or an order made under s. 52(4) (an order to provide samples).

225

The Powers of the Criminal Courts (Sentencing) Act 2000 s. 80 establishes the criteria for deciding the length of custodial sentences including discretionary life sentences and suspended sentences whether passed on adults or young offenders. Section 80(2)(a) provides that the length of a custodial sentence (other than one fixed by law or falling to be imposed under s. 109(2)) shall be commensurate with the seriousness of the offence or the combination of the offence with one or more associated offences. This provision enables the judge to pass a prison sentence which is longer than the sentence which would normally be regarded as commensurate with the offence as a deterrence provided it does not exceed the maximum permitted. Under s. 80(2)(b) the judge may also pass a longer custodial sentence than would usually be regarded as commensurate in order to protect the public where the offence is a violent or sexual offence.

An offender under the age of 18 at the date of conviction may not be sentenced to imprisonment but there are other types of custodial sentence that are applicable to these offenders. An offender aged 18 or over who has pleaded guilty to, or has been convicted of murder must be sentenced to life imprisonment and the judge must make a recommendation as to the minimum term to be served in prison after which the offender will be released on licence. Section 109 imposes a mandatory life sentence for any offender aged over 18 who is convicted of a second serious offence unless there are 'exceptional circumstances' relating to the offender or the offences where a mandatory life sentence would not be justified. For the purposes of s. 109, serious offences are listed in s. 109(5) and include attempted murder, manslaughter, wounding, causing grievous bodily harm with intent, and rape.

31. Pronouncing sentence

It is a basic principle that the offender should be sentenced only for those crimes for which he/she has pleaded guilty or has been convicted and not for anything else that the court thinks that he/she may have done. There are, nevertheless, three exceptions to this basic principle:

(a) where a secondary offence which does not appear on the indictment which is no more serious than the offence on the indictment involves an aggravating feature in relation to the offence that does appear;

(b) where the offender specifically asks for other offences to be taken into consideration by the court;

(c) where the prosecution case is that the offences on the indictment are merely examples of a continuing course of conduct and this is accepted by the defence.

In relation to (a) above, if the judge is satisfied that the prosecution version of the facts is accurate, then he/she may take into consideration the second-ary offence when passing sentence. In *R v Boswell* [1984], Lord Lane CJ, in the course of providing guidelines on sentencing for causing death by reckless driving, stated that an aggravating feature justifying a custodial sentence was where the offender's driving had involved other offences such as driving whilst disqualified or under the influence of drink. The judge may pronounce the sentence immediately but he/she may adjourn briefly to consider his/her decision. The Powers of the Criminal Courts (Sentencing) Act 2000 imposes a number of obligations on courts when passing sen-tence. Section 79(4) in particular requires that a judge, passing a custodial sentence for offences covered by the Act, must explain to the offender in open court and in ordinary language why he/she is passing a custodial sentence. Under s. 155(1) a sentence imposed by the Crown Court may be varied or rescinded within 28 days but any variation must be made by the judge who originally passed the sentence. A judge would be likely to exercise his/her powers under s. 155(1) in order to correct a technical error in the original sentence or to alter it to the advantage of the offender if he/she considers, on reflection, that he/she has been too severe.

APPEALS

32. Appeals from magistrates' courts

Less than 3 per cent of the decisions of a magistrates' court are ever appealed but those that are can be contested in one of three ways:

(a) by appeal to the Crown Court

(b) by appeal to the High Court by way of case stated for the opinion of the High Court

(c) by claim for judicial review to the High Court.

The appeal to the Crown Court mentioned in (a) above following a plea of not guilty may be against conviction and/or sentence. In general, a plea of guilty before a magistrates' court bars an appeal against conviction although there are certain exceptions to this rule – see *R v Huntingdon Crown Court ex p. Jordan* [1981]. If a guilty plea is entered, an appeal is normally restricted to the sentence handed down by the court.

The procedures outlined in (b) and (c) above are available to both a convicted accused and an unsuccessful prosecutor (usually the Crown Pro-secutor). Moreover, decisions of the Crown Court that do not arise from its

227

jurisdiction over trials on indictment may also be challenged by way of case stated for the opinion of the High Court or by way of a claim for judicial review. In all these instances the jurisdiction of the High Court is exercised by the Divisional Court of Queen's Bench.

33. Appeals to the Crown Court

Appeals to the Crown Court are governed by the Magistrates' Courts Act 1980 ss 108–110 and the Crown Court Rules 1982 (SI 1982 No. 1109). There is a right of appeal to the Crown Court not only against a fine or custodial sentence but also against the decision of a magistrates' court to place an offender on probation, to discharge him/her conditionally or unconditionally, to disqualify him/her from driving, to recommend him/her for deportation or to make a confiscation or compensation order. If there is to be an appeal, notice of an appeal must be given in writing to the clerk of the magistrates' court in question and to the prosecution within 21 days of sentence being passed or the offender being otherwise dealt with by magistrates (by being committed for sentence to the Crown Court). The notice must clearly state whether the appeal is against conviction or sentence or both but the grounds of the appeal need not be given. Permission to appeal is not required and the Crown Court has discretion to extend the time for giving notice of the appeal. If a convicted person gives notice of appeal where the magistrates have passed an immediate custodial sentence, the magistrates may grant bail under the Magistrates' Courts Act 1980 s. 113(1) subject to his/her appearing at the Crown Court at the time fixed for the hearing of the appeal. An application for bail can also be made to the Crown Court under the Supreme Court Act 1981 s. 81(1)(b) where magistrates have refused to grant bail.

The appeal will normally be listed for hearing by a circuit judge or recorder who must usually sit with two magistrates who were not concerned with the original case. An appeal against conviction will take the form of a rehearing of the case and the advocate for the prosecution will make an opening speech and call evidence. Previously unheard evidence may be called. Thereafter, the advocate for the appellant can make a submission of no case to answer. If this should fail, the advocate will then call the evidence for the defence, after which the advocate will make a closing speech. The court will announce its decision after this. If the appeal is against sentence only, the advocate for the prosecution simply outlines the facts and previous evidence together with any report compiled on the defendant for the court. The role of the advocate for the defence is largely confined to presenting a plea in mitigation. It is then for the Crown Court to decide how the appellant should be sentenced and the court will give reasons for its decision. If it takes the view that the appropriate sentence is at variance with the one imposed by the magistrates, then the appeal will be allowed and the sentence of the Crown Court will be substituted.

The Supreme Court Act 1981 s. 48 confers wide powers on the Crown Court when disposing of an appeal in that it may confirm, reverse or vary any part of the decision appealed against. It may increase the sentence imposed by the magistrates' court even in a case where the appeal is simply against a conviction, as well as impose a separate penalty for an offence for which the magistrates had decided not to impose a penalty. However, the Crown Court must not pass a sentence which exceeds that which the magistrates had the power to pass. It may also remit the case to the magistrates with its opinion on how it should be disposed of, particularly where it considers a guilty plea to be equivocal. In addition, it may make whatever order in relation to costs it considers just. For example, in the event of a successful appeal it may order that the costs of the defence in the magistrates' court are paid by the prosecution or paid out of central funds although there are limitations on the power to order costs.

34. Appeal by way of case stated

By means of this procedure, the aggrieved party invites the magistrates to state a case for consideration by a Divisional Court of Queen's Bench. The appeal must be on one of the two grounds mentioned in the Magistrates' Courts Act 1980 s. 111(1). Thus, an appeal must be on one or more point(s) of law or relate to jurisdiction and be identified in a document compiled by the clerk of the magistrates' court in consultation with the magistrates whose decision is being contested. An application must be made within 21 days of the day on which the magistrates' court sentenced or otherwise dealt with the appellant. Bail may be granted by magistrates where the appellant has been given an immediate custodial sentence, but if this was refused an application for bail can be made to a High Court judge in chambers. Usually two High Court judges will sit in a Divisional Court of Queen's Bench to hear the appeal, but sometimes three judges will sit, one of whom may be the Lord Chief Justice. In disposing of the appeal, the Divisional Court may reverse, affirm or amend the decision of the magistrates. If the prosecution has appealed, the Divisional Court can remit the case to the magistrates with instructions that they convict and proceed to sentence, but it may simply replace the acquittal with a conviction and impose the appropriate penalty. If an application is made to magistrates to state a case for the opinion of a Divisional Court of Queen's Bench, the appellant loses any right that he/she had to appeal to the Crown Court.

An appeal by way of case stated may be used to contest a decision of the Crown Court that does not relate to trial on indictment. Here the appellant has the responsibility for compiling an initial draft case to be put before a judge who presided in the proceedings where the disputed decision was arrived at.

35. Appeal by claim for judicial review

The procedure for instituting a claim for judicial review is set out in Chapter 15. An appeal by way of a claim for judicial review relates to jurisdictional disputes. The appellant may argue that the magistrates were in error in attempting to exercise jurisdiction. Since magistrates do not have the power to bail a person who is challenging their decision by claim for judicial review, an application for bail has to be made to the High Court to a judge in chambers. If the claim succeeds, the Divisional Court can issue one or more of the prerogative orders described in Chapter 15. The Supreme Court Act 1981 s. 29(3) permits a decision of the Crown Court to be challenged by way of a claim for judicial review provided it was not a decision that relates to a trial on indictment.

36. Appeals to the Court of Appeal (Criminal Division)

If a person has been tried on indictment, convicted and sentenced, any appeal has to be addressed to the Court of Appeal (Criminal Division) irrespective of whether the appeal is against conviction, sentence or both. Numerous types of error can be made in the course of a trial, any one of which may form the basis of an appeal against conviction. These errors may be summarised as follows:

(a) wrongful admission or exclusion of evidence by the trial judge

(b) erroneous exercise of discretion by the trial judge

(c) errors made by the advocate for the defence in presenting the case

(d) a ruling by the trial judge at the end of the prosecution case that 'there is a case to answer'

(e) defects in the form or wording of the indictment

(f) illogical and inconsistent verdicts given by the jury between separate counts on the indictment

(g) excessive intervention on the part of the trial judge

(h) errors and omissions in the summing up by the trial judge.

The Criminal Appeal Act 1968 s. 1 gives a person convicted of an offence a right to appeal against conviction, but an appeal is possible only with the permission of the Court of Appeal or if the trial judge grants a certificate that the case is fit for appeal. Where a certificate is granted at the initiative of the trial judge, he/she will draft the question that he/she considers ought to be raised on appeal and will read this to the advocates so that they can comment on it before it is actually certified. If the advocate makes the application for the certificate, the advocate will draft the question and the application will be made in chambers with a shorthand writer in attendance. For a certificate to be granted, there must be a particular basis for appeal on which the convicted person will have a substantial chance of succeeding.

If the trial judge has not granted a certificate that the case is fit for appeal, a prospective appellant needs permission to appeal. The power of the Court of Appeal (Criminal Division) to grant permission to appeal is one that is usually exercised by a single judge reading the papers, including the application for leave, without oral argument or even written representations from the advocates representing the parties. In the event that permission to appeal is refused by this judge, the applicant is entitled to have the application decided by a court subject the requirement on his/her part to serve notice upon the Registrar of Criminal Appeals. The entire process can be hastened where an appeal has obvious merit because the Registrar can list the application for a hearing by a court. Where the appeal is against conviction, both prosecution and defence will be represented at the hearing and if the application is granted, the court can proceed immediately to consider the appeal itself.

The Criminal Appeal Act 1968 s. 1 does not distinguish between persons convicted following a guilty plea and those convicted by a jury following a not guilty plea. However, in *R v Forde* [1923] Avory J. stated:

> A plea of guilty having been recorded, this court can only entertain an appeal against conviction if it appears (1) that the appellant did not appreciate the nature of the charge or did not intend to admit he was guilty of it, or (2) that upon the admitted facts he could not in law have been convicted of the offence charged.

Thus the Court of Appeal (Criminal Division) will grant permission to appeal if the applicant has pleaded guilty in the Crown Court only where there are exceptional circumstances, for example where the applicant's confession may be doubted because he/she is of low intelligence.

37. Determination of an appeal against conviction

The Criminal Appeal Act 1968 s. 2(1) as amended provides:

Subject to the provisions of this Act, the Court of Appeal –
(a) shall allow an appeal against conviction if they think that the conviction is unsafe; and
(b) shall dismiss such an appeal in any other case.

The simplification of the wording of s. 2(1) achieved by the enactment of the Criminal Appeal Act 1995 has not changed the effect of the statutory provision. Thus, for a conviction to be safe, it must be lawful. If it should transpire that the trial should never have taken place, the conviction cannot be regarded as safe. Moreover, a conviction can be quashed if it can be shown that it resulted from an abuse of process. In *R v McMullen* [2000] the Court of Appeal (Criminal Division) took the view that the conduct of the British authorities in procuring the deportation to England of the appellant was so unworthy and shameful that it amounted to an affront to the public conscience for the prosecution to succeed. In *Condron v UK* (the facts of which were set out in Chapter 10) the European Court of Human Rights stressed the necessity for the Court of Appeal to focus on the fairness of the trial rather than on the safety of the conviction when deciding whether to uphold an appeal from the Crown Court. The applicants contended before the European Court of Human Rights that their right to a fair trial under Article 6 had been violated when the 'no comment' interview was not excluded by the trial judge. The European Court of Human Rights took the view that there had been a violation of Article 6. Furthermore the Court rejected the Court of Appeal's conclusion that the exercise of the right to silence on the part of the applicants did not play a significant part in the jury's decision to convict. In the course of its judgement the Court stated:

> The question whether or not the rights of the defence guaranteed to an accused under Article 6 of the Convention were secured in any given case cannot be assimilated to a finding that his conviction was safe in the absence of any enquiry into the issue of fairness.

Since the Court of Appeal is required by the Human Rights Act 1998 s. 2(1) to take into account the jurisprudence of the European Court of Human Rights in determining a question that has arisen in connection with a Convention right, it should interpret the Criminal Appeal Act 1968 s. 2(1) in such a way as to embrace the notion that there should be no incompatibility between the Criminal Appeal Act 1968 s. 2(1)(a) and the Human Rights Act 1998 s. 3(1).

The Court of Appeal (Criminal Division) can decide the outcome of an appeal by majority of its members, but because of the necessity of certainty in criminal proceedings, only one judgement is given. The Supreme Court Act 1981 s. 59 allows a departure from this general practice if the presiding judge states that in his/her opinion the question is one of law on which separate judgements should be pronounced. If the appeal is successful, there will be one of two possible outcomes. The first is that the conviction is quashed and the Crown Court is instructed to substitute a verdict of acquittal for the conviction. If such is the case, a successful appellant cannot normally be retried for the offence for which the appeal was brought or for any other offence for which he/she could have been convicted by way of an alternative verdict. Nevertheless, a successful appeal does not rule out the possibility of a trial for a different offence based on the same facts and evidence.

The other possible outcome of a successful appeal is that the original conviction is quashed and a retrial is ordered. The Criminal Appeal Act 1968 s. 7(1) provides: 'Where the Court of Appeal allows an appeal against conviction and it appears to the court that the interests of justice require, they may order the appellant to be retried.' However, the retrial may not be for any offence other than the one for which the successful appeal was brought. The Court of Appeal (Criminal Division) relies on its powers under the Criminal Appeal Act 1968 in most criminal appeals but it also has a power independent of statute, inherited from the Court of Crown Cases Reserved, to quash a conviction and issue a writ of *venire de novo* the effect of which is to order a retrial.

38. Appeal against sentence

The Criminal Appeal Act 1968 s. 9(1) gives a person convicted on indictment the right to appeal to the Court of Appeal (Criminal Division) against any sentence passed on him/her for the offence that is not fixed by law. The Criminal Appeal Act 1968 s. 10 deals with the right to appeal when the offender was sentenced in the Crown Court following a summary conviction. He/she may appeal only if:

(a) he/she is sentenced to six months or more imprisonment

(b) the sentence is one that the magistrates had no power to pass

(c) the court in dealing with him/her for the offence

(i) recommends that he/she be deported, or
(ii) disqualifies him/her from driving, or
(iii) makes an order under the Powers of the Criminal Courts (Sentencing) Act 2000, or
(iv) makes an order under the Football Spectators Act 1989, or
(v) orders his/her return to prison.

In an appeal against sentence, it is unusual for the prosecution to be represented.

39. Appeal to the House of Lords

The Criminal Appeal Act 1968 ss 33 and 34 provides that the prosecution or the defence can appeal to the House of Lords from a decision of the Court of Appeal (Criminal Division) but the appeal is subject to both of the following conditions:

(a) that the Court of Appeal (Criminal Division) certifies that its decision which is being appealed against involves a point of law of general public importance;

(b) that either the Court of Appeal or the House of Lords gives permission to appeal because the point of law is one that should be considered by the House.

An application for permission to appeal to the House of Lords should be made to the Court of Appeal either orally immediately after it has delivered its decision or it should be made within 14 days of the decision. Notice of the application must be served on the Registrar in the requisite format. In hearing an appeal, the House of Lords may exercise any powers of the Court of Appeal (Criminal Division) or it may remit the case to it.

40. Application to the European Court of Human Rights

If a person considers that the national courts have failed to protect a right contained in the European Convention on Human Rights and Fundamental Freedoms, then he/she can petition the European Court of Human Rights in Strasbourg. The Court must consider the preliminary issue of admissibility, and in the region of nine out of ten applications are rejected on this basis. Article 35 of the Convention states that an application is inadmissible if:

(a) it is anonymous

(b) it concerns a matter that the Court has adjudicated upon

(c) it deals with a right not contained in the Convention

(d) the national remedies have not been exhausted

(e) it was not made within six months of the date of the decision complained of

(f) the applicant was not a 'victim' as required by Article 34

(g) it is an abuse of the right of petition

(h) it is manifestly ill-founded on its merits.

A committee of three judges can decide that the application is inadmissible acting under Article 28 and there is no appeal from this decision. If the application surmounts this first hurdle, the Court will attempt a 'friendly settlement' between the parties which may involve payment of compensation and/or a change in the law on which the complaint is founded. The procedure before the Court is mainly written in that affidavits and other documents are filed at the Court. If there is no settlement there will be a short oral hearing before a chamber comprising seven judges which thereafter may award a payment as 'just satisfaction' if it finds that there has been a violation. Quite often, however, the Court will direct that the finding of a violation of the Convention should be 'sufficient satisfaction' for the applicant. The judgement of the Court is by majority and dissenting judgements are quite common. The UK government, as a signatory to the Convention, is committed to implementing the judgements of the Court which may entail amending the offending legislation and amending the decision that caused the violation.

41. The Criminal Cases Review Commission

The Criminal Cases Review Commission was established by the Criminal Appeal Act 1995 as an independent body comprising 14 Commissioners appointed by the Queen on the recommendation of the prime minister. Its statutory remit is to investigate and process alleged miscarriages of justice in England, Wales and Northern Ireland. It is able to investigate convictions following trial on indictment, referrals regarding sentences imposed and it may even investigate convictions by magistrates. The Forensic Science Service is often called upon to assist the Commission with its investigative work.

References will be made to either the Court of Appeal or Crown Court only if it considers that there is a real possibility that the conviction, verdict, finding or sentence would not be upheld if the reference were to be made. Where the Commission decides to refer a case that was originally dealt with in the Crown Court, it will be treated as an appeal under the Criminal Appeal Act 1968 which will be referred to the Court of Appeal. Cases that were originally dealt with in a magistrates' court will be referred to the Crown Court. Details concerning recent references made by the Commission can be found on its website, and the annual report describes its working methods.

Progress test

1. How does the Criminal Law Act 1977 s. 14 classify criminal offences?

2. What is 'the information' that forms the basis of a summary trial?

3. Must the magistrates in a summary trial reach a unanimous verdict in order to convict the accused?

4. If a person is refused bail by magistrates, does he/she have a right of appeal?

5. What are the rules for establishing the mode of trial for the offence of criminal damage?

6. What is the purpose of a plea and directions hearing in a trial on indictment?

7. What is meant by the 'burden of proof' and 'the standard of proof' in a criminal trial?

8. What is the procedure for dealing with a submission of no case to answer in a trial on indictment?

9. What purpose is served by the judge's summing up in a trial on indictment?

10. Can the jury deliver a majority verdict or must it be unanimous?

11. What are the two possible outcomes of a successful appeal against conviction to the Court of Appeal?

12. What function does the Criminal Cases Review Commission serve?

Further reading

Books

Murphy, P. (ed.) (2001) *Blackstone's Criminal Practice* (London: Blackstone Press).
Sprack, J. (2000) *Emmins on Criminal Procedure* (London: Blackstone Press).
Wasik, M. (1998) *Emmins on Sentencing* (London: Blackstone Press).
Wasik, M., T. Gibbons and M. Redmayne (1999) *Criminal Justice: Text and Materials* (London: Longman).

Articles

Duff, P. (2000) 'The defendant's right to trial by jury – a neighbour's view', *The Criminal Law Review* February.
Duff, P. (2001) 'Criminal Case Review Commission and "deference" to the courts: the evaluation of evidence and evidentiary rules, *The Criminal Law Review* May.

Seago, P., C. Walker and D. Wall (2000) 'The development of the professional mag- istracy in England and Wales', *The Criminal Law Review* August.

Useful website

The website of the Criminal Cases Review Commission can be accessed at www.ccrc.gov.uk. The annual report of the Commission can be downloaded from this website.

12

Dispute resolution 1: Civil litigation

1. Introduction

It is an observable fact that disputes of various types arise from time to time in every area of human activity. In the business world, many firms and companies do their best to avoid disputes. They do so by taking care over the drafting of contracts and by attempting, at the outset, to provide for as many eventualities as possible in their contractual documentation. For example, in a building contract the main contractor might wish to exclude liability altogether for delays that are completely beyond his/her control (e.g. a strike at one of the ports where materials must be imported). Alternatively, the main contractor may seek to limit the amount of compensation payable for delay, caused by a particular event, to a fixed sum by agreement with the other party to the contract. This chapter deals with the resolution of disputes in the civil courts and begins by explaining the rationale for the Civil Procedure Rules. It will then be appropriate to consider a hypothetical scenario which will serve as a basis for the subsequent examination of the civil litigation process and the rules of procedure.

2. The quiet revolution

On 26 April 1999 a quiet revolution occurred in the procedure for conducting civil litigation in England and Wales. The sweeping changes ushered in were a response to the findings of an inquiry undertaken by Lord Woolf. In 1994, he had been commissioned by Lord Mackay of Clashfern (who was then Lord Chancellor) to conduct a review of the rules and procedures of the civil courts. His report, entitled *Access to Justice*, condemned the existing system as being too slow and too expensive. Its rules were too complex, the costs involved were too uncertain and, as a result, justice was inaccessible for many people.

The Civil Procedure Act 1997 had paved the way for the Civil Procedure Rules 1998 (CPR) which came into operation on 26 April when most of the old rules were revoked. These rules have been supplemented by a number of Practice Directions, and consequently both lawyers and judges have been obliged to acquaint themselves with a completely new set of civil procedural rules that aim to create a new climate of openness for the parties involved in litigation. However, it was not possible to devise new rules for all procedures in time, so it was necessary to incorporate some of the old rules of procedure into the new CPR and they have been incorporated in Schedules 1 and 2 of the CPR.

3. The scenario

Nine months ago David, the managing director of Modern Builders Ltd, was contacted by a firm of local architects who asked him to submit an estimate for a house extension that had been designed by the firm. The house is a detached property standing in half an acre of ground just outside Guildford, Surrey.

The house had been bequeathed to Alice on the death of her father in a road accident. She had recently returned from Hong Kong where she had given up her practice as a dentist so that she could look after her mother who had been seriously injured in the same accident. Alice's mother was undergoing a protracted course of treatment at Stoke Mandeville Hospital for her spinal injuries. In the meantime, Alice had decided to have the house modified so that her mother could live on the ground floor when she was finally discharged from hospital.

The contract to build the extension was awarded to Modern Builders Ltd because the company had submitted the most competitive tender for the work. The contract was for £30,000 but it allowed for stage payments to be made as work progressed and was inspected and 'passed' by the firm of architects. Work was to start on 1 March with completion set by 30 September. It was estimated that Alice's mother would be discharged from hospital in early October.

Although Modern Builders Ltd had a number of similar contracts under way at this time, work did commence on schedule but it became clear by the end of June that all the work would not be complete by the end of September as had been agreed. Although Alice protested to David that the work must be completed by the agreed date, he replied that he had been obliged to divert some of his workmen to deal with 'emergencies' and that there had been a very high rate of absenteeism due to illness. At this point, Alice offered to pay Modern Builders Ltd an additional £8,000 at completion if David would agree to engage additional workers and hire extra equipment so that the extension would be completed by the end of September. David agreed and promised that all the work, including decorating, would be finished by 30 September.

On 1 October, Alice wrote to the company stating that although the extension had been completed, there were aspects of the work with which she was dissatisfied. In the same letter she refused to pay the additional £8,000 and stated that she was withholding £4,500 of the original £30,000 to cover the cost of what she regarded as necessary rectification work. David considers that all the work has been satisfactorily completed and that the company is entitled to all the money that is being withheld.

If the parties adopt entrenched positions it will only be possible to re-solve the dispute by resorting to litigation. This would entail presenting the material facts to a judge whose role would be to apply the relevant law and give judgement for one of the parties to the dispute. However, under the CPR the parties are encouraged to achieve a settlement before proceedings are commenced. For certain types of claim there are pre-action protocols.

4. Pre-action protocols

The new climate of openness has been underpinned by the introduction of pre-action protocols. Prior to issuing proceedings, the claimant must write to the defendant informing him/her of the claim. A claim should not be commenced until three months have elapsed following the issue of this letter. There are four protocols in final form, namely:

(a) Personal Injury Protocol

(b) Clinical Negligence Protocol

(c) Construction and Engineering Protocol

(d) Defamation Protocol.

The Construction and Engineering Protocol has been devised to include professional negligence claims against architects, engineers and quantity surveyors. A number of working parties were convened by the Lord Chan-cellor's Department on pre-action protocols and it is now developing a general protocol for all users which will apply where no other approved protocol exists. The principal objective of all such protocols is to encourage the exchange of full information at an early stage about the potential legal claim with a view to encouraging the parties to avoid unnecessary litigation by achieving a settlement. It is also intended that they should support the efficient management of proceedings where litigation cannot be avoided. The *Civil Justice Reform Evaluation 2001* published by the Lord Chancellor's

Department reported that a survey was conducted by the Association of Personal Injury Lawyers of its members. According to this survey, 33 per cent of personal injury cases had been settled without the need for litigation. Of course, there are likely to be many instances of failure to comply with the appropriate protocol but the CPR enables the court to take non-compliance into account when making orders for costs. If the court takes the view that non-compliance has resulted in the commencement of proceedings unnecessarily or has led to additional costs being incurred, it has the power to order that the party at fault must pay the costs involved wholly or in part. Where there is no pre-action protocol in existence, each party is required to state whether they have exchanged information and/or documents with the other in order to facilitate the settlement of the claim. The *Civil Justice Reform Evaluation* indicated that there has been a fall in the number of claims issued following the introduction of the CPR.

5. Issue and service of proceedings

Apart from certain types of case (such as insolvency proceedings, non-contentious probate, proceedings under the Mental Health Act 1983 and family proceedings), there is no distinction between the procedure that obtains in the High Court and that which applies in the county courts. A common process applies to commencement of most claims (apart from Admiralty claims, claims in the Commercial Court and applications for judicial review) in that the same claim form is used. It is form N1 which can be obtained free of charge from any county court office together with a set of guidance notes to assist with completion. However, forms N394, N396 and N397 are used for county court applications under the Landlord and Tenant Acts 1927 and 1954. The claimant will be provided with three copies of the blank form N1 (see Figure 12.1 on pages 242–3). The form N208 is used where there is no dispute over the essential facts of a case or if the claim requires an authoritative interpretation of a document or where the claimant seeks a declaratory judgement. A claim for less than £15,000 cannot normally be issued from the High Court in London and personal injury claims must normally exceed £50,000 to be issued from the High Court. Nevertheless, cases involving complex issues of law and fact may exceptionally be commenced in the High Court below these limits.

As can be seen, the N1 claim form must state on its face the name of the claimant and the claimant's address. The defendant's name and address (or place of business) must also appear. Brief details of the claim and its monetary value must be given (unless a remedy other than financial compensation is being sought). On the reverse of the form, the claimant should provide more detailed particulars of the claim that is being made. However,

Claim Form

In the

Claim No.

Claimant

SEAL

Defendant(s)

Brief details of claim

Value

£

Defendant's name and address

Amount claimed	
Court fee	
Solicitor's costs	
Total amount	
Issue date	

The court office at

is open between 10 am and 4 pm Monday to Friday. When corresponding with the court, please address forms or letters to the Court Manager and quote the claim number.

N1 Claim form (CPR Part 7) (10.00)   *Printed on behalf of The Court Service*

Figure 12.1 N1 claim form.

Claim No.	

Does, or will, your claim include any issues under the Human Rights Act 1998?   ☐ Yes   ☐ No

Particulars of Claim (attached)(to follow)

Statement of Truth
*(I believe)(The Claimant believes) that the facts stated in these particulars of claim are true.
* I am duly authorised by the claimant to sign this statement

Full name _____

Name of claimant's solicitor's firm _____

signed _____ position or office held _____
*(Claimant)(Litigation friend)(Claimant's solicitor)   (if signing on behalf of firm or company)
*delete as appropriate

Claimant's or claimant's solicitor's address to which documents or payments should be sent if different from overleaf including (if appropriate) details of DX, fax or e-mail.

if he/she does not complete this section, these 'particulars of claim' must then be submitted to the defendant within 14 days after service of the claim form on the defendant. If the particulars are served separately on the defendant, a copy of the particulars of claim must be filed with the court within seven days of their service (on the defendant), together with a certificate of service. In any event, the particulars of claim must be a precise statement of the facts on which the claimant relies and must state the remedy or remedies sought. The court now has the power, of its own motion and without conducting a hearing, to strike all or part of a statement of case on form N1, on the basis that no reasonable ground for bringing the claim is disclosed. The court can also, of its own motion, give a summary judgement *against a claimant* if it is considered that the claimant has no real prospect of success with the claim. If the claimant wishes to recover interest on a sum of money claimed, this must be detailed and the claimant must sign a statement on form N1 to the effect that he/she believes that the facts alleged are true. A false declaration would amount to a contempt of court which, in this context, is a criminal offence. If the claimant has entered into a conditional fee agreement, a notice (using form N251) must also be filed at the court offices. Copies of form N1 will be numbered and sealed with the court seal by the court staff upon payment of the appropriate fee and one copy of the claim form will be posted to the defendant by the court office with a response pack. Under the CPR, the proceedings are officially commenced when the claim form is issued by the court and it must be served on the defendant within four months (or six months if it is to be served out of the court's jurisdiction). Once the initial proceedings have been served they can be amended only with permission of the court. The response pack includes an admission form, a defence form and an acknowledgement of service form.

6. Responding to the particulars of claim

The defendant has a number of options which can be conveniently summarised as follows:

(a) Admit liability and make an offer to pay.

(b) File a defence to the whole or part of the claim within 14 days of service of the particulars of claim.

(c) File an acknowledgement of service within 14 days of service of the particulars of claim *and then file a defence* within 28 days of service of the particulars of claim.

If the defendant does nothing, 'judgement by default' can be entered against him/her for the figure stated on the claim form, but if the defendant has applied for a summary judgement under Part 24 of the CPR, a default judgement cannot be entered in favour of the claimant until that application has been disposed of. Also, judgement by default cannot be entered if the proceedings were commenced using form N208. If no precise sum is specified on the claim form and judgement by default is to be entered for the claimant, the judge can award an appropriate sum without the need to convene an assessment hearing. In many instances a defendant will admit the claim and make an offer to pay, but a defendant who wishes to defend the claim must file a defence. A defendant who has not acknowledged service may not participate in the hearing of the claim without permission of the court even though he/she may attend the hearing. According to CPR r. 16.5(1) the defendant must state which of the allegations contained in the particulars of claim he/she denies or which he/she is unable to admit or deny but requires the claimant to prove. In addition, he/she must indicate those allegations which he/she admits. If the defendant denies an allegation he/she must state his/her reasons for doing so and state his/her own version of events if it is different from the claimant's. A bare denial of the claimant's allegations contained in form N1 or an incoherent defence is liable to be 'struck out' on the court's own initiative so the defendant will not help his/her cause by resorting to delaying tactics. If the defendant disputes the value of the claim stated in form N1, he/she must state why he/she disputes it giving his/her own value of the claim. Where the defence relates to a personal injury claim and the claimant has attached a medical report pertaining to his/her injuries, Practice Directive 16 para. 13.1 requires that the defence should state whether the defendant:

(a) concurs with the medical report

(b) disputes it (and if so, giving reasons why)

(c) neither agrees nor disputes it but has no knowledge of the details comprising the report.

Where a medical report has been obtained by the defendant which is to form part of his/her defence, this must be attached to the defence form. Of course, if both parties have complied with the pre-action protocol for personal injury, the medical report will usually have been agreed and it is unlikely that the defendant will have procured his/her own report.

Under the CPR it is possible for a defendant to raise a counterclaim by which he/she asserts that it is really him/her that has a claim against the claimant. If the defendant does raise a counterclaim, the original claimant must file a defence to the counterclaim. Where a defence is filed with or without a counterclaim it must be accompanied by a statement of truth, as must any counterclaim. If the statement of truth is to be signed by the legal advisor rather than the client, the latter should give an assurance to the former in respect of the details of the case to be verified. Moreover, a legal advisor should not sign the statement of truth unless he/she is specifically authorised to do so; nor should he/she sign without having explained the consequences of a false declaration to the client. If a legal advisor should fail to observe these precautions he/she might be open to an allegation of professional misconduct.

One's understanding of this process will be aided by refering back to the scenario outlined at the beginning of this chapter. The company (Modern Builders Ltd) would be the claimant for £12,500 and Alice, as defendant, would have to consider her options. She could admit liability in full in respect of the company's claim. She might take the view that she is in the right and decide to defend the action by completing and filing a defence to the effect that she is not legally obliged to make the payment of £8,000. In addition, she might counterclaim under CPR r. 20.4(1) regarding the £4,500 stating that she has the right to retain this sum to cover the cost of what she considers to be rectification work. If so, she must file her counterclaim with the court and pay the appropriate fee. The counterclaim should normally form a single document in which the counterclaim follows the defence. Were Alice to ignore the sealed copy of the claim form that is served on her, judgement would be entered against her *by default* on the application of the claimant. If Alice were to file a defence, the company would not be obliged to file a 'reply' but it could. A reply is simply a response to any of the issues raised in the defence and if a counterclaim is raised by the defendant, the claimant may wish to file a reply and a defence to the counterclaim. Failure to file a reply would not operate to the company's detriment because it is not deemed to have admitted the matters raised in a defence filed by Alice. The various documents referred to above constitute the statement of case.

Under Part 18 of the CPR and Practice Direction 18, any party to the proceedings can obtain from the other party:

(a) further clarification of any matter in dispute regarding the proceedings, and

(b) further information relating to any matter in dispute.

This may be done by directing a request to the other party in accordance with Practice Direction 18 without involving the court. It is only if the party does not respond, or if the response is inadequate, that an application can be made for an order under CPR r. 18.1 requiring disclosure.

7. Agreed settlements: Part 36 Offers and Payments

The CPR encourage the parties to settle their dispute even before the commencement of legal proceedings and certainly long before the actual trial takes place. There is an incentive for them to do so by way of saving of costs. Part 36 of the CPR is quite complex. At the outset it is important to distinguish between a pre-action offer which is not a Part 36 offer and a pre-action offer that comes within the ambit of the CPR Part 36. Whilst both are mentioned in Part 36 of the CPR, a formal Part 36 offer has more serious potential cost consequences for a defendant than an ordinary pre-action offer to settle. A pre-action offer to settle may be made by either side to the dispute and, if it complies with the requirements set out in r. 36.10, the court will take it into consideration together with the surrounding circumstances when making any order as to costs in any subsequent proceedings. The circumstances referred to include whether the person making the offer (offeror) has complied with a relevant pre-action protocol or, in the absence of a protocol, whether the offeree was given sufficient information to assess whether to accept the offer. It is quite possible that if the offeror ignored a relevant protocol that the court may refuse to allow him/her any cost benefit. The offer may consist of a proposal to settle for a specified sum or for some other remedy. It must be clear to the offeree whether the offer is indeed a Part 36 offer. Thus to comply with the requirements of r. 36.5, it has to be in writing and be signed stating:

(a) whether it relates to all or part of the claim being made

(b) whether it takes account of any counterclaim that has been made

(c) whether it is inclusive of interest and giving details of interest to be paid.

According to CPR r. 36.10(2)(a), the offer must also be expressed to be open for 21 days after it has been made, but thereafter it will lapse. The party who would be the claimant, if proceedings were to be initiated, should normally consider making a pre-action offer 21 days before commencing proceedings in virtually every case. He/she should do so with a view to putting financial pressure on the party who would be the defendant to resolve the dispute. If the defendant is held liable for more than what was contained in the claimant's offer (or judgement against the defendant is more advantageous to the claimant), r. 36.21 will apply. This means that the court may order interest on the entire or any part of any sum awarded to the claimant from the date on which the defendant could have accepted the offer. Interest will not, however, be due on the interest already payable. In addition, the court may order that the defendant must pay the claimant's costs from the latest date on which he/she could have accepted the offer. The court does, however, have the discretion not to make such an order if it considers that it would be unjust. In considering whether it would be unjust, it will take into account all the circumstances of the case including:

(a) the terms of the Part 36 offer

(b) the stage in the proceedings an offer (or payment) was made

(c) the information available to the parties at the time

(d) the conduct of the parties in relation to the giving or refusing to give information for the purpose of evaluating the offer (or payment).

If the claimant has not made a pre-action offer to settle, the defendant should take the initiative as soon as he/she can evaluate the substance of the claim being brought against him/her. Such an offer should include an offer to pay the costs of the claimant (offeree) for 21 days after the offer was made. These costs could be considerable and could include the costs of reviewing documents, compiling witness statements, expert evidence together with draft particulars of claim. If the claimant decides to accept an offer from the defendant relating to every aspect of claim made, he/she will be entitled to recover his/her costs up to the date of the notification of acceptance. A realistic Part 36 offer from the defendant should focus the claimant's mind on the advisability of resolving the dispute as early as possible. If the claimant declines the offer, then fails to obtain a more advantageous judgement in court, he/she could be held liable for the costs the defendant incurred after the latest date on which the pre-action offer could have been accepted. The permission of the court is not required for a pre-action settlement and, if accepted, the case will be closed.

If proceedings, as described above, are started after a pre-action offer that complies with CPR r. 36.10 has been made, that offer cannot be accepted without the court's permission. Where the defendant in a money claim makes a pre-commencement offer but proceedings are then commenced, a defendant seeking to avail himself/herself of the costs advantage must make a payment into court. This must be done within 14 days of the service of the claim form. Moreover, the amount of the payment must not be less than the sum offered before the proceedings began. Thus, in the scenario above, Alice could make a payment into court as indicated but it must equal or exceed the amount offered before proceedings were commenced. The payment, however, cannot be accepted by the claimant without the court's consent.

A new Part 36 offer can be made any time after proceedings have been commenced because the parties have not settled. A defendant's Part 36 offer or payment made 21 days or more before the start of the trial may be accepted by the claimant without the necessity of obtaining the court's permission if the claimant gave the defendant notice of acceptance in writing no later than 21 days following the offer or the making of the payment. In the event that the defendant should make a Part 36 offer or payment less than 21 days before the trial, or if the claimant does not accept it within the 21-day period, the claimant may still accept without the necessity of obtaining the court's consent provided both reach agreement on the liability for costs. If a claimant accepts a defendant's Part 36 offer or payment that does not require the approval of the court, the defendant, as offeror, must pay the claimant's costs up to the date of serving notice of acceptance of the offer. If the defendant accepts a Part 36 offer made by the claimant that does not require the approval of the court, the defendant, as offeree, must pay the claimant's costs up to the date of the serving of the notice of acceptance.

The incentive for the claimant to settle resides in the fact that if he/she should be awarded less at the end of the trial than the amount offered by the defendant, the court will not usually allow him/her to recover costs incurred after the date on which the offer could have been accepted. If the claimant makes an offer to the defendant to settle for *less* than the amount claimed, but the defendant decides to decline the offer, and then the claimant is awarded *more* at the trial, the defendant will be penalised in costs and by the interest that is payable in respect of the claim.

Part 36 offers do not apply to the small claims track but this does not operate to bar a party from making an offer or a payment in such a case but the consequences set out in Part 36 will not apply in a small claim. The fact that a Part 36 offer has been made will not be communicated to the trial judge until the issues of liability and the amount of damages payable (if any) have been determined, except where:

(a) the defence of tender before claim has been raised

(b) the proceedings have been stayed under r. 36.15 after acceptance of a Part 36 offer (or payment), or

(c) the issue of liability has been decided before any assessment of the money claimed and the fact that there has or has not been a Part 36 payment could be relevant to the question of costs on the issue of liability.

The essence of (a) above is that, before a claimant starts proceedings the defendant unconditionally offers him/her the amount due or, if no specified sum is claimed, an amount sufficient to satisfy the claim.

8. Allocation of the case

Although a claimant largely has a free choice over which court to use when commencing proceedings (High Court or county court) this may not be the court that ultimately hears the case. This is because every defended claim has to be allocated to one of the three tracks: small claims, fast track or multi track – by a procedural judge. Although there are several factors to be considered when allocating a case to a track (the nature of the remedy sought, the number of parties involved, the complexity of the facts, law or evidence, the amount of oral testimony to be given and the views and circumstances of the parties), in practice it is normally the amount of the claim that will be the deciding factor. Usually cases involving amounts up to £5,000 will be allocated to the small claims track in the county courts. CPR r. 26.6(1) provides that the following claims will normally be allocated to the small claims track:

(a) Those with a financial value of no more than £5,000.

(b) Personal injury cases where the damages claimed do not exceed £5,000 in total and where general damages do not exceed £1,000.

(c) Breach of covenant to repair cases where both the cost of repair and the value of any other claim for damages do not exceed £1,000.

Cases involving amounts up to £15,000 will be placed on the fast track and will be heard in a county court where both district and circuit judges have jurisdiction. The fast track is also appropriate for non-monetary claims comprising applications for injunctions, declarations and claims for specific performance that are unsuitable for the small claims track but which are too straightforward for the multi track. For those cases involving a fixed sum, these will be transferred to the county court that has jurisdiction for the area where the defendant lives or carries on business. Most of those cases involving more than £15,000 are allocated to the multi track whereby they are transferred to a trial centre. These are the venues for multi track trials and a proportion of fast track trials, and are the county courts for England and Wales. If, however, a case simply entails the assessment of damages because liability has been admitted, then it may or may not be allocated to a track.

A procedural judge makes the first case management decision by deciding which is the most appropriate court to hear the case. In the Royal Courts of Justice (High Court) the procedural judges are High Court Masters, whereas in the civil trial centres they are circuit judges or district judges. If a claim, which is for a specified sum and is against an ordinary person, is defended, it will automatically be transferred to the defendant's home court by the court that received the defence. Thus, when Alice filed her defence, the case would have been transferred to Guildford County Court. In other cases, transfers are governed by CPR Part 30. The criteria for deciding whether to transfer is set out in the High Court and County Court Jurisdiction Order 1991 (SI 1991 No. 724). In order to assist the court with the allocation process, each party is normally required to complete and file an allocation questionnaire using form N150 soon after the defence is filed. It is always the court where the proceedings were commenced that has the responsibility for serving the allocation questionnaires. The questionnaire asks each side or their legal representative:

(a) whether they would like proceedings to be stayed (suspended) for a month in order to achieve a settlement by means other than litigation

(b) if there is some reason why the claims should be heard at a particular court

(c) whether a pre-action protocol (if appropriate) has been complied with or whether the party has exchanged information and/or documents with the other side to assist in settling the claim.

In the Case Management Information section (part d), each party is required to state what amount of the claim is in dispute, whether application has been made for summary judgement and what expert witnesses and other witnesses are to be called. In the guidance notes, the parties are reminded to include themselves as witnesses of fact if they will be giving evidence. Each party is then asked which is the most suitable track for the claim and thereafter:

(e) how long the trial is expected to last

(f) whether a list of directions has been attached and if the directions have been agreed with the other side

(g) what costs have been incurred to date and what are the estimated overall costs. (This is addressed to solicitors and is completed only for fast track and multi track claims.)

In relation to (a) above, if both parties consent to a stay, the court will expect them to use the time in a genuine effort to resolve the dispute without the necessity of a court hearing. The allocation questionnaire will specify the date by which it must be filed and, on receipt, the court will be able to decide the most appropriate venue and the most appropriate track. It will also assist the court in deciding on the nature of any appropriate directions and whether a case management conference will be required in the event that the case is to be allocated to the multi track. Allocation questionnaires are not usually used in specialist cases that are automatically allocated to the multi track such as cases involving applications under the Companies Act 1985 and claims allocated to the Technology and Construction Court. These courts have their own procedures for dealing with case management. If one of the parties fails to file an allocation questionnaire, the court may give any direction it deems appropriate, but if it takes the view that it does not have sufficient information at its disposal, it will list the case for an allocation hearing. The claimant is obliged to pay a fee on filing his/her allocation questionnaire unless the claim is for a sum of money of not more than £1,000. Under CPR r. 3.7, the claim will be struck out automatically if the allocation fee is not paid after the court has served a warning notice using form N173.

Once the court has decided which track to allocate the case to, it sends an allocation notice to the parties with copies of their allocation questionnaires. This allocation notice gives directions and the reasons for the judge's allocation decision. The form of directions that the court makes at the allocation stage is dependent on the track that the case is allocated to and the particular circumstances of the case. In cases that are allocated to the small claims track the court will make standard directions contained in Practice Direction 27. These basic standard directions require the parties to serve copies of documents on each other and provide copies for filing with the court. The original documents must be brought to the hearing. For cases allocated to the fast track or multi track it will consider making directions covering the disclosure of documents, the exchange of witness statements, disclosure of experts' reports and narrowing the scope of the expert evidence as well as listing the claim for trial. Under CPR r. 26.6(5), cases will not normally be assigned to the fast track unless oral expert evidence at trial can be limited to two separate fields of expertise and where each party is limited to one expert for each area of expertise. For cases allocated to the multi track, the court will consider if a case management conference is necessary and whether a pre-trial review is required. Under CPR r. 32.1, the court has the power to give directions limiting the issues in which it wishes to be addressed and on the evidence that may be produced at trial on these issues. However, this power will normally be exercised only in accordance with the overriding objective of the CPR, namely that cases must be dealt with justly and fairly.

In fast track cases, the court will normally order disclosure of documents at the allocation stage and the order will be limited to what is known as standard disclosure. This requires a party to disclose only:

(a) the documents on which he/she relies

(b) the documents which:

    (i) adversely affect his own case

    (ii) adversely affect the other party's case, or

    (iii) support the other party's case

(c) the documents that he/she is required to disclose by a Relevant Practice Direction.

In a multi track case, an order for disclosure will usually be made by the court at a case management conference. However, if the case does not merit a case management conference, disclosure will be dealt with by the court as part of the case management directions given at the allocation stage. Each side will normally give disclosure by making a list using form N265 and by serving it on the other side. Once a document has been disclosed in this way, each side can then make arrangements to inspect and copy any document which the other side possesses, provided it is still within their control. Inspection of particular documents has been refused if one of the parties asserts that it is a privileged communication.

9. The small claims procedure

Under CPR r. 27.4(1)(d) the court may fix a date for a preliminary hearing although CPR r. 27.6 states that a preliminary hearing of a small claim may only be convened in one of three situations:

(a) if the court considers that special directions are necessary under r. 27.4 to ensure a fair hearing, or

(b) where one of the parties has no real prospect of success, to facilitate disposal of the claim, or

(c) so that the court can strike out the whole or part of a statement of case that discloses no reasonable basis for bringing or defending a claim.

At the end of the preliminary hearing the court will set a date for the final hearing and inform the parties, giving them any further directions necessary. The hearing itself is normally conducted in public before a district judge (unless a hearing in private is justified by the Convention rights enshrined in the Human Rights Act 1998) who may require that all or part of the proceedings shall be tape-recorded. Nevertheless, the proceedings are likely to be relatively informal and the strict rules of evidence are not applied. The district judge will have read the papers beforehand and may adopt any method of proceeding which he/she considers fair and he/she may even adopt an inquisitorial approach, questioning witnesses before even the parties themselves can do so. Expert evidence can only be given with the court's consent and the court may also limit cross-examination to a fixed time or to a particular subject. Alternatively, the court can, with the consent of the parties, dispose of the case without a hearing at all. The judge must always give reasons for his/her decision. This can be done at a subsequent hearing or orally at the hearing but subsequently confirmed in writing.

A hearing may be conducted in the absence of one of the parties because either party may now give notice at least seven days prior to the hearing

253

that he/she does not propose to attend, requesting that the court deal with the case in his/her absence on the basis of documents submitted. A party not present at the hearing or represented and who has neither given notice of non-attendance nor consented to disposal without a hearing is able to apply for the judgement to be set aside and the case reheard. The appropriate application must be made no later than 14 days after notice of judgement was served on him/her. However, the application will only be successful if he/she can satisfy the court that:

(a) he/she had a good reason for not attending (or being represented) or for not giving notice of non-attendance, and

(b) that he/she has a reasonable prospect of success at the hearing.

A party may not make such an application where the court dealt with the claim without a hearing, with the consent of the parties. The court can grant the same final remedies under the small claims procedure that can be granted in cases on the fast track or the multi track. There is, nevertheless, a limit imposed by CPR r. 27.14 and Practice Direction 27 para. 7 on the costs that can be recovered under the small claims procedure.

A party who is dissatisfied with the outcome of the case can appeal from the decision of a district judge to a circuit judge by serving notice of appeal using form N161 but only on grounds of a serious irregularity affecting the proceedings or a mistake of law. This must usually be done within 14 days of the original decision. Particulars of the grounds of appeal must be given in the notice, and on hearing the appeal the court can make any order it considers appropriate.

10. The listing questionnaire

For cases allocated to the fast track or multi track, a listing questionnaire will be sent out to the parties either at the allocation stage with the case management directions given or, at the very latest, shortly before the hearing date. If it was sent with the directions given at the allocation stage, this document has to be returned (usually with 14 days) by the parties. If neither party returns the listing questionnaire then the court will usually make an order to the effect that if the questionnaires are not filed within three days from the service of the order, the claim and any counterclaim will be stuck out. If only one party is at fault, the court will give listing directions based on the questionnaire that is received. The listing questionnaire asks:

(a) whether all previous directions given by the court have been complied with and whether any further directions are required to prepare the case for trial

(b) whether the court has already given permission to use written expert evidence and whether permission has been granted for oral testimony from experts to be given at the trial

(c) for information concerning the availability of other witnesses and whether interpreters will be required

(d) whether a solicitor/barrister will be presenting the case

(e) for an estimate of the length of time the trial will take and the number of pages of evidence to be included in the trial bundle.

11. Trials on the fast track

The dispute between Modern Builders Ltd and Alice would be allocated to the fast track. Further directions may be given at the listing stage when the parties have filed their listing questionnaires. Under CPR r. 28.6(1) the court will:

(a) set the date for the trial or confirm one already given,

(b) give any additional directions deemed necessary and, if appropriate, set a trial timetable, and

(c) detail any further steps that need to be taken prior to a trial of the action.

Fast track trials are supposed to conform to a strict timetable of 30 weeks between the allocation of the case and the trial of the action. The underlying assumption is that the solicitors acting for the parties will have sufficient time to undertake the necessary preparatory work for the trial. Thus claimants need to ensure that their cases are already well prepared even before they issue proceedings lest they fall behind schedule once the very strict timetable starts to apply. Defendants too will find themselves under pressure, although compliance with a relevant pre-action protocol should ensure that they are well prepared. Normally, trials are limited to a single day, but if a trial is not finished on the day for which it is listed the judge will normally sit on the next court day to complete it. As indicated previously, trials must usually be conducted in public (unless a hearing in private is justified by the Convention rights enshrined in the Human Rights Act 1998). Hearings in private may be justified on the grounds of morals, public order, national security, where the interests of juveniles are involved, for the protection of private life and in instances where a public hearing would prejudice the interests of justice.

Although the entire rationale of the fast track procedure is to have a swift resolution of the dispute, the judge will bear in mind that under Schedule 1

Article 6(1) of the Human Rights Act 1998 the parties have a right to a fair trial, which means that each must be given an equal opportunity to present his/her case. Time will nevertheless be saved because expert witnesses will normally give their evidence in writing – indeed, jointly instructed experts are becoming established practice. The judge will have read the papers which must have been submitted in a properly indexed and paginated trial bundle beforehand. A case summary not exceeding 250 words may also have been prepared by the procedural judge. Thus the trial judge may decide to dispense with opening addresses by the advocates representing the parties. Witness statements will normally stand as 'evidence in chief' and the extent of cross-examination is likely to be limited by the judge. At the end of the trial the judge will deliver his/her judgement and summarily assess costs. In order to assist the trial judge in assessing the costs, the parties are required to file signed statements of their costs using form N260 at least 24 hours before the trial. Should they fail to do so without reasonable excuse, this will be taken into account in deciding the costs order relating to the claim, the trial and any subsequent assessment hearing that might be necessary as a result of the failure. The trial judge is responsible for ensuring that the costs claimed are not disproportionate or otherwise unreasonable.

If the claimant recovers between £3,000 and £10,000 the sum recoverable by the advocate for preparing and appearing at the trial is currently £500. If the sum recovered is more than £10,000 the sum recoverable for preparing and appearing at the trial is currently limited to £750. Since the costs of the trial are fixed in relation to the amount claimed with no discretion permitted, it is likely that all but the most junior members of the Bar will find it not financially worthwhile to appear as advocates and so solicitors will probably do most of this advocacy.

12. Multi track trials

The multi track is intended for a very wide range of cases. These include relatively straightforward cases, such as contractual disputes where the amount claimed exceeds the financial limit for fast track trials, to the most difficult cases that involve complex issues of law and fact with amounts at stake that could run into millions of pounds. All Part 8 claims (those commenced using form N208) are allocated to the multi track, as are those raising points of law of great public importance.

The straightforward cases involving amounts just over the limit for fast track trials will be the subject of standard case management directions, but really complex cases will be subject to more active case management by way of case conferences and pre-trial reviews. At a case management conference the agenda is in effect set by Practice Direction 29. A judge can ask probing questions in relation to a party's case with a view to narrowing the issues to be tried so that minor ones are eliminated by agreement with the parties. At the conclusion of a pre-trial review, the court must draw up a trial timetable if one has not been set earlier. Rule 1.4(2) of the CPR requires courts, as part of the process of active case management, to encourage and facilitate the use of alternative dispute resolution (ADR) where appropriate (*see* Chapter 14). Moreover, rule 26.4 allows the court to stay proceedings to permit the use of ADR, either where the parties themselves request it or where the court of its own initiative considers it to be appropriate because both sides seem prepared to reach an agreed settlement. If a case involves less than £50,000 it will usually be heard at a civil trial centre, but if it exceeds that amount it will normally be heard at the Royal Courts of Justice.

13. Conduct of the trial

According to CPR r. 39.2(1), trials must be conducted in public, but r. 39.2(3) states that hearings may be conducted in private under certain circumstances. Practice Direction 39 gives a list of the proceedings that will be conducted in private. Most civil trials at first instance take place before a judge sitting alone but there is a statutory right to a jury trial for certain tort actions. The County Courts Act 1984 s. 66 and the Supreme Court Act 1981 s. 69 allow for jury trial in actions in the torts of deceit, defamation, malicious prosecution and false imprisonment unless the court takes the view that the trial requires prolonged examination of documents, scientific or local investigation that cannot be conveniently carried out with a jury. If there is to be a jury trial, High Court juries have 12 members and county court juries have 8 members.

As previously stated, the CPR require judges sitting at first instance to assert greater control over the preparation and conduct of hearings. The judge will have read the relevant documents comprising the trial bundle beforehand as well as the skeleton arguments submitted by the advocates. The barrister/solicitor representing the claimant may be allowed to make a short opening speech setting out the background to the case but immediately afterwards he/she must call the witnesses that are appearing for the claimant, who are duly sworn or make an affirmation. Since every witness statement will now stand as evidence in chief, witnesses can be cross-examined without delay by the advocate for the defendant to expose any inconsistencies or gaps in the evidence given. The court may, however, allow a witness to amplify the content of a witness statement under CPR r. 32.5 and give evidence in relation to new matters that have arisen since the witness statement was served on the other side. Nevertheless, the judge may limit cross-examination if he/she considers that it is achieving no useful purpose. Witnesses may also be asked questions by the judge who may wish to clarify certain points. When the advocate for the claimant has called all the witnesses for his/her client, he/she makes his/her submissions on the relevant law to the judge. In doing so he/she will cite all relevant case law precedents and legislation but not in detail. Although he/she is required to cite all the relevant law, even though this may lend some support to the defendant's case, he/she is at liberty to interpret it to the claimant's advantage and to attempt to persuade the judge that this body of law really advances and supports the claimant's case.

The advocate for the defence will then call the witnesses for his/her client who are duly sworn or affirmed and then cross-examined by the advocate for the claimant. Once the advocate for the defendant has called all the witnesses for the defence and has cited all the evidence for the defence, he/she will cite all the relevant law, but not in detail, in support of the defendant's case to the judge. If the defendant's advocate elects not to cite evidence at the trial, the advocate for the claimant will make a closing speech and the advocate for the defendant will follow this with a statement of the defendant's case.

14. Delivering judgement

At the end of the trial, the judge must give a reasoned judgement stating the conclusions he/she has reached on any factual issues in dispute. If the evidence given is conflicting, he/she must state which version of the facts is the most likely to be accurate and therefore on which he/she will rely. In giving his/her judgement, the judge will recite the material (important) facts of the case as established in evidence and state how the relevant law (statute and/or precedent) is to be applied to those facts. The end result must be that judgement is given in favour of one party and the other party loses. A copy of the judgement is normally completed by the court and sealed so that it can be served on the parties. The costs of the action are, for the most part, borne by the losing party, but as has been seen, this is not an invariable rule.

15. Remedies

A court may make both interim remedies and final remedies at the conclusion of the trial. The interim remedies that may be granted are set out in r. 25.1 and include interim injunctions and interim declarations. The most usual final remedy given by a court will entail the payment of money to settle a debt or settle some other unpaid, ascertained sum. (If the court were to give judgement for Modern Builders Ltd against Alice it might order her to pay the entire £12,500). Alternatively, the claimant may simply have asked for an award of damages in the claim form to be settled by the court, but if there has been an infringement of a legal right that has not resulted in any real loss, the court will only award nominal damages. Compensatory damages can be divided into pecuniary and non-pecuniary damages. The former compensates the claimant for measurable financial loss caused by the defendant's wrongdoing. Non-pecuniary (or general) damages are awarded in recognition of the suffering that the wrongdoing has caused the defendant. The amount awarded as non-pecuniary damages will be assessed according to what the court considers appropriate in the particular case, but it will take into account what has been awarded in similar cases. In tort claims, the amount awarded is that which will restore the claimant (in so far as it is possible to do so) to the position he/she would have been in had the wrongful act not been committed. In a claim for breach of contract, the damages sought can be awarded on two different bases:

(a) to restore the claimant to the position he/she would have been in had the contract been performed properly, or

(b) to compensate for expenditure rendered futile by the breach of contract.

The claimant can choose on which basis to claim. Sometimes a court may award aggravated damages (as defined in the CPR glossary) for the defendant's objectionable behaviour, but a claim for such damages must be made separately in the particulars of claim. Very occasionally a court may award exemplary damages (as defined in the CPR glossary). These must also be claimed separately in the particulars of claim, and are awarded to show the court's disapproval of the defendant's behaviour. Orders for the payment of a debt and damages are the basic common law remedies but sometimes a court can give a declaratory judgement: defining the parties' rights, without granting any other remedy. Damages are not always the most appropriate remedy and the court may award one of the equitable remedies discussed in Chapter 4, if requested by the claimant. These remedies are injunction, specific performance, rectification and rescission. Various other remedies are available in special proceedings, for example, in insolvency proceedings bankruptcy orders and winding-up orders for companies can be obtained, as can company director disqualification orders.

16. Enforcement of judgements

Obtaining a judgement from the court involving the payment of money by the losing party is one thing, enforcing it, if he/she is reluctant to pay, is quite another matter. Judgements requiring the payment of money may be enforced by warrant of execution but in only one case in three are the bailiffs able to recover anything that can be sold. Sometimes this may be due to the fact that they are unable to gain access to premises – as the law currently stands they must be invited on to the premises unless they find an open door. Garnishee proceedings (where a claim can be made on a person's bank account) may be a possibility, but the claimant would need to have very precise details relating to the defendant's bank account. There must also be cleared funds on the account. Another possibility exists in the form of a bankruptcy notice (or an order to wind up a company) but that will entail additional expense. Where the judgement has been given against a private individual there is the possibility of an attachment of earnings by the court. This is usually done through the county court. The Attachment of Earnings Act 1971 s. 6(1) provides that:

> An attachment of earnings order shall be directed to a person who appears to the court to have the debtor in his employment and shall operate as an instruction to that person –
> (a) to make periodic deductions from the debtor's earnings . . . and
> (b) at such times as the order may require, or as the court may allow, to pay the amounts deducted to the collecting officer of the court, as specified in the order.

Once the money has been paid over by the employer to the court, the court will then pay it to the party that has sought to enforce the judgement.

17. Appeals

The system for civil appeals can be conveniently summarised as follows:

(a) An appeal from the decision of a district judge may be made to a circuit judge of the county court provided notice of appeal is filed within 14 days of the date of the decision and permission to appeal is obtained.

(b) An appeal from a preliminary decision of a High Court master or a district judge may be made to a High Court judge.

(c) An appeal from the decision of a circuit judge in the county court should be made to the High Court within 14 days of the date of the decision and permission to appeal is required either from the lower court or the appeal court.

(d) A final decision in a multi track case or in specialist proceedings must be appealed to the Court of Appeal within 14 days of the date of the decision and permission to appeal is required either from the lower court or from the appeal court.

(e) An appeal from the decision of a High Court judge must be made to the Court of Appeal within 14 days of the date of the original decision and it is necessary to obtain permission to appeal either from the lower court or from the appeal court.

(f) Decisions of the Court of Appeal can be appealed to the House of Lords within one month of the order being made or within three months if permission to appeal is granted by the Court of Appeal itself.

According to CPR r. 52.3(6), permission to appeal will be given only where:

(a) the court takes the view that the appeal would have a real prospect of success, or

(b) there is some compelling reason why the appeal should be heard.

CPR r. 52.11(10) states that every appeal will be limited to a review of the decision of the lower court unless:

(a) a Practice Direction requires otherwise for a particular category of appeal, or

(b) the appeal court takes the view that in the particular circumstances it would be in the interests of justice to hold a rehearing.

The appeal court will permit an appeal to go ahead only if the decision of the lower court was wrong or unjust because of a serious procedural or other irregularity in the proceedings. It will not make original findings of fact. Indeed, a finding of fact of a lower court can be overturned only if there was no evidence to support it or if the finding of fact goes against the weight of the evidence. According to the earlier ruling in *Ladd* v *Marshall* [1954], fresh evidence can only be admitted on appeal if:

(a) the evidence could not have been obtained with reasonable diligence for the hearing in the lower court,

(b) it would probably have an important influence on the outcome, and

(c) it is apparently credible.

Even in the era of the CPR the appeal court will be unwilling to allow fresh evidence to be introduced at the appeal stage unless there are special reasons. Under CPR r. 52.10(2) the appeal court has the power to:

(a) affirm, set aside or vary any order or judgement made or given by a lower court

(b) refer any claim or issue for determination by the lower court

(c) order a new trial

(d) make orders for the payment of interest

(e) make a costs order.

In some circumstances an appeal may occasionally be made directly from the High Court to the House of Lords thereby 'leapfrogging' the Court of Appeal. This is only likely to happen when the Court of Appeal is bound by one of its existing precedents and an advocate for one of the parties considers that the House of Lords may be willing to overrule the Court of Appeal. There is also a possibility of an appeal to the European Court of Human Rights at Strasbourg if it can be shown that one of the parties did not receive a fair hearing either at first instance or on appeal. On the other hand, a complaint to the European Court of Human Rights under the Convention can only be made if the complainant has exhausted his/her rights under national law. There is also a time limit of six months, after which complaints will not be entertained.

Progress test

1. What criticisms did Lord Woolf make of the old civil justice system in his report *Access to Justice*?

2. What function is the pre-action protocol intended to serve?

3. Are there any sanctions that may be imposed on litigants who fail to observe the requirements of a pre-action protocol?

4. How does a claimant normally set about commencing legal proceedings against someone? To which courts may the relevant form(s) be taken?

5. On receipt of the claim, what options are open to the defendant?

6. What is a Part 36 offer?

7. Why might a claimant make a pre-action Part 36 offer?

8. What is the function of the allocation questionnaire and what questions does it ask?

9. What are the tracks to which a case may be allocated and what is normally the determining factor?

10. What is the function of the listing questionnaire?

11. What are the main objectives in allocating a case to the fast track?

12. What types of case will be allocated to the multi track, and can a judge suspend proceedings to refer the dispute to some form of alternative dispute resolution?

Further reading

Books

Bramley, M. and A. Gouge (2000) *The Civil Justice Reforms One Year On* (London: Butterworths).

Grainger, I. and M. Fealy (2000) *The Civil Procedure Rules in Action* (London: Cavendish).

Rose, W.M. His Honour Judge (1999) *Pleadings Without Tears* (London: Blackstone Press).

Rose, W. His Honour Judge, S. Sime and D. French (eds) (2001) *Blackstone's Civil Practice* (London: Blackstone Press).

Sime, S. (2000) *A Practical Approach to Civil Procedure* (London: Blackstone Press).

Slapper, G. and D. Kelly (1999) *The English Legal System* (London: Cavendish Publishing, chapter 7).

Article

Harrison, R. (2001) 'First principles and witness statements', *New Law Journal* Vol. 151, No. 6982.

Useful website

The Court Service website at www.courtservice.gov.uk is a useful source of up-to-date information. Forms used in civil litigation can be downloaded from this site.

13

Dispute resolution 2: The role of tribunals

1. Introduction

The courts are not the only places where disputes may be resolved, and where individuals may be disciplined for lapses from accepted norms of behaviour. There are, in fact, a large number of tribunals of various types whose status is lower than that of the ordinary courts that deal with such matters. Some of these tribunals have been created by Acts of Parliament. Others exist because certain organisations have discovered the need for a forum in which complaints about members can be aired and, if necessary, members can be sanctioned for infringing the rules. These inferior tribunals are not (with the exception of the Lands Tribunal) presided over by judicial appointees as in the ordinary courts. In *Attorney General* v *BBC* [1981], Lord Scarman distinguished between the ordinary courts and certain tribunals when he said:

> I would identify a court in (or 'of') law i.e. a court of judicature, as a body established by law to exercise, either generally or subject to defined limits, the judicial power of the state. In this context judicial power is to be contrasted with legislative and executive (i.e. administrative) power. If the body under review is established for a purely legislative or administrative purpose, it is part of the legislative or administrative system, even though it has to perform duties which are judicial in character.

In this case, the House of Lords held that a valuation court was in fact a tribunal because it performed an administrative function. It is not easy to devise a perfect system of classification for such a diverse range of quasi-judicial bodies but one that is commonly adopted by most legal commentators entails drawing a distinction between:

(a) administrative tribunals

(b) employment tribunals

(c) domestic tribunals.

264

This is the classification that has been adopted in the interests of investigating and comparing their respective roles in the area of dispute resolution.

2. Administrative tribunals

Many of these tribunals have been established by statute in response to a perceived need to have a review process that is quite separate from and independent of government. There are nearly seventy of these tribunals whose function is to deal quickly and cheaply with grievances against government departments and other agencies of the state. In fact they deal with more cases annually than the ordinary courts and collectively they are responsible for administering the system of administrative justice that obtains in England and Wales. The more important administrative tribunals include the Parole Board, the Criminal Injuries Compensation Authority (which exists to decide claims for compensation for victims of crime), the Immigration Appeal Tribunal, the Lands Tribunal, Mental Health Review Tribunal(s), Rent Tribunal(s), Social Security and Child Support Commissioners (which hears appeals from Social Security Appeal Tribunals, Child Support Appeal Tribunals, Medical Appeal Tribunals and Disability Appeal Tribunals) and the Special Commissioners of Income Tax. The composition of these tribunals varies in terms of the number of persons who sit to hear a case and determine its outcome.

For the most part, the procedure in these administrative tribunals is far less formal than in the ordinary courts. For this reason, individuals were originally expected to be able to do without legal representation. In very straightforward cases they may still choose to do so, but in more complex matters (e.g. disputes before the Lands Tribunal and in tax cases before the Special Commissioners of Income Tax) legal representation may be advisable unless the complainant is particularly articulate and competent. The chairperson of an administrative tribunal will normally be legally qualified (either as a solicitor or barrister) and he/she will be assisted by two (or more) other persons who are empanelled because of their specialist knowledge. These lay experts normally vote with the chairperson in deciding the outcome of cases. A Committee on Administrative Tribunals and Enquiries (the Franks Committee) was established in the aftermath of the maladministration highlighted by the Crichel Down affair. Crichel Down is a piece of land in Dorset that had been compulsorily acquired by a government department. When it was no longer required for the purpose for which it had been acquired, various civil servants then frustrated the attempts of the former owner to repurchase it. The Committee's 1957 report in paragraph 42 stated:

265

In the field of tribunals openness appears to us to require the publicity of proceedings and knowledge of the essential reasoning underlying the decisions; fairness to require the adoption of a clear procedure which enables parties to know their rights, to present their case fully and to know the case which they have to meet; and impartiality to require the freedom of tribunals from the influence, real or apparent, of government departments concerned with the subject matter of their decisions.

With a view to achieving a greater coherence within the tribunal system and achieving a better method of surveillance, the Committee recommended that there should be a standing council on tribunals. Soon afterwards, the government of the day enacted the Tribunals and Inquiries Act 1958 which created the Council on Tribunals. This legislation and subsequent legislation was consolidated in the Tribunals and Inquiries Act 1992. Those tribunals that come under its remit are listed in Schedule 1 of the Act. The Council functions as a part-time body comprising fifteen persons who are appointed by the Lord Chancellor and Lord Advocate for Scotland and it meets on a monthly basis. Although it has a full-time secretariat, it has no executive powers and operates mainly as an advisory and consultative body but it can receive complaints from the public in relation to public inquiries. Although the Council maintains a 'watching brief' and produces an annual report, the real task of supervision of administrative tribunals resides with the Administrative Court, which is part of the High Court, rather than with the Council on Tribunals. In this respect, the Administrative Court exercises a long-standing common law jurisdiction whereby it can grant one or more of the prerogative orders in response to a claim for judicial review (*see* Chapter 15).

If an administrative tribunal makes an error of law, the statute that created it may have provided for a specific right of appeal to the High Court. Alternatively, if an individual considers that an error of law has been made or that his/her case has not been dealt with in accordance with the principles of natural justice, he/she can apply to the Administrative Court for judicial review. This is not an appeal as such but rather a review of the decision-making process as is explained in Chapter 15. Even if a right of appeal has been stipulated in a particular Act of Parliament, the High Court may still entertain a claim for judicial review if this is advantageous to the complainant. Where a judge is satisfied with the substance of a claim, he/she can make a quashing order which nullifies the earlier decision. A mandatory order will require a tribunal to rehear the case and it is therefore often applied for at the same time as a quashing order. A prohibiting order can also be made by the Administrative Court to prevent a tribunal from exceeding its jurisdiction and it can also be used to prevent a tribunal from ignoring the principles of natural justice when hearing a case.

3. Employment tribunals

Employment tribunals were originally established as industrial tribunals under the Industrial Training Act 1964 s. 12 to adjudicate over the legality of industrial training levies. Employment tribunals now have the power to determine over 50 different types of complaint arising from the employment relationship. They are supported by the Employment Tribunals Service (ETS) which is an executive agency of the Department of Trade and Industry. The ETS operates from 34 permanent offices across Britain but tribunal hearings are conducted at numerous locations to accommodate the needs of employers and employees.

It is interesting to chart the unplanned and rather haphazard expansion of the jurisdiction of employment tribunals since 1964. The Industrial Training Act 1964 sought to improve the skills levels in UK industry by forcing employers to provide funding for industrial training. An early reported case on the application of the legislation was that of *Hotel and Catering Industry Training Board* v *Automotive Proprietary Ltd* [1969] which was considered in Chapter 7. However, the first extension of the jurisdiction of employment tribunals (or industrial tribunals as they were then known) came with the Redundancy Payments Act 1965. The aim of the legislation was to cushion the blow of redundancy by providing state compensation – via the employer – to those who lost their jobs through no fault of their own. The Act contained the legal definition of what constituted a redundancy situation but it was necessary to have a tribunal of some kind to decide whether a redundancy situation had arisen before the issue of compensation could be considered.

In 1963, the International Labour Organisation (ILO) in Geneva had adopted Recommendation 119 on the Termination of Employment at the Initiative of the Employer. As a member state of the ILO, the UK was obliged to give 'consideration with a view to effect being given to it by national legislation . . .'. References were made in the parliamentary debates over the Redundancy Payments Act 1965, to the desirability of including control over arbitrary or, as they came to be known, unfair dismissals, but nothing was done at the time. The Conservative government of Edward Heath (1970–74) wanted to introduce a legal framework for the conduct of industrial relations. Although the government was concerned to comply with its ILO obligations, as contained in Recommendation 119, it obviously thought that the inclusion of the right not to be unfairly dismissed in the Industrial Relations Act 1971 would persuade the trade unions to accept its statutory framework for industrial relations. The Conservatives were defeated in the election in February 1974. Although the incoming Labour government repealed the Industrial Relations Act

1971, it re-enacted the unfair dismissal provisions with the right to complaint to an industrial tribunal in the Trade Union and Labour Relations Act 1974. The relevant provisions have since been re-enacted and are to be found in the Employment Rights Act 1996. Alleged unfair dismissals still account for the bulk of all claims brought before employment tribunals to this day.

4. Discrimination in employment

The Labour Government of 1974 to 1979 was responsible for three important pieces of anti-discrimination legislation that expanded the jurisdiction of industrial tribunals. These were:

(a) Equal Pay Act 1970

(b) Sex Discrimination Act 1975

(c) Race Relations Act 1976

The pressure to enact the Equal Pay Act 1970 initially came from the Trades Union Congress who wanted the government to ratify the ILO Convention 100 requiring equal remuneration for men and women doing work of equal value. Although it was enacted in 1970, the Act did not come into operation until 1975. This gave employers the necessary 'breathing space' to alter discriminatory pay systems and it was also intended that the commencement of the Equal Pay Act 1970 should be synchronised with the coming into operation of the Sex Discrimination Act 1975. This Act aimed to combat forms of sex-based discrimination other than pay. Although this was ground-breaking social policy at the time, neither statute was entirely satisfactory and both have been amended since to take account of rulings in the European Court of Justice on Article 119 of the EC Treaty and Directive 76/207/EEC on equal treatment of men and women. As the UK was becoming a multi-ethnic society it was considered essential that there should be legislation to combat racial discrimination in employment. The Race Relations Act 1968 had extended non-discrimination to the employment sphere and there was further legislation in the form of the Race Relations Act 1976.

5. Expansion of jurisdiction under the Conservatives

The incoming Conservative government's priority was to reduce what it viewed as the abuse of power by the trade union movement and a start was made in the Employment Act 1980. In a series of Employment Acts enacted from 1982 the power of trade unions was reduced by means of conferring rights on individual trade unionists (such as the right not to be expelled and the right not to be unjustifiably disciplined) that could be enforced before industrial tribunals. Although extending individual employment rights was not part of its agenda, the government was obliged to transpose the Acquired Rights Directive (77/187/EEC) in the Transfer of Undertakings (Protection of Employment) Regulations 1981 (known as TUPE). These regulations attempted to safeguard the interests of employees upon a sale or disposal of a business by allowing employees to complain to an industrial tribunal if their rights were infringed. The Local Government Act 1988 had ushered in the policy of compulsory competitive tendering for local authority services. As these services were contracted out, this exercised downward pressure on the wages of lowly-paid workers but many were able to invoke the TUPE regulations before tribunals to safeguard their existing terms and conditions of employment. Claims continue to be brought under the regulations every year. The Wages Act 1986 (since consolidated in the Employment Rights Act 1996) gave employees the right to complain to an industrial tribunal if they had suffered unauthorised deductions from their wages. If a complaint is well founded, the tribunal will order payment of the amount unlawfully withheld.

The Pregnant Workers Directive (92/85/EEC) required the UK government to amend its legislation relating to maternity leave. As a result, every woman now has a statutory right to 14 weeks' maternity leave and a right to return to work irrespective of length of service. A woman also has a right not to be unreasonably refused time off during working hours to enable her to keep antenatal appointments irrespective of length of service. If an employer decides to suspend a woman on maternity grounds for health reasons, the Employment Rights Act 1996 s. 67 confers on her the right to be offered suitable alternative employment by her employer where there is an available vacancy. In the event that a woman is suspended on maternity grounds, she has the right to be paid her normal remuneration during suspension in accordance with s. 68. A woman whose rights are infringed may bring her employer before an employment tribunal.

Long-standing legislation, requiring employers to give written particulars of contracts of employment, had to be amended in 1993 in the light of Directive 91/533/EEC. Consequently, if the employer fails to provide the employee with a written statement of particulars under the Employment Rights Act 1996, he/she can complain to an employment tribunal and the tribunal is empowered to issue a statement of particulars to the employee should the employer refuse to do so.

Having unsuccessfully challenged its legality in the European Court of Justice, the government was obliged to implement Directive 93/104/EC (Working Time Directive). The directive attempted to establish a limit for the number of hours that could be worked and also provided for paid annual leave and for rest periods. The Working Time Regulations 1998 (SI 1998 No. 1833) were made rather belatedly and the industrial tribunals were designated as the forum for hearing complaints. Then, as a result of a successful campaign waged by the disability lobby, the government was persuaded to enact the Disability Discrimination Act 1995. The legislation is aimed at helping disabled people to find gainful employment and to prevent their being discriminated against. As with grievances under the Working Time Regulations, employment tribunals became the chosen forum for hearing complaints and dispensing remedies.

6. Expansion in jurisdiction since 1997

In its first term of office commencing in 1997 the Labour government steered the following legislation through Parliament: National Minimum Wage Act 1998, Public Interest Disclosure Act 1998 and Employment Relations Act 1999.

All complaints under the National Minimum Wage Act 1998 are brought before employment tribunals as are complaints of dismissal arising under the Public Interest Disclosure Act 1998. The Employment Relations Act 1999 creates a new right to parental leave (13 weeks) for male and female employees with one year's service. This innovation was necessary to implement the Parental Leave Directive (96/34/EC). If an employee works part-time, the entitlement is proportionate to the time that the employee normally works. There are provisions relating to leave for family and domestic reasons (ss 7–9); the right to be accompanied in disciplinary and grievance hearings (ss 10–11); as well as protection of employees taking industrial action that has the support of a ballot (s. 16). Also the Part-time Workers (Prevention of Less Favourable Treatment) Regulations 2000 (SI 2000/1551) have been operative since 1 July 2000 to implement Directive 97/81/EC. These regulations will improve the terms and conditions of part-timers, most of whom are women. Thus, the very diverse nature of the jurisdiction of employment tribunals is now apparent.

The most recent Report and Accounts of the Employment Tribunals Service covering the period 1999–2000 gives a breakdown of the various categories of complaint that were made to employment tribunals during this period (Table 13.1). As previously indicated, the largest category by far is that of unfair dismissal complaints. Not all of these applications result in a tribunal hearing. Some are conciliated by the Advisory, Conciliation and Arbitration Service (ACAS) to the mutual satisfaction of both sides. Some complaints are withdrawn and do not therefore proceed to a tribunal hearing.

Table 13.1   Employment tribunal statistics 1999–2000

Complaint	No. of applications
Unfair dismissal	44,538
Wages Act	21,285
Breach of contract	9,725
Redundancy pay	5,911
Sex discrimination	4,926
Race discrimination	3,246
Equal pay	2,391
Working time	2,314
Disability discrimination	1,743
Transfer of undertaking – dismissal	771
Transfer of undertaking – failure to inform and consult	679
Written statement of terms and conditions	676
Unfair dismissal for pregnancy	648
Unfair dismissal – exercise of a statutory right	386
National minimum wage	357
Unfair dismissal – health and safety	255
Unfair dismissal – union membership/activities	132
Other	3,952
Total	**103,935**

7. Employment tribunal procedure

Every tribunal panel consists of a legally qualified chairperson who may be outvoted by the two other lay members – one representing the employer's side and one representing the trade union side of industry. The two lay members are selected from lists kept by the Secretary of State for Education and Employment whereas the chairperson, who must be a barrister or solicitor, is appointed by the Lord Chancellor. Employment tribunals look very similar in many respects to the 'labour courts' that are found in other European countries and can no longer be regarded as purely administrative tribunals.

It is a relatively simple matter to bring a complaint to the attention of an employment tribunal. A simple form (an IT1) can be obtained from a Job Centre or from an office of the Benefits Agency. The completed form is sent to the Central Office of Employment Tribunals for processing. The application is then sent to the respondent employer who should normally 'enter an appearance' within 14 days of receiving the application, although this period can be extended. A copy of the application document will be sent to ACAS which is legally obliged to try to find an agreed settlement through conciliation (without the need for a tribunal hearing). Employment tribunals set themselves the target of hearing all claims within 26 weeks of the

271

date of registration and for publishing their decisions within five weeks of the hearing. Often, cases can be heard in a day or less.

Although legal representation is not essential, many complainants choose to be legally represented. This is because there is some evidence to indicate that those that are represented are more likely to win their cases. For the most part, claimants do not have to worry about the prospect of an award of costs being made against them, should they lose, unless the tribunal takes the view that a claim is frivolous or vexatious. Tribunals can now award up to £10,000 in costs against the applicant for claims that are deemed unreasonable or vexatious and they will have power to strike out ill-founded claims. If complainants do not have legal insurance or are not supported by a trade union, they are obliged to meet their own costs including the costs of being legally represented.

Of the total of 103,935 applications in 1999–2000 (*see* Table 13.1), 83,409 cases were disposed of in one way or another. ACAS conciliated 32,192 cases and 27,536 were withdrawn by the applicants. Whilst 13,332 cases were dismissed at a tribunal hearing or disposed of otherwise, 10,349 applicants were successful at the tribunal hearing. Included within these aggregates were the 36,197 unfair dismissal claims which were disposed of in one way or another. ACAS conciliated 16,251 and a further 10,013 were withdrawn; 6,765 were dismissed at a tribunal hearing or disposed of otherwise. Only 3,168 applicants were successful at the conclusion of the tribunal hearing, which is less that 10 per cent. Although 42 applicants were awarded compensation exceeding £20,000, the median (statistical average) award was £2,515. The median awards for racial and sex-based discrimination respectively were £2,378 and £2,180.

8. Appeals from employment tribunals

Appeals from the decisions of employment tribunals go straight to the Employment Appeal Tribunal (EAT) which was originally brought into being by the Employment Protection Act 1975 but is now governed by the Industrial Tribunals Act 1996. The EAT is situated in London and has the status of a division of the High Court (notwithstanding its title) because it is presided over by a High Court judge and is a superior court of record.

Appeals are restricted to points of law so as to restrict the number of possible appeals and therefore an appellant must be able to show that the tribunal went wrong in law. Guidance was given by the Court of Appeal in *British Telecommunications Plc* v *Sheridan* [1990] on what is considered to amount to a point of law. Unless the original tribunal decision was made by the chairman sitting alone, the presiding judge in the EAT will sit with two laypersons who can outvote him/her in deciding the appeal. In 1999–2000 there were 888 appeals, but of these, only 271 were successful in overturning the decision of the tribunal that originally heard the case. In *The Post Office* v *Lewis* [1997], the Court of Appeal made it clear that where a decision of an employment tribunal was neither perverse nor affected by an error of law, it was not permissible for the Employment Appeal Tribunal to interfere on the basis that the tribunal had failed to refer in its decision to the main part of the applicant's defence. The applicant was dismissed by his employer when 59 items of mail destined for a block of flats were found in a postbox in Tooting, south west London. Since these items of mail had already been through the sorting process they should not have been in the postbox, and since the applicant was the only postman on that round on that day he was dismissed following an internal inquiry. The tribunal had found that the decision to dismiss was unfair due to insufficient investigation but it concluded that even if the Post Office had investigated the matter more thoroughly, it would still have dismissed the applicant and acted fairly in doing so. It also found, on the balance of probability, that he had willfully delayed delivery of the mail and ruled that his conduct was blameworthy so that it would not be just and equitable to make any award of compensation or, for that matter, award reinstatement. The Employment Appeal Tribunal allowed an appeal by Lewis because the tribunal's decision did not deal with the 'main plank' of Lewis's defence. In giving the judgement of the Court of Appeal, Henry LJ stated that the employment tribunal had not found it necessary to resolve the 'main plank' issue because of the weight the tribunal gave to another matter. He emphasised that the weight that should be given to evidence was a matter for the original tribunal (the tribunal of fact) and the EAT should not have interfered with the tribunal's decision. Even though two or more employment tribunals reach different conclusions on the same facts does not mean that one or other has made an error of law particularly where the conclusions relate to questions of reasonableness. A further appeal on a point of law from the decision of the EAT to the Court of Appeal is possible with the permission of that court. Very occasionally there can be a further appeal on a point of law to the House of Lords but again only with the permission of the House of Lords.

9. Domestic tribunals

This category is really a convenient 'hold all' for all those tribunals that are not administrative tribunals or employment tribunals. Within this category are found tribunals ranging from disciplinary and grievance committees at the workplace to the disciplinary committees established by organisations such as the Law Society, Bar Council, Institute of Chartered Accountants in

England and Wales and Chartered Association of Certified Accountants. Universities and trade unions too have disciplinary bodies which decide whether a member should be disciplined if an allegation of an infringement of the rules is established. When actions amounting to gross misconduct are substantiated, the member may be expelled, although in the case of trade unions, there are now restrictions contained in the Trade Union and Labour Relations (Consolidation) Act 1992 on the right to expel a member. These disciplinary tribunals are usually established by the organisations concerned. Their jurisdiction over their members usually arises out of the 'contract of membership' which is deemed to exist between the organisation (if it is a legal entity) and the individual members or between the person concerned and his/her fellow members if the organisation is not a legal entity. Certain tribunals that have been set up to deal with misconduct by members of the medical profession have been established by statute. For example, the Professional Conduct Committee of the General Medical Council (GMC) exercises a disciplinary function over doctors and was established by the Medical Act 1978. It may suspend or remove a doctor's name altogether from the Medical Register for serious professional misconduct. In recent years, it has been heavily criticised for being too lenient especially with Dr Harold Shipman, the general practitioner from Greater Manchester who was subsequently convicted of the murders of a number of his elderly patients. The GMC established an interim orders committee in 2000 which can suspend doctors or restrict the scope of their practice, pending a full hearing of a complaint, in an effort to restore public confidence in the medical profession. An article in the *Independent* of 6 March 2001 reported that one doctor a week is suspended by the interim orders committee pending a full investigation of a complaint. Disciplinary tribunals have also been created by Acts of Parliament for dentists and opticians. The Solicitors' Disciplinary Tribunal was established by the Solicitors Act 1974 to deal with misconduct by members of the profession and it too has often been criticised for its leniency.

10. Procedural fairness

Since the majority of domestic tribunals are not presided over by a judge, or for that matter by a person who is legally qualified (except those dealing with the legal profession), it is essential that the proceedings are conducted fairly. Otherwise the courts can, and do, intervene to ensure that a minimum degree of procedural fairness is observed. This is often referred to as applying the 'principles of natural justice'. There are two basic principles: the first is that the person making the decision should be independent and unbiased. This is sometimes expressed in the maxim 'no person should be a judge in his/her own cause'. The second principle is that both sides must be given a proper hearing, and this is particularly important with regard to someone accused of wrongdoing who must be allowed to explain his/her conduct. In addition, the tribunal should give reasons for the decision it has reached at the end of the proceedings to demonstrate that its decision is not irrational. The observance of these principles will normally ensure minimum standards of procedural propriety. The same high standards obtaining in an ordinary court are not expected of a domestic tribunal, but the proceedings must be conducted as fairly as possible and a decision can be challenged in the courts if it is blatantly unfair. There is an automatic right of appeal to the Judicial Committee of the Privy Council from the decisions of those tribunals dealing with complaints against doctors, dentists and opticians.

Domestic tribunals are not supervised by means of the prerogative orders. Nevertheless, their decisions may be reviewed by the High Court where an injustice has been done. This was established in *Lee* v *Showmen's Guild* [1952] where Frank Lee owned and operated a fairground ride which he called Noah's Ark. He was a member of the guild which was a registered trade union and under its rules, no member should apply for the use of a site at a fairground which another member had occupied for two years previously if that other member wished to use the position again. Moreover, rule 14a enabled the committee to impose a fine on a member who was then deemed to have forfeited his membership within a month if he did not pay the fine that was imposed. Rule 15c provided that no guild member should engage in 'unfair competition' with regard to the taking of a position at a fairground. However, rule 26 stated that all members of the guild should have the option at the termination of the Second World War (1939–1945) of taking up their pre-war positions at all fairs. From 1934 to 1943, one William Shaw occupied the no. 2 site at the Bradford Summer Fair, but in 1945 and 1946 this position was occupied by Frank Lee. Although no fair was held in 1947, Shaw applied to the guild committee to have the option of taking up the no. 2 site, and the committee acting under rule 26 granted him the right to take up his pre-war position at the Bradford fair. Notwithstanding this decision, it seems that Frank Lee occupied the no. 2 site in 1949 and Shaw complained to the guild's committee who fined Lee £100 and ordered him give up the position to Shaw. When Lee failed to pay the fine, the committee decided that he was no longer a member of the guild. This decision operated to deprive Lee of his livelihood because he could not work on any fairgrounds controlled by the guild. He successfully challenged the decision of the guild's committee in the High Court and there was a subsequent appeal to the Court of Appeal by the guild. The judges of the Court of Appeal decided that they had jurisdiction to examine any decision of the committee which involved a question of law and this would extend to the interpretation of the committee's rules and it upheld Frank Lee's claim. It decided that the committee had misinterpreted its rule 15c and its decision to expel him was, in the circumstances, beyond its powers and therefore devoid of legal effect.

In *Bonsor* v *Musicians' Union* [1955], the appellant joined the respondent union because he was a professional musician and it was difficult for him to obtain paid work without union membership. Although he had been a member for many years, during 1948 he omitted to pay his weekly union subscriptions and, by the end of June 1949, he had accumulated 52 weeks' arrears. The branch secretary of the union expelled him from the union at the end of June under rule 27(7) of the rule book. Bonsor asked to be reinstated so that he could obtain paid work but the branch secretary refused to reinstate him unless he paid all his outstanding subscriptions together with fines. He offered to pay the amount in question from his first week's earnings but the branch secretary refused. As a result, Bonsor was unable to obtain work (except with the few non-union bands) and he applied to the High Court claiming:

(a) a declaration that his actual expulsion from the union in November, 1949 was null and void

(b) a declaration that he was entitled to be reinstated as a member of the union

(c) an injunction restraining the union and its officers from acting on the assumption that he was not a union member

(d) damages from the union for breach of contract

(e) other unspecified relief.

In the High Court, Bonsor abandoned claims (b) and (d) although he reserved the latter claim for argument in the event of a subsequent appeal. The High Court held that a proper interpretation of rule 27(7) meant that only a branch committee could expel a member. Thus the apparent exercise of the power in the rules by a branch secretary was *ultra vires* and devoid of legal effect. It therefore granted the declaration requested in (a) and the injunction sought in (c) but the claim for damages was dismissed. The union appealed to the Court of Appeal and Bonsor cross-appealed over the rejection of the claim for damages for breach of contract. Bonsor then appealed to the House of Lords on the issue of whether damages could be awarded against the union arising from the branch secretary exceeding his powers and expelling him. Having conducted an extensive review of the case law, the House of Lords held by majority that the union could be liable in damages for breach of contract with one of its members. Thus not only may the courts review the decision-making process to ensure that a rule book or similar constitutional document has been interpreted and applied properly, they may also award damages to compensate individual members of an organisation who suffer loss as a result of officials abusing their powers.

Progress test

1. What differences are there between a domestic tribunal and an administrative tribunal?

2. What is the basis of the authority and jurisdiction of a non-statutory domestic tribunal?

3. What do you understand by the phrase 'procedural fairness'?

4. Is it more likely that a non-statutory domestic tribunal might depart from the principles of procedural fairness than an administrative tribunal? If so, why? If not, why not?

5. How is the membership of an administrative tribunal usually composed?

6. How do administrative tribunals differ from the ordinary courts?

7. How and by what means does the High Court exercise supervisory jurisdiction over administrative tribunals?

8. Are administrative tribunals really quicker and cheaper than the ordinary courts?

9. How important is the role of the Council on Tribunals and what are its specific functions?

10. If you were dismissed by your manager for refusing to work overtime in order to cover for an absent colleague who was sick, how would you go about obtaining legal redress assuming that you had worked for your former employer for one year and that working overtime was voluntary?

Further reading

Books

Deakin, S. and G. Morris (1998) *Labour Law* (London: Butterworths, chapter 2).

Denning, Lord (1979) *The Discipline of Law* (London: Butterworths, part 4).

De Smith, S. and R. Brazier (1998) *Constitutional and Administrative Law* (Harmondsworth: Penguin, chapter 31).

Parpworth, N. (2000) *Constitutional and Administrative Law* (London: Butterworths, chapter 15).

Smith, I.T. and G.H. Thomas (2000) *Industrial Law* (London: Butterworths, chapter 8).

Ward, R. (1998) *Walker and Walker's English Legal System* (London: Butterworths, chapter 9).

Useful websites

The website of the Council on Tribunals can be accessed on: www.council-on-tribunals.gov.uk/

Judgements of the Employment Appeal Tribunal can be accessed on www.employmentappeals.gov.uk/

14

Dispute resolution 3: Alternative forms of resolution

1. Introduction

As has been seen in Chapter 12, most disputes can be resolved through litigation by the application of rules of law to the facts as agreed and/or established at a trial. Litigation, however, may not always be the best method of dispute resolution. This is because it usually involves some delay, considerable cost and is adversarial to some extent even in the new climate of civil litigation engendered by the Woolf reforms. At the conclusion of the litigation process there will normally be a clear 'winner' and a clear 'loser' and this may serve to further embitter the relationship between the parties which may have taken many years to foster. For this reason, litigation is often the worst possible means of resolving a business dispute because of the damage done to a long-standing commercial relationship. A costly civil trial may even fail to resolve the matter to the total satisfaction of the 'winning' party especially if the remedy sought has not been obtained because it is discretionary or if all the costs cannot be recovered from the other side. Indeed, a victory may prove hollow in that the amount, if any, recovered may be dwarfed by the costs of the action. Even if damages are awarded to the winning side, it may be necessary to commence another set of legal proceedings to enforce the judgement if the losing side does not pay up immediately.

Firms and companies can always resolve any disputes on a purely informal basis by means of a compromise with the other side by making concessions with a view to preserving business relationships. They may do this by themselves or they may seek to involve neutral outsiders as 'facilitators' and formalise the process to a degree but without adopting the very high degree of formality which attends legal proceedings. This may be done through a process that has become known as alternative dispute resolution, or ADR for short.

ADR is an overarching term for a variety of forms of dispute resolution but there is no agreed terminology covering these dispute resolution processes. The simplest form of ADR to understand is mediation. Some writers and commentators use the term 'mediation' interchangeably with the term 'conciliation'. Some important providers of ADR distinguish between mediation and conciliation but would also include arbitration within the ambit of ADR since it is an alternative to litigation in the courts. Others would exclude arbitration on the basis that it is a form of legal proceeding. As has been seen in Chapter 12, the prevailing ethos pervading the Civil Procedure Rules is that litigation should be avoided if at all possible and the parties are actively encouraged to consider ADR instead. Parties to a dispute have always been able to refer their dispute to arbitration which is a far older and more formal means of dispute resolution than either mediation or conciliation. Although arbitration is conducted outside the court system it is nevertheless an 'imposed' solution but it is less formal than litigation and it is also conducted in private. In this chapter, attention focuses firstly on mediation and then on conciliation before moving on to consider other forms of ADR. Arbitration has been singled out for separate treatment at the end of the chapter.

2. Mediation

Mediation is defined by Mediation UK (which describes itself as an umbrella organisation for all initiatives concerned with conflict resolution in the UK) as 'a process whereby an impartial third party helps two disputing parties to sort out their disagreement. The parties, not the mediator, decide the terms of the subsequent agreement'. Mediation UK is mainly concerned with community mediation services that deal with excessive noise, refuse dumping, harassment and other annoyances in a community context. It is also engaged in victim/offender work by bringing both together to help mutual understanding and to discover whether there is scope for reparation to take place.

Mediation is by no means confined to community initiatives and is used by firms and companies seeking an alternative to litigation. All mediations are conducted in private at a time and place to suit the parties. A hotel meeting room would be a suitable venue. The person appointed as mediator should have some experience and have the confidence of the parties to the dispute so that he/she can be effective in the role. Where this is the case, both sides are more likely to be open with the mediator and to trust him/her. In some instances it may be desirable to appoint as mediator someone who is legally qualified.

When the parties come to a mediation they should ideally sit opposite each other at a rectangular table with the mediator sitting at the head of the table. The mediator will normally have read all the relevant papers beforehand and will usually commence by explaining how the process will be conducted. If required by the mediator, each side (or their legal representatives) will then explain what is in dispute and state their aspirations for the outcome of the process. In order to facilitate the discussion it is then usually necessary for the mediator to separate the parties and place them in rooms near the main meeting room. Thereafter, the mediator will act as a go-between to explore the possibility of a solution that is acceptable to both sides. These individual meetings with the parties are known as caucuses. The mediator must treat what is said by each side as confidential. He/she must not try to impose his/her views on the parties and confidential information can be disclosed to the other side only if consent has been given. Information given to the mediator is not given under oath or affirmation and there is no scope for cross-examination given the nature of the process. Once it seems to the mediator that the gap between the parties is narrowing, he/she may then attempt to bring about another joint session with a view to achieving an agreement. If a settlement is agreed it will be because the parties themselves wish to resolve their dispute as amicably as possible.

If an agreement has been reached that is embodied in the form of a contract it will be binding on the parties, but unless an agreement incorporates what in contract law is known as 'consideration', it will not be legally binding on the parties. If a settlement is achieved it is not limited to the normal remedies available from a court and may include the provision of replacement goods or the provision of additional services free of charge. Should the process prove to be inconclusive, the mediator will not act as a witness in any subsequent arbitration or litigation.

Mediation is not always successful. It is less likely to be successful where the dispute centres on one or more issues of law rather than facts, or where precedent (or legislation) favours one of the parties. Where it is successful, it will usually have resulted in the repairing of a business relationship that would otherwise have irretrievably broken down. An article in the *Financial Times* of 28 October 1997 reported a survey conducted by the Royal Institute of Chartered Surveyors in which almost 70 per cent of the UK's leading property lawyers favoured mediation as an alternative to litigation for resolving property or construction disputes.

Although mediation offers the prospect of a speedy settlement it is not a 'free service' because the mediator will expect to be paid. A relatively straightforward mediation could cost between £1,500 and £2,000. Moreover, if companies are in dispute they may have briefed lawyers to represent them in the mediation and the lawyers too will have to be paid.

In the UK, organisations such as the Centre for Effective Dispute Resolution (CEDR) and the ADR Group have devised Model Mediation Procedures. It was reported in the *Financial Times* of 3 November 1996 that at a conference run by the CEDR and the Confederation of British Industry that Keir International, an international construction company, had settled a £15 million dispute following a five-day mediation. It was estimated that this had saved at least £250,000 in legal costs. Lord Alexander QC, chairman of NatWest Bank, reported that a hire purchase transaction with a corporate client had been settled by mediation in less than a day whereas the bank's lawyers had estimated that the cost of legal action in the courts would have been £150,000 on each side. It had also saved £40,000 in court costs to say nothing of management time saved. Organisations such as CEDR and the ADR Group have drafted suitable clauses that can be incorporated into commercial contracts which rule out recourse to litigation until the potential for ADR has been adequately explored by the parties.

3. Conciliation

Mediators can adopt one of two distinct approaches: a facilitative approach which has already been described above or an evaluative approach which is sometimes referred to as conciliation. Some of the groups promoting ADR do not distinguish between mediation and conciliation. CEDR and the Chartered Institute of Arbitrators, on the other hand, do make a distinction. Whilst CEDR views Conciliation as an informal attempt to achieve an agreed settlement between the parties, the Chartered Institute of Arbitrators, defines it as

> a process whereby a conciliator investigates the facts of the case, attempts to reconcile the opposing contentions of the parties and prompts them to formulate their own proposals for settlement of the case by indicating the strong and weak points of their arguments and the possible consequences of failure to settle. The conciliator will not usually make a recommendation of his/her own for settlement of the dispute, however he/she acts as a catalyst for settlement by the parties themselves.

On the other hand, the Institution of Civil Engineers have a slightly different view of the process. Its Conciliation Procedure 1999 is an important ADR scheme; the preface to the scheme states:

> The main difference between conciliation and adjudication or arbitration is that the outcome of conciliation is not imposed and only becomes binding with the consent of each party. Conciliation therefore allows the parties to the dispute the freedom to explore ways of settling the dispute with the assistance of an independent impartial person – the Conciliator.

The Institution of Civil Engineers Conciliation Procedure allows for the appointment of a conciliator by the president of the Institution, and on taking up his/her appointment the conciliator issues instructions regarding the date and place for the conciliation meeting. Each side then informs the conciliator of the name of its representative. The representative must have full authority to act on behalf of the party in question. According to para. 4.5:

The Conciliator may:
(a) issue such further instructions as he considers to be appropriate;
(b) meet and question the parties and their representatives, together or separately;
(c) investigate the facts and circumstances of the dispute;
(d) visit the site;
(e) request the production of documents or the attendance of people whom he considers could assist in any way.

Paragraph 4.6 states:

The Conciliator may conduct the proceedings in any way that he/she wishes, and with the prior agreement of the parties obtain legal or technical advice, the cost of which shall be met by the parties, in accordance with Paragraph 5.4, or as may be agreed by the parties and the Conciliator.

If an agreement cannot be arrived at, the conciliator will make a recommendation. Under the Institution of Civil Engineers contracts, a recommendation is a distinct stage in the dispute resolution process. Paragraph 5.1 goes on to state:

The Conciliator shall advise all parties accordingly and prepare his recommendation forthwith:
(a) if, in the opinion of the Conciliator, it is unlikely that the parties will achieve an agreed settlement to their disputes; or
(b) if any party fails to respond to an instruction by the Conciliator, or
(c) upon the request of any party.

The nature of a recommendation in this context is specified in para. 5.2 as follows:

The Conciliator's Recommendation shall state his solution to the dispute which has been referred for Conciliation. The Recommendation shall not disclose any information which any party has provided in confidence. It shall be based on his opinion as to how the parties can best dispose of the dispute between them and need not necessarily be based on any principles of the Contract, law or equity.

The Conciliator is not required to give reasons for his/her recommendation: it is simply his/her opinion of how the dispute might be resolved in the most practical way. Nevertheless, should he/she choose to do so, his/her reasons will be issued as a separate document, within seven days of giving the recommendation.

Thus, a person acting as a conciliator can be more proactive in exploring a basis for a settlement and may suggest ideas that have not occurred to the parties. If requested by the parties, he/she may sometimes offer a non-binding legal opinion if this is likely to assist with a settlement. Such a non-binding legal opinion may progress discussions that have become stalled. It may focus on a single issue or the likely outcome of the case were it to be litigated. If the conciliator is likely to be called upon to give a legal opinion, he/she must be legally qualified.

The Chartered Institute of Arbitrators has devised a Consumer Dispute Resolution Scheme in consultation with the Office of Fair Trading and the National Consumer Council which applies to claims made by private consumers of goods and services. The scheme does not extend to claims for physical injury, illness and nervous shock and different trade associations set different financial ceilings for the monetary amounts of claims by consumers. It operates in two stages: firstly there is a conciliation process which is controlled by the Institute, and if conciliation fails there is provision for arbitration. According to para. 2.1 of the 2000 edition:

> Where a written complaint by a consumer to a supplier has been rejected or where there has been no reply or where the parties have not been able to settle their dispute within four weeks of the date of the written complaint that matter can be referred to conciliation.

The process begins after both sides have signed and submitted the Institute's application form together with the appropriate fee and the president or a vice-president of the Institute has appointed a conciliator. According to para. 3.1:

> The Conciliation procedure will be at the discretion of the Conciliator. However, each party will be requested to submit case statements and all relevant supporting evidence. These will be reviewed by the Conciliator who may ask the parties for clarification of their cases either in writing or at a meeting.

Paragraph 3.2 then goes on to state:

> The Conciliator will provide the parties with a report which, together with the Conciliator's suggestions for a settlement, will form the basis of a possible agreement. If accepted by the parties the Conciliator will incorporate the settlement terms in a written agreement to be signed by both parties.

It is clear from para. 3.3 that if the parties do not settle within six weeks of the conciliator's appointment, the dispute may be referred to arbitration and the documents submitted to the conciliator will be passed on to the arbitrator with the conciliator's report. However, unless the parties request it, the conciliator cannot act as arbitrator nor must he/she divulge to the arbitrator information given to him/her in confidence. Moreover, the conciliator must not act as an advocate, advisor or witness for any party in the course of the arbitration.

4. Other forms of ADR

Mediation and conciliation often do, but need not, focus on clearly defined points of law. If a point of law or the interpretation of the wording of a contract lies at the heart of a dispute, the parties involved may apply to bodies like CEDR for an 'early neutral evaluation'. This will often entail a QC giving an indication of the likely outcome of the dispute were it to be litigated. The person appointed as the 'neutral' will issue his/her non-binding written opinion at the end of the process with a view to encouraging the parties to settle. As long ago as 1990, the Chartered Institute of Arbitrators devised guidelines for a supervised settlement procedure. Under these guidelines most business disputes can be submitted to a panel comprising one or more senior executives from both sides who will be assisted by a neutral chairperson who need not be a lawyer. This procedure is sometimes referred to as a 'mini trial' but this is a misnomer because the normal rules of procedure and evidence do not apply and, as stated above, the chairperson need not be legally qualified. The process aims at the achievement of a workable compromise rather than a legal solution as such. The opening paragraphs of the explanatory notes to the guidelines state:

> Most bona fide disputes between reputable parties are capable of settlement in a manner that is business orientated, thus avoiding or at least curtailing legal expenditure, the loss of executive time and the deterioration of a valuable business relationship.
>
> Such a settlement can be facilitated by the use of a structured procedure which ensures that authorised management representatives are presented with the facts, viewed from both sides, and can then enter into negotiations under the guidance of a neutral adviser experienced in conciliation, mediation and arbitration techniques.
>
> This procedure can be invoked at an early stage when there is goodwill and a history of good relationships or after litigation or arbitration has been initiated.

Included with the guidelines is a draft agreement for the signature of those wishing to embark on a supervised settlement procedure. A compromise agreement must normally be concluded within 60 days of the date of the agreement unless the parties agree to an extension of time. All statements and documents produced are treated 'without prejudice' and are

285

therefore inadmissible in any subsequent legal proceedings if the process should prove be inconclusive.

5. Arbitration

Although arbitration is a method of dispute resolution which occurs outside the normal court structure, the arbitrator's decision (or 'award' as it is technically known) can be enforced through the courts if necessary, as stipulated in the Arbitration Act 1950 s. 26. It is therefore legally binding on the parties. All the detailed rules governing arbitrations are set out in the Arbitration Acts 1950 and 1996 but some can be modified by agreement between the parties. There are a number of significant advantages to be gained from trying to resolve a dispute through arbitration as opposed to litigation. These are as follows:

(a) There is a greater degree of flexibility in the procedure in arbitration as compared with litigation in that the rules of evidence need not be so strictly applied in an arbitration and the entire matter can be decided on the basis of written submissions if the parties agree to this.

(b) The parties are at liberty to decide upon the location, together with the date and time of proceedings, whereas in litigation the parties have only limited opportunities to request that the case be heard at a court in a particular locality.

(c) A person with the appropriate technical qualifications can be appointed by the parties where a dispute arises in a particular trade or business and it involves technical issues so that the arbitrator(s) can bring his/her (or their) specialist knowledge to bear when arriving at a resolution of the dispute.

(d) The parties will avoid the attention of the press and media because the proceedings will be conducted behind closed doors.

(e) There can be a saving of time and therefore expense although the parties themselves must bear the cost of the arbitration proceedings (but there will undoubtedly be a saving of court fees and lawyers' fees if the parties are not legally represented).

(f) The decision of the arbitrator may be given more quickly than the judgement of a court which may be reserved for weeks or even months.

In relation to (e) above, if the parties decide upon a full-scale hearing and on being represented by lawyers, the cost may be as high as litigation in the courts and may therefore confer no financial advantage. Savings are likely, however, if the dispute is a technical one and the arbitrator is a technical expert who can dispose of the matter without the need for lawyers and expert witnesses. Often the parties will agree that the issue can be decided upon on the basis of the documentation that they submit to the arbitrator and this will be likely to result in considerable savings of time and money. Even if lawyers are involved, they may be able to narrow the area of dispute as well as shorten the preparation time and time taken up with the hearing.

Arbitration will not be an appropriate method of dispute resolution in all cases. For example, if the case involves a completely novel set of facts for which there is no existing precedent or relevant statute law, arbitration will be inappropriate. On the other hand, if a dispute simply requires an authoritative interpretation of a statutory provision, this can be obtained from a court as specified by the Arbitration Act 1996 s. 45.

Many contracts today contain arbitration clauses. For example, the Royal Institute of British Architects has a standard form contract for minor building works which contains such a clause. Even if there is no arbitration clause in a contract there is nothing to prevent the parties from submitting their dispute for resolution by arbitration. The agreement to do so must itself be in writing as required by the Arbitration Act 1950 s. 32 and should contain a provision governing the appointment of the arbitrator. At the outset the parties may agree on the powers that will be exercisable by the arbitral tribunal (a single arbitrator or a panel of arbitrators). Where one party is a UK national and the other is a foreign national it would be common practice to provide in the contract for a panel of three arbitrators to be appointed. One would be appointed by each side and a third person would be appointed as an 'umpire' to guarantee a majority decision of 2:1 in the event that unanimity was not possible.

The Chartered Institute of Arbitrators (whose president is often a judge from the Court of Appeal) can provide a list of suitable persons from among its 7,500 members to act as competent arbitrators in virtually any dispute. An arbitrator need not be a barrister or solicitor but parties in dispute do often nominate lawyers to act as arbitrators. In high-value commercial contracts (those involving the hire of ships and aircraft or large-scale civil engineering projects), it would not be uncommon to find a term in the contract requiring the parties to submit all disputes to Arbitration before resorting to litigation. The Arbitration Act 1996 s. 9(1) provides:

> A party to an arbitration agreement against whom legal proceedings are brought (whether by way of claim or counterclaim) in respect of a matter which under the agreement is to be referred to arbitration may (upon giving notice to the other parties to the proceedings) apply to the court in which the proceedings have been brought to stay the proceedings so far as they concern that matter.

Section 9(4) further provides that

> On an application under this section the court shall grant a stay unless satisfied that the arbitration agreement is null and void, inoperative, or incapable of being performed.

The party making the application must demonstrate that the legal proceedings brought against him/her deal with a dispute that can be referred to arbitration under the arbitration clause or agreement. The Arbitration Act 1996 s. 1(a) and (b) states that

> (a) The object of arbitration is to obtain the fair resolution of disputes by an impartial tribunal without unnecessary delay or expense;
> (b) The parties should be free to agree how their disputes are resolved, subject only to such safeguards as are necessary in the public interest;

This means that the parties and/or their legal representatives must identify their priorities. If it is important that the dispute is resolved quickly it must be decided whether full pleadings are really necessary or whether an opening statement of case with skeleton arguments will suffice. Similarly, opening and closing submission can be given in writing. Where time is of the essence, s. 33(b) requires that the Arbitrator

> adopt procedures suitable to the circumstances of the particular case, avoiding unnecessary delay or expense, so as to provide a fair means for the resolution of the matters falling to be determined.

If the Arbitrator fails to deal with matters quickly, the parties, acting together, are at liberty under s. 23 to terminate his/her appointment or any one party may apply to the court under s. 24 to remove the arbitrator. Unlike mediation and conciliation, the Arbitration Act 1996 normally requires the arbitral tribunal to apply the relevant law to the facts as agreed by the parties and/or established at the arbitration hearing. Thus the role of an arbitral tribunal is similar to that of a judge in a civil trial but the arbitrator can be a little more inquisitorial than a judge. According to s. 46(1), the arbitral tribunal must decide the dispute

> (a) in accordance with the law chosen by the parties as applicable to the substance of the dispute, or
> (b) if the parties agree, in accordance with such other considerations as are agreed by them to be determined by the tribunal.

Apart from the ability of an arbitral tribunal to award damages it may grant other remedies under the Act. The Arbitration Act 1996 s. 48(5) specifies that a tribunal has the same powers as a court to:

(a) order a party to do or refrain from doing anything, or

(b) order specific performance of a contract other than one relating to land, or

(c) order rectification, setting aside or cancellation of a deed or other document.

6. Arbitration schemes

The Chartered Institute of Arbitrators has assisted the Office of Fair Trading in the setting up of a wide range of consumer arbitration schemes and there are over fifty of these schemes in operation sponsored by various trade associations. The arbitration itself will be administered by the Chartered Institute of Arbitrators (CIA) and can take up to 14 weeks as indicated below:

1 week	The Institute sends out a claim form to the applicant and the arbitrator.
4 weeks	The applicant's claim must be received by the Institute which will copy it to the respondent.
3 weeks	The defence and any counterclaim is submitted to the Institute by the respondent and a copy will be forwarded to the claimant from the Institute.
2 weeks	Any reply to the defence must be submitted to the Institute and a copy will be forwarded to the respondent from the Institute.
1 week	All documents are to be sent to the arbitrator.
3 weeks	The arbitrator gives his/her decision (award).

The claimant pays only a modest registration fee and legal representation is not strictly necessary. The trade body pays the CIA's fee and the arbitrator's fee. The arbitration is usually conducted on the basis of written argument and evidence, but if either party requests it, or if the arbitrator considers it appropriate, a meeting can be held between the parties and the arbitrator. The arbitrator can use such a meeting to ask questions in order to clarify the matters in dispute. The Institute will send a copy of the award to each party and to the organisation acting as a sponsoring body for the scheme. If the award entails the payment of money it must normally be paid within 21 days of the posting of the award. Such schemes are intended to be a real alternative to litigation but they cannot operate to exclude the right of consumers to take legal action in the courts.

Arbitration a Commercial Initiative (ACI) operates from Gray's Inn, London, and offers a variety of arbitration schemes to industry and commerce. Disputes can be transferred between the various ACI schemes when appropriate. These schemes are:

(a) fixed fee arbitration

(b) standard arbitration

(c) fast track arbitration.

Fixed fee arbitration is designed for parties who are able to cooperate with a view to obtaining a speedy resolution of their dispute. Those cases that are not suitable for fixed fee arbitration are conducted under the rules for standard arbitration, whilst fast track arbitration will be appropriate when there is urgency and ACI is able to provide arbitrators who will hear a dispute as soon as the parties are ready to be heard. In addition, ACI also offers individually designed arbitration schemes where firms and companies have similar recurring disputes and wish to have them resolved by a neutral body.

The International Chamber of Commerce (ICC) offers an arbitration service for the resolution of business disputes through the International Court of Arbitration whose secretariat is based in Paris, although it operates in and through the major international financial centres including London. It is not, however, attached to the ordinary English court system. Indeed, the International Court is truly international in that its members are drawn from some sixty countries. This body ensures that the rules of arbitration of the ICC are properly applied and provides a highly supervised form of arbitration in that it:

(a) ascertains whether there is an agreement to arbitrate

(b) decides on the number of arbitrators

(c) appoints the arbitrators

(d) decides challenges to the appointment of arbitrators

(e) ensures that the arbitration is conducted according to the ICC rules

(f) decides the location for the arbitration if the parties cannot agree

(g) fixes and extends time limits

(h) decides the fees and expenses of the arbitrator(s)

(i) scrutinises the award.

The members of the International Court of Arbitration do not adjudicate on the issues submitted to the ICC because this is the province of the arbitrator(s) appointed. Instead, the Court supervises the arbitration process from the initial request to the making of the final award. The staff of the secretariat receive copies of all pleadings and other communications exchanged between the parties. Under the ICC rules, the Court must approve all awards to ensure that they conform to its high standards so that they are unlikely to be annulled in national courts thereafter.

7. Appeals from an arbitrator's award

According to the Arbitration Act 1996 s. 68(1), an application can be made to the High Court where there is a 'serious irregularity' in respect of the tribunal's conduct of the proceedings or in the award itself. Any application is made under the Civil Procedure Rules PD49G on notice to the other party/parties and to the tribunal. The appeal must be brought within 28 days of the award. The phrase 'serious irregularity' is defined in s. 68(2) as follows:

(a) Failure by the tribunal to comply with s. 33 which is the requirement to observe the normal standards of procedural fairness sometimes known as the principles of natural justice.

(b) The tribunal exceeding its powers other than by exceeding its substantive jurisdiction.

(c) Failure by the tribunal to conduct the proceedings in accordance with the procedure agreed by the parties.

(d) Failure by the tribunal to deal with all the issues that were put to it.

(e) Any arbitral or other institution or person vested by the parties with powers in relation to the proceedings or the award exceeding its powers.

(f) Uncertainty or ambiguity as to the effect of the award.

(g) The award being obtained by fraud or the award or the way in which it was procured being contrary to public policy.

(h) Failure to comply with the requirements as to the form of the award.

(i) Any irregularity in the conduct of the proceedings or in the award which is admitted by the tribunal or by any arbitral or other institution or person vested by the parties with powers in relation to the proceedings or the award.

In the event that there should be any serious irregularity affecting the tribunal proceedings or the award, the court may, under s. 68(3):

(a) remit the award wholly or in part to the arbitral tribunal for reconsideration, or

(b) set the award aside wholly or in part, or

(c) declare the award to be of no effect, wholly or in part.

Any matters that do not come within s. 68(2), as specified above, may not be challenged under that section. An appeal on a point of law is possible under the Arbitration Act 1996 s. 69 which states:

> Unless otherwise agreed by the parties, a party to arbitral proceedings may (upon notice to the other parties and to the tribunal) appeal to the court on a question of law arising out of an award made in the proceedings.

A question of law is defined by s. 82(1) as meaning a question of the law of England and Wales or Northern Ireland as appropriate. Consequently, if the parties have chosen to conduct the proceedings under foreign law, no appeal is possible. The tribunal's findings on questions of fact are conclusive and final, and if there is to be an appeal on a question of law it must arise from the award. Even then, s. 69(2) provides that an appeal can be brought only with the agreement of the other party/parties or with the permission of the court. Moreover, s. 70(2) provides that such an appeal may not be brought unless the applicant has exhausted recourse under s. 57 which empowers the tribunal to correct its award and make an additional award. According to s. 69(3) the court must be satisfied:

(a) that the determination of the question will substantially affect the rights of one or more of the parties

(b) that the question is one which the tribunal was asked to determine

(c) that on the basis of the finding of fact in the award

(i) the decision of the tribunal on the question is obviously wrong, or
(ii) the question is one of general public importance and the decision of the tribunal is at least open to serious doubt, and

(d) that, despite the agreement of the parties to resolve the matter by arbitration, it is just and proper in all the circumstances for the court to determine the question.

The content of an application and the procedure for making an appeal are set out in s. 69(4)–(6). On hearing the appeal the court may, under s. 69(7):

(a) confirm the award

(b) vary the award

(c) send the award back to the arbitral tribunal, wholly or in part, for reconsideration in the light of the court's determination

(d) set aside the award wholly or in part.

It should be noted that the parties are free under s. 69 to agree beforehand that there will be no right of appeal whatever.

8. ADR and arbitration compared

At the end of the mediation or conciliation process there is a sense in which the parties 'own' the solution that has been arrived at through discussion. At the conclusion of an arbitration the party who has 'lost' may nevertheless harbour resentment and this may ultimately serve to damage a business relationship that has taken many years to foster. At the conclusion of a successful mediation or conciliation there is no 'loser' but, as has been stated, not all attempts at mediation and conciliation succeed. Arbitration does at least offer the prospect of finality.

Progress test

1. Why might the management of a business be reluctant to take a dispute to court?

2. What do you understand by the term 'mediation' and does it differ from 'conciliation'? In general, are both suitable for resolving business disputes?

3. Do lawyers favour mediation and conciliation as methods of dispute resolution?

4. How does arbitration differ from mediation and conciliation?

5. Is arbitration really an alternative to litigation? If so, why? If not, why not?

6. What advantages do you see for a business in submitting a dispute to arbitration?

7. Are there any disadvantages?

8. Is it more likely that the parties will preserve a cordial business relationship by referring a dispute to arbitration than by resorting to litigation?

9. In arbitration, how is natural justice ensured?

10. On what grounds is it possible to appeal from an arbitrator's award? Can an appeal be precluded from the outset?

Further reading

Books

Harris, P. (1997) *An Introduction to Law* (London: Butterworths, pp. 118–27).
Newman, P. (1999) *Alternative Dispute Resolution* (Welwyn Garden City: CLT Professional Publishing).
Palmer, M. and S. Roberts (1998) *Dispute Processes* (London: Butterworths).

Stone, M. (1998) *Representing Clients in Mediation* (London: Butterworths).
Tweeddale, K. and A. Tweeddale (1988) *A Practical Approach to Arbitration Law* (London: Blackstone Press).

Useful websites

The website of the Chartered Institute of Arbitrators is www.arbitrators.org/ and the Centre for Dispute Resolution has a website at www.cedr.co.uk/

The website of the ADR Group is at www.adrgroup.co.uk/ and the International Chamber of Commerce at www.iccwbo.org/ Details of the new ICC ADR scheme can also be found on this website.

The website of Arbitration a Commercial Initiative can be found at www.aciarb.com

15

Dispute resolution 4: Judicial review

1. Introduction

Judicial review is a process whereby the superior courts examine official acts, alleged omissions, decisions and orders of those persons and institutions under a legal duty to perform public functions. Viewed in this way, it may be said that judicial review is concerned with the maintenance of the rule of law in a democratic society by ensuring that government, national and local, does not exceed its powers and exercises those that it has when under a common law or statutory duty to act.

Both national and local government are held accountable to the governed through the mechanism of periodic elections. Another control over government is the rather ill-defined constitutional principle of 'ministerial responsibility' by which ministers are politically accountable to Parliament such that they can be embarrassed into resigning for their political mistakes following a vote of 'no confidence' in the House of Commons. Constituency MPs hold regular 'surgeries' for their constituents and have long been accustomed to pursuing grievances on their behalf relating to the conduct of government departments, local authorities and certain public officials. In addition, there are now well established ombudsman schemes to deal with complaints of maladministration against both national and local government. Within this framework of accountability the superior courts, through the process of judicial review, protect individuals and groups against the abuse of official power. The process of judicial review has evolved over centuries. It has been closely tied to the development of the remedies that the superior courts devised to supervise the decisions and acts of inferior courts and administrative bodies (these are discussed fully in 13). The jurisdiction of the courts in judicial review is supervisory rather than appellate in that they oversee the exercise of discretionary powers, as was made clear in *Associated Provincial Picture Houses Ltd* v *Wednesbury Corporation* [1948].

This chapter begins by examining the form of the action before proceeding to consider the established categories for judicial review. Some space is then devoted to an explanation of the modern procedural aspects under the Civil Procedure Rules and the available remedies.

2. Form of the action

Prior to 1977, when the Rules of the Supreme Court were revised, persons seeking to challenge the acts and decisions of governmental bodies and public officials had some degree of choice. They had the option to proceed on a public law basis when seeking a public law remedy in the form of one of the prerogative orders (discussed in **13**). Alternatively, they could pursue an ordinary civil action for a declaratory judgement and/or an injunction. Public law actions have always proceeded on the basis that the individual litigant is, in theory, acting on behalf of the monarch in seeking to ascertain whether there has been an infringement of the law. Thus the action is styled *R v Secretary of State . . . ex parte* followed by the name of the litigant. An ordinary civil action has long taken a form with the applicant's name (now the claimant's name) appearing first, followed by the name of the defendant; for example, *Ridge* v *Baldwin*. There were a number of procedural advantages in taking the ordinary civil action route, not least of which was that the time allowed for the commencement of proceedings was far more generous than for the public law action which was time-barred after six months.

The new procedural rules cured the procedural disadvantages associated with the public law action but still seemed to leave open the possibility of a choice for litigants. This was retained when the rules were put on a statutory basis in the Supreme Court Act 1981 s. 31. However, no doubt motivated by a desire to prevent abuse of the ordinary civil law process, the House of Lords in *O'Reilly* v *Mackman* [1983] sought to curtail this choice. The case arose as a result of a riot that took place at Hull Prison but the action was not begun until three years after the decision of the board of visitors to punish certain of the participants by reducing their remission. Under the new rules governing claims for judicial review, any claim to challenge the decision of the board of visitors would have to have been brought within three months; so a public law action was time-barred. In refusing to permit a challenge in an ordinary civil law action, Lord Diplock giving the judgement of the House of Lords said:

> it would in my view as a general rule be contrary to public policy, and as such an abuse of the process of the court, to permit a person seeking to establish that a decision of a public authority infringed rights to which he was entitled to protection under public law to proceed by way of an ordinary action and by this means to evade the provisions of Order 53 for the protection of such authorities . . .

Within months of delivering its judgement in *O'Reilly* v *Mackman* the appeal in *Cocks* v *Thanet County Council* [1983] came before their Lordships. The claimant applied to the council for permanent housing for himself and his family in September 1981 under the Housing (Homeless Persons) Act 1977 whilst living with a friend. He then commenced proceedings against the council in the county court in January 1982 for a declaration that the council was in breach of its obligation to provide permanent housing for himself and his family under the Act. A High Court judge ruled that he could proceed with his claim in the county court but the council then appealed directly to the House of Lords arguing that, amongst other matters, the court could only consider the claim by way of an application for judicial review. The House of Lords applied its ruling in *O'Reilly* v *Mackman* and held that the claimant could only proceed by way of judicial review. Although the House of Lords indicated that challenges to governmental decisions should normally proceed by way of a public law action for judicial review, it made it clear at the time, and has done since, that its guidance is not to be applied in a rigid fashion especially where it might result in a denial of justice. In *Wandsworth Corporation* v *Winder* [1985], the council tried to argue that the defendant could not raise a public law issue as a defence in a civil action. It had let a flat to the defendant under Part V of the Housing Act 1957 on a weekly tenancy at a rent of £12.06. Under a newly incorporated schedule to this statute, the council was obliged to review its rents and increase them from time to time. In 1981 the council resolved to increase its rents, and in March it served notice on the defendant that the rent of his flat would be increased to £16.56 weekly. He objected to this increase and continued to pay the former amount so that arrears gradually accumulated. In the following year the council passed a further resolution to increase its rents and it served notice on the defendant on March 1982 to the effect that his rent would rise to £18.53. He again refused to pay any increase and the council began legal proceedings for possession of the flat and recovery of the arrears of rent. In his defence, Winder claimed that he was not liable to pay the arrears because the resolutions passed by the council were *ultra vires* and therefore void. The council applied to have this defence struck out as an abuse of process of the court and at first instance this was done on the basis that the conduct of a local authority should be challenged by way of an application for judicial review. The Court of Appeal allowed the defendant's subsequent appeal but the council then appealed to the House of Lords. Their Lordships held that it was a paramount principle that a private citizen's recourse to the courts to determine his rights could not be excluded except by very clear words in a statute. Moreover, there was nothing in the Supreme Court Act 1981 s. 31 or in the Rules of the Supreme Court that could be interpreted as abolishing the citizen's right to challenge a decision of a local authority in the course of defending an action.

The right to raise a point of public law is not limited to instances where a person is a defendant in an action, as was demonstrated in *Roy* v *Kensington and Chelsea and Westminster FPC* [1992]. Dr Roy was a general practitioner in the area administered by the Family Practitioner Committee (FPC) who had reduced his practice allowance as it was legally entitled to do if it was satisfied that he was not devoting a substantial amount of his time to his NHS practice. The statement of fees and allowances made by the Secretary of State under regulation 24 of a statutory instrument, required that all FPCs make payments to NHS general practitioners, providing for basic and supplementary practice allowances. Although Dr Roy was abroad for between one-third and one-half of each year, he did arrange cover for his NHS patients by securing the services of a locum doctor, and so he sought to challenge the FPC's decision and assert that he was indeed devoting a substantial amount of his time to general practice. He therefore commenced an ordinary civil action for breach of contract against the FPC in the High Court. The court struck out certain parts of his statement of claim on the basis that it was an abuse of the process of the court because the issues involved matters of public law that should have been pursued by way of an application for judicial review. However, the Court of Appeal allowed Dr Roy's appeal, but the FPC then appealed to the House of Lords which availed itself of the opportunity to conduct an exhaustive review of the relevant case law. In giving the leading judgement, Lord Lowry stated that the rule in *O'Reilly* v *Mackman* was subject to many exceptions based on the nature of the claim and on the undesirability of erecting procedural barriers. At the close of his judgement he said:

> it seems to me that unless the procedure adopted by the . . . party is ill-suited to dispose of the question at issue, there is much to be said in favour of the proposition that a court having jurisdiction ought to let a case be heard rather than entertain a debate concerning the form of the proceedings.

Accordingly, the House of Lords unanimously dismissed the appeal brought by the FPC.

In *Boddington* v *British Transport Police* [1999] the House of Lords made it clear that, in principle, a public law defence can be raised in criminal proceedings to ensure that a conviction is not based on an invalid legal instrument. It is important to note that the decisions of private bodies that do not derive their powers from statute cannot normally be challenged in a claim for judicial review, as is illustrated by the ruling in *R* v *Disciplinary Committee of the Jockey Club ex p. Aga Khan* [1993]. However, in *R* v *Panel on*

Takeovers and Mergers ex p. Datafin [1987] the Court of Appeal permitted an application by way of judicial review because of the special functions exercised by the Panel in the City of London.

3. Exclusion of judicial review

In the past, successive governments have steered statutes through Parliament that contained express provisions which seemed to exclude any scope for judicial review of administrative action. These provisions have come to be known as 'ouster of jurisdiction' clauses since they appear to remove official acts and decisions from judicial scrutiny. In *Anisminic Ltd* v *Foreign Compensation Commission* [1969] the House of Lords devised an ingenious way of circumventing such clauses. The Commission was established to administer claims under the Foreign Compensation Act 1950 in respect of assets owned by UK nationals that had been confiscated by foreign governments. The company owned property in Egypt that was confiscated by the government and it made a claim for compensation to the Commission which declined to accept the claim. Not surprisingly, the company sought to challenge the Commission's decision. The Foreign Compensation Act 1950 s. 4(4) contained the following provision:

> The determination by the Commission of any application made to them under this Act shall not be called in question in any court of law.

The House of Lords held that the Commission's decision was not a determination but rather a 'purported determination' and since the above provision made no reference to purported determinations, their Lordships were not precluded from inquiring whether or not any order or decision of the Commission was a legal nullity.

4. The established categories

In the case of *Council for Civil Service Unions* v *Minister for the Civil Service* [1985] Lord Diplock set out the modern basis for judicial review in terms of 'illegality', 'procedural impropriety' and 'irrationality'. More recently, 'proportionality' has emerged as a fourth basis to justify judicial review although it has yet to become as well established as the other three. In the exposition that follows, these general headings will be used to expound the basic principles pertaining to judicial review. However, the first three should not be thought of as being self-contained because, in practice, there is sometimes a degree of overlap between them. For example, a decision-making body (or an official) that unlawfully fetters its discretion may have its decision reviewed on the grounds of illegality or procedural impropriety.

5. Illegality

At common law, a decision may be illegal if it infringes a basic right. For example, in *Raymond* v *Honey* [1983] the Home Secretary had power to make rules for the regulation and management of prisons under the Prison Act 1952 s. 47. Raymond, a prison governor, was under the impression that the Prison Rules 1964 r. 33 and r. 37A empowered him to prevent mail being sent by prisoners in certain circumstances and he prevented some of Honey's mail being sent to his solicitors. Honey was advised to initiate contempt of court proceedings against the governor, which Lord Russell in *R* v *Gray* [1900] defined as:

> Any act done which is calculated to obstruct or interfere with the due course of justice or the lawful process of the courts.

The governor's action came within this definition but his defence was that he had been authorised to intercept prisoners' mail under the prison regulations. This then focused attention on whether the Home Secretary was empowered under the Prison Act 1952 s. 47 to make regulations granting the governor such powers. The House of Lords took the view that it did not and ruled accordingly. In the course of his judgement Lord Wilberforce said:

> under English law, a convicted prisoner, in spite of his imprisonment, retains all civil rights which are not taken away expressly or by necessary implication . . . There is nothing in the Prison Act 1952 that confers power to make regulations which would deny, or interfere with, the right of the respondent, as a prisoner, to have unimpeded access to a court. Section 47 . . . is quite insufficient to authorise hindrance or interference with so basic a right.

An administrative act or decision is illegal if it goes beyond the scope of the authority that has made the act or decision possible. It will also be illegal if it contravenes that authority in any way or if the person acting or deciding pursues an objective other than the one for which the power to act or decide was conferred. In the sphere of administrative law there are a number of instances where an Act of Parliament confers a discretionary power on a government minister, a public body or an official, and the courts have long taken the view that the exercise of this discretion must be according to the law. This principle was clearly established in the landmark, if somewhat controversial, judgement of the House of Lords in *Padfield* v *Minister of Agriculture, Fisheries and Food* [1968]. A milk marketing scheme had been introduced by Act of Parliament that required milk producers to sell all their output to regional Milk Marketing Boards. The various boards included both consumers' and producers' representatives. Subsequent legislation in the form of the Agricultural Marketing Act 1958 made provision for two separate bodies to hear complaints about the operation of the scheme. Most complaints were to be referred to a consumers' committee, but s. 19(3) provided that:

> A committee of investigation shall . . . (b) be charged with the duty, if the Minister in any case so directs, of considering and reporting to the Minister on . . . any . . . complaint made to the Minister as to the operation of any scheme which, in the opinion of the Minister, could not be considered by a Consumers' Committee.

The minister had refused to exercise his discretion to empanel a committee to investigate complaints made by the south eastern producers that the majority of the board had fixed prices in a way that was particularly unfavourable to them. They therefore applied for a court order that would require the minister to do so. The House of Lords held that the minister's discretion was not unfettered (unlimited) and that the reason that he had given for his refusal showed that he had gone beyond his powers not only by taking into account factors that were irrelevant from a legal standpoint but also by using his powers in a way that was calculated to frustrate the policy behind the Act as interpreted by their Lordships. On this basis, the House of Lords considered that it was entitled to intervene and declare the minister's decision illegal. Although their Lordships made a mandatory order requiring the minister to empanel a committee, the minister subsequently declined to follow the committee's advice – he was legally entitled to do this. For the milk producers who brought the action it was a hollow victory.

Even where an Act of Parliament confers an unfettered discretion on a minister, the courts may still assert their right to review a ministerial decision because Lord Upjohn said in *Padfield* v *Minister of Agriculture, Fisheries and Food*:

> [T]he use of that adjective [unfettered], even in an Act of Parliament, can do nothing to unfetter the control which the judiciary have over the executive, namely, that in exercising their powers the latter must act lawfully and that is a matter to be determined by looking at the Act and its scope and object in conferring a discretion upon the Minister rather than by the use of adjectives.

Nevertheless, the courts will decline to review decisions involving matters of economic and social policy that involve difficult choices between competing priorities because they recognise that this is not their sphere. Such decisions are matters requiring the exercise of political judgement.

Statute law is not the only source of the UK government's legal authority. The government also possesses a number of common law powers which lawyers refer to as 'prerogative powers', that is, powers exercised under the royal prerogative. These prerogative powers were largely defined at the time of the 1688 revolutionary settlement, and although the monarch does still have some prerogative powers that she is able to exercise, most of these are exercised by Her Majesty's government. In *Council for Civil Service Unions* v *Minister for the Civil Service* [1985], the House of Lords held that most prerogative powers are now subject to judicial review. Such a review occurred in *R* v *Secretary of State for the Home Department ex p. Bentley* [1994], the applicant being the sister of Derek Bentley. Derek Bentley and Christopher Craig were convicted in 1952 of murdering a police officer but the jury had recommended mercy. The prosecution had argued that both were engaged in a joint criminal endeavour. Although Craig had fired the fatal shot, this had occurred after Bentley, who had been arrested, uttered the ambiguous sentence 'Let him have it, Chris'. Since Bentley was aged 19 at the time, he was sentenced to death, whereas Craig who was aged 16 was ordered to be detained at Her Majesty's pleasure. After the trial, the judge wrote to the Home Secretary stating that he could find no mitigating circumstances in Bentley's case. In spite of a campaign and the advice of the senior civil servants to the contrary, the Home Secretary declined to reprieve Bentley who was then executed. Following a long campaign for a posthumous pardon by the applicant, the case was reviewed by a later Home Secretary. He concluded in October 1992 that there were no grounds for recommending a free pardon on the basis that he could not substitute his judgement for the Home Secretary at the time. In addition, he stated that it had been a long established policy of successive Home Secretaries that a free pardon in relation to a conviction for an indictable offence should be granted only if moral as well as technical innocence of the convicted person could be established, which was not possible in the particular case. On considering the substantive application for judicial review, the Divisional Court held that decisions taken under the royal prerogative were susceptible to judicial review if their nature and subject matter were amenable and in so far as the challenge did not require the court to review questions of policy. Moreover, even though the formulation of the criteria for the exercise of the royal prerogative of mercy, by the grant of a free pardon, was probably not justiciable, failure by the Home Secretary to recognise that the prerogative of mercy could be exercised otherwise than by way of a free pardon was subject to judicial review. The court took the view that the Home Secretary had not given sufficient consideration to the possibility of granting a form of pardon suitable to the circumstances of the case and that he should consider the matter afresh.

The subsequent case *R* v *Secretary of State for the Home Department ex p. Fire Brigades Union* [1995] centred on a scheme for compensating victims of crime. The Criminal Injuries Compensation Scheme had originally been introduced under the Crown's prerogative in 1964 but was then to be placed on a statutory basis under the Criminal Justice Act 1988 ss 108–117 and

Schedules 6 and 7. The aim was to provide compensation to victims on a case by case basis applying the compensatory principles of the law of torts. According to the Criminal Justice Act 1988 s. 171(1) the statutory scheme was to come into force 'on such day as the Secretary of State may . . . appoint'. In fact, the Secretary of State did not make a commencement order and in 1993 he indicated that the statutory provisions would not be brought into operation but that the non-statutory scheme would be replaced by a non-statutory tariff scheme. This meant that awards to victims would be made on an *ex gratia* basis by reference to a tariff fixed according to particular categories of injury. In July 1994 the House of Commons in the Appropriation Act 1994 approved supply estimates which included funding for the Home Office to operate the revised scheme. In an application for judicial review, the union representing persons liable to suffer injury as victims of violent crime sought two declarations: (a) that the Secretary of State by failing or refusing to bring the statutory scheme into operation has acted unlawfully and in breach of his duty under the 1988 Act, and (b) that by implementing the non-statutory tariff scheme he had acted unlawfully in breach of a duty under the Act and accordingly had abused his prerogative powers. The Divisional Court dismissed the application but the Court of Appeal allowed the appeal in part by granting the second declaration. The Secretary of State then appealed to the House of Lords. By majority the House of Lords dismissed the appeal by the Secretary of State and a cross-appeal by the union. In relation to the second declaration, their Lordships held that the Criminal Justice Act 1988 s. 171(1) imposed a continuing obligation on the Secretary of State to consider whether to bring the statutory scheme into operation. They also took the view that he could not lawfully bind himself not to exercise the discretion conferred on him and that the non-statutory tariff scheme was inconsistent with the statutory scheme. Thus the decision of the Secretary of State not to bring ss 108–117 into operation but to introduce the non-statutory tariff scheme was unlawful. However, in dismissing the union's cross-appeal their Lordships indicated that the 1988 Act did not impose a legally enforceable duty on the Secretary of State to bring ss 108–117 into operation at any particular time.

Where a power has been granted for one purpose but is exercised for another, the courts will normally take the view that the power has not been validly exercised. This principle was established initially in relation to the exercise of powers of compulsory purchase but it has since been developed to the point that it is now a fundamental principle of administrative law of general application. It was applied in *Hazell v Hammersmith & Fulham LBC* [1992]. In this case the local authority had power to borrow money under the Local Government Act 1972 on both a long-term and a short-term basis. It exercised these powers to finance certain capital projects. However, from

1987 to 1989, it entered into a number of interest rate swap contracts with banks. The swap market enables a borrower to raise funds in the market to which the borrower has best access but then to make interest and capital repayments in its preferred form of currency. From April 1987 to February 1989 the local authority did this mainly with a view to boosting its income because if it swapped from a fixed interest rate to a variable rate, it stood to make considerable financial gains if interest rates went down, but if they rose, it stood to make serious losses. If it swapped from a variable rate to fixed rate the opposite result would obtain. In July 1988, the district auditor challenged the validity of these interest rate swap transactions on the basis that they amounted to speculative trading for profit because the authority had made no attempt to match its actual debts and investments with any of the transactions. The auditor applied, under the Local Government Finance Act 1982, for a declaration that the items appearing in the local authority's capital market fund account for 1987 and 1988 were contrary to law and for an order for rectification of the accounts. The case eventually reached the House of Lords which ruled that the local authority had no power to enter into the interest rate swap transactions with a view to increasing its financial resources because such transactions were inconsistent with its borrowing powers in the Local Government Act 1972.

In *R* v *Secretary of State for Foreign Affairs ex p. World Development Movement Ltd* [1995] the Foreign Secretary was empowered under the Overseas Development and Cooperation Act 1980 s. 1(1):

> for the purpose of promoting the development or maintaining the economy of a country . . . outside the UK, or the welfare of its people, to furnish any person or body with assistance whether financial, technical or any other nature.

The Malaysian government had identified the Pergau River as an appropriate site for a hydroelectric power station. A consortium that included GEC and Balfour Beatty informed the Department of Trade and Industry that it would be seeking financial assistance under the 'aid and trade provision' in the Act, and in November 1988 it submitted a formal application that gave its indicative costs for the project amounting to £315 million to the Overseas Development Administration (ODA). Then, in January 1989, it produced a firm contract proposal for £316 million with a UK content of £195 million. Following the report of an appraisal mission that was sent to Malaysia by the ODA, the UK government made an oral offer of £68.25 million for the project conditional upon a full economic appraisal. A subsequent appraisal mission reported that at the consortium's price of £316 million, the economic viability of the project was marginal. In March 1989 the consortium informed the ODA that its budget estimate had been revised upwards from £316 million to £397 million and the ODA minuted that the project was no longer marginal but uneconomic. Nevertheless, the UK government gave the Malaysian government written notice of an offer of assistance based on the original estimate of £316 million with an indication that it would be willing to discuss the possibility of further financial assistance. By early 1990 the ODA completed yet another economic appraisal which concluded that, at £397 million the project would be a 'very bad buy' and a burden on Malaysian consumers. In spite of advice from the ODA that the project was an abuse of the aid programme and was not a sound development project, the Foreign Secretary approved the financial support under the 'aid and trade provision' in the legislation, on the basis that a contrary decision would affect the credibility of the UK abroad. The World Development Movement (WDM), which functions as a non-partisan pressure group dedicated to improving the quantity and quality of British aid to developing countries, sought an assurance from the Foreign Secretary that no further funds for the project would be provided. When he refused to give such an assurance the WDM applied for judicial review of his decision to grant financing under the 'aid and trade provision' and his decision to refuse to withhold outstanding payments. The Foreign Secretary argued that s. 1(1) did not limit aid to projects that were viable in narrow economic terms but allowed aid to be granted which served wider political and economic considerations such as the promotion of regional stability and good government. The Divisional Court held that the Foreign Secretary was fully justified under the legislation, when making decisions of whether to grant assistance, to take account of political and economic considerations and to consider the impact on the UK's credibility of the withdrawal of an offer already made. However, it ruled that on the evidence no development purpose under the Act existed. Accordingly, the Foreign Secretary's decision was unlawful.

Even though an Act of Parliament may confer a discretionary power without expressly referring to a particular purpose, this will not prevent the courts from insisting that the discretionary power is exercised in accordance with what they regard as the implied purpose of the legislation. If the exercise of a discretionary power has been influenced by consideration that ought not to have been taken into account, the courts will usually rule that the power has not been validly exercised where these extraneous considerations have influenced the decision.

In *R v Liverpool University ex p. Caesar-Gordon* [1991] the University of Liverpool Conservative Association applied for, and was granted provisional approval by the university to hold a meeting to be addressed by a South African diplomat in November 1988. Having consulted with the local police, the university then withdrew its approval because it was not reasonably practicable to make adequate arrangements for the maintenance of good order at the meeting and in the adjacent residential area. The Association appealed to the university vice-chancellor who rejected the appeal but the Association then sought permission for a meeting in January 1989 to be addressed by two South African diplomats. Permission was granted provided that entry would be restricted to staff and students of the university and that whilst the Association could issue invitations to its own members, there would be no other publicity apart from notices within the university on the day of the meeting. Attendance was to be limited by the size of the venue and admission was to be on proof of identity. On the day of the meeting, the university revoked its permission because of fear of public disorder outside the university precincts. The chairman of the Association applied for judicial review requesting a declaration that the university had acted contrary to the Education (No. 2) Act 1986 s. 43 by failing to take such steps as were reasonably practicable to ensure freedom of speech. The Divisional Court held that, in the performance of its duty to ensure freedom of speech, the university was not acting beyond its powers by restricting publicity and admission; however, it was not entitled to take into account threats of public disorder outside the university precincts.

Under the general heading of illegality, particular difficulties arise in relation to the delegation of discretionary powers. There is a general principle that a discretionary power should be exercised only by the body or official to whom it has been entrusted unless there is an express power to delegate it to another. The case *Ellis* v *Dubowski* [1921] involved an appeal by a local authority inspector following the refusal of the local magistrates to convict the respondents for an infringement of the Cinematograph Act 1909. County councils were empowered under the Act to impose conditions on the granting of licences to operate cinemas. A licence was granted to the respondents on the basis that no film was to be shown which was likely to be injurious to morality or to encourage or incite crime or to lead to disorder. In addition, the respondents were prohibited under the terms of their licence from showing a film that had not been certified for public exhibition by the British Board of Film Censors (BBFC), a body which then had no statutory or constitutional authority. The respondents had failed to comply with this latter requirement but argued that the county council had no authority to delegate its powers under the Cinematograph Act 1909 other than in accordance with s. 5 which permitted delegation to a council committee or to local magistrates. In essence, their case was that the condition in the licence was *ultra vires* and void in so far as the council had delegated its powers to the BBFC. Lawrence CJ ruled that this condition in the licence was unlawful on the basis that 'The condition sets up an authority whose *ipse dixit* is to control the exhibition of films. The effect is to transfer a power which belongs to the County Council...'. Later in his judgement he stated: 'a condition putting the matter into the hands of a third person or body not possessed of statutory or constitutional authority is *ultra vires* the committee'.

More recently in *R v DPP ex p. Association of First Division Civil Servants The Times* 24 May 1988 the delegation of a power to review prosecutions in order to decide whether there was sufficient evidence to proceed was held to be illegal because the Act of Parliament conferring the power on the Director of Public Prosecutions envisaged that it would be delegated only to a member of the Crown Prosecution Service who would be a lawyer. Nevertheless, the courts have recognised that special considerations arise where a statutory power is conferred on a Secretary of State but is exercised by a senior departmental official. Under what has become known as the Carltona principle, formulated by Lord Greene MR in *Carltona Ltd v Commissioners of Works* [1943], the courts have accepted that powers entrusted to senior ministers can normally be exercised by senior officials of the department acting under the authority of the Secretary of State. However, the Carltona principle can be expressly excluded by the wording of the legislation. For example, the Immigration Act 1971 ss 13(5), 14(3) and 15(4) all refer to action by the minister 'and not by a person acting under his authority'.

As was stated in Chapter 8, all public authorities are now required by the Human Rights Act 1998 s. 6 to act in accordance with the Convention rights as set out in Schedule 1 of the Act. The case of *R v North and East Devon Health Authority ex p. Coughlan (Secretary of State and another intervening)* [2000] (to be considered below) illustrates how a Convention right can arise in relation to decisions made by agencies of the NHS. Should public authorities fail to act in accordance with the Convention rights, their decisions can be reviewed by the courts on the basis of illegality because they will either have contravened or have exceeded the provisions of the statute. Although the Act has great constitutional importance it has to be remembered that the European Convention on Human Rights and Fundamental Freedoms has not been incorporated into UK law in the same way as has the EC Treaty. Moreover, the European Court of Human Rights has not devised a doctrine of direct effect. Thus the scheme of the Human Rights Act 1998 requires that legislation should be interpreted and applied in a way that is compatible with the Convention rights set out in Schedule 1. If, because of the very precise wording of the statute, this is not possible, the courts are limited to the making of a declaration of incompatibility. They are not at liberty to suspend the operation of an Act of Parliament where one or more provisions conflicts with rights contained in Schedule 1. The courts will nevertheless be required to review their previous case law. For example, in the case *Brind and others v Secretary of State for the Home*

Department [1991] the House of Lords held that there was no presumption that the courts would review the exercise of an administrative discretion on the basis that the discretion had to be exercised in accordance with the Convention. In the light of the Human Rights Act, however, a similar case today may have a different outcome; the House of Lords would have to review its previous decision and take into account the principle of proportionality. In *Raymond* v *Honey* [1983] the House of Lords upheld the rights of a prisoner on common law principles but today it is likely that the judgement in a similar case would be based on the relevant Convention right in the Schedule.

As was stated in Chapter 7, certain provisions of the EC Treaty have direct effect in the legal systems of member states. Individuals and private corporations (as well as foreign nationals) may have recourse to these Treaty provisions and challenge governmental decisions in the courts of England and Wales. For example, Article 87(1) of the EC Treaty states:

> Save as otherwise provided in this Treaty, any aid granted by a Member State or through State resources in any form whatsoever which distorts or threatens to distort competition by favouring certain undertakings or the production of certain goods shall, in so far as it affects trade between Member States, be incompatible with the common market.

The European Court of Justice has declared that Article 87(1) has direct effect and if a UK company is to receive illegal state aid (aid that has not been approved by the European Commission) a competitor may make an application to the courts to have the payment of the aid suspended pending an investigation by the Commission.

As has been stated, directives can have vertical direct effect provided the criteria are satisfied, and where this occurs they can form the basis for challenging official decisions. In *R* v *Secretary of State for the Home Department ex p. Dannenberg* [1984] the applicant was a German national who entered the UK in 1981 and in 1982 was given a resident's permit for five years. On 29 April 1983 he appeared before Mid Sussex Magistrates' Court charged with a number of offences to which he pleaded guilty. The magistrates had before them a copy of a notice that had been given to the applicant pursuant to the Immigration Act 1971 s. 6(2) to the effect that they should recommend him for deportation. Having sentenced the applicant, the magistrates made a recommendation under s. 6(1) of the Act for deportation. Following the recommendation, the applicant was ordered to be detained until the Secretary of State could consider the recommendation. In due course the Secretary of State was able to do so and he made an order for deportation under s. 5(1) of the Act. Neither the magistrates nor the Secretary of State gave reasons for the recommendation or the deportation order. Although the Civil Division of the Court of Appeal held that the refusal of the Divisional Court to quash the recommendation was a judgement in a criminal matter and no appeal could be addressed to the Civil Division concerning it, the Court of Appeal still allowed the appeal. It did so on the basis that the deportation order did not contain any information relating to the grounds on which it was made and nor did the magistrates' recommendation. This was an infringement of Articles 6 and 9 of Directive 64/221/EEC. Accordingly the deportation order was invalid and was therefore quashed.

Parliamentary legislation may also be challenged for illegality by way of judicial review where it conflicts with EU law, and it will be recalled from Chapters 5 and 7 that a successful challenge to the legality of the Merchant Shipping Act 1988 Part II and the regulations created thereunder was made in *R* v *Secretary of State for Transport ex p. Factortame Ltd.*

6. Procedural fairness in general

Whilst illegality focuses mainly on the need to ensure that decisions are made within the scope of the powers that have been delegated and that the powers themselves have been properly exercised, procedural fairness focuses on the decision-making process. Firstly, the courts require that decision-makers should not be biased or in any way prejudiced, otherwise there is a real likelihood that their judgements will be flawed as proper consideration will not have been given to the representations put forward by those most concerned. Secondly, individuals and groups should have the opportunity, in so far as this is practicable, to make representations and thereby influence the outcome of the decision-making process. Thus under the heading of procedural fairness, the courts impose a duty on those acting in an official capacity to act fairly. Accordingly, they will examine the consultation process, if any, with a view to determining whether it is adequate and whether it contributes towards the administration process rather than hindering it. In so doing the judges are motivated to ensure the quality and rationality of the decision-making process. The requirement of procedural fairness has generated a vast amount of case law and some of the more significant cases are considered in **7** and **8**.

7. Procedural fairness: the rule against bias

If administrative decisions are to be intrinsically fair it is essential that the decision-maker is not biased or prejudiced. Bias or prejudice on the part of the decision-maker is likely to have the result that a proper consideration of the arguments put forward by interested parties is precluded. Bias may arise because of a financial or proprietary interest but other factors too give rise to actual bias. In practice, the rule against bias is concerned with the risk of bias just as much as the fact of actual bias to ensure that justice is not only done, but is also seen to be done. Although an administrative decision must be invalidated if actual bias on the part of the decision-maker is established, the same result will obtain if there appears to have been a real danger of bias, as was stated by the House of Lords in R v *Gough* [1993]. This was not an application for judicial review as such but an appeal to the House of Lords against conviction, albeit on the flimsiest grounds. The appellant and his brother were charged on indictment with conspiracy to rob, but his brother was discharged on the application of the prosecution. However, in the course of the trial, the brother was referred to by name and a photograph of him and the appellant was shown to the jury and a statement containing the brother's address was read to the jury. At the conclusion of the trial the brother caused a disturbance in the courtroom and one of the jurors recognised him as her next door neighbour. The brother then informed the defence of the connection. Soon afterwards the juror was interviewed by the police and she swore an affidavit to the effect that she was unaware of the connection until after the jury had delivered its verdict. The Criminal Division of the Court of Appeal had ruled that the correct test was whether the appellant had a fair trial. Since it concluded that he had, it dismissed the appeal. The basis of the appeal to the House of Lords was that the presence of the brother's neighbour on the jury was a serious irregularity. In giving the leading judgement of the House of Lords dismissing the appeal, Lord Gough stated that the test for bias to be applied by courts and administrative tribunals should be stated in terms of whether there was a real danger rather than just a real likelihood of bias.

In the later case of R v *West London Coroner ex p. Dallagho and another* [1994] the Court of Appeal seems to have applied this guidance strictly. The applicants were mothers of two of the victims of the *Marchioness* tragedy. In 1989 the vessel had been chartered for a night-time pleasure cruise on the River Thames with a discotheque and licensed bar. The *Marchioness* collided with the dredger *Bowbelle* near Southwark Bridge and the *Marchioness* sank very quickly. Of the passengers and crew, who numbered 131, there were only 80 survivors. Most of those who died were between the ages of 18 and 30. All the 51 bodies recovered were taken to the Westminster mortuary which was within the jurisdiction of HM Coroner for Inner West London. Inquests into these deaths were opened and adjourned in the weeks immediately following the disaster. In February 1990 the coroner indicated that he would commence the inquest hearings on 23 April, taking them in two parts: part one dealing with forensic and identification evidence relating to who had died, when and from what cause; part two would deal with eye witnesses and technical evidence on how the deceased met their deaths.

When the hearings began on 23 April, relatives of seven of the deceased, including the applicant, objected to this two-stage inquest so that the coroner heard only 44 part one inquests and soon afterward the inquests were adjourned pending criminal proceedings. Following a misunderstanding, Mrs Lockwood-Croft, a bereaved mother, was denied sight of her son's body by persons claiming to be, but who were not, acting on the coroner's instructions. On her subsequent request for an exhumation order because she was having nightmares that the interred body was not that of her son, the coroner expressed his belief to the appropriate authorities that she had been deeply psychologically affected in her grief and was not acting rationally and that other relatives were mentally unwell. By late June 1992 all the criminal proceedings had concluded and the coroner had to decide whether to resume the inquest under the provisions of the Coroners Act 1988 s. 16(3) the relevant text of which is: 'After the conclusion of the relevant criminal proceedings . . . the coroner may . . . resume the adjourned inquest if in his opinion there is sufficient cause to do so.'

On 22 July 1992 the coroner announced his decision not to resume the adjourned inquests and he decided in late 1992 not to grant the exhumation order to Mrs Lockwood-Croft. She and the first applicant joined forces to challenge the coroner's decision not to proceed with the inquests on the grounds that he had shown apparent bias towards them by the comments that he made about their mental condition. The Court of Appeal quashed the coroner's decision and the matter was remitted to another coroner in a different district for a fresh decision. Referring to the decision of the House of Lords in *R v Gough*, Simon Brown LJ in the Court of Appeal stated the following propositions:

1. Any court seized of a challenge on the ground of apparent bias must ascertain the relevant circumstances and consider all the evidence for itself so as to reach its own conclusion on the facts.
2. It necessarily follows that the factual position may appear quite differently as between the time when the challenge is launched and the time when it comes to be decided by the court. What may appear at the leave (permission) stage to be a strong case of 'justice [not] manifestly be[ing] seen to be done', may, following the court's investigation, nevertheless fail. Or, of course (although perhaps less probably), the case may have become stronger.
3. In reaching its conclusion the court 'personifies the reasonable man'.
4. The question on which the court must reach its own factual conclusion is this: is there a real danger of injustice having occurred as a result of bias? By real is meant not without substance. A real danger clearly involves more than a minimal risk, less than a probability. One could, I think, as well speak of a real risk or a real possibility.

5. Injustice will have occurred as a result of bias if 'the decision maker unfairly regarded with disfavour the case of a party to the issue under consideration by him'. I take unfairly regarded with disfavour to mean 'was predisposed or prejudiced against one party's case for reasons unconnected with the merits of the issue'.

6. A decision maker may have unfairly regarded with disfavour one party's case whether consciously or unconsciously. Where, as here, the applicants expressly disavow any suggestion of actual bias, it seems to me that the court must necessarily be asking itself whether there is a real danger that the decision maker was unconsciously biased.

7. It will be seen, therefore, that by the time that legal challenge comes to be resolved, the court is no longer concerned strictly with the appearance of bias but rather with establishing the possibility that there was actual although unconscious bias.

The rule against bias must not be taken to absurd lengths, as necessity may sometimes dictate that a person who is not completely neutral and totally objective makes an official decision. Moreover, in matters of policy, public officials may have previously indicated their position on a particular issue but this does not necessarily preclude them from giving proper consideration to representations before a decision is made.

8. Procedural fairness: the duty to act fairly

Particular Acts of Parliament may set out a consultation procedure, and where this is the case the procedure must be followed otherwise there will be scope for a successful challenge of the decision in the courts. In other circumstances the court may infer that a fair hearing is required because of the need to safeguard some right or interest. In *Ridge* v *Baldwin* [1964] the House of Lords reasserted the principle that public bodies must observe certain standards of procedural fairness in their decision-making. The appellant was appointed chief constable of Brighton in 1956. The appointment was made subject to the Police Act 1919 and the regulations made under it. On 25 October 1957, he was arrested and charged, with others, of conspiracy to obstruct the course of justice and three days later he was suspended from duty by the local Watch Committee (the forerunner of the modern Police Authority). He was subsequently acquitted of the charges against him by a jury on 28 February 1958, but Donovan J on passing sentence on his co-accused, said that the facts disclosed in the course of the trial

establish that neither of you had that professional and moral leadership which both of you should have had and were entitled to expect from the Chief Constable of Brighton . . .

After his acquittal, the appellant applied to be reinstated, but on 7 March 1958 the Watch Committee met and decided that he had been negligent in the performance of his duties as chief constable. The committee also decided to dismiss him from office in the apparent exercise of its powers under the Municipal Corporations Act 1882 s. 191(4). Under that subsection it could dismiss him if he was negligent in the discharge of his duty or otherwise unsuitable to hold office. Whilst no specific charge was formulated against him, either at that meeting or at another on 15 March, when the committee was addressed by the appellant's solicitor, the committee in arriving at its decision considered his own statements in evidence and the observations of Donovan J above. The appellant then addressed an appeal to the Home Secretary who decided that there was sufficient material on which the committee could, in purporting to exercise its power under s. 191(4), dismiss him. The appellant then brought an action against members of the committee for a declaration that his dismissal was illegal, *ultra vires* and void. He also claimed arrears of remuneration and damages. The House of Lords held that the decision of the committee to dismiss him was null and void and that notwithstanding the fact that the decision of the Home Secretary was final and binding on the parties under the Police Appeals Act 1927, that decision could not give validity to the decision of the committee. As the appellant was not an employee of the committee and the latter could dismiss him only on the grounds set out in s. 191(4), that is for neglect of duty (as opposed to breach of contract), three of the five Law Lords held that the committee had not observed the principles of natural justice by informing him of the charge against him and giving him an opportunity to be heard.

Public administration abounds with instances where administrative decision-making must be preceded by a formal consultation process. For example, planning legislation requires public participation in the drafting of development plans. It also provides for appeals to be made against the refusal of planning applications or against any conditions that might be attached to such applications. Even in the absence of a statutory requirement to consult, the courts will often, in the interests of procedural fairness, presume that an opportunity is to be afforded for consultation or at least a chance to make representations where an individual's or entity's common law or statutory rights are at stake. In *R v Liverpool Corporation ex p. Liverpool Taxi Fleet Operators' Association* [1972] the corporation had power under the Town Police Clauses Act 1847 to 'license . . . such number of hackney coaches or carriages . . . as they think fit' in its area. In exercise of this power it limited the number to 300. Then, in 1970 and 1971 when many private minicabs were operating for hire in the streets, the applicants who represented the interests of the 300 existing licence-holders were assured by the town clerk that they would be consulted if any change in the number of licences was contemplated. In 1971, a special subcommittee of the corporation recommended increases for 1972 and 1973 and no restriction in numbers thereafter, but it heard the applicants case against its proposals. At a public meeting of the full corporation on 4 August 1971, the committee chairman gave a public undertaking that the numbers would not be increased above 300 until provision controlling minicabs had been enacted by Parliament and had come into force. This undertaking was confirmed orally by the chairman and then by letter dated 11 August 1971 from the town clerk. However, in November 1971 the subcommittee decided to increase the number of licences for 1972, and on 22 December the corporation confirmed this resolution. An application for judicial review to the Divisional Court was declined but the Court of Appeal allowed an appeal and granted the relief sought on the basis that the corporation had not acted fairly by failing to fulfil the terms of the assurance it had given.

More recently, in R v *Secretary of State for Health ex p. United States Tobacco International Inc.* [1992] an American company had received financial support to establish a factory in the UK to manufacture oral snuff from tobacco. Subsequently, having inquired into its possible detrimental effects, the Secretary of State for Health made regulations banning the product but without affording the company an opportunity to challenge the evidence. Although it was held that the company, prior to the ban, had no legitimate expectation of a continuation of the government's original policy, the negative impact of a ban on the company's business interests required a fair hearing. The fact that no opportunity had been provided rendered the regulations in question void and they were quashed by order of the court.

The principle of legitimate expectation seems to have become established in administrative law with the case of *Schmidt* v *Secretary of State for Home Affairs* [1969]. A legitimate expectation of consultation may arise as a result of the past conduct of the decision-maker, and this was recognised in the case of *Council for the Civil Service Unions* v *Minister for the Civil Service* [1985]. Although the House of Lords ultimately decided against the civil service unions on the basis of a risk to national security certified by a government minister, it confirmed that the principle of legitimate expectations existed in administrative law. Indeed, Lord Fraser said that a legitimate expectation could arise 'either from an express promise given on behalf of a public authority or from the existence of a regular practice which the claimant can reasonably expect to continue'.

Although the protection of legitimate expectations is an important aspect of procedural fairness, it should not mean that officials are prevented from ever changing their policies and practices. If they were, they would be falling foul of another requirement of procedural fairness in that they would be fettering their discretion for the future. If there is to be a change to a long-standing policy, some form of notice should be given with an opportunity afforded for comment and for objections to be raised by those affected.

Apart from those instances where the form of hearing is prescribed by statute, the degree of consultation deemed appropriate will vary depending on the nature of the decision and the context. In *R* v *Secretary of State for the Home Department ex p. Doody* [1994], Lord Mustill said:

> The principles of fairness are not to be applied by rote identically in every situation. What fairness demands is dependent on the context of the decision, and this is to be taken into account in all aspects. An essential factor of the context is the statute that creates the discretion, as regards both its language and the shape of the legal and administrative system within which the decision is taken. Whilst the statute is an essential factor, it is not the only feature and the courts will supplement the statutory code or if the statute is silent imply a code.

In general it may be said that a party who is likely to be directly affected by a proposed administrative act or decision should be given adequate notice of what is proposed so that he/she may be in a position to make representations and/or appear at any official inquiry. Such notice should afford him/her the time to prepare his/her case or responses to allegations that are to be made. Where the words 'hearing' or 'an opportunity to be heard' are used in a statute they will normally require that an oral hearing is conducted and interested parties may be entitled to call witnesses to support their case and they may also be legally represented (unless there is a statutory provision to the contrary). Where witnesses are called there must normally be provision for cross-examination unless this serves no useful purpose. In *Bushell* v *Secretary of State for the Environment* [1981] the Secretary of State published two draft schemes for the construction of motorways and access roads under the Highways Act 1959 s. 11. As a result of objections to the scheme, a public local inquiry was held, but at the time the Highways (Inquiries Procedure) Rules 1976 were not in force although the Secretary of State had announced his willingness to comply with similar rules. In the course of the inquiry, counsel for the Department of the Environment indicated that a departmental publication known as the Red Book had been used as the basis for assessing future traffic growth and was the foundation for the Department's case for the new motorways. The applicant and other objectors who sought to challenge the Department's case wished to cross-examine the witnesses that gave evidence for the Department, to test the accuracy of the traffic predictions contained in the Red Book. The inspector presiding over the inquiry ruled that he would not permit these witnesses to be cross-examined as to the need for the motorways or on the reliability of the Red Book. He did, nevertheless, permit the objectors to call their own evidence questioning the need for the motorway scheme. In drafting his report, he recommended that the scheme go ahead. However, following the closure of the inquiry but before the inspector made his report, the Department of the Environment issued new design and flow standards that demonstrated that the existing roads in the area could take much more traffic than had been previously estimated. Although this revised method of predicting traffic growth indicated a slower rate of growth than had been predicted by the Red Book, the Secretary of State refused the objectors' request for the inquiry to be reopened so that this new information could be considered. He did indicate that such representations as they wished to make regarding the need for new motorways against the background of the new estimates could always be considered by him as part of the ongoing consideration of any part of the Department's proposals. He assured them that if the new information led him to disagree with the inspector's recommendation, they would be given an opportunity to comment on it. Nevertheless, he went on to state that he had fully taken into account the general changes relating to design flow standards and traffic forecasts that had taken place since the inquiry and that he was satisfied that they did not materially affect the evidence on which the inspector had made his recommendations. He then went on to approve the scheme. The applicants then applied under the Highways Act 1959 Schedule 2 for his decision to be quashed on a number of grounds. These included that the inspector had been wrong in law to disallow cross-examination of the Department's witnesses on the Red Book and that since the inquiry the Secretary of State had taken account of undisclosed information which affected the fundamental issue, namely whether the motorways were needed. On the basis of this new information, it was argued, the inspector might have reached a different set of conclusions. Initially the application was dismissed by the Divisional Court but the Court of Appeal, by majority, allowed the appeal. The Secretary of State then appealed to the House of Lords and their Lordships allowed the appeal. They did so on the basis that, in the absence of statutory rules as to the conduct of the inquiry, the Act required only that the procedure had to be fair to all parties concerned. Moreover, the issue of whether the procedure, particularly the lack of cross-examination, was fair depended on the subject matter and the practical realities. Their Lordships took the view that the inspector's refusal to allow cross-examination as to the reliability of the Red Book was not a breach of natural justice and that the Secretary of State had not been bound to communicate the new departmental advice received after the close of the inquiry.

In many instances the decision-maker is merely placed under a duty to consult. However, this is still interpreted by the courts as requiring the decision-maker to afford those affected an opportunity to make representations or comments upon proposals that have been announced previously. Even in the absence of a duty to consult, the courts will often impose such a duty.

In *Chief Constable of North Wales* v *Evans* [1982] the applicant, Evans, was a probationary member of the North Wales Constabulary and until January 1978 he received good progress reports. On 31 January a report was conveyed to the divisional chief superintendent that contained a number of spurious allegations relating to his private life. It also transpired that when he had been given police accommodation in the form of a council house he asked whether it would be in order for him to keep his four dogs there and was informed that this would be acceptable provided nobody complained. In the autumn of 1978, the council informed him that he would have to get rid of the dogs and he indicated that he would try to find alternative homes for them. In a memorandum to the chief constable, the deputy chief constable who had interviewed Evans concerning the dogs expressed his view that people who flouted the terms of their tenancy agreements were unsuitable to be in the police service. The chief constable interviewed the applicant briefly on 8 November and informed him that he had made a mistake in accepting him and gave him the opportunity of resigning as an alternative to being dismissed. Despite his resignation, he subsequently applied for judicial review of the chief constable's decision. Woolf J in the Divisional Court held that the chief constable was bound to act fairly in exercising his discretion and the Court of Appeal largely upheld this ruling. When the chief constable appealed to the House of Lords, their Lordships applied their earlier ruling in *Ridge* v *Baldwin*. They took the view that the chief constable's discretion under the Police Regulations 1971 was not absolute but qualified and that he had not dealt with the applicant fairly because he had not put the adverse factors on which he acted to the applicant before deciding to dispense with his services.

With regard to legitimate expectations, mention was made of the requirement of a public decision-making body (or official) entrusted with discretionary power not to fetter its discretion. If it does so, its decision may be reviewed on the grounds of both illegality and procedural impropriety. The decision will be illegal if the decision-maker fails to utilise the discretion that has been conferred and instead imposes restrictions on himself/herself. There will be an infringement of procedural propriety if the persons affected are not permitted to influence the use of that discretion. In *R* v *Herrod ex p. Leeds County Council* [1976] local authorities had passed resolutions under the amended Betting and Gaming and Lotteries Act 1963 Schedule 6 para. 3, stating that permits would not be granted or renewed under s. 49 of the Act for the provision of amusements with prizes on specified premises.

As a result, applications for the grant or renewal of a permit for prize bingo on the premises in question were refused by the local authorities in line with the resolutions that had been passed. Appeals had been allowed by the Crown Court on the basis that, under para. 4 of Schedule 6, the resolutions could not take effect because the premises were to be used wholly or mainly for a 'pleasure fair' consisting wholly or mainly of amusements. The Divisional Court quashed the ruling of the Crown Court, but in a subsequent appeal the Court of Appeal held that the local authorities were not at liberty to pass a resolution that resulted in a 'blanket refusal' and that they had to consider each application on its merits.

This does not mean that a public decision-making body cannot formulate a policy in the interests of efficient administration but it does mean that such a policy must normally allow for exceptional cases. Moreover, it must afford interested individuals the opportunity to persuade the decision-maker to amend or deviate from a policy or rule in appropriate cases. The rationale for the rule against the fettering of discretion is, therefore, to ensure that there is some degree of responsiveness on the part of the decision-maker so that justice may be done in individual cases. In *R* v *Law Society ex p. Reigate Projects* [1993] the applicants had engaged a solicitor to act for them in the acquisition of a set of premises for future development. They paid over to him £250,000 but the solicitor used only £25,000 of this sum for a deposit on the property and he stole the remainder. He subsequently committed suicide and it emerged that he had defrauded many of his clients and that his practice was really in ruins. The initial £25,000 that had been paid to the vendors was forfeit and in an attempt to rescue the development project, the applicants faced both an increased purchase price and increased development costs. Therefore, they applied for compensation totaling £981,991 from the compensation fund operated by the Law Society under the Solicitors Act 1974 s. 36. The Law Society awarded them £315,672 comprising £225,000 (the balance of the purchase price of the premises), £4,380 (costs) and £86,292 (money previously deposited with the solicitor by the applicants).

The applicants were informed that the balance of their claim was regarded by the adjudication committee as consequential loss and therefore beyond the scope of the compensation fund. When the applicants commenced their application for judicial review of the decision, the committee reconsidered the application for compensation. The applicants were subsequently informed that under the policy guidelines for the administration of the fund it was not usual practice to award compensation for consequential loss and that there were no special reasons in the applicants' case to justify a departure from the policy. On hearing the application for judicial review the Divisional Court decided that the Law Society was entitled to have a policy for the administration of the fund provided it was made known, was reasonable and did not unwarrantably fetter its discretion. The Court took the view that the Solicitors Act 1974 s. 36(2)(a) provided for the payment of compensation mainly for the loss resulting from a solicitor's dishonesty of clients' money entrusted to him/her and that the Law Society's policy guidelines were not improper and did not impose an unwarranted fetter on its discretion. Since there had been no flaw in the way in which the decision had been arrived at or in the reasons provided, the decision could not be invalidated.

Although there is no general rule requiring the decision-maker to give reasons for an administrative decision, there are a number of recognised exceptions. The Tribunals and Inquiries Act 1971 s. 12 imposes an obligation on a large number of statutory tribunals and ministers notifying official decisions following the holding of a statutory inquiry, to supply reasons for a decision upon request. Where reasons are necessary they must be intelligible and meet the substance of the arguments put forward in order to avoid the impression that the decision was based on extraneous considerations rather than on matters raised at the hearing.

In other circumstances, fairness may require that reasons for an administrative decision are given. In R v *Civil Service Board ex p. Cunningham* [1991] the applicant was, until February 1988, the physical education officer at one of HM detention centres. He was dismissed from the prison service following an alleged attack on a prisoner. Although the alleged incident was investigated by the police, the applicant was not prosecuted. At the time of his dismissal he was 45 years of age and had worked for the prison service for 23 years. The applicant first appealed to the Civil Service Appeal Board which, in November 1988, ruled that his dismissal had been unfair and recommended that he be reinstated. As it was entitled to, the Home Office refused to accept the recommendation of the Board and so the Board assessed compensation for unfair dismissal at £6,500. The applicant had been in receipt of full pay until January 1989 but thereafter the only payment he received from the Home Office was £6,500. Had he been an ordinary employee as opposed to a civil servant, he would have received between £14,240 and £16,374 in similar circumstances. The Board declined to give reasons for its award of compensation beyond its assertion that it employed simple and informal procedures. The applicant was granted judicial review of the Board's decision on the basis that it was irrational and there had been a failure to observe the principles of natural justice. The judge granted the application on the failure to give reasons alone and this was upheld on appeal by the Court of Appeal.

In R v *Secretary of State for the Home Department ex p. Fayed* [1997] the Court of Appeal, by majority, steered its way around a statutory provision that appeared to exclude review by the courts to require some reasons to be given for a decision. The applicants were two brothers, Mohammed and Ali, both of whom were born in Egypt. The first brother had lived in the UK since 1964 and was granted leave to remain indefinitely. At the time of this litigation, he was married to a citizen of Finland and had dependent children who were British citizens. The second brother had come to live in the UK in the late 1960s and in 1977 was granted indefinite leave to remain. At the time he was married to a British citizen and his children were British citizens. They both had substantial business interests in the UK and were residents for tax purposes. On 29 January 1993, the second brother submitted an application for naturalisation as a British citizen under the British Nationality Act 1981 and the first brother made a similar application soon afterwards. The application forms requested limited information, but on 23 February 1995, in separate letters, both brothers were informed that 'after careful consideration your application has been refused'. No reasons were assigned and so the brothers made applications to the Home Office asking for reasons for the refusals but these were declined. Although permission for a judicial review was granted, Judge J dismissed the applications on the basis that British Nationality Act 1981 s. 44(2) did not require the Secretary of State for the Home Department to give reasons for the granting or refusal of any application involving the exercise of his discretion. Thus, according to the ruling of Judge J the failure to give the brothers an opportunity to deal with factors that might be adverse to their applications was not unlawful. However, the Court of Appeal allowed the subsequent appeal. Lord Woolf MR accepted that the Secretary of State was not required under s. 44(2) to give reasons for refusing an application for British citizenship where the decision involved the use of his discretion, but he ruled that he was required to exercise his discretion reasonably and was not relieved of the obligation to be fair in arriving at his decision. Furthermore, until the areas of concern were identified which caused the Secretary of State to doubt that the applicants were of good character (so that they would be in a position to make further representations) justice had not been seen to be done.

9. Irrationality or unreasonableness

The assertion of irrationality requires the courts to consider whether the decision-maker who acts under a discretionary power has improperly exercised that power, and so the applicant must surmount a high threshold of proof. This is because a claim of irrationality or unreasonableness takes the courts very close to the line beyond which it would be examining the merits of the decision. In *Council of the Civil Service Unions* v *Minister for the Civil Service* [1985], Lord Diplock described irrationality in terms of a decision which is so outrageous in its defiance of logic or accepted moral standards that no sensible person who had applied his mind to the question to be decided could have arrived at it.

Although this formulation is by no means perfect because it hints at a degree of mental incapacity, it does convey the notion of an abuse of power on the part of the decision-maker. It is necessary to establish such an abuse of power in judicial review proceedings.

The courts assume that certain principles apply to the exercise of all powers, even where a decision-maker is invested with a wide discretion. They take the view that the discretion is to be exercised according to these principles unless an Act of Parliament clearly indicates to the contrary. The governing principle is the rule of law. This encompasses the principle of legal certainty and the principle of equality. The essence of legal certainty is that legitimate expectations in the substantive sense (as distinct from the procedural sense) are to be upheld. An example of this can be seen in the case *R v North and East Devon Health Authority ex p. Coughlan (Secretary of State for Health and another intervening)* [2000]. The applicant was a patient at an NHS hospital for the chronically sick and disabled that was administered by the Exeter Health Authority, the predecessor of the appellant health authority. In 1993, the applicant and seven other similarly disabled patients were moved with their agreement to Mardon House, a purpose-built NHS facility, after receiving assurances from Exeter Health Authority that they could live there for as long as they wished. However, five years later the health authority decided to close Mardon House and to transfer responsibility for the applicant's care to a local authority social services department. In arriving at its decision, the health authority relied on a policy statement in which it had classified the type of nursing care required by the applicant as standard nursing care. The classification was apparently based on NHS policy guidance which distinguished between general nursing care (to be provided by local authorities as a social service for which the patient paid according to means) and specialist nursing services which were to be provided free by the NHS. When the applicant applied for judicial review of the decision to close Mardon House, the judge ruled that the health authority was bound by the assurances given previously by the Exeter Health Authority.

In his ruling he held that both general and specialist nursing care were the sole responsibility of the health authorities and therefore granted the application and quashed the decision of the Exeter Health Authority. The health authority appealed and the Secretary of State for Health intervened because he was concerned by the judge's decision that both general and specialist nursing care were the sole responsibility of the NHS. The Court of Appeal therefore had to consider the duties of the Secretary of State under the National Health Act 1977 ss 1 and 3 in respect of the provision of health services and a local authority's powers under the National Assistance Act 1948 s. 21 to provide accommodation for persons who were in need of care and attention.

The Court of Appeal held that although the Secretary of State was entitled to exclude some nursing care from the nursing services provided by the NHS, the health authority's criteria of eligibility were flawed. In addition, the court ruled that the disabilities of the applicant and her fellow patients went far beyond the scope of local authority services and that the error made by the health authority called into question the closure decision. The assurances given by the health authority had induced a legitimate expectation of a substantive benefit, the negation of it would be so unfair as to amount to an abuse of power. It is also interesting to note that the Court of Appeal stated that, in revoking its promise, the health authority had infringed the applicant's rights under Article 8 of the European Convention on Human Rights and Fundamental Freedoms to respect for her home.

Not every statement by a public official will give rise to a legitimate expectation that will be upheld by the courts, especially where it has been given on the basis of misleading information provided by or on behalf of the applicant. In *R v Inland Revenue Commissioners ex p. Matrix Securities Ltd* [1994] the applicant sought a declaration that the Inland Revenue Commissioners were not entitled to revoke a clearance that had been given at a local level after the Court of Appeal had refused to grant such a declaration. The applicant's solicitor had given information that was inaccurate and misleading to a tax inspector. On the basis of the information received, the inspector gave an assurance, on which the applicant sought to rely regarding the acceptability to the Revenue of a certain tax avoidance scheme. The House of Lords held that the Revenue was entitled to withdraw the clearance that it had given.

The principle of equality embraces formal equality and substantive equality. The former simply requires that public officials apply the law in an even-handed way. Thus persons similarly situated will be treated equally. Substantive equality is concerned more with non-discrimination and is closely associated with the notion of equality as a general principle of EU law. An example of formal equality arose in *R v Port Talbot B.C. and others ex p. Jones* [1988], where a local councillor applied to the council for a house. The Divisional Court held that the preferential allocation of a council house to a councillor with a view to putting her in a better position to contest a local election in her own ward was an abuse of power because it was unfair to others on the housing list. It is also an example of a decision based on irrelevant considerations. The courts have also declared invalid instances of substantive inequality. In *James v Eastleigh Borough Council* [1990] the House of Lords held that the adoption by a local authority of the statutory pensionable ages (then 65 for men and 60 for women) as the qualification for free admission to a leisure centre was a breach of the statutory prohibition against sex discrimination.

It is essential that administrative decisions should not be tainted with impropriety of any kind. In *Victoria Square Property Co. Ltd* v *Southwark LBC* [1978] the owners of a house let the house to a tenant under an agreement pursuant to the Housing Act 1957. The local authority was not satisfied that it was suitable for human habitation and served a notice on the owners requiring an extensive schedule of repairs and renovations to bring it up to the required standard. The owners appealed against the notice contending that the house could not be rendered fit for human habitation at reasonable expense. A county court judge allowed the appeal and quashed the notice. The local authority then decided to compulsorily purchase the property and execute the necessary work. It therefore made a compulsory purchase order but then realised that it had not obtained an express finding from the county court judge that the house was not capable of being rendered fit for human habitation at reasonable expense. This was an essential precondition to accompany the compulsory purchase order. When the judge refused to make such an order, the local authority realised that the minister could not confirm the compulsory purchase order and so it attempted to achieve its aim by another route. It served notice on the owners specifying a time and place when it would consider the condition of the property and any offer that the owners might wish to submit in connection with the work. The owners did not submit a notice of intention to execute work but offered a formal undertaking not to let the house until the local authority was satisfied that it had been rendered fit for human habitation. The local authority refused to accept this undertaking and served notice on the owners to purchase the property. The owners appealed and the judge found:

(a) the intention of the local authority on acquiring the house was to rehouse the existing tenant and render it fit for human habitation for a period of more than 30 years by carrying out not only the work specified in its notice but also extra work to bring it up to an even higher standard;

(b) that its reasons for wishing to acquire the house were to avoid the loss of residential accommodation and to ensure that it was occupied by a person on its waiting list;

(c) that the owners would suffer a financial loss if the local authority compulsorily purchased the house.

The judge ruled that the local authority had no statutory power to acquire the house to increase its existing stock of housing. The local authority then appealed to the Court of Appeal which held that although it could acquire property under the Housing Act 1957 s. 17(2) prior to demolition where its condition fell short of the standard set for human habitation, the subsection could not be stretched to cover an acquisition made with the intention of restoring the property for long-term occupation.

If inadequate weight has been attached to an important and relevant consideration by a decision-maker, the courts will be prepared to declare the administrative decision to be invalid, as can be illustrated by the case of *Glamorgan C.C.* v *Rafferty* [1987]. Under the Caravan Sites Act 1968 s. 6(1) the council was obliged to exercise its powers to provide adequate accommodation for gypsies residing or regularly resorting to its area. However, for more than 10 years the council had ignored its statutory duty to provide adequate accommodation for the gypsies in its area. On 16 September 1985, it resolved to commence proceedings to evict a number of gypsy families who were trespassing on a site in Neath owned by the council. On 2 October, a High Court judge made an order that enabled the council to recover possession of the site. A writ of possession was issued in November 1985 but was not served because a local solicitor interceded on behalf of the gypsy families. In December 1985 the order for possession was set aside by another High Court judge who directed that the council's claim for possession should proceed by way of a trial in the High Court on the basis that the council was in breach of its statutory duty to provide adequate accommodation. At this time one of the gypsies had applied for judicial review of the council's decision of 16 September 1985. The council then appealed against the order and the judgement given in judicial review proceedings. The Court of Appeal held that the council had not given adequate weight to the breach of its statutory duty and the consequences before proceeding to evict the gypsies. It therefore confirmed that the council's decision to evict should be quashed.

Taking into account irrelevant considerations will tend to bring about the same result as was illustrated by the decision in *R* v *Secretary of State for the Home Department ex p. Venables* [1997]. Venables and Thompson murdered a young child when they were both aged 10. The trial judge imposed the mandatory sentence provided by the Children and Young Persons Act 1933 s. 53(1) of detention during Her Majesty's pleasure. In his report to the Home Secretary the trial judge recommended that the penal element of their sentence should be set at 8 years. The Lord Chief Justice subsequently advised the Home Secretary that the penal element should be increased to 10 years. Having received this advice the Home Secretary, acting pursuant to his discretion under the Criminal Justice Act 1991 s. 35 and a policy statement of 27 July 1993, deliberated over the penal element of the sentence and ultimately decided that it should be increased to 15 years. In a letter announcing his decision, he stated that he had taken account of the widespread public concern about the case which was evidenced by petitions and other correspondence that he had received. At the time there was an intense media campaign in the popular press urging that the applicants should be detained for life. In an application for judicial review by the boys, the Divisional Court quashed the Home Secretary's decision who then appealed to the Court of Appeal but without success. The House of Lords then heard a final appeal from the Home Secretary and a cross-appeal from the boys in relation to the imposition of the penal element. In a long and detailed judgement their Lordship's held, among other things, that the Home Secretary ought not to have taken account of the public protests in fixing the penal element of the sentence. Accordingly, he had misdirected himself in giving weight to irrelevant considerations which influenced his decision to the detriment of the applicants.

If there is no evidence for a finding on which an administrative decision depends or where the evidence cannot be regarded as supporting a finding of fact, there will be a basis for impugning the decision. Official decisions may be invalidated by the courts on grounds of irrationality or unreasonableness if they are unduly oppressive because they subject an individual to excessive hardship. In *R* v *Hillingdon LBC ex p. Royco Homes Ltd* [1974] the applicants were granted outline planning permission for the construction of seven blocks of three-storey flats within the borough subject to certain conditions. Conditions 4 and 5 required that the dwellings built should be occupied by persons on the local authority's housing list for a guaranteed period of 10 years. This effectively required the company to assume, at its own expense, part of the local authority's housing obligations as a housing authority. The Divisional Court took the view that these conditions were quite unreasonable and the grant of planning permission embodying them was quashed.

In general, even though it is pleaded more often than the other grounds for judicial review, it is more difficult for an applicant to challenge an official act or decision on the basis of irrationality.

10. Proportionality

Both the European Court of Justice and the European Court of Human Rights recognise proportionality as a general principle of law. In the European context there are two aspects to be considered:

(a) the balancing test

(b) the necessity test.

The balancing test requires a balancing of the ends to be achieved by an official decision and the means adopted to achieve them. An application of this balancing test has already been considered in Chapter 7 in Case 114/76 *Bela-Muhle Josef Bergmann KG* v *Grows-Farm GmbH & Co. KG* [1977] where an action was brought to impugn the validity of a Community regulation which sought to reduce the vast stocks of skimmed milk powder by turning it into animal feed. The price at which the intervention agencies sold the milk powder for conversion into animal feed was more than three times that of alternative animal feedstuffs with similar nutritional value which imposed a disproportionate burden on farmers who were required to purchase it. The ECJ ruled that the regulation was null and void.

Where a particular objective can be achieved by more than one means, the necessity test requires that the least harmful of these should be adopted to achieve a particular objective. Proportionality has long been applied in English administrative law under the guise of what has become known as 'Wednesbury reasonableness', or irrationality or abuse of power. In relation to (a) above, in *R* v *Secretary of State for Transport ex p. Pegasus Holidays (London) Ltd and Airbro (UK) Ltd* [1988], proportionality was employed to test the government's suspension of the permits of Romanian pilots who were flying aircraft for the applicant travel company. In relation to (b) above, in *Hall & Co. Ltd* v *Shoreham by Sea UDC* [1964] the plaintiffs were the owners and occupiers of land that lay between the main Brighton road and the estuary of the River Adur that was suitable for industrial development. They therefore sought planning permission from the council to develop the site. Permission was granted but it was made subject to a number of conditions, the last two of which were the subject of the application for judicial review. Condition 3 required that the plaintiffs construct a road over the entire frontage of their land at their own cost. They were also required to give free access along it to traffic from ancillary roads. Condition 4 stated that the access referred to in condition 3 would be for a period of five years but may be ended when there was an alternative access to the main Brighton road. The council would then be obliged to maintain the road at public expense once it was opened. The plaintiffs challenged the validity of the conditions imposed because the council would obtain the benefit of having the road constructed for it at the plaintiffs' expense and would not have to pay compensation to them for the land used when it took over the responsibility of the road. The Court of Appeal held that the grant of planning permission was *ultra vires* and therefore void. It was not necessary for the local authority to impose such onerous conditions in granting planning permission because it could in fact achieve its aims in relation to a road widening scheme by using its powers of compulsory purchase and paying compensation to the plaintiffs for the land that was used.

Where the courts in England and Wales apply directly effective EU law embodied in a Treaty provision or in a regulation, the general principle of proportionality may be invoked to challenge official action in appropriate cases on the basis that it has been disproportionate.

11. Procedure: making an application

The Lord Chancellor appointed a committee under the chairmanship of Sir Jeffery Bowman with instructions to undertake a review of the operation of the procedure for the Crown Office list at the High Court in relation to applications for judicial review. The committee reported in March 2000 and new rules of procedure were laid before Parliament on 2 August which came into effect on 2 October 2000. The Crown Office list has since become the Administrative Court list. Unfortunately the new rules do not implement all the recommendations of the Bowman Report. Applications for judicial review are now referred to as claims for judicial review and are governed by the Civil Procedure Rules Part 8 as modified by a new Part 54 and supplemented by Practice Direction 54. A claimant in judicial review proceedings is expected to give prior warning of a claim to the party who would be the defendant. The defendant too is required to display a considerable degree of openness when dealing with the claimant. If the claimant does not at least communicate by letter with the defendant prior to the commencement of proceedings, the defendant is likely to raise this omission if the case is resolved without a hearing when costs are considered. Moreover, failure to communicate by letter might result in a 'wasted costs' order being made against the lawyer acting for the claimant. A claimant must still obtain permission from the Administrative Court to proceed by submitting:

(a) a claim form (form N461)

(b) written evidence in support of the claim

(c) a copy of any order that the claimant wishes to have quashed

(d) an approved copy of the reasons for reaching the decision where the claim relates to a decision of an inferior court or tribunal

(e) copies of any documents on which the claimant intends to rely

(f) copies of any relevant statutory material

(g) a list of essential documents for advance reading by the court.

If the claimant seeks to raise an issue under the Human Rights Act 1998 or seeks a remedy under that legislation, the claim form must include the information required by Practice Direction 16 para. 16 (Statements of Case).

There is a general requirement that all claims for judicial review are made promptly. This means that an application must normally be made within three months of the date when the basis for the application arose. All pending applications are placed on the Administrative Court list and are usually considered by a single judge from a specially nominated group of High Court judges, of whom there are currently 25. The requirement that the claimant must first obtain permission operates as a filtering device in that spurious and frivolous applications can be eliminated. All claimants are required to display the utmost good faith because the permission to proceed will be revoked if there has been any misrepresentation or concealment of material facts. The first hurdle that the claimant must surmount is to show that he/she has the required 'standing' which is sometimes referred to as *locus standi*. The Supreme Court Act 1981 s. 31(3) provides that a claimant who has sufficient interest in the matter to which the application relates should be accorded standing. In the *Inland Revenue Commissioners* v *National Federation of Self Employed and Small Businesses* [1982] the majority of the House of Lords took the view that standing should no longer be seen as a preliminary issue or a threshold issue. The Federation wanted to challenge the validity of a tax amnesty granted to casual workers who had worked in newspaper production in Fleet Street. Their Lordships indicated that any applicant who approaches the court with what appears to be a convincing legal argument to the effect that a national or local governmental body has committed an illegal act should expect to be granted permission even if he/she had only a remote personal interest in the matter. On the facts of this particular case, the House of Lords unanimously decided that the Federation did not have standing in the case because their Lordships considered that the Inland Revenue Commissioners (IRC) were within the ambit of their statutory discretion and that in any event the relationship between the IRC and individual taxpayers was confidential.

In the past, the courts have not always shown themselves to be sympathetic to actions initiated by interest groups. In *R* v *Secretary of State for the Environment ex p. Rose Theatre Trust* [1990] property developers were granted planning permission to erect an office block on a site where, in the course of preliminary work, the remains of the old Rose Theatre were discovered. Two of Shakespeare's plays were premiered there and it was the venue for most of Marlowe's plays. A group of distinguished archaeologists and thespians formed a company to campaign for the preservation of the archaeological remains and the company applied to the Secretary of State to have the site included in the schedule of monuments maintained by him under the Ancient Monuments and Archaeological Areas Act 1979 s. 1(1). Although the Secretary of State agreed that the archaeological remains were of national importance, he declined to schedule the site as requested, not least because it was being preserved and protected voluntarily. In giving his judgement, Schieman J denied that the company had 'sufficient interest' to be accorded the necessary standing. Since then the courts have been more sympathetic to applications for judicial review brought by interest groups. As has been seen, an application by an interest group was allowed to proceed in *R* v *Secretary of State for Foreign Affairs ex p. World Development Movement Ltd.*

The usual grounds for refusal of an application is that the claimant has not taken a more appropriate route to pursue his/her grievance. For example, the 'case stated procedure' is the most suitable method for appealing from an administrative decision of magistrates. In addition, the Administrative Court imposes a more stringent test when considering applications for judicial review in relation to decisions on immigration, homelessness and child protection. It is aware that allowing challenges to these types of decision by way of judicial review is detrimental to good public administration. The application takes the form of a full statement that identifies the applicant and sets out the relief sought. It is necessary to set out the facts and the legal grounds for challenge supported by precedent and statute law. According to Practice Direction 54 the question of permission will usually be considered without an oral hearing. If the initial application is refused, this refusal can be challenged before the Court of Appeal under the Supreme Court Act 1981 ss 16 and 18 but it is necessary for the applicant to obtain permission to do so from the Court of Appeal or from the Administrative Court. If the Court of Appeal should refuse the application there cannot be a further appeal to the House of Lords. See *R* v *Secretary of State for Trade and Industry ex p. Eastway* [2001]. Even if permission to proceed is granted, the respondent may apply to have the permission revoked on the grounds that the application discloses no arguable case or because there has not been full and frank disclosure of all the material facts and relevant law. All such applications are examined carefully because they tend to be regarded unfavourably.

Once permission has been granted, the substantive application is commenced by serving the order granting permission on the defendant and on all persons directly affected who filed an acknowledgement of service. Any of those persons who wish to contest the claim (or support it on additional grounds) must do so within 35 days following service of the permission file. They must serve the detailed grounds for contesting (or supporting) together with their written evidence. It should be noted that permission to proceed with a judicial review is permission to proceed on specified grounds only since the claimant will not be permitted to rely on other grounds without the consent of the court. The full hearing of the claim will often be heard before a single High Court judge or, where the Administrative Court Office requires, before the Administrative Court comprising two High Court judges. In very important cases, the court may comprise three High Court judges. Criminal matters are always referred to a Divisional Court. In general, the parties are not cross-examined although the court does have the discretion to order cross-examination where there is a conflict of evidence or where the applicant alleges that a precondition to the making of a decision did not exist. If the facts are agreed, the court will be concerned only with the inferences that can be drawn from them and the legal consequences that follow.

12. Appeals

There can be an appeal from a decision of the Administrative Court. The rules relating to appeals differ depending on whether the matter is civil or criminal. In a criminal matter an appeal can be made to the House of Lords where the provisions of the Administration of Justice Act 1960 s. 1 are satisfied. These are as follows:

(a) The Administrative Court certifies that a point of law of general public importance is involved.

(b) Either the Administrative Court or House of Lords gives permission.

In civil matters, permission is required to appeal to the Court of Appeal except in proceedings arising from a decision made pursuant to the Immigration Act 1971, the British Nationality Act 1981, the Asylum and Immigration Appeals Act 1993 or any other decision relating to nationality or immigration. Unless permission to appeal has been granted, a valid notice of appeal cannot be served.

13. Remedies

The powers of the superior courts to grant remedies are contained in the Supreme Court Act 1981 s. 31. Even before the hearing of the substantive claim, a claimant may ask the court to grant an interim remedy. This could take one of two forms:

(a) An interim injunction to preserve the *status quo* prior to the conclusion of the full hearing or a stay of proceedings to prevent the public body (or official) from continuing with its disputed conduct when the remedy sought is one or more of the prerogative orders.

(b) An interim declaration to prevent some imminent danger to himself or his property.

These interim remedies will be granted only at the discretion of the court.

If the applicant is successful at the conclusion of the substantive hearing, the court will consider the remedy or remedies sought in the claim. It is usual for an applicant to ask for one or more of the prerogative orders, but he/she may have asked for an injunction in final form and/or a declaration. In its 1994 report *Administrative Law: Judicial review and statutory appeals*, the Law Commission recommended that the prerogative orders should be renamed, and this finally occurred in 2000. They are now known as mandatory orders, quashing orders and prohibiting orders. A court may grant these individually or in combination but they are always granted at the discretion of the court.

If, prior to submitting a claim for judicial review, the applicant requested a public body (or official) to perform a duty imposed by law, the court can make a mandatory order requiring that the duty be performed. A mandatory order is also appropriate to require a tribunal to 'state a case' and give reasons for its decision where this is required by statute. Applicants often apply for a quashing order and a prohibiting order at the same time. The quashing order operates to nullify the decision that has been impugned and the prohibiting order operates to prevent the body in question from exceeding its jurisdiction.

In many ways, injunctions and declaratory judgements are more flexible forms of relief and can be granted in those situations where the prerogative orders are available if the court considers it just and convenient. The jurisdiction of the High Court to grant injunctions in judicial review cases is to be found in the Supreme Court Act 1981 s. 31(2). The court may do so taking into account:

(a) the nature of the matters in respect of which relief may be granted by prerogative orders

(b) the nature of the persons and bodies against whom the relief may be granted by such orders

(c) the other circumstances of the case.

Injunctions, whether interim or in final form, may be either mandatory, requiring an act to be done, or prohibitory, requiring the addressee to refrain from acting in a certain way. In final form they may be granted for a fixed period with permission granted to apply for an extension. Alternatively, they may be granted for an indefinite period with provision for subsequent termination.

A declaration at the conclusion of the substantive hearing is simply a formal statement by the court of the legal position and the respective rights of the parties. It does not contain any order that can be enforced against the respondent.

14. Liability in tort

In general, public officials and bodies that fail to act in accordance with the principles considered in this chapter when exercising their discretion do not commit a tort such that they would be liable at common law to pay damages. Moreover, the careless performance of a statutory duty does not itself give rise to any cause of action unless there is a right of action for breach of statutory duty or a situation exists where a common law duty of care arises in the tort of negligence. In relation to negligence claims at common law, many of the powers and duties conferred on departments of national and local government involve a substantial policy component and for this reason it is difficult for the courts to establish whether a duty of care arises in the first place and, if it does, the standard of care required. The High Court does, nevertheless, have power under the Supreme Court Act 1981 s. 31(4) to award damages in judicial review proceedings where appropriate, but it will usually deal with the public law issues first. If the applicant's claim is successful, the claim for damages will be considered at a separate hearing. Such claims are often for financial loss only (referred to in legal parlance as economic loss) and the courts are usually reluctant to award damages for economic loss unless there is a contractual relationship. Whether there is a cause of action capable of giving rise to a claim for damages very much depends on the facts of the particular case.

A public official or public body could incur liability in the tort of 'misfeasance in public office' where the official or public body acts/decides or refrains from acting/deciding but is activated by malice towards the applicant. Alternatively it may arise if the actor/decision-maker knows that his/her act or omission or decision is unlawful and the result is that the applicant is deprived of a benefit or suffers loss. Thus, if a decision-maker takes account of irrelevant matters he/she could be liable in damages for the tort of misfeasance in public office provided that it can be established that the act was done maliciously or he/she knew that he/she was acting unlawfully. Apart from the personal liability of the individual, the public authority may be liable (through the doctrine of vicarious liability) for officials who commit the tort. There have been few successful claims and magistrates and those exercising judicial functions normally have immunity from actions in tort.

Some statutes (for example, Highways Act 1980) specifically create a right of action for breach of statutory duty for which damages can be claimed. In the absence of a clear, express statutory provision the courts are reduced to drawing an inference whether it was intended that there should be a right of action. This is made all the more difficult by the fact that most statutory duties in the area of public administration are owed not to individuals but to the public at large. In such cases the courts are unlikely to conclude that there is a private right of action. Procedural impropriety does not automatically give rise to the tort of breach of statutory duty or misfeasance in public office. A statement of a public official might create a legitimate expectation and thereby give rise to a claim in damages for negligent misstatement but only if the statement transpires to be untrue and was given in response to a specific request. Excessive delay by a public body in making a decision may occasionally give rise to a claim in the tort of negligence but it will be essential for the court to be able to infer a duty of care from the facts of the case.

Where, in a claim for judicial review, the court is prepared to admit a claim for compensation on the basis of a right of action in tort, damages will be assessed to place the applicant as nearly as possible in the position he/she would have been in had the tort not been committed.

Progress test

1. What is the purpose of judicial review of administrative action?

2. Have the exceptions to the rule in *O'Reilly* v *Mackman* effectively destroyed the rule?

3. In what circumstances may an official act or decision be challenged on the grounds of illegality?

4. In what circumstances will the courts accept that there must be delegation of the exercise of a discretionary power?

5. What do you understand by the 'rule against bias'?

6. In relation to procedural fairness, when may the courts infer that a fair hearing is necessary?

7. In what circumstances may a public body or official be required to give reasons for an act or decision?

8. When may an official act or decision be challenged in the courts on the basis that it is irrational or unreasonable?

9. What do you understand by the term 'proportionality' in the context of a claim for judicial review?

10. What is meant by 'standing' in the context of a claim for judicial review, and what test is applied?

11. What are the prerogative orders? Are these remedies available as of right?

12. What are the conditions of liability for the tort of misfeasance in public office and what remedy, if any, is available?

Further reading

Books

Craig, P. (1999) *Administrative Law* (London: Sweet & Maxwell).

De Smith, S.R. Brazier (1998) *Constitutional and Administrative Law* (Harmondsworth: Penguin, chapters 28–30).

Loveland, I. (2000) *Constitutional Law: A critical introduction* (London: Butterworths, chapters 14–17).

Parpworth, N. (2000) *Constitutional and Administrative Law* (London: Butterworths, chapters 12–14).

Wade, H.W.R. and C.F. Forysth (2000) *Administrative Law* (Oxford: Oxford University Press).

Woolf, Lord, Jowell, J. and A.P. Le Sueur (1999) *Principles of Judicial Review* (London: Sweet & Maxwell).

Articles

Cornford, T. and M. Sunkin (2001) 'The Bowman Report, access and the recent reforms of judicial review procedure', *Public Law* Spring.

Fordham, M. (2001) 'Judicial review: the new rules', *Public Law* Spring.

Useful website

A summary of the recommendations of the Bowman Committee can be found at www.Open.gov.uk/lcd/civil/bowman2000/bowman2000Fr.htm

16

Law reform and the Law Commission

1. Introduction

In terms of the functional analysis of law put forward by the American jurist Karl Llewellyn, the law and its administration must always be in a state of continual evolution to prevent social implosion and economic retardation. The truth of this proposition is well demonstrated by two periods of particularly rapid change in the history of the UK. The period of almost breakneck industrialisation from 1786 to 1875 was one of unprecedented upheaval. In 1750 the economy was still largely agricultural and the combined population of England and Wales hovered steadily around the 6 million mark. The manufacturing sector was comparatively small and was largely craft based. Overseas trade was also on a relatively minor scale. By 1811 the population of England and Wales had more than doubled, and by the time of the 1851 census it had reached 18 million. The factory system of production was well established by the end of the eighteenth century and continued to extend itself into newer industries during the nineteenth. The drift of population from the countryside to the new industrial towns was well under way by the first decade in the nineteenth century and was set to continue apace. Overseas trade almost doubled between 1750 and 1800, from £22 million to £42 million. London became the hub of this vast colonial empire with its banking, insurance and control over shipping. This massive transformation in national life generated the pressure for a thorough reform of all the institutions of the state. Parliament was reformed in 1832 after a campaign of popular agitation to make it more representative of the newer centres of population. The new manufacturing interests were represented in Parliament for the first time through the redistribution of seats in the House of Commons, and male members of the new industrial middle class were given the vote. The long ascendancy of the House of Lord's chamber at Westminster could now be challenged and further reforms of the franchise were to follow, as were reforms in local government and in the civil service. The reforms of the law and its administration from 1850 to 1875 have already been outlined in Chapter 4.

A second period of rapid change has occurred since 1945. Prior to 1939, the UK was a great world power and the Westminster Parliament legislated not only for the UK but also for its extensive colonial empire. After 1945, most of the former colonies gained their independence, although a few very small former colonies remain linked to the UK as dependent territories. Since 1945 the UK has become a 'welfare state' and government has become more involved in the active management of the economy. As indicated in Chapter 5, there has been constitutional change too. The major political parties have long accepted the political philosophy of 'pluralism' as UK society has become multi-ethnic and multicultural. Such rapid change has subjected existing institutions to stresses and strains and the law and legal system have struggled to keep pace with the rate of change. At the beginning of the third millennium it would seem that the future of the UK is closely bound up with the future of the European Union in which it is just one of fifteen member states and it is not even the largest economy.

Until the mid-1960s the approach of successive governments to the need for law reform was not at all systematic. The nineteenth century practice of setting up Royal Commissions to investigate and report on pressing problems of the day was continued into the twentieth century. This hardly represents a systematic approach to the problem of law reform. Two part-time committees were then established to deal with the more technical aspects of the civil and criminal law respectively that were considered to be in need of reform. This chapter deals briefly with these before moving on to consider the role and work of the Law Commission.

2. Royal Commissions

The Royal Commission, as an independent advisory committee to government, was completely revamped in the 1830s with the emergence of social scientific techniques of inquiry. It has since proved to be a popular method, used by successive governments, for dealing with particularly pressing problems. The nomenclature 'Royal' derives from the fact that the Commission is established by Royal Warrant addressed to the Commissioners themselves. It is a convenient piece of make-believe that the appointments appear to be made by the Queen, but the reality is that they are made by the government of the day and confirmed by the Queen. Examples include: the Royal Commission chaired by Lord Beeching that resulted in the Courts Act 1971 (establishing the Crown Court) and the Royal Commission on Criminal

Procedure 1980 which resulted in the enactment of the Police and Criminal Evidence Act 1984 and the establishment of the Crown Prosecution Service. The Royal Commission chaired by Sir Henry Benson on the provision of legal services proved to be something of a disappointment in that it did not result in a radical change in the existing working practices of the legal profession. In 1991 a Royal Commission on criminal justice was established to consider reforms to the criminal law arising from certain highly publicised miscarriages of justice such as those of the 'Guildford four', the 'Birmingham six' and the Judith Ward case. Its recommendations found expression in the Criminal Justice Act 1993. Although a Royal Commission can call upon the resources and expertise of a wide range of people in public life and from the learned professions to collect evidence and produce an authoritative report, there is no guarantee that the government of the day will heed the recommendations contained therein and it is certainly not obliged to do so. Once the Commission has reported it is disbanded and its personnel revert to their former activities and occupations. Therefore, by its nature it is not a very suitable means for dealing with the need for comprehensive ongoing law reform, yet the Royal Commission is still likely to be used by governments in the twenty-first century if only for political reasons to demonstrate that 'something is being done' about a particular problem.

3. The Law Reform Committee

The Law Reform Committee was initially established in 1934 by Lord Sankey (then Lord Chancellor) as the Law Revision Committee. It was revived in 1952 by Lord Simonds and renamed the Law Reform Committee. The Committee comprised six judges, three professors of law, two QCs and two solicitors. Its secretariat was provided by the Lord Chancellor's Department but it had no research facilities. Its terms of reference were

> to consider, having regard especially to judicial decisions, what changes are desirable in such legal doctrines as the Lord Chancellor may from time to time refer to the Committee.

Its ability to put forward proposals for changes to the civil law was therefore restricted to proposals received from the Lord Chancellor. Since all members of the Committee had other full-time occupations and responsibilities, the Committee functioned only on a part-time basis and therefore its contribution to law reform was on a very small scale. It is now defunct. However, some of its notable achievements were the Law Reform (Frustrated Contracts) Act 1943 and the Occupiers' Liability Act 1957.

4. The Criminal Law Revision Committee

The Criminal Law Revision Committee was established in 1959 by the Home Secretary, Mr Butler, and was the equivalent, in the sphere of the criminal law, of the Law Reform Committee. It too functioned as a part-time body that met at the request of the Home Secretary – on average 10 times a year. In its time it did produce a number of controversial reports, some of which resulted in new statute law such as the Theft Act 1968 and later the Theft Act 1978, but it is now defunct.

5. The Law Commission

Traditionally, particular government departments have assumed responsibility for certain branches of the law but they were usually preoccupied with new legislative initiatives rather than with the need to reform the existing law. For example, the Department of Trade and Industry has long considered itself to be responsible for company and commercial law. The Home Office has considered itself responsible for the criminal law and for aspects of the criminal justice system. The case for a permanent, full-time statutory law reform body was made cogently in a book entitled *Law Reform NOW* edited by Gerald Gardiner QC and Andrew Martin which appeared in 1963. The 1960s was an era during which there was a widespread desire for a break with the past and a desire for innovation. The book was largely a response to the authors' perceived inaction on the part of government to the pressing need for law reform. The proposal put forward by Gerald Gardiner QC and Andrew Martin was inspired by the work of the New York Law Revision Commission which had been established in the 1930s. In 1964, Gerald Gardiner became Lord Chancellor in Harold Wilson's first Labour government and it is reported that he agreed to accept the post only on condition that the incoming government would establish a Law Commission for the UK. In due course the government published a White Paper entitled *Proposals for English and Scottish Law Commissions* which subsequently resulted in the enactment of the Law Commissions Act 1965.

6. Personnel of the Law Commission

Each Law Commission (one for Scotland and one for England and Wales) consists of five commissioners who are appointed by the Lord Chancellor for a period of five years initially. The chair is always a High Court judge and there is usually one barrister and one solicitor together with two university academics. The work of the Commission is supported by about 15 civil servants from the government's legal service and by some personnel from the Office of Parliamentary Counsel to the Treasury on two-year second-ments. The Law Commission advertises annually for between 10 and 12 well qualified graduates to work as full-time research assistants to research in the areas of common law, company and commercial law, criminal law, property and trust law, and statute law revision. Employment has been offered initially for a year with the possibility of an extension to a maximum of two years.

7. The statutory remit of the Law Commission

The Law Commissions Act 1965 s. 3(1) states:

> It shall be the duty of each of the Commissions to take and keep under review all the law with which they are respectively concerned with a view to its systematic development and reform, including in particular the codification of such law, the elimination of anomalies, the repeal of obsolete and unnecessary enactments, the reduction of the number of separate enactments and generally the simplification and modernisation of the law, and for that purpose –
> (a) to receive and consider any proposals for the reform of the law which may be made or referred to them;
> (b) to prepare and submit to the Minister from time to time programmes for the examination of different branches of the law with a view to reform, including recommendations as to the agency (whether the Commission or another body) by which any such examination should be carried out;
> (c) to undertake, pursuant to any such recommendations approved by the Minister, the examination of particular branches of the law and the formulation, by means of draft Bills or otherwise, of proposals for reform therein;
> (d) to prepare from time to time at the request of the Minister comprehensive programmes of consolidation and statute law revision, and to undertake the preparation of draft Bills pursuant to any such programme approved by the Minister;
> (e) to provide advice and information to government departments and other authorities or bodies concerned at the instance of the Government with proposals for the reform or amendment of any branch of the law;
> (f) to obtain such information as to the legal systems of other countries as appears to the Commissioners likely to facilitate the performance of any of their functions.

The Commission has the statutory right to put forward proposals for law reform which it does in the form of programmes. However, these proposals must be approved beforehand. Thus, the government of the day can exercise a veto on any proposal, although it has done so on only a few occasions since 1965. To date, the Lord Chancellor has laid seven of its programmes for law reform before Parliament, in 1965, 1968, 1973, 1989 (two programmes), 1995 and 1999. The inclusion of an item in a programme does not guarantee that the reform proposals can be successfully carried through, and in any event the programmes have not been slavishly adhered to in the past by the commissioners. The published programmes have really been declarations of intent.

8. Methods of working

At any particular point in time the Commission is likely to be engaged on between 20 and 30 law reform projects. A project normally commences with a study of the particular area of law in order to identify defects and anomalies. The Commission then consults extensively by issuing one its consultation papers (working papers) which describes the present law and its shortcomings and sets out possible reforms. According to the Seventh Programme, its initial proposals are based on:

> thorough and thoughtful research and analysis of case law, legislation, academic and other writing, law reports and other relevant sources of information both in the United Kingdom and overseas. Its preliminary research seeks to establish the existing legal position here and, if appropriate, in comparable jurisdictions. It highlights the current short comings and considers ways in which other juris-dictions have tried to overcome them and ways in which commentators have suggested overcoming them. Most usually we look to the law of other jurisdic-tions and we often gain considerable assistance from the reports of their Law Commissions.

The consultation process itself covers a wide range of people and groups. It includes the legal and other professions, members of special-interest groups, businesspeople, consumer groups, central and local government, and even the public at large. Its consultation documents are available on the Internet and it is making use of its website to elicit opinions from interested members of the public via e-mail. Where a Commission proposal is likely to have significant social or economic repercussions, the Commission may use empirical research of a social scientific nature to underpin its work. For example, during 1999, research was commissioned in the areas of non-pecuniary loss in personal injury cases which subsequently formed the basis of the Commission's report. It was this report that led to the landmark ruling by the Court of Appeal in *Heil* v *Rankin* [2000] that has resulted in an increase in the level of awards. The Law Commission also maintains links with university departments engaged in socio-legal research.

At the end of the consultation stage the Law Commission prepares a report for the Lord Chancellor which sets out its final conclusions and recommendations. At the end of this report there will usually be a draft Bill that can be introduced into Parliament if the Commission is proposing a change in the law. The subsequent fate of the Bill is largely in the hands of the government of the day. Its chances of being enacted depend on whether the government accepts the recommendations contained in the report. Although the Bill can be introduced in the House of Lords by the Lord Chancellor, it cannot be put forward for the Royal Assent unless the government is prepared to allow time for its stages in the House of Commons. Although a private member could, in theory, champion a Law Commission Bill, this not very likely to happen. Generally, private members usually prefer to support measures that are more newsworthy than law reform measures and, in any event, the government would still have to make space in the crowded parliamentary timetable.

9. The Seventh Programme and beyond

The Seventh Programme was published in June 1999 and was conceived as a rolling programme intended to cover the period April 1999 to March 2001. The 35th annual report (2000) gives an indication of the progress achieved up to March 2000, and the 36th annual report (publication April/May 2002) covers the period to the end of March 2001. Discussions were under way in March 2001 with government departments and others bodies on the work that should be undertaken to form part of the Eighth Programme of reform proposals. This will be published in the second half of 2001 following approval by the Lord Chancellor and should become available on the Commission's website.

10. An evaluation of the Law Commission

The Law Commission has accomplished a great deal since 1965. In the early years, a good deal of its time was taken up with identifying obsolete and unnecessary statutes relating to a bygone era that should have been repealed, although it did find time for other projects. It seems to have abandoned its early ambitious plans for a codification of the law of contract and the law relating to landlord and tenant. However, there remains an urgent need for the codification of the criminal law. In an article entitled 'Law reform: the shape of change' published in the *JSB Journal* in 1999, Mrs Justice Mary Arden (the outgoing chairman of the Law Commission) has stated that once the core areas of the substantive criminal law have been brought up to date it should be possible to consolidate all the relevant statute law into a single criminal code. In the same article she stated that over 70 per cent of the Commission's reports had been implemented either wholly or in part since 1965. According to the Commission's 34th annual report, this amounted to 102 of its reports. By implementation is meant that legislation has been enacted by Parliament. The 35th annual report states that two more statutes were enacted based on its reports, namely the Trustee Act 2000 and the

Powers of the Criminal Courts (Sentencing) Act 2000. Since 1965, the Law Commission had been responsible for some important pieces of legislation, including the Unfair Contract Terms Act 1977, the Children Act 1989, the Computer Misuse Act 1990, the Criminal Justice and Public Order Act 1994, the Family Law Act 1996 the Land Registration Act 1997, the Trustee Delegation Act 1999 and the Contracts (Rights of Third Parties) Act 1999. Its reports on corruption, involuntary manslaughter and business tenancies were broadly accepted by government in 2000 and legislation may be forthcoming. A ministerial committee has been established at the Lord Chancellor's Department to consider what can be done about the Commission's unimplemented reports where they have been accepted in principle by government.

It is clear that the Law Commission could achieve more if it were adequately resourced. The 35th annual report states that, from 1995, there was no increase in the funds allocated to the Commission via the Lord Chancellor's Department and that in financial year 2000/01 it received only a 2 per cent increase in its resources. The cost of the Commission in 2000 was just over £3.3 million. Although it makes much of its independence from government, the latter controls its purse strings via the Lord Chancellor's Department and thereby indirectly limits what it is able to achieve. That said, very little would have been achieved by way of law reform since 1965 without the dedicated work of the Law Commission.

Progress test

1. Is law reform necessary? If so why; if not, why not?

2. What contribution do Royal Commissions make to the process of law reform and what are the advantages and disadvantages of using this type of agency as a means of law reform?

3. How does the Law Commission differ from the other law reform agencies that preceded it?

4. Is the Law Commission truly independent? Does this matter?

5. Are the Commissioners appointed for far too short a period?

6. What do you consider to be the main problems facing the Law Commission?

7. Is there a case for increasing the size of the Law Commission's budget?

8. Has the Law Commission made a significant contribution to law reform in England and Wales?

Further reading

Books

Zander M. (1999) *The Law Making Process* (London: Butterworths, chapter 9).
Zellick, G. (ed.) (1988) *The Law Commission and Law Reform* (London: Sweet & Maxwell).

Articles

Cretney, S. (1985) 'The politics of law reform', *Modern Law Review* vol. 48, No. 5.
North, P. (1985) 'Law reform, processes and problems', *Law Quarterly Review* Vol. 101 (July), p. 338.

Useful websites

Useful up-to-date information on the work of the Law Commission can be obtained from its website at www.lawcom.gov.uk/ and copies of its Seventh Programme can be obtained from this source or from www.open.gov.uk/lawcomm/

PART FOUR

Legal skills

17

Legal skills 1

1. Introduction

The initial encounter with the law section of a university learning resources centre (LRC) can be a daunting and intimidating experience. Having read this chapter, you should be able to navigate about the law section to locate the material that you need in the shortest possible time. This is a useful transferable skill to acquire. Once you have learned how to navigate the law section in your own LRC, you will be able to find source material in other universities quickly because this material tends to be organised according to similar principles in all universities. You should always bear in mind that the staff in your own LRC are there to help students in difficulty and you should never be afraid to ask for assistance even if the person behind the desk looks formidable. It is quite likely that he/she will prove to be very helpful. If a member of staff of the LRC organises a special session for new undergraduates, you should endeavour to attend because you will pick up a great deal of helpful information, as well as, perhaps, a useful booklet on the particular features of the law collection and the online research facilities that are available to students.

In recent years, some excellent texts have been published on how to use a law library. Once you have read this chapter, you will have acquired most of the basic knowledge that you will need as a first-year undergraduate. These texts will give you far more detailed information and will be particularly helpful with research that you have to undertake if you are required to complete a dissertation or similar project as part of your course of studies. Two of these texts have been listed at the end of this chapter.

Apart from the various texts written by legal scholars and collections of legal periodicals (journals), the law collection at your university will contain three types of primary source material, namely law reports, statutes and subordinate legislation. You need to be able to access these original sources quickly.

2. Older law reports

So much of English law is case law and it will be necessary for you to look up the more important precedents in the branches of the law that you are currently studying. In Chapter 4 you will have read about the history of law reporting and will recall that, prior to 1865, law reporting was undertaken by individual barristers who published reports of varying quality. Only in the late eighteenth century were particular barristers appointed to record the decisions of the superior courts with some editorial assistance from the judiciary, but usually these reports were published under the name of the reporter. It is unlikely that you will have to venture further back in time than the nineteenth century but you may occasionally have to consult a report that was compiled in the seventeenth century or even earlier. For instance, the date of Pinnel's case is 1602 (published in a report by Chief Justice Coke) and it is still cited in all the standard student texts on the law of contract. If you are a student at one of the newer universities it is unlikely that you will have copies of the original editions of these reports, but fortunately most of the older cases are to be found in one of five collections:

The English Reports
The All England Law Reports Reprint series
The Revised Reports
The Law Journal Reports 1822–1949
The Law Times Reports (Old Series 1843–60) and (New Series 1859–1947).

The LRCs of most newer universities have the English Reports series and/or the All England Law Reports Reprint series where you will be able to find most of these old cases.

The English Reports usually have a distinctive pale olive green binding but some of the volumes may have been rebound in another colour if the original binding has become shabby. Each volume has the series title embossed in gold within an upended rectangle at the top of the spine and each is between 2.5 and 3.5 inches thick with the volume number underneath the series title within the rectangle. The volume numbers run from 1 to 176 together with the name of a court and names of the original reports or reporter in smaller print on the spine. Your tutors will usually ensure that you are given the full citation for all cases to which you are required to refer, but the citation is likely to be in its original form for these old cases, for example *Adams v Lindsell* (1818) 1 B. & Ald. 681. You can locate this case quickly in the English Reports (even without the citation given above) by consulting the index of case names in volumes 177–8. The crucial information for you is the volume number which appears in bold type and the page number next to it. Once you have these, you will be able to find the report of the case in this series. The entire series of the English Reports is available on CD-ROMs, and if your LRC has them, you will be able to access the relevant reports very quickly (especially if the CD-ROMs have been networked) and print off copies for you own use.

The All England Law Reports Reprint series is bound in dark blue buckram. This series covers a period from 1558 to 1935 and contains about five thousand cases. From 1843 the cases reprinted in this series are from reports that appeared originally in the Law Times Reports or Times Law Reports. The cases have been selected for reprint because they have been subsequently referred to in the All England Law Reports after 1935 and because they are mentioned in *Halsbury's Laws of England* (a type of legal encyclopaedia). Provided you know the year of the case, you should also be able to find it quickly in the All England Law Reports Reprint series because the dates appear on the spines of the various volumes embossed in gold. If you do not have the date, look for the name of the case in the alphabetical list of cases in the bound index which you should find on the shelf at the end of this series.

Most of the pre-1866 cases can be traced by using a bound publication known as *The Digest*, which is an encyclopaedia of case law in summary form. It is an easy publication to find because the volumes are hardbound in a deep red. The entire series comprises approximately seventy main volumes with a number of continuation volumes. In addition, it has a con-solidated table of cases and a consolidated index. The current edition is the third and is known as the Green Band Reissue after the green horizontal stripe on the spine. The four volumes comprising the consolidated table of cases give an alphabetical list of about 500,000 cases (not all of them Eng-lish) that are included in *The Digest*. The reference in bold print is to the volume in which a summary of the case will be found. You will probably find that there is a card mounted within a hard, clear plastic covering near the volumes that tells you how to use *The Digest*. It is important to note that the references in the consolidated table of cases are not to a page number but to *case numbers* in the appropriate volume. When you have located the case summary, you will find at least one other citation where the full text of the report is to be located. In order to discover the meaning of the various abbreviations that are used for the citations given, you should consult the table of abbreviations in the cumulative supplement.

3. Reports of the ICLREW

As stated in Chapter 4, the Council for Law Reporting for England and Wales (later to become the Incorporated Council) was established to produce authoritative law reports for legal practitioners and others. When it began publishing in 1866, it initially produced 11 separate series of reports, each covering a different superior court. These originally had calf leather bindings on the spines, with each volume embossed with the volume number and with the relevant year of Queen Victoria's reign. When the civil court structure was revamped in 1875, the number of separate series was reduced and it was reduced further after 1880.

The reports of appeals heard in the House of Lords and Privy Council respectively were published in separate volumes between 1866 and 1874. Thereafter a series officially entitled Appeal Cases commenced in 1875 and contains reports of appeals to both the House of Lords and Privy Council. The original bindings were in calf leather but it is likely that they will have been rebound since then in a light tan binding. Each of the early volumes covers two years of reports. The official citation that you will have been given for reports from 1875 to 1890 is such that the year appears enclosed in round brackets followed by the volume number of the report in the series. After that, the abbreviation App. Cas. appears followed by the page reference. An example would be the contract law case of *Adam* v *Newbigging* (1888) 13 App. Cas. 308. Only after 1891 did the year become part of the citation and it therefore appears in square brackets followed by the abbreviation AC and then the page number, for example *Baumwoll Manufacturers* v *Furness* [1893] AC 8.

Equity cases and Chancery Appeal cases appear first in a series dating from 1866 to 1875. Thereafter, the reports of the Chancery Division of the High Court appear as a separate series. The official citation has the year enclosed in round brackets followed by the volume number of the report in the series. After that, comes the abbreviation Ch. D. followed by the page number. An example is provided by the contract law case of *Arnison* v *Smith* (1899) 41 Ch. D. 348. Only after 1891 did the year become part of the citation. It appears in square brackets followed by the abbreviation Ch. and the page number, for example *Bonhote* v *Henderson* [1895] 1 Ch. 742.

From 1866 to 1875, reports of the cases of the Court of Crown Cases Reserved and the Court of Queen's Bench were each reported in separate series as were those of the Court of Common Pleas and the Court of Exchequer. These two latter series continued to be published separately until 1880, but after 1875 they were published as the reports of the Common Pleas Division and the Exchequer Division respectively. These may be in their original calf leather spine bindings but they have since been rebound in a material similar to those used for the Appeal Cases. The Incorporated Council has since reissued sets in light green bindings.

The Queen's Bench Division of the High Court was created in 1875. The series bearing this title appeared and for a time incorporated the reports of the Court for Crown Cases Reserved. From 1875 to 1890 the citations that you will have been given for the reports of the Queen's Bench Division at this time start with the year enclosed in round brackets followed by the volume number. After the abbreviation QBD comes the page number, for example *Canning* v *Farquhar* (1885) 16 QBD 722. As with the Appeal Cases and those of the Chancery Division, from 1891 the year became part of the citation and so it appears in square brackets thus: *Cullen* v *Knowles* [1898] 2 QB 380. The volumes in this series may be in their original calf leather spine bindings but they may have since been rebound using material similar to those used for the Appeal Cases but the series title will appear prominently on the spine.

From 1866 to 1875 there was a separate series of reports combining Admiralty with ecclesiastical cases and another series combining reports of probate and divorce cases. After 1875, with the reorganisation of the civil courts, these were all merged as the reports of the newly created Probate, Divorce and Admiralty Division of the High Court. From 1875 the citations for cases reported in this series commence with the year enclosed in round brackets followed by the volume number. The abbreviation PD for Probate Division is followed by the page number. When the year in which the cases was reported became part of the official citation in 1891 it began to appear in square brackets followed by the abbreviation PD and the page number, Following a further reorganisation in 1972, the Probate, Divorce and Admiralty Division became the Family Division. The former series ended and a new series of Family Law Reports came into being. The citation you will be given for this series will have the year in square brackets followed by the abbreviation FLR followed by the page number.

4. Modern reports of the ICLREW

The more recently published volumes of Law Reports series are often hard bound in a greyish brown scrim cloth which is very hard wearing. The Appeal Cases bear the words Law Reports, the year (and volume number if there is more than one) in black on the spine with the series title embossed in gold over a light tan horizontal stripe. In some LRC collections they may have light brown bindings. Those of the Chancery Division are easily identified because the series title is embossed in gold over a red horizontal stripe, but in some LRC collections they may appear in bright red bindings. The horizontal stripe for the Queen's Bench Division is green, as is that of the Family Division series. The reports of the Queen's Bench Division often extend to two volumes because they contain reports of appeals heard by the Court of Appeal, and in some LRC collections they may appear in green bindings. You will find indexes for the Law Reports series nearby covering ten-year spans commencing with the period 1951–60 in hard red bindings.

5. Other law reports

Apart from the All England Law Reports, you will find that some commercial and shipping cases are only reported in a series known as Lloyd's Law Reports. Like the bound volumes of the Weekly Law Reports, these are hardbound in black with gold blocking on the spine indicating the series title, the year and volume number. This series started in 1952 as Lloyd's List Reports and there is a cumulative case citator that goes up to 1999. The series now appears in monthly parts and these can normally be located next to the bound volumes. The Criminal Appeal Reports is another specialist series of reports that contains judgements of the Divisional Court of Queen's Bench, Court of Appeal (Criminal Division) and the House of Lords and are readily identifiable by their bright red bindings with gold blocking on the spine for the series title, year and volume number.

6. Using the *Current Law Case Citator*

If, for some reason, you have written down the name of a case without the accompanying citation, you will be able to find the latter by using the *Current Law Case Citator*. It not only provides a full list of citations for the Law Reports series but it also gives a history of the case in terms of whether it was taken on appeal. In addition, you will discover whether the decision has been applied, considered, approved, disapproved or followed by other courts subsequently. This information will be particularly useful to you if you become involved in moots organised by your students' law society. The work is in a number of parts as follows:

(a) A bound volume covering the period 1946–76.

(b) A second bound volume covering the period 1977–97.

(c) A softbound volume for the period after 1998 which is replaced each year by an updated Volume.

(d) The latest Current Law Monthly Digest containing a cumulative list of cases reported in the current year. The December issue for the previous year will have a list of all the cases reported in that year.

You should work through the parts of the *Citator* in chronological order unless you know that you are looking for a recent case that will be located in the Monthly Digest. The *Current Law Case Citator* is also available on

CD-ROM and there is an Internet version. However, the Internet version is available only on subscription, although many universities do have subscriptions. If your LRC has a subscription you will need to obtain a username and password to gain entry into the website.

7. Locating recent case reports

Case law continues to develop as cases with novel fact situations arise or the application of existing principles may be extended to new situations. The courts are also called upon from time to time to give authoritative interpretations of statutory provisions or evaluate existing legislative provisions in the light of the Human Rights Act 1998. Thus new judgements cascade from the superior courts every week that they are in session, although only a fraction of these are ever reported. It may be necessary for you to consult some of these cases in the course of your studies. The broadsheet newspapers regularly carry reports of judgements the day after they are delivered in the superior courts. The most widely known are those published in *The Times*. Sometimes tutors cut these out and pin them on noticeboards for students to read. A member of the LRC staff may also be tasked with cutting them out of the newspapers and placing them in a file for student access. There is a publication known as the Daily Law Reports Index which contains references for all these reports since 1986 which is probably available on request. The red quarterly paperbound indexes are hardbound at the end of the year. These reports tend to be rather brief owing to considerations of space but often serve as an early indication of a more detailed report to come later in either the Weekly Law Reports or the All England Law Reports. As was indicated in Chapter 4, both of these series are published in weekly parts throughout the year. If you are given a reference to a report in either of these series for the current calendar year, the citation will be in the same format as for one of the bound volumes.

The Weekly Law Reports are always hardbound at the year-end in a very distinctive black binding with the title of the series blocked in gold on the spine. The weekly parts for the current year will usually be filed near to those volumes that have been most recently bound. They have buff covers with the series title printed on the spines in dark green. Unfortunately, experience confirms that the weekly parts will rarely be in order (although they should be) and so you may have to sort through until you find the one that you are looking for. Each part of the Weekly Law Reports contains some cases that will appear in volume 1 of the bound set for the year in question. All the parts will be bound into three volumes at the end of the year. The cases that will not appear in volume 1 will appear in either volume 2 or volume 3, and the index on the cover of each weekly part indicates the eventual destination of every report. The cases that eventually appear in volumes 2 and 3 will be republished in the Law Reports of the Incorporated Council with a summary of the arguments put forward by the advocates once the judges have checked and, if necessary, edited their judgements. If you are doing research, you may need to check whether there are divergences between the report of the judgement in the Weekly Law Reports and the version that appears in the Law Reports in the following year. The cases that will appear in volume 1 will not subsequently be republished in the Law Reports.

The weekly parts of the All England Reports are published by a commercial publisher (Butterworths). They have a distinctive binding in the form of a vertical dark blue stripe parallel to a pale greenish-blue stripe. The cases are listed in alphabetical order against the background of the greenish-blue stripe. As with the Weekly Law Reports, these too will be hardbound at the end of the year, in dark blue buckram, and will be accompanied by a bound annual review. Some older volumes may have been bound in beige.

Reports of recent cases may also be found in periodicals such as the *New Law Journal*, the *Solicitors Journal* and the *Law Society Gazette*. Transcripts of recent judgements from the House of Lords can be obtained from the Westminster Parliament website at www.parliament.uk and Court of Appeal judgements can be obtained from the Court Service website at www.courtservice.gov.uk/judgments/judge_home.htm

8. Legislation

The ICLREW has published volumes of statutes from 1866 to 1965. In your LRC, the nineteenth century volumes may still have their original calf leather spine bindings. Statutes dating from the thirteenth century to 1865 have been collated in a series known as Statutes at Large. The volumes in this series are as thick as those comprising the English Reports and are sometimes hardbound in black with the series title embossed in silver with the relevant regnal years of the reigning monarch. From 1966 (or perhaps from 1940) the modern statutes in your LRC will be in annual volumes, hardbound in red in a series entitled Public General Acts and General Synod Measures. If you are engaged in historical research, all these provide excellent resource material because they are in the original form in which they received the Royal Assent. Of course, many will since have been repealed, whilst many others will have been amended. *Consequently, you should not rely upon these series as being up to date.* The same can be said of the series known as Current Law Statutes Annotated which is hardbound in blue volumes with the series title embossed in gold on the spine. This series is not updated after it appears in bound volumes and you should not rely on the statute law contained in it as being current unless you are certain that the statute in question has not been amended since it was first enacted.

The most reliable publication in book form on statute law currently in force is *Halsbury's Statutes of England*. This publication is now in its fourth edition and can be easily located in the law section by its distinctive markings. The volumes are hardbound in grey with a red horizontal stripe at the top of the spine with the series title and edition number embossed in gold. It provides up-to-date versions of all Public General Acts of Parliament except Consolidated Fund Acts in force in England and Wales. There is also a valuable commentary on the various provisions making up each statute with any judicial interpretations of words and phrases in decided cases. Unfortunately there are six parts to this publication as indicated below:

(a) The 50 bound volumes which are arranged alphabetically by subject matter – when the law on a particular topic has undergone a considerable amount of change the volume will be replaced by an updated reissue with the date appearing at the bottom of the spine.

(b) The Current Statute Service which is housed in six loose-leaf, grey, plastic binders containing the texts of statutes not yet incorporated into the main volumes.

(c) The Cumulative Supplement comprising a single bound volume that is issued annually which records the changes affecting statutes contained in (a) and (b) above.

(d) The Noter-up which is contained in a slim, grey, loose-leaf binder that records very recent changes in (a) and (b) above.

(e) Table of Statutes and General Index in the form of a single volume issued yearly that provides the index to (a) and (b) above – the number in bold print refers to the main volume number (unless it is followed by an *S* which is a reference to the Current Statute Service) and the last number is the page reference.

(f) Is It in Force? This is a single volume issued every year located in the Noter-up service binder giving details of when a statute came into force.

There is an online version of the volume known as 'Is It in Force?' which can be accessed free via the Butterworths website at www.Butterworths.com

9. Strategy for using *Halsbury's Statutes of England*

Although you will probably find a 'How to use Halsbury's Statutes Guide' encased in clear, hard plastic near the work, if it is not available you should proceed as follows:

(a) Look up the name of the statute in the Statutes and General Index, but if it is more recent than the date of this table you should refer to the alphabetical list of statutes at the beginning of the Current Statute Service.

(b) Locate the statute in the relevant main bound volume or Current Statute Service having made a note of the reference from the Statutes and General Index.

(c) Look in the Cumulative Supplement to see if there is an entry for the volume and page reference. If there is, this means that there has been a change in the law which must be investigated.

(d) Irrespective of whether there is a relevant entry in the Cumulative Supplement you should also refer to the Noter-up to ascertain whether there are any entries for the volume and page reference and investigate any changes.

10. Subordinate legislation

The best source of up-to-date information on statutory instruments in force is *Halsbury's Statutory Instruments* which comprises 22 hardbound volumes in which the statutory instruments are arranged by broad subject categories. However, this work may contain only summaries of the statutory instruments you need. The hardbound volumes are easy to locate because of their grey binding with the series title embossed in gold vertically along the spines. In addition to the bound volumes, there are two grey, loose-leaf Service binders. Binder 1 contains notes of changes in the law and binder 2 contains the texts of some new statutory instruments. If you have been given the year and number you should be able to locate it quickly in binder 1 which gives a chronological list. If you have not been given the full citation and know only the name, you can look this up in the annual Consolidated Index and Alphabetical List of Statutory Instruments. You will probably find a 'How to Use Halsbury's Statutory Instruments Guide' encased in clear, hard plastic on the shelf near the work. If you need the full text of a statutory instrument that you cannot obtain in *Halsbury*, you could try the HMSO website at www.hmso.gov.uk/

11. Locating European materials

The *Official Journal of the European Communities* for the current year can be located on the Europa website. You will probably find copies of the 'L' series (Legislation) for previous years hardbound in bright blue volumes to distinguish them from the 'C' series (Information and Notices) which may be bound in a greyish-blue material. Each volume is about three inches thick with gold blocking on the spine indicating the year with volume and series letters. Next to these you will find the parts for the current year filed in cardboard containers. The law reports of the European Court of Justice are to be found hardbound in distinctive mauve volumes. Another commercially produced series by Sweet & Maxwell, known as the Common Market Law Reports, are hardbound in maroon and should be found nearby. The individual volumes have the series title blocked in gold on the spine with the year and volume number. The weekly parts can normally be located next to the bound volumes stored in plastic or cardboard files. Your LRC may subscribe to the All England European Cases Reports series instead.

12. Legal textbooks

The legal textbooks that are housed in the law section of the LRC at your university will be organised by subject. The texts themselves can be considered as falling into three broad categories – practitioners' works, other academic texts including philosophical works, and the standard student texts – although they will all appear on the same shelves arranged by subject. The practitioners' works can be subdivided into bound texts and loose-leaf works and are usually available for reference only. A number of the bound practitioners' texts are published by Sweet & Maxwell in a series known as the Common Law Library which includes such well known and authoritative works as:

Benjamin's Sale of Goods
Bowstead and Reynolds on Agency
Chitty on Contract
Charlesworth and Percy on Negligence
Clerk and Lindsell on Torts
Phipson on Evidence.

Other well known bound practitioners' texts include *Archbold – Criminal Pleadings, Evidence and Practice, Blackstone's Criminal Practice* and *Blackstone's Civil Practice*. In recent years there has been a proliferation of loose-leaf works from the major legal publishers. These have the advantage that they are updated at least three or four times a year. As such, they have an advantage over the hardbound works which have to be updated by way of new editions. There are yearly editions of works such as *Archbold – Criminal Pleadings, Evidence and Practice, Blackstone's Criminal Practice* and *Blackstone's Civil Practice* but the texts that appear in the Common Law Library series are not updated that frequently. Well established loose-leaf works include publications such as:

Emmet on Title
Goode on Consumer Credit Legislation
Harvey on Industrial Relations and Employment Law
Hill and Redman's Law of Landlord and Tenant
Kemp and Kemp on Damages.

At the back of the final binder will be found a filing card which tells the reader when the work was last updated. In the first binder, the publisher sometimes produces a bulletin covering developments since the last updating of the work. This is particularly helpful for those students taking courses where there are likely to have been important legislative developments and judgements that have occurred since the last update. This is a valuable service to students of fast-moving areas of law such as labour and employment law. Some of the academic texts may be available only on reference, but the student texts are there to be borrowed.

The LRC at your university may classify its textbooks according to the Dewey decimal system of classification or the Library of Congress system. In the Dewey system, law books fall within the classification numbers 340 to 349. Books on the English Legal System usually start with the classification number 340, but you will need to become familiar with the computerised catalogue in your LRC so that you can search for books you need by author and title.

13. Legal periodicals

The law section of your LRC will have bound collections of a number of legal periodicals. A distinction needs to be made between refereed journals and other periodicals. The latter contain articles by practising lawyers and legal academics on matters of topical interest and include titles such as the *Legal Action, New Law Journal, Solicitors Journal, Law Society Gazette, Counsel* and *The Barrister*. The current editions of these help you to keep up to date with the latest developments in the various branches of the law and the bound collections may prove helpful to those doing research some years later on views being expressed at the time. However, it is the refereed journals that contain the most authoritative articles on different aspects of the law as each article has to be passed for publication by an editorial panel of distinguished academics and practising lawyers. You may be referred to articles in journals such as the *Cambridge Law Review, Common Market Law Review, Criminal Law Review, European Law Review, Industrial Law Journal, Journal of Business Law, Law Quarterly Review, Modern Law Review, Oxford Journal of Legal Studies* and *Public Law*. If you are, make sure that you are given the year the article was published and the page reference so that you can locate it quickly. The current editions of these publications should appear on free-standing racks so that the covers are clearly visible. A label bearing the title of each journal will appear at the appropriate place so that it is obvious whether the latest edition has been removed temporarily. To assist you in your search for journal articles there is a Legal Journals Index covering over four hundred periodicals for the period 1986–2000. From 2001 this continues to be available on CD-ROM and there is an Internet version as part of the Current Law Information database but it is available only on subscription so you must ask whether your university has taken out a subscription to the service.

14. Legal dictionaries

As you are likely come across the occasional word or phrase that is unfamiliar, you will need to locate a legal dictionary. There are a number of these, the most authoritative being *Stroud's Judicial Dictionary*. There is a new edition of *Stroud* and you will probably find it in the reference section. *Mozley and Whiteley's Law Dictionary* is now in its 12th edition and is well worth consulting, and the same may be said of *Osborn's Concise Law Dictionary*. Both are more 'user friendly' for the undergraduate than *Stroud*. Although there is a glossary of legal terms at the beginning of this book, you may find it useful to acquire your own copy of *Osborn's Concise Law Dictionary* or *Mozley and Whiteley's Law Dictionary* to help you with your substantive law courses.

Further reading

Clinch, P. (2001) *Using a Law Library: A student's guide to legal research skills* (London: Blackstone Press).
Dane, J. and P.A. Thomas (1996) *How to Use a Law Library* (London: Sweet & Maxwell).

18

Legal skills 2

1. Introduction

The aim of the chapter is to help you with your research for seminars and essays. Some general words of advice have also been included on the preparation of seminar papers, essays writing and examinations. Few modular degree schemes are assessed solely by unseen examinations. Although some of the courses comprising your degree scheme may be assessed solely by coursework, most will be assessed by a combination of coursework and examinations. Depending on the weighting allocated to it, coursework of a very good standard can boost your overall performance significantly. Therefore, it is well worth investing time and effort in your assignments, particularly if you do not normally perform well under the stress of examinations. Seminars are an essential part of the learning process because they encourage you to undertake some research even when you are not required to present a seminar paper. Drafting and delivering seminar papers will improve your presentational skills and enhance your ability to speak in public even if it is just to a group of 20–25 fellow students.

Essay and seminar questions for your English Legal System (ELS) course will usually be different from those on substantive law courses. Typically on an ELS course, you will be required to answer questions on those aspects of the legal system that are of topical interest. However, even on substantive law courses, you may be asked to prepare a seminar paper or write an essay dealing with some legal concept or legal doctrine. In the unlikely event that you have been fortunate enough to have been provided with all the resource material that you need, you will have to spend time in the LRC looking for relevant material so that you can answer the question(s) set. What distinguishes the good student from the average student is the willingness of the former to look for references and material beyond what is in the course text and in addition to those he/she has been given by a member of the academic staff.

2. Locating material

Law is a vast area of scholarship and new material is being published all the time on a wide range of legal subjects. Sometimes articles are inspired by judgements that have been delivered in the superior courts but they may also be reporting the findings of empirical research. The online database *Lawtel* holds details of about fifty journal titles from 1998 and this should save you time looking through a number of printed indexes for articles. There is a daily update service that provides summaries of the latest articles as well as information on new legislation and case law. The website can be accessed at www.lawtel.co.uk but it is a subscription service and you will need to obtain a username and password before you can access it.

The Current Law Monthly Digest gives details of periodical articles by subject but you need to look through all the monthly parts, starting with the most recent unless you are able to search online. The information in each monthly part is arranged under subject headings so that you can focus on the relevant subject area quickly. At the end of each subject division you will see a paragraph headed 'Articles'. The articles that appear are selected from the Legal Journals Index database, but only major articles appear. Thus it may worthwhile checking the Index database at www.smlawpub.co.uk/product/abbrevs/abbrevs.cfm In addition to the journal articles listed in the Current Law Monthly Digest, you will discover references to government circulars and consultative documents which may not be available in your LRC. There is also a separate European Current Law Monthly Digest giving extensive coverage of developments in EU law. An Internet version of entire Current Law service exists but it is only available to subscribers. Many of the universities and colleges offering law courses now have a subscription but you will need to ask the LRC staff for a username and a password to gain access to the site if your institution has a subscription.

You could also access Butterworths Law Direct at www.Butterworths.com which is a free online legal newspaper if the topic you are researching is receiving some media attention currently. You should also use the web addresses included at the end of the chapters of this book to obtain up-to-date information on the various subjects. Most of these sites are updated regularly and some have a What's New? section.

If you have an extended essay or special project to write as part of the assessment for your course, you could make use of the ISI Social Science Citation Index which is available via the Web of Science website through the Internet. You will need a short course of instruction lasting about an hour and a half but it is well worth the time spent and at the end of it you will be given a username and password. These will give you unsupervised access to several thousand journal articles and conference papers, many of them from the USA and Canada. This will be particularly useful if you are undertaking a comparative study.

3. Researching legal problems

When it comes to researching legal problems for seminars and essays on courses where substantive law is taught, many hard-pressed students are content to rely on their course texts and lecture notes. Lecture notes should update the course texts but you cannot assume that all lecture notes will be completely up to date unless there is a clear indication to this effect. It is always worthwhile checking the current edition of the Current Law Monthly Digest to see if there have been any recent cases in the area of law that you are studying or the *Lawtel* database if this is available to you. The commercial publisher Butterworths offers a wide range of online services that can be accessed from a PC but these are all subscription services and they are not available in all universities. Where these are available, they provide an excellent means of keeping completely up to date. The ICLREW, however, offers a free 24-hour law reporting service at www.lawreports.co.uk. Every item starts with a series of key words followed by the names of the parties, date of judgement, the composition of the court and a brief summary of the decision. It is also worthwhile accessing the BAILII website at www.bailii.org/databases.

4. Using *Halsbury's Law of England*

If you are intending to enter legal practice it is a good idea to try to develop whilst you are an undergraduate those research skills that you will require to be a competent professional. All practising lawyers use *Halsbury's Laws of England* when researching legal problems. You should try to become accustomed to using it too, because it is a highly authoritative reference work that is kept completely up to date. It is now in its fourth edition and is easy to locate in the LRC because of its distinctive brown binding and the red patch bearing the title of the work that appears at the top of the spine. There are seven parts to the work as follows:

(a) The 50 main volumes contain an exposition of the law of England and Wales arranged by subject from administrative law to wills. The volumes usually cover more than one subject. Every so often, a main volume will be reissued when there have been significant changes in the law covered by that volume. Volumes 51 and 52 cover the European Communities.

(b) The Annual Abridgements are published in April each year and are a comprehensive statement of the law of any one year. There are summaries of cases as well as legislation.

(c) The Cumulative Supplement which is a bound two-volume set that is issued every year that records the changes that affect the main volumes and the Annual Abridgements.

(d) The Current Service is contained in two loose-leaf binders. The first binder contains a Monthly Review that gives outline summaries of recent cases and legislation. The second contains the Noter-up service which has references to decisions and legislation arranged by subject for the main volumes and Annual Abridgements.

(e) The two-volume Consolidated Index of subjects in the main volumes.

(f) The Consolidated Table of Statutes arranged alphabetically for those cases cited in the main volumes.

(g) The Consolidated Table of Cases arranged alphabetically.

The strategy for using this legal encyclopedia is as follows:

(a) Start with the appropriate volume of the Consolidated Index to look up a key word or phrase, noting the volume number (given in bold print) and the paragraph number in the main work. If you are sure that the problem that you are researching involves an aspect of contract law you will look for that in the Index. The Consolidated Tables of Cases and Statutes respectively will, of course, give you references for cases and statutes in the main work but it is unlikely that you will need to use them.

(b) Since it is possible that the information in the main work may be out of date, you will need the volume number and paragraph number to check the latest Cumulative Supplement and Noter-up to see if there have been any changes since the main volume was published. If there has, you must read the information in the Cumulative Supplement together with that contained in the main work.

(c) The Noter-up will be found in the second binder of the Current Service. It is arranged in the same way as the Cumulative Supplement, by volume and paragraph number, and you must check there to see if there have been any changes since the publication date of the Cumulative Supplement.

You will probably find that there is a thin, paperbound user's guide near the work that will take you through these various steps. As an exercise, you might like to tackle the problem that you encountered in Chapter 12 that centred on the dispute between Alice and Modern Builders Ltd. As key words and phrases, try looking in the Consolidated Index for: variation of contract – consideration – performance of existing duty – benefit to promisor.

Some universities have subscriptions to *Halsbury's Laws Direct* which is an online version and is far easier to use than the printed version of the work. If your institution does have a subscription, you will have to check whether it is available to undergraduates. If it is not, you will not be unduly disadvantaged by using the printed version.

5. The Lexis and Westlaw databases

Lexis is a massive legal database located at Dayton, Ohio, which is accessed from the UK via the Butterworths website. It contains hundreds of thousands of cases from 1945 to the present. The software it uses enables it to search for words and names anywhere in a law report and consequently it is able to retrieve relevant cases that would not normally be identified by conventional searching by subject heading in printed indexes. Although it is updated weekly, there could be a delay of some weeks before the text of a judgement is added. It can be quite expensive to use and you are likely to need permission from a member of the academic staff if you wish to conduct a search. Some members of the LRC staff may be authorised to carry out searches on your behalf but you would need to attend a training course before you would be allowed to use it unsupervised. It is a very powerful research tool and is used extensively by practitioners because it also contains the full texts of Acts of Parliament and EU legislation.

Westlaw UK is another web-based legal information retrieval system providing primary and secondary sources of UK and EU law, but user training is essential.

6. Format of a modern law report

Modern law reports tend to follow a standardised format. At the beginning will appear the names of the parties. Immediately underneath will be found the name of the court and the names of the judges who decided the case, together with the dates on which the case was heard and the judgement delivered. Usually, judges take time to consider and formulate their judgements and so some time will have elapsed between the hearing and the judgement. A series of key words and phrases then appears in italics which conveys an impression of what the case is about. After that, there will be what lawyers call the 'headnote', which is a summary of both the facts of the case and the judgement by the editor or reporter. There will be a list of the cases that were referred to by the advocates in argument and those that were referred to by the judge(s) in the course of delivering judgement. If the report is of an appeal, there will be some brief information concerning the trial of the case at first instance. Immediately before the detailed judgement(s) will appear the names of the advocates who represented the litigants. Only in reports prepared by the ICLREW is there a summary of the arguments deployed by the advocates.

7. Reading case law

One of the questions that hard-pressed first-year law students often ask when presented with a worksheet containing a long list of cases is: Which cases *must* I read? Hopefully your course convener will have indicated the really important cases that you must read week by week. You should endeavour to read these in the Law Reports or All England Law Reports (if the former are not available to you) rather than in a case book and make notes. Case books are very useful when you are working away from the LRC but they should not be regarded as a substitute for reading full versions of cases in the Law Reports. Decisions of the Court of Appeal and House of Lords are well worth taking time over because these have often defined or developed particular aspects of the law. This is not to say that judgements of the High Court are unimportant – far from it.

Students who find themselves pressed for time also ask: How much of the report should I read? It may be that you only have time to read the headnote which is the editor's or reporter's summary of the facts and what he/she considers is the reason for the decision or *ratio decidendi*. It is better to spend your limited time reading this carefully than to try to skim-read all three (or more) judgements at great speed in the hope that you will recall some points. However, you must bear in mind that the headnote is only the editor's or reporter's considered view and that another court at a later date may take a different view of the *ratio decidendi*, and it is this which is definitive – not the headnote. Having read the headnote carefully you may have time to return to the report later to read it in full and make notes.

If you are not under a severe time constraint, on your initial reading you should try to absorb the leading judgement, if it is clear that there is one. Where the other judges have agreed with the judge who has given the most detailed judgement, it will be sufficient for you to read this leading judgement and ignore the few comments and observations that the other judges have made. However, it does sometimes happen that the judges agree on the outcome but differ in their reasoning. If you have been asked to analyse the judgments, there are no short cuts. Not infrequently, you will come across a Court of Appeal decision where there is a dissenting judgement, and where a case has gone on appeal to the House of Lords there may be one or even two dissenting judgements. If the case gave rise to academic controversy at the time, it is a good idea to read the dissenting judgement(s) if time permits or return to the report later. You may, of course, be asked specifically to discuss the dissenting judgement(s) in a seminar paper or essay, in which case you have no choice.

8. Preparing and delivering a seminar paper

Seminars are usually timetabled for slots of between 45 minutes and an hour. The person leading the seminar will have indicated previously how many papers are to be presented. If two papers are to be presented in one hour, you should prepare your paper so that it can be read out loud within ten minutes, leaving ample opportunity for discussion before the second paper is due to be read. The main purpose of the seminar is to generate relevant discussion. No one will thank you if you use up all the allotted time for discussion by producing a text that is so lengthy that its delivery precludes any subsequent discussion. Remember that your fellow students will want to make notes for the discussion that is to follow so you must not speak too quickly. This means that the word length of your paper should be between 1,000 and 1,200 words if it is to be delivered at a rate that your audience can assimilate within ten minutes. Seminar papers that focus on the solution of a hypothetical legal problem are likely to be shorter. If your seminar paper provides a solution to such a problem, make sure that you include the full citations to all relevant statutes and cases. Often it is helpful to make a slide for use with an overhead projector that contains all the references. The projector can be switched on and off as necessary.

As when writing an essay, you must select and arrange the material gained from your research so that you answer the question that has been set and not one of your own devising. Nor must you just blurt out a mass of information in the hope that some of it is relevant to the question that has been asked. When you have produced what you regard as a coherent answer to the question set, it is a good idea to record it on to a cassette tape or minidisc. When you replay it you will gain an impression of how it will sound to your audience. If possible, ask a fellow student to listen to it and offer constructive criticism. As a result of the playback, make some changes to improve the overall fluency of the presentation. This will also help you to fix the material in your memory so that you do not have to over-rely on your script and can make frequent eye contact with your audience as you speak. Sometimes it can help to present the outline of your paper as a set of bullet points on an overhead projector slide, but if you do this, make sure you use a large enough font so that the slide can be read without difficulty.

If you have researched your paper thoroughly, you are likely to have the satisfaction of having your fellow students ask you to e-mail it to them once you have incorporated any corrections or observations made by the seminar leader. It is always a good idea to ask the seminar leader for feedback at the end of the session. This will help you to improve your presentational skills for next time. If you intend to practise and make regular court appearances, you must hone your presentational skills.

9. Essay writing

An essay is a valuable form of assessment because it forces you to synthesise the material you have uncovered through your researches. It can also help to develop your ability to argue – an essential skill if you intend to practise. It must therefore have an identifiable structure. The introductory paragraph should define the main concepts and/or issues and indicate how the subject matter will be developed through the subsequent paragraphs. These paragraphs should link together logically and be organised around a main theme or concept and will consist of more than a single sentence. Relevant case law and statute law should be cited as appropriate in support of the propositions that are put forward. The case law should not be set out in great detail; a short statement of the facts and the decision will suffice. Likewise, it is usually unnecessary to quote statutory provisions in full. Just give the essence of the relevant provisions. Every essay should have a concluding paragraph which draws the strands in the argument together or summarises the answer to the question. In general, law essays are of two types:

(a) a general discursive-type question

(b) a hypothetical scenario or case study requiring the student to advise one of the parties.

If you are tackling a general discussion-type question you should present both sides of the argument as ably as you can, setting out the facts and supporting evidence or authority before presenting your conclusion. Advocates should be able to argue both sides of an argument, and this is a useful skill for you to acquire. For other forms of type (a), you must have regard to the way in which the question is framed. If you are asked to 'compare and contrast', you must set out the similarities and the differences as you see them before presenting your conclusion. If you are asked to 'critically appraise' the performance of some aspect the English legal system, you must do exactly that, setting out the merits and shortcomings. If you are asked to critically analyse a judgement, you will be required to expose any flaws in the underlying logic.

Having conducted your research for type (a) it is likely that you will have accumulated more material and notes than you need for your essay and they are unlikely to be in an order in which you can use them. It is good practice, therefore, to take a large piece of unlined paper and write the question in a rectangle in the centre and build up a Buzan (after Tony Buzan) diagram or 'mind map' linking various concepts, ideas and authorities so that eventually a structure emerges in your head. Since you must remain within the word limit and use your 'word budget' to best advantage, you will have to jettison the material that is not directly relevant. Before you start writing, it is a good idea to see if you can write a draft of the concluding paragraph in three or four sentences. Do not shy away from this. It is a very good discipline because it will remind you that you must produce a considered concluding paragraph and, just as important, it will help to keep you focused as your write.

The hypothetical scenario (b) may be stated in just a few lines or it may be set out as a highly detailed scenario, perhaps taking up an entire sheet of A4 paper. In either event you must accept the truthfulness of the facts as presented and not question them. Where the scenario is set out in detail it is less likely that there will be omitted facts on which you would be required to speculate. This may be contrasted with the real word of professional practice where it is necessary to extract all the information in an interview and to remind yourself at the end that the client's version of the facts may not be complete and may not even be totally reliable. When you are tackling a scenario that is highly detailed you should underline all the key words and phrases and ensure that you construct your essay in such a way that you address all these key points before summarising your advice to X or Y in your concluding paragraph. Where the scenario has been presented in just a few lines of text you must make sure that you cover any important issues or matters in the body of your essay that have not been specifically mentioned. For example, if you were given a very short scenario in which someone working in a shop had been dismissed for being late and you are asked to comment on whether he/she could bring a claim for unfair dismissal, it would be pertinent to mention in your answer the need to establish 'employee status' and the requisite continuity of service, otherwise there is no basis for a claim. It would be fatal to devote all your word budget to disciplinary sanctions that can be exercised by management and cases on dismissals for lateness. In all legal writing, the mode of citation from law reports is important and you must make sure that you give the *full citation*, not just the year. Ideally, all your citations should be to the reports of the ICLREW where the report has been published in the Law Reports series.

Do not overlook the bibliography. This should contain a list of all the books and articles (also conference papers and radio programmes) that you have cited in the essay. The convention is to prepare the list in alphabetical order by the first author's surname. For a book, the surname of the author appears first, followed by his/her initials and (the date of publication) in brackets. The title of the book is underlined and there is a comma, after which the place of publication appears followed by the name of the publisher. An example would be:

Treitel, G.H. (1999) <u>The Law of Contract</u>, London: Sweet & Maxwell.

Some universities prefer that the title of a text is placed in italics rather than underlined. You would be wise to check any rubric that has been prepared for students and conform to the requirements stated. In the case of journal articles, these should be set out as follows:

Worthington, S. (2000) 'Corporate governance: remedying and ratifying directors' breaches' *Vol. 116 Law Quarterly Review*, 638.

10. Examinations

Law course conveners who set examinations do so in the hope that the students to be assessed will do well, and they are invariably disappointed if students perform indifferently or badly. On a modular degree scheme, teaching time is at a premium and most lecturers struggle to teach the course material in the 12 weeks that are normally available. Thus there is unlikely to be teaching time for special revision sessions. The onus is therefore on the student to make space in his/her study programme to conduct regular reviews of the course material and cases. There is research evidence that shows this is the most effective way of remembering subject matter because it is transferred from short-term into long-term memory. On the whole, lawyers tend not to be 'team players', but you might find it useful to form a small study group with two or three others that meets weekly so that you can revise together and share material. This can be a good way of revising because normally you will be unaware of the gaps in your knowledge until someone asks you a question that you cannot answer. If you cannot always meet face to face, there is always e-mail and the conferencing software such as First Class that many universities now make available to students.

At the end of the semester you are likely to have only a week or two available for examination revision and so this must be used to best advantage. In the time available it will not be possible to revise the entire syllabus and so it is best to focus on the main topics. If you obtain past examination papers you will be able to construct a matrix from which you will see if there is some pattern to the way in which certain topics recur. Remember that the external examiner would be more than a little annoyed with a course convener who sets questions on exactly the same topics as last time and would probably complain about this in his/her report to the university. Thus, it is most likely that the topics to be examined will be somewhat different from those examined last time, and this knowledge may help you decide what you will revise.

Examinations at degree level are not designed solely to test knowledge of certain facts. Thankfully, the amount of rote learning required of students has been substantially reduced by allowing them to bring unannotated statutes into the examination. Degree-level examinations assess the ability to analyse, argue and apply knowledge, particularly when candidates are called upon to solve legal problems. If you have obtained some past examination papers, you should try to formulate some outline answers supported by relevant examples and authority to some of the questions you think might be asked. Check your answers against the course text, lecture notes and other relevant resource material you have to hand. There are now some very good published texts of questions and answers and you may wish to use these, but make sure that they were published very recently.

In the examination hall you may be allowed some reading time, especially if your paper contains a number of lengthy problem-type questions. You must use this to best advantage by reading over the paper quickly to identify those questions that you think you can answer. You should then reread the paper carefully, underlining key words and phrases in those questions you have selected, noting the names of any relevant cases as they occur to you. There is no need to give the citations, and if you can only remember the name of one of the parties that is better than no reference to authority. You must always answer the number of questions that you have been asked to attempt, but no more. Bearing in mind that you may have to answer one question from each section of a divided paper, a successful strategy dictates that you must make your final selection on the basis of those questions to which you can produce the 'best' answers. If all questions carry equal marks you must divide your time equally. If the mark weighting is unequal you must allocate your time proportionately. Do not 'borrow' time from another question. For your first answer, choose the question on the paper to which you think you can give the best answer. There is no requirement that questions be answered in a particular order. This will help to build your confidence from the outset. If you have allocated 45 minutes in total for answering this question, you should spend at least 10 minutes jotting down your ideas and then arranging them into a coherent structure before starting to write your answer. Always meet the question 'head on' and tailor your information accordingly. The inclusion of irrelevant material will not gain you any marks and will use up valuable time that you could put to good use elsewhere on the paper. If you have left the most difficult question to the end and time is running out, do not continue to write in continuous prose. Set out your remaining points in brief note form, developing them as best you can. Although revision is essential to examination success, so is examination technique.

Further reading

Farrar, J.H. and A.M. Dugdale (1990) *Introduction to Legal Method* (London: Sweet & Maxwell).

Tunkel, V. (1992) *Legal Research* (London: Blackstone Press).

Index

ACAS 32, 271–2
Access to Justice 238
Act of Union 1707 82
Act of Union 1800 82
acte clair 142
actus reus 215
Administrative Court 32, 327–30
Admiralty Court 32
ADR Group 282
advocates-general in ECJ 97
affirmative resolution procedure 32
alibi evidence 209, 214, 219
allocation questionnaire 251, 252
appeals against conviction 230–3
appeals against sentence 233
appropriate adult 181, 189
Arbitration
  ACI 289–90
  advantages 286
  agreement 287
  CIA scheme 289
  ICC scheme 290
Arden (Mary) J QC 341
arraignment of accused 213
arrest
  nature of 176
  use of force 179
  warrant 176
attachment of earnings 260
Attorney General 197

Bacon, Francis 56
Bail
  granted by Crown Court 206
  granted by magistrates 204–6
  nature of 204
  police bail 184
Bar complaints system
Bar Council 20, 23
BarDIRECT 19
Bar Vocational Course 27

barrister(s) 16, 18
  chambers 16
  professional negligence 19
Bentham, Jeremy (1752–1832) 57
Bowman Report 327
breach of statutory duty 333
burden of proof
  in criminal trial 220
bye law 80

Carltona principle 307
case management conference 252
case stated 32, 229, 329
caution, on admitting guilt 192, 195
cautioning prior to questioning 188
Central Criminal Court (Old Bailey) 30
Central Office of Employment
    Tribunals 271
Centre for Effective Dispute Resolution
    (CEDR) 282, 285
Chancery (Amendment Act) 1858 57
Chancery Division of High Court 31
Chartered Institute of Arbitrators 284,
    285, 287, 289
circuit judge
  appointment 30
  in county court 31
Citizens' Advice Bureau 157, 159, 168
citizen's power of arrest 177
Civil Justice Reform Evaluation 240–1
Codes of Practice under PACE, Codes
    A–E 171
codification of case law 71
Coke, Sir Edward 56
Commercial Court 32
Commissioners of Inland Revenue 33
common law
  history of 52–3
  nature of 52
Common Law Procedure Act 1854 57
Common Professional Examination 10

Community Legal Service Directory 158
Community Legal Service Quality Task
Force 158
community punishment 224
conditional fee agreement 164–7
consolidation of statutes 71
contempt of court 244
contingency fees 167
Council for Legal Education 9
Council on Tribunals 266
counterclaim in civil proceedings 246–7
counts on indictment 212
county courts 31
Court of Appeal (Civil Division) 33–4,
46
Court of Appeal (Criminal Division)
230–3
Court of Chancery 41
Court of Common Pleas 52
Court of Exchequer 52
Court of King's/Queen's Bench 52
Court of Protection 33
Criminal Cases Review Commission
235
Crown Court circuits 30, 228
Crown Prosecution Service 194, 200,
202
Curia Regis 52
custodial sentences 224–6
custody record 180

damages
aggravated 259
compensatory 259
nominal 259
defence of tender before claim in civil
proceedings 249
depositions as evidence 217
Deregulation Committee 84
deregulation orders 83
direct effect in EU law 102, 111–14
Director of Public Prosecutions 194, 197
discharging jurors 215
disclosure of documents in civil
proceedings 252
Divisional Courts
Chancery 33
Family 33
Queen's Bench 32

district judges 30
district judges of magistrates' courts 30,
204

either way offences 201
employed Bar 18
Employment Appeal Tribunal 272
equality principle in public law 322
equitable remedies 59
injuction 56, 59
recission 60
rectification 59
specific performance 59
equity, development of 54–8
EU (European Union)
citizenship 125
first pillar
Coal and Steel Community 92
Euratom 92
European Community 92, 98–9
Institutions
Commission 92, 94, 95
Council 92, 93, 94
Court of Auditors 93, 98
Court of Justice 93, 97
Parliament 93, 98
second pillar 92
secondary legislation
Decisions 108
Directives 108
Regulations 107
third pillar 92
European Convention on Human
Rights 119–20, 121, 137, 145–9
European Court of First Instance 97
European Court of Human Rights
139–40
evidence via video link 217
evidential test for prosecutions 194
extended detention in custody 186
extrinsic aids to interpretation 132

Family Division of High Court 33
formal caution following an admission
of guilt 192
Franks Committee 265
fundamental rights in EU law
equality 121–2
generally 119–20

fundamental rights in EU law
 (*continued*)
 legal certainty 121–2
 procedural justice 123
 proportionality 121
fusion of two branches of legal
 profession 24

Gardiner, (Gerald) Lord QC 338
garnishee proceedings 260

habeas corpus 32
Henry II (1154–1189) 52
High Court 33
High Court judges
 appointment 33
 eligibility for appointment 33
 mode of address 31
House of Lords
 chamber of the legislature 63
 judicial committee 34

implied repeal, doctrine of 72
indictable only offences 201
industrial tribunals, *see* Employment
 Appeal Tribunal
inns of court 16–17
Institute of Legal Executives 13
interim injunction 258
International Chamber of Commerce
 290
International Labour Organisation 267
intrinsic aids to interpretation 131

Joint Committee on Statutory
 Instruments 87
judgement by default 244
Judicial Committee of Privy Council 34
Judicial Review of decision not to
 prosecute 195
Judicial Studies Board 36
jury foreman 218, 221

Law Commissioners 64
Law Reports 50–1
Law Society 9–12
Law Works 168
leap-frogging appeals 262
legal advice in custody 186, 188

legal aid 155
legal certainty in public law 321
legal executive 13
 rights of audience 13
legal help and representation 159
Legal Practice Course 10
Legal Services Commission 156
 Funding Code 159
 Special Cases Unit 160
Legal Services Ombudsman 14, 20–3
legislative procedure
 committee stage 68
 first reading 67
 report stage 69
 royal assent 70
 second reading 67
 third reading 69
life peers 63
locus standi 328
Lord Chancellor 27–36, 339–40
Lord Chancellor's Department 35, 37
Lord Chief Justice 33, 37
Lord Ellesmere 55
Lord Justices of Appeal 34
Lords of Appeal in Ordinary (Law
 Lords) 34

MacPherson Report 170
magistrates
 appointment 28
 training 28
magistrates' courts 27–9
Magna Carta 1215 52
mandatory order 331
Master of the Rolls 16, 33
maxims of equity 58
Mediation UK 280
medieval Chancellors 54
mens rea 215
misfeasance in public office 332
Modernising Justice 155

National Mode of Trial Guidelines 207
negative resolution procedure 82
Newton hearing 222

Obiter dicta 43–5
Office for the Supervision of Solicitors
 15

Office of Votes and Proceedings 81–2
Order in Council 86

parliamentary counsel 66
per incuriam 46–7
police bail 184
precedent
    disapproving of 50
    factual distinguishing 49–50
    over ruling 50
    restrictive distinguishing 50
prerogative orders 266
prerogative powers 301
presentment in an indictment 212
President of Family Division 34
primary prosecution disclosure 209
principles of natural justice 274–5
Private members' Bills 64
Pro Bono unit of Bar 168
Professional Conduct Committee of the
    Bar 21
prohibiting order 331
prosecuting agencies 196
Provisions of Oxford 53
Public Defender Service 163
Public General Acts 67, 79
pupillage 17
purposive interpretation of statutes 133,
    155

quashing order 331
Queen's Bench Division of High Court
    31–2
Queen's Counsel 19
Queen's speech 65

Ratio decidendi 43–5, 365
Remedial orders 85–6
Reprimanding/warning of young
    children 193
rights of audience
    barristers 11
    solicitors 12
Royal Commission on Criminal
    Procedure 170, 184

Royal Commissions 64
Royal prerogative 301–2

search warrant 174
solicitor(s) 9, 10
Solicitors' Costs Information and Client
    Care Code 15
Solicitors' Disciplinary Tribunal 16
Solicitors' Pro Bono Group 168
standard of proof in criminal trial 220
State liability in EU Law 115–18
statement of incompatibility 139–40
statutory charge of Legal Services
    Commission 162
statutory instruments 80–1, 86–7
standard directions in civil procedure
    252
strip searches by police 182
Stroud's Judicial Dictionary 359
subsidiarity in EU Law 103
summary judgement 245
summary offence 201
supremacy of EU Law 74, 101
Supreme Court of Judicature Act 1873
    58
Supreme Court of Judicature Act 1875
    58

tape recording of police interviews
    189
'the information' in summary trial
    201–2
Thring, Henry 79
tort of negligence 333
tort damages 259
Treaty of Nice 95, 97, 107

ultra vires doctrine
    and statutory instruments 88–90
United Kingdom defined 62

Visitors of Inns of Court 23

writ of *venire de novo* 233
writs, medieval form 53